**JOURNAL FOR THE STUDY OF THE OLD TESTAMENT SUPPLEMENT SERIES**

326



Sheffield Academic Press

*Paul-Eugène Dion*

# The World of the Aramaeans III

## Studies in Language and Literature in Honour of Paul-Eugène Dion

edited by
P.M. Michèle Daviau, John W. Wevers
and Michael Weigl

Journal for the Study of the Old Testament
Supplement Series 326

Published by
Sheffield Academic Press Ltd
Mansion House
19 Kingfield Road
Sheffield S11 9AS
England

www.SheffieldAcademicPress.com

Typeset by Sheffield Academic Press
and
Printed on acid-free paper in Great Britain
by Antony Rowe Ltd,
Chippenham, Wiltshire

British Library Cataloguing-in-Publication Data

A catalogue record for this book is available
from the British Library

ISBN 1 84127 179 9

## CONTENTS

# PREFACE

The languages and literature of the Bible have been of lifelong interest to Paul-Eugène Dion in his teaching, research and public lectures. In the course of his academic life, Paul took a broad view of the biblical world when he added the dialects, epigraphy and history of the Aramaeans of Syria to his research and teaching. In his research, he investigated the political activities, social structures, religious beliefs and culture of the Aramaeans and the ways in which these people interacted with those of Mesopotamia in the east, Phoenicia in the west, Israel, Judah and the states of Transjordan to the south. Their language had an even greater influence than individual cultural characteristics, extending in the Persian period as far south as Upper Egypt and continuing in later Syriac literature.

The essays presented here include biblical, historical and cultural studies, most of which reveal the richness of the world of the Aramaeans and examples of the extent of Aramaean cultural influence. These studies are presented in admiration and affection for the work of Paul-Eugène Dion, and as a contribution to the study of the Aramaeans of Syria and their neighbours.

The response to our call for contributors was overwhelming. So many essays of quality, sometimes very detailed, were submitted, that it proved necessary to divide the Festschrift into three volumes, each containing several essays related to the Aramaean world, but reflecting a different province of Paul Dion's interests and scholarship: biblical studies; historical and archaeological research; language and literature.

More than in the two previous volumes, contributors to the present volume represent an even mix of former students (Weigl, Leonhard, Morrow), teaching colleagues (Harrak, Frame, Lutz), and other specialists and long-time friends (Tropper, Pardee, Bordreuil, Lindenberger). All these are active in areas—ancient law and wisdom, Assyriology, Ugaritology and other fields of Semitic Epigraphy—in which Professor Dion developed his own research, or found stimulation for the wide array of his literary interests, from the poetry of Second Isaiah, Job and the Psalter, through the formulas of ancient letter-writing, and the dialects of Old Aramaic.

This book is the gift of all those who have contributed their scholarship, friendship and respect for Paul Dion, including his colleagues and former students in the Near Eastern Studies Department (now the Department of Near and Middle Eastern Civilizations) at the University of Toronto, as well as colleagues in North America, Europe and the Near East with whom he has maintained an active exchange of students and offprints. Invaluable was the contribution of John W. Wevers, who not only wrote an important article, but also reviewed all manuscripts with his unfailing standards for precision and excellence. Other contributors also deserve a word of thanks: original artwork on the cover and before the index of each volume is the contribution of Isabelle Crépeau (Montréal); Wilfrid Laurier University student assistants, Erin Mitchell and Daniel Lewis, prepared bibliographies in a standard format, and inserted Hebrew and Greek characters where needed. Funding for this work was provided by Wilfrid Laurier University through a book preparation grant and by private gifts. Special thanks are also due to resources of the Archive of the Royal Inscriptions of Mesopotamia, the University of Toronto online catalogue, and the Karlsruher Virtueller Katalog; their extraordinary collections made available complete publication information for the preparation of bibliographies and footnotes. Finally, M. Daviau is especially grateful to all the contributors and to her students for their patience during the busy months needed to complete this work.

# ABBREVIATIONS

| | |
|---|---|
| *5R* | H.C. Rawlinson and T.G. Pinches, *The Cuneiform Inscriptions of Western Asia.* V. *A Selection from the Miscellaneous Inscriptions of Assyria and Babylonia* (London: British Museum, 1880–84) |
| *AAAS* | *Annales Archéologiques Arabes Syriennes* |
| *ABD* | David Noel Freedman (ed.), *The Anchor Bible Dictionary* (New York: Doubleday, 1992) |
| *ADAJ* | *Annual of the Department of Antiquities of Jordan* |
| *ADD* | C.H.W. Johns, *Assyrian Deeds and Documents Recording the Transfer of Property* (4 vols.; Cambridge: Deighton, Bell & Co., 1898–1923) |
| *AfO* | *Archiv für Orientforschung* |
| *AHw* | Wolfram von Soden, *Akkadisches Handwörterbuch* (Wiesbaden: Harrassowitz, 1959–81) |
| *AJ* | *Antiquités Judaïques* |
| *AJA* | *American Journal of Archaeology* |
| *AJSL* | *American Journal of Semitic Languages and Literatures* |
| *AJT* | *American Journal of Theology* |
| ALASPM | Abhandlungen zur Literatur Altsyrien-Palästinas und Mesopotamiens |
| AnBib | Analecta biblica |
| *ANET* | James B. Pritchard (ed.), *Ancient Near Eastern Texts Relating to the Old Testament* (Princeton, NJ: Princeton University Press, 1950) |
| AnOr | Analecta orientalia |
| AnOr 8 | A. Pohl, *Newbabylonische Rechtsurkunden aus den Berliner Staatlichen Museen* (Analecta orientalia, 8; Rome: Pontificio Instituto Biblico, 1933). |
| AOAT | Alter Orient und Altes Testament |
| *AoF* | *Altorientalische Forschungen* |
| *AP* | A. Cowley, *Aramaic Papyri of the Fifth Century B.C.* (Oxford: Clarendon Press, 1923) |
| *ARAB* | D.D. Luckenbill (ed.), *Ancient Records of Assyria and Babylonia* (Chicago: University of Chicago Press, 1927) |
| ARES | Archivi Reali di Ebla Studi |
| ARET | Archivi Reali di Ebla Testi |

| | |
|---|---|
| *ARI* | A.K. Grayson (ed.), *Assyrian Royal Inscriptions*, II (Wiesbaden: Harrassowitz, 1976) |
| ARM | Archives royales de Mari |
| *ArOr* | *Archiv orientálni* |
| ATD | Das Alte Testament Deutsch |
| *AuOr* | *Aula orientalis* |
| AUWE 11 | E. Gehlken, *Uruk: Spätbabylonische Wirtschaftstexte aus dem Eanna-Archive.* II. *Texte verschiedenen Inhalts* (Ausgrabungen in Uruk-Warka, Endberichte, 11; Mainz am Rhein: Von Zabern, 1996) |
| *BA* | *Biblical Archaeologist* |
| BAH | Bibliothèque archéologique et historique |
| *BAR* | *Biblical Archaeology Review* |
| *BASOR* | *Bulletin of the American Schools of Oriental Research* |
| BETL | Bibliotheca ephemeridum theologicarum lovaniensium |
| *Bib* | *Biblica* |
| BibOr | Biblica et orientalia |
| BIN 1 | C.E. Keiser, *Letters and Contracts from Erech Written in the Neo-Babylonian Period* (Babylonian Inscriptions in the Collection of James B. Nies, 1; New Haven: Yale University Press, 1918) |
| *BIFAO* | *Bulletin de l'Institut français d'archéologie orientale* |
| *BiOr* | *Bibliotheca orientalis* |
| *BJRL* | *Bulletin of the John Rylands University Library of Manchester* |
| BKAT | Biblischer Kommentar: Altes Testament |
| *BMAP* | E. Kraeling, *The Brooklyn Museum Aramaic Papyri* (New Haven: Yale University Press, 1953) |
| *BN* | *Biblische Notizen* |
| BoSt | Boghazköi-Studien |
| BRM 1 | A.T. Clay, *Babylonian Business Transactions of the First Millennium B.C.* (Babylonian Records in the Library of J. Pierpoint Morgan, 1; New York: privately printed, 1912) |
| *BSO(A)S* | *Bulletin of the School of Oriental (and African) Studies* |
| BTAVO | Beihefte zum Tübinger Atlas des Vorderen Orients |
| BWANT | Beiträge zur Wissenschaft vom Alten und Neuen Testament |
| *BZ* | *Biblische Zeitschrift* |
| BZAW | Beihefte zur *ZAW* |
| *CAD* | Ignace I. Gelb *et al.* (eds.), *The Assyrian Dictionary of the Oriental Institute of the University of Chicago* (Chicago: Oriental Institute, 1964–) |
| CAT | Commentaire de l'Ancien Testament |
| CBOT | Coniectanea Biblica, Old Testament |
| *CBQ* | *Catholic Biblical Quarterly* |
| *CIS* | *Corpus inscriptionum semiticarum* |

| | |
|---|---|
| *CIS II* | *Corpus inscriptionum semiticarum. Pars secunda: Inscriptiones aramaicas continens* (Paris: Academie des Inscriptions et Belles Lettres, 1888) |
| *CRAI* | *Comptes rendus de l'Académie des inscriptions et belles-lettres* |
| CSCO | Corpus scriptorum christianorum orientalium |
| CSCO.Sub | Corpus scriptorum christianorum orientalium. Subsidia |
| CT 55 | T.G. Pinches, *New-Babylonian and Achaemenid Economic Texts* (Cuneiform Texts from Babylonian Tablets in the British Museum, 55; London: British Museum Publications, 1982) |
| CT 56 | T.G. Pinches, *Neo-Babylonian and Achaemenid Economic Texts* (Cuneiform Texts from Babylonian Tablets in the British Museum, 56; London: British Museum Publications, 1982) |
| *CTA* | *Corpus des tablettes en cunéiformes alphabétiques découvertes à Ras Shamra – Ugarit de 1929 à 1939* (Paris: Geuthner, 1963) |
| *Cyr.* | J.N. Strassmaier, *Inschriften von Cyrus, König von Babylon (538–529 v. Chr.)* (Babylonische Texte, 7; Leipzig: Pfeiffer, 1890) |
| *Dar.* | J.N. Strassmaier, *Inschriften von Darius, König von Babylon (521–485 v. Chr.)* (Babylonische Texte, 10–12; Leipzig: Pfeiffer, 1897) |
| Ebib | Etudes bibliques |
| *ED* | *Euntes Docete* |
| *EI* | *Eretz-Israel* |
| *Eisl* | *Encyclopedia of Islam* |
| *ETL* | *Ephemerides theologicae lovanienses* |
| GAG | *Grundriss der Akkadischen Grammatik* (von Soden) |
| GCCI 1 | R.P. Dougherty, *Archives from Erech, Time of Nebuchadnezzar and Nabonidus* (Groucher College Cuneiform Inscriptions, 1; New Haven: Yale University Press, 1923) |
| GCCI 2 | R.P. Dougherty, *Archives from Erech, Neo-Babylonian and Persian Periods* (Groucher College Cuneiform Inscriptions, 2; New Haven: Yale University Press, 1933) |
| GCS | Griechische christlichen Schriftsteller |
| GDK | Gottesdienst der Kirche. Handbuch der Liturgiewissenschaft |
| *GGA* | *Göttingische Gelehrte Anzeigen* |
| *GTJ* | *Grace Theological Journal* |
| *HALAT* | Ludwig Koehler *et al.* (eds.), *Hebräisches und aramäisches Lexikon zum Alten Testament* (5 vols.; Leiden: E.J. Brill, 1967–1995) |

| | |
|---|---|
| *HNE* | M. Lidzbarski, *Handbuch der nordsemitischen Epigraphik: nebst ausgewählten Inschriften* (Weimar: E. Felber, 1898) |
| HSAO | Heidelberger Studien zum Alten Orient |
| HSM | Harvard Semitic Monographs |
| HSS | Harvard Semitic Studies |
| *HTR* | *Harvard Theological Review* |
| *HUCA* | *Hebrew Union College Annual* |
| *IEJ* | *Israel Exploration Journal* |
| *JANES* | *Journal of the Ancient Near Eastern Society (of Columbia University)* |
| *JAOS* | *Journal of the American Oriental Society* |
| *JBL* | *Journal of Biblical Literature* |
| *JCS* | *Journal of Cuneiform Studies* |
| *JEOL* | *Jaarbericht...ex oriente lux* |
| *JewEnc* | *Jewish Encyclopedia* |
| *JJS* | *Journal of Jewish Studies* |
| *JNES* | *Journal of Near Eastern Studies* |
| *JNSL* | *Journal of Northwest Semitic Languages* |
| *JSOT* | *Journal for the Study of the Old Testament* |
| JSOTSup | *Journal for the Study of the Old Testament*, Supplement Series |
| *JSS* | *Journal of Semitic Studies* |
| JSSSup | *Journal of Semitic Studies*, Supplement Series |
| *JTS* | *Journal of Theological Studies* |
| *KAI* | H. Donner and W. Röllig (eds.), *Kanaanäische und aramäische Inschriften* (3 vols.; Wiesbaden: Harrassowitz, 1962–64) |
| KAT | Kommentar zum Alten Testament |
| *KTU* | M. Dietrich, O. Loretz and J. Sammartin (eds.), *Die keil-alphabetischen Texte aus Ugarit* (Neukirchen–Vluyn: Neukirchener Verlag, 1976) |
| *LA* | *Studii Biblici Franciscani Liber Annuus* |
| LAPO | Littératures anciennes du Proche-Orient |
| LCL | Loeb Classical Library |
| LD | Lectio divina |
| *LdÄ* | *Lexikon der Ägyptologie* |
| *LZD* | *Literarisches Zentralblatt für Deutschland* |
| *MEE* | *Materiali Epigrafici di Ebla* |
| *MUSJ* | *Mélanges de l'université Saint-Joseph* |
| *NABU* | *Nouvelles Assyriologiques Brèves et Utilitaires* |
| *Nbk.* | J.N. Strassmaier, *Inschriften von Nabuchodonosor, König von Babylon (604–561 v. Chr.)* (Babylonische Texte, 5–6; Leipzig: Pfeiffer, 1889) |
| *Nbn.* | J.N. Strassmaier, *Inschriften von Nabonidus, König von Babylon (555–538 v. Chr.)* (Babylonische Texte, 1–4; Leipzig: Pfeiffer, 1889) |

| | |
|---|---|
| *Ner.* | B.T.A. Evetts, *Inschriften of the Reigns of Evil-Merodach (B.C. 562–559), Neriglissar (B.C. 559–555) and Laborosoarchod (B.C. 555)* (Babylonische Text, 6/B; Leipzig: Pfeiffer, 1892) |
| *NSI* | G.A. Cooke, *A Text-Book of North-Semitic Inscriptions* (Oxford: Clarendon Press, 1903) |
| NTTS | New Testament Tools and Studies |
| OBO | Orbis biblicus et orientalis |
| OLP | Orientalia lovaniensia periodica |
| *OLZ* | *Orientalistische Literaturzeitung* |
| *Or* | *Orientalia* |
| OrChrA | Orientalia Christiana Analecta |
| *OrNS* | *Orientalia New Series* |
| *OrSuec* | *Orientalia Suecana* |
| OTP | James Charlesworth (ed.), *Old Testament Pseudepigrapha* |
| *OTS* | *Oudtestamentische Studiën* |
| PBS 2/1 | A.T. Clay, *Business Documents of Murashu Sons of Nippur Dated in the Reign of Darius II* (Publications of the Babylonian Section, University Museum, University of Pennsylvania, 2.1; Philadelphia: University Museum, 1912) |
| *PEQ* | *Palestine Exploration Quarterly* |
| *PET* | M. Krebernik, *Die Personennamen der Ebla-Texts. Eine Zwischenbilanz* (Berlin: Reimer, 1988) |
| *PS* | *Patrologia Syriaca* |
| *RA* | *Revue d'assyriologie et d'archéologie orientale* |
| *RB* | *Revue biblique* |
| RCA | L. Waterman, *Royal Correspondence of the Assyrian Empire* (Ann Arbor: University of Michigan Press, 1930–36). |
| *RevSém* | *Revue sémitique* |
| *RHPR* | *Revue d'histoire et de philosophie religieuses* |
| *RHR* | *Revue de l'histoire des religions* |
| RIH | Ras ibn Hami |
| *RivB* | *Rivista biblica* |
| *RlA* | *Reallexikon der Assriologie u. Vorderasiatischen Archaeologie* |
| *RQ* | *Revue de Qumran* |
| RS | Ras Shamra |
| SAA | State Archives of Assyria |
| SAA 6 | T. Kwasman and S. Parpola, *Legal Transactions of the Royal Court of Nineveh*, Part I: *Tiglath-Pileser III through Esarhaddon* (State Archives of Assyria, 6; Helsinki: Helsinki University Press, 1991) |
| SAAS | State Archives of Assyria. Studies |
| SANT | Studien zum Alten und Neuen Testament |
| SBAB | Stuttgarter Biblischen Aufsätzbände |

| | |
|---|---|
| SBF.CMi | Studium Biblicum Franciscanum. Collectio major |
| SBF.CMa | Studium Biblicum Franciscanum. Collectio minor |
| *SBFLA* | *Studii biblici franciscani liber annuus* |
| SBLDS | SBL Dissertation Series |
| SBLMS | SBL Monograph Series |
| SBLTT | SBL Texts and Translations |
| SBT | Studies in Biblical Theology |
| *SCT* | C.H. Gordon, *Smith College Tablets: 110 Cuneiform Texts Selected from the College Collection* (Smith College Studies in History, 38; Northampton, MA: Department of History of Smith College, 1952) |
| *SE* | *Studia Evangelica I, II, III* (= TU 73 [1959], 87 [1964], 88 [1964], etc.) |
| *SEL* | *Studi Epigrafici e linguistici* |
| SH | Šēḫ Ḥamad |
| SHAW | Sitzungsberichte der Heidelberger Akademie der Wissenschaften |
| SHCANE | Studies in the History and Culture of the Ancient Near East |
| SHANE | Studies in the History of the Ancient Near East |
| *SJOT* | *Scandinavian Journal of the Old Testament* |
| *SMEA* | *Studi Micenei ed Egeo-Anatolici* |
| *SR* | *Studies in Religion/Sciences religieuses* |
| SS.NS | Studia Semitici Nuova Serie |
| StSemNeerl | Studia Semitica Neerlandica |
| *TA* | *Tel Aviv* |
| *TAD* A-D | B. Porten and A. Yardeni, *Textbook of Aramaic Documents from Ancient Egypt* (4 vols.; Winona Lake, IN: Eisenbrauns, 1986–1999) |
| TCL 12 | G. Contenau, *Contrats néo-babyloniens.* I. *De Téglath-phalasar III à Nabonide* (Texts cunéiformes du Louvre, 12; Paris: Geuthner, 1927) |
| TCL 13 | G. Contenau, *Contrats néo-babyloniens.* II. *Achéménides et Séleucides* (Texts cunéiformes du Louvre, 13; Paris: Geuthner, 1927) |
| *TDNT* | Gerhard Kittel and Gerhard Friedrich (eds.), *Theological Dictionary of the New Testament* (trans. Geoffrey W. Bromiley; 10 vols.; Grand Rapids: Eerdmans, 1964–) |
| *THAT* | Ernst Jenni and Claus Westermann (eds.), *Theologisches Handwörterbuch zum Alten Testament* (Munich: Chr. Kaiser Verlag, 1971–76) |
| ThB | Theologische Bücherei |
| *TLZ* | *Theologische Literaturzeitung* |
| TM | Texte Massorétique |
| *TSSI* | J.C.L. Gibson, *Textbook of Syrian Semitic Inscriptions* (3 vols.; Oxford; Clarendon Press, 1971–82) |

| | |
|---|---|
| TuM 2/3 | O. Krückmann, *Neubabylonische Rechts- und Verwaltungstexte* (Texte und Materialien der Frau Professor Hilprecht Collection, 2/3; Leipzig: J.C. Hinrichs, 1933) |
| *ThWAT* | G.J. Botterweck and H. Ringgren (eds.), *Theologisches Wörterbuch zum Alten Testament* (Stuttgart: W. Kohlhammer, 1970–) |
| *TynBul* | *Tyndale Bulletin* |
| *TZ* | *Theologische Zeitschrift* |
| UET 4 | H.H. Figulla, *Business Documents of the New-Babylonian Period* (Ur Excavations Texts, 4; London: British Museum, 1949) |
| *UF* | *Ugarit-Forschungen* |
| *UIOM* | *Sumerian and Akkadian Cuniform Texts in the Collection of the World Heritage Museum of the University of Illinois* |
| VA | Collection signature of the Vorderasiatische Abteinlung of the Berlin museums |
| *VT* | *Vetus Testamentum* |
| *VTE* | D.J. Wiseman (ed.), *The Vassal Treaties of Esarhaddon* (London: British School of Archaeology in Iraq, 1958) |
| VTSup | *Vetus Testamentum*, Supplements |
| WMANT | Wissenschaftliche Monographien zum Alten und Neuen Testament |
| WSS | N. Avigad and B. Sass (eds.), *Corpus of West Semitic Stamp Seals* (Jerusalem: Israel Academy/IES, 1997) |
| WVDOG | Wissenschaftliche Veröffentlichungen der Deutschen Orient-Gesellschaft |
| *WZKM* | *Wiener Zeitschrift für die Kunde des Morgenlandes* |
| YOS 6 | R.P. Dougherty, *Records from Erech, Time of Nabonidus (555–538 BC)* (Yale Oriental Series, Babylonian Texts, 6; New Haven: Yale University Press, 1920) |
| YOS 7 | A. Tremayne, *Records from Erech, Time of Cyrus and Cambyses (538–521 BC)* (Yale Oriental Series, Babylonian Texts, 7; New Haven: Yale University Press, 1925) |
| YOS 17 | D.B. Weisberg, *Texts from the Time of Nebuchadnezzer* (Yale University Series, Babylonian Texts, 17; New Haven: Yale University Press, 1980) |
| *ZA* | *Zeitschrift für Assyriologie* |
| *ZAW* | *Zeitschrift für die alttestamentliche Wissenschaft* |
| *ZDMG* | *Zeitschrift der deutschen morgenländischen Gesellschaft* |
| *ZDPV* | *Zeitschrift des deutschen Palästina-Vereins* |
| *ZS* | *Zeitschrift für Semitistik und verwandte Gebiete* |
| *ZTK* | *Zeitschrift für Theologie und Kirche* |

## LIST OF CONTRIBUTORS

Pierre Bordreuil, Institut d'Etudes Semitiques, Collège de France, Paris, France

Grant Frame, Department of Near and Middle Eastern Civilizations, University of Toronto, ON, Canada

Amir Harrak, Department of Near and Middle Eastern Civilizations, University of Toronto, ON, Canada

Clemens Leonhard, Institut fur Litergiewissenschaft, Vienna University, Austria

James Lindenberger, Centre for the History of Biblical Interpretation, Vancouver School of Theology, BC, Canada

R. Theodore Lutz, Department of Near and Middle Eastern Civilizations, University of Toronto, ON, Canada

William Morrow, Queen's Theological College, Kingston, ON, Canada

Dennis Pardee, Department of Near Eastern Languages and Civilization, University of Chicago, IL, USA

J. Tropper, Freie Universitat Berlin, Germany

Michael Weigl, Department of Old Testament Studies, Vienna University, Austria

# PAUL-EUGÈNE DION: AN APPRECIATION

John William Wevers

I consider it a privilege to write a few words in appreciation of my colleague and friend, Paul-Eugène Dion, whom I have known since 1972, first as a brilliant and mature graduate student in my Septuagint seminar, and later, since 1980, as my colleague and close associate in the Department of Near Eastern Studies (now the Department of Near and Middle Eastern Civilizations) at the University of Toronto.

His graduate studies culminated in his PhD dissertation, entitled *La langue de Ya'udi: Description et classement de l'ancien parler de Zencirli dans le cadre des langues sémitiques du nord-ouest*, which appeared in 1974. Prior to his Toronto studies he had been teaching Bible and theology at the Collège Dominicain d'Ottawa (1964–70), as well as serving as visiting professor or part-time instructor at l'Université de Montréal, Queens University and St Paul University in Ottawa. From that period I personally knew only one publication of his, which dealt with the Servant Songs in Deutero-Isaiah in *Biblica* 51. From his bibliography it is apparent that he had concerned himself with New Testament studies as well as with Old Testament. His earlier training had been at the École Biblique et Archéologique Française in Jerusalem, but his graduate studies at Toronto were undertaken to broaden his background in the Semitic environment of the Hebrew Scriptures, and he concentrated largely in cuneiform studies, viz. Asssyro-Babylonian languages and texts, as well as Northwest Semitic language and culture, as his above-mentioned dissertation written under the late Professor Ernest Clarke illustrates.

A few years later he left Le Collège Dominicain d'Ottawa to join the teaching staff in the Department of Near Eastern Studies at Toronto, where his broader graduate studies received full play. He quickly became our resident authority on the history and culture of the Aramaeans of pre-Christian times, was acknowledged as such far beyond the borders of Canada, and his detailed knowledge of the ancient Semitic world was communicated freely to his graduate students in seminars on Deuteronomy, the Psalter, and Deutero-Isaiah, his triennial offerings in the Graduate School.

Professor Dion had an amazingly wide bibliographic knowledge, and colleagues and students alike never approached him in vain for current bibliography on anything connected with the biblical world. His bibliographic database was and is immense and contemporary. I was myself often the beneficiary of his briefing on some difficult exegetical problem in the Pentateuch; he would inevitably give me references to discussions which I had overlooked, even in my own field of expertise.

He is truly a Renaissance-type scholar. For example, he fully kept up on archaeological matters of the Near Eastern world even though he had never had extensive training in archaeology (digging only for one season at Tall Jawa, in Jordan); he was able to hold his own in discussions with professional archaeologists. He could discuss intelligently with Jack Holladay details of Iron Age pottery characteristics of some site, or neolithic levels of digs in Iran with Cuyler Young. But his central interest dealt with historical and textual matters, such as early Old Aramaic inscriptional materials, the Tel Dan Stele, the bilingual inscription of Tell Fekherye, the Seal of Ariyaramna, the *ktym* of Tel Arad. These interests were in due course capped by his encyclopaedic study of the Aramaeans of the Iron Age in his 1997 Etudes bibliques volume: *Les Araméens à l'âge du fer: Histoire politique et structures sociales*.

Paul Dion, however, always remained faithful to his early devotion to Old Testament studies. His graduate courses in exegesis produced numerous articles on Deutero-Isaiah, the Psalter, and Deuteronomy in various French or English journals and Festschriften throughout North America and Europe. Typologically, these reflect his catholic interests, historical insights, exegetical matters, poetic structures, legal matters, ritual perspectives, archaeological details—anything which might clarify our understanding of the Old Testament text, history and culture was important to our friend, whose retirement we now recognize by this volume of studies, but whose retirement which this necessitates we deplore.

May I be permitted a personal reflection on my friend and colleague. For many years we have had adjacent offices in the Department, and have eaten our brown bag luncheons together at 12.30 daily. Our discussions have roamed widely, not only on our particular academic interests, but on literature, classics, history, theology, classical music, drama, painting, architecture, even food, but I don't believe he ever referred to the Stanley Cup finals in hockey, the Grey Cup rivalries, or the World Series. I suppose that Paul may have known the difference between hockey, football and/or baseball, but he never to the best of my recollection ever thought it of sufficient interest to mention it. I shall miss him.

# Compositional Strategies in the Aramaic Sayings of Ahikar: Columns 6–8

Michael Weigl

## *Recent Research on the Composition of the Book of Proverbs*

The past decades have seen rising scholarly interest in the compositional arrangement and structural unity of proverb collections, especially within the biblical book of Proverbs, thus ending an unduly long period of neglect of this important issue. There had been a long-standing and almost unanimous consensus among scholars about the arrangement of the individual sayings contained within the older collections of the book of Proverbs (10.1–22.16; 25–29). Editorial coincidence and very loose, mostly thematic connections between individual sayings were widely acknowledged as the only discernible criteria of composition.[1] This rather imprecise device was mostly deemed of minor importance for the final and canonical arrangement of the text. Besides that, there was no reckoning with other, more elaborate compositional techniques that could have served as unifying components binding together the vast thematic and formal spectrum. Likewise, context was barely considered relevant for interpretation. As a consequence, exegetes predominantly followed the lines of the individual proverbs.[2] In many cases the

1. Even the most outstanding authorities on Old Testament Wisdom literature shared this common view, cf. G. von Rad (1992: 151-52): 'Das Sprüchebuch präsentiert uns...eine zunächst schwer überschaubare Vielfalt von einzelnen Wirklichkeiten [...] Besonders erschwerend empfinden wir das Fehlen irgendeiner sachbedingten Ordnung, einer Disposition in den Sammlungen der Sentenzen und Lehren. Nur selten stößt der Leser einmal auf eine Spruchgruppe, in der sich Zusammengehöriges zusammengefunden hat. Für das Verständnis des Ganzen der aufgereihten Sentenzen sind diese kleinen Ordnungsorganismen ohne Bedeutung, weil sie zu vereinzelt auftreten.'

2. For example, this rather extreme approach has been adopted by W. McKane

results were unsatisfactory and shallow. Only a few scholars opted for a different approach. History of interpretation attests persistent efforts by a handful of commentators to demonstrate at least a minimum of compositional intention behind the seemingly chaotic corpus.[3] None of them argued for a consistent compositional concept stretching over the entirety of the individual collections. However, important observations were made about smaller clusters of text. In general, though, these opinions were not well received. Learned agreement remained with the more dominant exegetical tradition.

It was exactly this well-established *opinio communis* that has been transformed quite dramatically in recent scholarship. Rising interest[4] in matters of compositional techniques incited a series of detailed studies which were initially founded on remarks and observations of earlier commentators. Without giving a complete bibliography, only a brief overview illustrates the intensity of research on this issue. One may refer to the most important monographs and essays of the past two decades: Perry 1987; Hildebrandt 1988; Van Leeuwen 1988; Krispenz 1989; Whybray 1992; Snell 1993; Goldingay 1994; Hildebrandt 1990; Whybray 1994; Krüger 1995; Pola 1995; Skoralick 1995; Scherer 1997a, 1997b, 1999; compare also the recently published Heim 1999. Over a relatively short period of time, the once far-reaching consensus has lost its plausibility. Commonly shared assumptions were entirely

in his commentary on the book of Proverbs (1970: 10, 413): 'I argue...that there is, for the most part, no context in the sentence literature and that the individual wisdom sentence is a complete entity [...] The atomistic character of sentence literature may be modified to some extent by a secondary grouping of sentences, whether this is based on purely mechanical considerations [...] or derives from editorial groupings based on the common content in several sentences.'

3. An excellent résumé about different trends in research on the composition of the book of Proverbs can be found in Skoralick (1995: 91-159).

4. One of the first scholars who systematically devoted attention to matters of inner structural and compositional coherence in the book of Proverbs was U. Skladny (1962). He intended to present a clear outline of the older collections of Proverbs by assessing their thematic peculiarities. In order to achieve this, he carefully analysed repetitions and grouped them into semantic fields. However, the final presentation of his results proved to be most controversial. Despite the questionable method of the employment of word statistics and percentages to argue for the thematic cohesion of an individual collection, Skladny's treatment proved to be a source of inspiration for many further investigations; cf. also J. Conrad (1967: 67-76).

reversed. In the meantime, several painstaking articles and monographs have become available which confirm the opposite. It may suffice to point to R.N. Whybray's *The Composition of the Book of Proverbs* (1994) to prove that the fragmentation of the collections into individual proverbs and their interpretation without considering the greater editorial context are a matter of the past.

The earliest and most widely acknowledged compositional technique that was recognized as such turned out to be the most elusive one. Early on, similarity of content was understood as a device to group sayings into larger units. However, closeness of related topics is sometimes the hardest to grasp since it always remains dependent on the criteria the individual commentator is willing to establish. It is not always easy to verify, and in fact can be misleading. Proverbs are not always grouped by similar content. There are also many examples which demonstrate that a second proverb develops the content of the first, sometimes giving the first one a totally different meaning. Also, seemingly unrelated proverbs can be arranged in a sequence to set a new horizon of interpretation for both, thus avoiding monotonous repetition or boring reiteration of a certain topic. Therefore, one has to be very cautious in claiming similarity of content as compositional technique. There definitely is a need for more precise criteria.[5]

Recent studies have developed a lot of very useful instruments for analysis. Firstly, form and content of a proverb need to be acknowledged as two distinct constituents. This distinction must not be overstressed, though,[6] since both in mutual interaction contribute to the individuality of a specific saying. Without doubt the most basic methodical differentiation is that between nominal sayings and instruction. However, in many cases it remains insufficient to appreciate fully the variety of forms present in sentence/instruction literature.[7] As has been

5. Aptly Skoralick (1995: 94). She warns against subjective distortions of possible relations between individual proverbs: 'Ordnung…ist ein vielschichtiges Phänomen.'

6. At the level of a comprehensive interpretation, form and content together are, of course, inseparable. The methodological distinction between both must not cut this delicate link, cf. Bjørndalen (1970: 347-61).

7. Useful as this differentiation is for a basic assessment of literary forms, it is too imprecise to satisfy the demands of a detailed investigation. Furthermore, if considered the *only* admissible criterion, the distinction between the literary forms of sentence/saying and instruction may direct scholarly attention into wrong conclusions about compositional issues. This was the main criticism against McKane's

shown by various investigations, a careful evaluation of forms remains a desideratum for any profound analysis. Very important monographs dealing with matters of form are at hand already: cf. Schmidt 1936; Richter 1966; Hermisson 1968; Nel 1982. In addition, any analysis of compositional techniques ought to be aware of the fundamental features of syntax and grammatical structure of the individual units of each single saying. Only then is it feasible to correlate larger units and envisage potential compositional devices such as syntactic or semantic parallelism. Often the effectiveness of a saying emerges as a combination of these two aspects of parallelism. This is even more true if one investigates larger compositional units.

Having recognized the significance of affinities between proverbs in form, syntax and semantics one needs to consider other structural devices. The outstanding value of paronomasia as an indicator for compositional units was detected a long time ago (Boström 1928). The repetition of significant words or phrases, clusters of derivations from the same roots can be considered very meaningful compositional devices as well. Sometimes there is a marked shift in meaning between two occurrences of the same lexeme ('wordplay'). However, not only the fact of repetition is significant. Much depends on the distribution of the re-occurrences. They can serve as a simple verbal link between two adjoining proverbs, but sometimes also create an extensive framework of larger compositional units (cf. esp. Skoralick 1995; Scherer 1999). Twice-told proverbs constitute the extreme and most obvious mechanism which gives structure to comprehensive units of text, regardless as to whether or not they serve as outright repetitions or variants of the same proverb (cf. Snell 1993). Finally, there are a lot of very refined stylistic indicators such as sound patterns (cf. McCreesh 1991) which need to be taken into account for a profound compositional investigation. A final assessment of editorial principles leading up to the canonical collections within Proverbs is a goal which still needs a considerable amount of research.

'new approach' towards his otherwise very inspiring commentary on Proverbs. It is based on a methodological differentiation between the 'Instruction Genre', the 'Sentence Literature', and 'Poems and Numerical Sayings' in the book of Proverbs. The material is then classified into different categories, leading up to a new arrangement of the text. This methodology rests on a specific and 'atomistic' theory about the nature of the proverb collections, cf. above and McKane (1970).

### *The Aramaic Ahikar Papyri*

The validity of hypotheses about the guiding principles of editorial activity in the book of Proverbs has been counter-checked against the background of Egyptian Wisdom literature.[8] Thereby it became apparent that the book of Proverbs does not stand as an isolated example for an otherwise unattested phenomenon. Yet there exists an additional, hitherto underestimated corpus of sayings which shares even more common traits with Proverbs than any of the most frequently quoted Egyptian collections: the Aramaic sayings of Ahikar. Not long after the turn of the century (1907–1908), German excavations at the Judaeo-Aramaean military colony of Elephantine, situated on an island in the River Nile, brought to light a considerable amount of papyrus fragments containing texts of very different literary character. The most interesting and only literary corpus among them was a papyrus containing 14 columns of text in Aramaic. Even though the papyrus had been seriously damaged and some of the original columns had been lost, the document was quickly identified as an Aramaic version of the story and the sayings of Ahikar which until then had only been known from much later traditions.[9]

The Elephantine version of the Ahikar tradition consists of two parts: an introductory narrative and a corpus of sayings. Five columns of the Ahikar tale and nine columns containing proverbs of different literary forms were preserved. The narrative is superficially situated at the court of the Assyrian kings Sennacherib and Esarhaddon. It tells the reader about the fate of Ahikar, a wise courtier who, being childless, adopted his nephew Nadin and brought him up with the utmost love and devotion, only to be the ungrateful young man's victim after a change in power at the court. Slandered and without legal defence he was thrown into prison to await his execution. There, however, he met Nabušumiškun, a young man whom he had once saved from the same

8. This is especially true for Prov. 22.20–23.11 and their relation to the Instruction of Amenemope (cf. recently Römheld 1989).

9. The authoritative edition of the later Ahikar tradition still remains that of Conybeare, Harris and Lewis (1913). The most valuable and packed with detailed observations are Nau (1909) and Charles (1963). The interrelations and dependencies of all these younger versions represent a very complex problem that is not yet entirely understood. The most convincing theory was developed by Fales (1993: 39-60).

fate. The said Nabušumiškun recognized his former benefactor and hid him, and by this courageous act saved Ahikar. At this point, the Aramaic papyrus breaks off without revealing the story's end.[10] After a gap of four columns the Elephantine Papyri contain a collection of proverbs of very diverse literary character that are partly incomprehensible due to the papyrus's bad state of preservation. Clearly fictitious, the original relationship between the story and the proverb collection has been a matter of serious scholarly disagreement in the past. There are strong indicators that both elements did not form a compositional unity from the beginning but were only connected with one another at a later stage.[11] The sayings themselves represent without doubt a homogenous tradition that can be dealt with independently of the narrative.

Shortly after the discovery of the Elephantine Papyri and their version of the story and the proverbs of Ahikar, the full importance of the find became clear. The texts were published quickly by E. Sachau (1911). They immediately attracted intense scholarly attention (cf. esp. Ungnad 1911; Grimme 1911; Perles 1911, 1912; Seidel 1912; Epstein 1912, 1913a, 1913b, 1916; Wensinck 1912; Nöldeke 1913; Baneth 1914; Stummer 1914a, 1914b, 1915; Cowley 1923; and many others) which since has never totally subsided. Euphoria about the fact that the papyri contained the oldest known version of the Ahikar tradition enticed many a savant to localize close connections to the older

10. Younger traditions tell about the probable continuation of the tale. There, the proverb collection is stylized as the instruction Ahikar gave to his adopted son to enable him 'to stand before the king' in his place. After being freed again in a moment of crisis, Ahikar is restored to his former position and helps the Assyrian king to remain victorious over the Egyptian pharaoh. Finally, Nadin is handed over to Ahikar who confronts him with a long series of 'woes' that in the end cause the death of the ungrateful nephew. Without doubt, this extensive plot exceeds the original limits of the Aramaic story, whose original delimitation is impossible to determine. Also, there is no consensus as to whether the Aramaic story formed a frame around the block of sayings (so Kottsieper 1991: 320-24) in the same way the younger traditions did. The extant columns of Aramaic text do not favour this hypothesis. They contain the narrative and the proverbs in a linear continuation. Still, the last part of the papyrus is missing, so there can be no definitive decision.

11. There is an ongoing discussion about the relationship between the narrative and the proverbs. It is widely accepted that the tale shows traits of a much later stage in development of the Aramaic language and must therefore be subsequent to the more archaic dialect of the proverb collection (cf. esp. Kutscher 1970: 347-412; Greenfield 1968: 359-68; Lindenberger 1983: 17-20, 292).

traditions contained in the book of Proverbs. Affinities in form and content even led some scholars to claim the whole Ahikar tradition for Judaism (cf., e.g., Conybeare, Harris and Lewis 1913: xviii-xx; Schmitt 1913–14).[12] The depiction of Ahikar in the book of Tobit as the pious Jew who saved his relative from utter despair in times of hardship certainly favoured such an interpretation in the beginning. Eventually, though, scholarly interest in the Aramaic Ahikar Papyri declined sharply. Other exegetical controversies became more important. This is reflected by the decreasing number of publications, save in a few smaller studies with a rather limited scope on the Aramaic text.

The first scholar to resume this almost forgotten topic of research on a large scale was James M. Lindenberger (1983, 1985). His invaluable and thorough study of the sayings represents the first systematic treatment of the entire Aramaic proverb collection. The author not only dedicated a considerable amount of attention to possible restorations of the damaged sayings, he also evaluated the tradition-critical importance of the younger Ahikar traditions. Besides an extensive philological treatment, Lindenberger moreover considered thematically related texts of Old Testament and Akkadian Wisdom literature. In doing so, he became the first researcher to analyse systematically the Aramaic corpus in association with Old Testament texts. He recognized a series of substantial analogies both in form and content which had not yet been detected as such before. Nevertheless, Lindenberger was very careful not to over-stress these affinities and avoided comprehensive hypotheses about the relationship between the Aramaic and the biblical Wisdom collections. Undoubtedly, philological considerations make up the centrepiece of Lindenberger's monograph (1983). The results of this investigation convinced him to assume a northern Syrian genesis of the proverb collection. This hypothesis immediately aroused new scholarly curiosity. It positioned an important collection of sentence literature in close proximity to the Israelite monarchy from which, according to the overwhelming learned consensus, Prov. 10.1–22.16 and 25–29 had originated.

In 1990, the German scholar Ingo Kottsieper published a further study dedicated to the Aramaic proverbs. His priority was to examine

12. Schmitt, with respect to the Syriac version of the Ahikar story, notes: 'Wir haben in diesem Roman mit seiner didaktischen Weisheit einen wohl aus den Jahren 100 v. Chr. bis 100 oder 200 nach Christus aus jüdischen Kreisen stammenden schriftlichen Versuch, unter den Heiden Propaganda zu machen…' (1913–14: 90).

the proverb collection's grammatical and philological traits, founding his considerations on a totally new arrangement of the extant columns of text and on partly very original, partly rather controversial restorations of broken lines. The objective of his investigation was limited and strongly focused—a legitimate approach, to be sure.[13] Consequently, the author did not concern himself with problems originating from the literary characteristics of the sayings. Neither did he raise questions about their poetical structure, their composition or possible parallels in other literary traditions. The endeavour resulted in the first elaborate grammar, as well as in an extensive and helpful dictionary, of the Aramaic proverbs.[14] Kottsieper finally arrived at the conclusion that the Aramaic proverbs originated in the southern Lebanon of the mid-eighth to the mid-seventh centuries BCE (cf. esp. 1990: 241-46), in even closer geographical and chronological proximity to the Israelite monarchy than implied before him by Lindenberger. It is evident that the author's conclusions about the origins of the Aramaic proverbs—which I personally do not share!—have many important implications for biblical studies. If Kottsieper is right, the local and temporal vicinity of the (older) biblical and the Aramaic proverbs must be judged in a totally new light. Kottsieper did not take up on that aspect at all. Not much later, a number of scholars did, presupposing the accuracy of Kottsieper's theories without further consideration (e.g. Engelken 1996: 403-405; Scherer 1997b: 28-30). Indeed, the fascination of a possible acquaintance of Old Testament and Aramaic Wisdom is tempting biblical scholars to determine direct connections, not excluding outright literary dependency. This is not the place to opt for a more cautious and restricted approach in detail. Methodological restraint is advisable in any case.

13. His German translation (1991) in *Texte aus der Umwelt des Alten Testaments* (eds. G. Burkard *et al.*) and a series of other publications were even more influential. There, the author concentrated on literary aspects of the proverbs, thus supplying information underlying, but not given in his original study, cf. 1992, 1997a, 1997b.

14. The basic flaw of this study, however, is to be seen in the way it is presented. There is (almost) no discussion of the frequently very eccentric restorations, let alone a satisfying elucidation of the new arrangement of the preserved columns on which the entire grammar is based. Frequently, Kottsieper's etymologies are debatable. This is especially true where he turns to the Arabic to explain early Aramaic lexicography.

Given this context, the issue of composition in the Aramaic proverbs attained significant importance for Old Testament research. With a lot of detailed analysis and information at hand, several biblical scholars began to raise corresponding questions, taking the new results about compositional techniques in Prov. 10.1-22.16 and 25-29 as their point of departure: Are the Ahikar sayings just a random collection of individual and formally unrelated sayings? Were they grouped in any discernible, intended fashion? What—if any—were the editorial principles? Does this bear any consequences for assessing the origin of a single saying or a more comprehensive assemblage? Whereas Lindenberger (1983) only touched the issue and Kottsieper (1991: 323) rejected major compositional activity,[15] Porten and Yardeni (1993: xv-xvi) and especially Scherer (1997b: 28-45) considered it an important factor. The latter author was the first explicitly to try to correlate the biblical and the Aramaic proverbs with regard to composition (1997b). Scherer's advance cannot be underestimated. It may serve as an important directive for future research by indicating that the transferral of a specific exegetical methodology is an important step towards a better understanding of the sayings of Ahikar in this respect as well. By outlining selected aspects of compositional criteria employed in the extant Aramaic sayings, the present contribution in honour of my friend and teacher Paul-Eugène Dion is meant to prompt further discussion.[16]

15. Kottsieper 1991: 323: 'Die Spruchsammlung besteht aus vielen Einzelsprüchen zu den verschiedensten Themenbereichen, die nur zum Teil in Gruppen zusammengefaßt sind. Dabei scheint kein durchgängiges Redaktionsprinzip geherrscht zu haben.'

16. Before proceeding with a detailed analysis of selected passages a few methodological remarks are in place. One of the most annoying aspects of dealing with the Aramaic sayings is the wide range of different reference systems. Virtually every new edition introduced a new numbering of the proverbs, partly because of the different views about the sequence of the columns on the papyrus, partly because of a new syntactical segmentation of individual proverbs. Sachau, Cowley, Lindenberger and Kottsieper all developed a system of their own, so did the final and unquestionably authoritative edition by Porten and Yardeni (1993). Their approach will be adopted in this essay. Each saying is quoted by a reference to the column, followed by the number of the given line and a proverb number. Where necessary, syntactic segmentation will be indicated by lower case letters.

## *Composition in the Aramaic Proverbs of Ahikar, Columns 6–8*

Without doubt the corpus of the Aramaic proverbs preserved on the extant columns of the Elephantine Papyri lacks a consistent compositional concept that would have been applied throughout the whole collection. However, one has to take into account that our perception of compositional elements could be seriously distorted by the fragmentary preservation of the text. Different factors may have had an influence on the actual arrangement of the preserved sayings.[17] On the other hand there are certain indicators for the attempt to create larger units by mere scribal techniques, for example the use of separation marks of different kinds written either between individual sayings as asterisks in the form of an א or as lines drawn at the right margins of the papyrus to indicate a larger context in which two or more sayings were grouped. These scribal annotations cannot easily be ignored, even if they remain minor editorial devices and are not employed consistently throughout the entire text. Certainly they remain on the surface structure of the text and do not express a more sophisticated and substantial compositional process.

Principles of composition become more evident after a detailed analysis of the individual sayings, bearing in mind that the context of each saying might be a relevant factor for determining its meaning as well as its place in a larger compositional unit. At many points sayings were grouped into pairs, triplets or even more extensive assemblages. Similarity in form and syntax was of high importance in this process. Catchwords and repetitions of words or roots as well as semantic fields pertain to the level of semantics and content. Often synonyms and antonyms between single syntactical elements served as a substantial mechanism to constitute a larger compositional unit. At some points in the collection more refined stylistic figures such as chiasm or inclusio were employed to connect two or more sayings. One might also consider

17. The availability of space might have been a factor, for example. The first lines of a column usually coincide with the beginning of a new saying. This is clear evidence of the scribe's attempt to present his object in a well-structured form. Nevertheless, the boundaries between the individual proverbs are less evident the further a column has been inscribed. In the lower third of a column the proverbs usually do not start at the beginning of a line any more, but wherever the previous proverb ended. This is less evident in the first columns of the collection but becomes the rule towards its end.

an arrangement along existing word-pairs or even reckon with more extended standing lists. A detailed inquiry aptly follows the arrangement of the sayings on the papyrus according to the perspective of the intended reader.

*Column 6*

Despite its fine state of preservation column 6 does not easily reveal an obvious and consistent editorial concept. At first sight it only contains a rather diffuse mixture of formally and thematically diverse sayings, showing no apparent deliberate compositional arrangement. Do the form and content of these 17 diverse sayings collected in column 6 reveal any traits of editorial principle at all?

6.79 (1), the first unit, can be considered to be a fragment of a hymn about something or someone precious to the gods. It is followed by a short proverb about the necessity to take a careful and deliberate approach towards the reality of time, cf. 6.80 (2). 6.81 (3) unfolds an entirely different, new context. Its main characteristics are rather complex combinations of admonitions and embedded nominal elements which substantiate the importance of the foregoing exhortations and warnings and a common topic, dealing with considerate speech. 6.82 (4) and 6.83 (5) develop this theme in detail. They are cast in the form of admonitions ensued by motive clauses. Both of them share an identical literary form and characteristic imagery.

The transition between 6.83 (5) and 6.84 (6) marks an important shift in content. The sayings following 6.84 (6) still deal with the same topic, but presuppose a different setting. The royal court replaces the private sphere. Now, either the king or his subject speak. All admonitions are directed towards the courtier; the king himself is never addressed. Sayings 6.84 (6)–6.89-90 (12) almost exclusively deal with the commanding 'word of a king'. A loosely related statement about the bitter taste of poverty in 6.89 (11) and an admonition not to overestimate the importance of progeny in 6.90 (13) interrupt the otherwise homogenous unit twice. The topic 'king' is resumed in 6.91 (14)–6.92 (15). At this point his commands are of no importance any more. Instead, these two sayings now contemplate the king's almost divine character and the consequences that his affinity to the gods bears for his people.

The last two sayings of the column, 6.93 (16) and 6.94 (17), are of a totally different character in form as well as in content. Saying 6.93

(16) is stylized as a statement and makes use of very distinct imagery. Implicitly, its constitutive metaphor refers back to 6.81 (3)–6.83 (5) and resumes the topic of considerate speech. It shows no apparent connection with the adjoining and final saying 6.94 (17), where animals interact about something we have no way of telling due to the damage the papyrus suffered.

6.79 (1)

אף לאלהן יק[י]רה הי
עמ[ה] למ[ראהם] מלכותא
בשמ[י]ן שימה הי
כי בעל קדשן נשא[ה]

(a) Moreover, to the gods she is precious.
(b) With her master[18] she shares kingship.
(c) She is put into heaven,
(d) for the lord of the holy ones exalted her.

A short hymn situated in the realm of heaven serves as the introductory unit at the head of column 6. Following the rearrangement of the text by Porten and Yardeni, the hymn comes to be the exposition of the entire proverb collection. Traditionally, 6.79 (1) has been regarded as the continuation of 12.189 (97). There, the wisdom of the gods (חכמתהם) and its bestowal upon humankind are mentioned explicitly. In combination with 6.79 (1), this saying would have formed a perfect hymnal unit exalting the gods and their favourable attitude towards humankind (cf. Lindenberger 1983: 68-70; and the cautionary remarks by Gianto 1995: 88-89). However, without a direct juxtaposition between the end of column 12 and the beginning of column 6 there is no indication as to the subject of the hymn in 6.79 (1) whatsoever. A reference made by הי in the first statement 6.79 (a) could be regarded as an indication that indeed wisdom is the subject to which the hymn

18. Here, the papyrus was severely damaged. Only the initial ע of the preposition in (b) was preserved unambiguously. After it traces suggest מ. A detached fragment contains a ל, followed again by a tiny segment of מ. None of the previously proposed reconstructions is entirely satisfactory. Lindenberger (1983: 499) and most of the other commentators follow a reading already suggested by Baneth (1914: 297): עד לעלמן לה מלכותא, 'forever the kingdom is hers'. However, the width of the lacuna advises a shorter reading. Kottsieper (1990: 12) introduced a conjecture which is based on a more realistic judgment of the available space. It has been adopted above.

refers. Certainty about this pronominal reference cannot be achieved on the basis of internal criteria alone. It might allude to something precious to the gods that had been mentioned at the end of a lost column, but it is also possible that it refers to a concluding element of the preceding narration. If one is willing to consider comparable texts of a different literary setting, one could infer that indeed חכמה (wisdom) is the topic of 6.79 (1).[19]

In terms of compositional criteria, 6.79 (1) certainly remains detached from what follows. The solemn, descriptive language, as well as the nominal style and total absence of any reference to an addressee, distinguish this unit from the bulk of text arranged in column 6. However, in its greater context 6.79 (1) does not remain totally isolated. With regard to its syntax and its nominal, descriptive and hence rather dignified style one can notice a certain affinity with the sayings about the king, grouped almost at the end of the column in 6.91 (14) and 6.92 (15). Taking into account a certain number of significant repetitions, which will be mentioned in the context of these sayings further below, there is clear evidence that those three texts share a lot of common features. All three of them are either situated in or allude to the heavenly sphere. They are to some extent concerned with eternal rule and the splendour of kingship.

One wonders if this combination is merely coincidental. It could also express a deliberate editorial concept which purposely associated the king with the gods. A reflection on the eternal rule granted to someone or something by the gods, placed right at the beginning of a textual unit dealing extensively with human kingship, positively has a bearing on the reader's understanding of what follows. A certain amount of repetition in 6.91 (14) and 6.92 (15) assists in securing the effectiveness and perceptibility of this notion. If this is true, there must be a new assessment of the hymn's function. 6.79 (1) emerges as an introductory hymn, praising the deeds of the gods and at the same time establishing the authority of a human king by associating him with the divine sphere, a phenomenon well known from related Near Eastern literatures.[20]

19. Cf. Job 28; Prov. 8.22-31; Ecclus 1.9-10; 24.1-7; Wis. 7.25-29 and Lindenberger 1983: 68.

20. Introductory hymns placed at the beginning of many a Sumerian or Akkadian composition might illustrate this, e.g. the fable of the encounter between the date palm and the tamarisk, cf. Lambert 1996: 155, 163 and Wilcke 1989: 171, 178. Moreover, it would seem rewarding to consider also the mythological introductions

When envisioning the entire ensemble of proverbs, the structural importance of the hymn becomes even more striking.

6.80 (2)

ברן[י] אל תלן[ו]ט יומא
עד תחזה [סו]פה

(a) My son, do not curse the day
(b) until you see its end.[21]

The strong orientation of 6.80 (2) alongside the semantic field of speech, as well as the essential component of the right timing of an utterance, affiliate 6.80 (2) with the following group of sayings. 6.83 (5) and its exhortation to utter one's opinions at the appropriate time only (cf. אחרי כן הנפק מלתך בעדדה in 6.83 [b]), resumes the very same basic concept in different wording. In its briefness 6.80 (2) states the hermeneutic principle by which 6.81 (3)–6.83 (5) have to be understood. It functions as a kind of superscription and interpretative key for the following compositional unit, and even extends its range to the sayings about the king which follow later. The lexeme יום, as used here to express the notion of untimeliness, also helps establish this remote connection. Anyone who unfittingly opposes the king's command will not be able to savour life in its entirety (cf. ותהך ולא ביומיך in 6.86 [f]).

It is generally assumed that this short warning about careful judgment is not connected with the units that surround it. Besides its simple syntactic structure which distinguishes it from its context, there is neither a reference to the gods nor to considerate speech figuring predominantly in the next saying. However, the first part of the warning already gives indisputable evidence against this assumption. לוט יומא ('to curse the day') in 6.80 (a) undoubtedly constitutes a very forceful act of speech. Even though the root לוט itself is not resumed in any of

of the great Akkadian myths. However, a detailed comparison is beyond the scope of this essay.

21. Traditionally, the last word of (b) is read as לילה, cf. Lindenberger 1983: 73 and Porten and Yardeni 1993: 36. However, this interpretation causes serious problems. לילה is otherwise unknown in early Aramaic; the reading of the initial consonant ל remains more than uncertain. Puech (1988: 589-90) proposed סופה instead. It fits the traces extant on the papyrus much better. At the same time it also ascertains a very consistent interpretation.

the following sayings, and the form of a simple warning without a substantiating clause is not repeated either, 6.80 (2) serves as a short introduction to the subsequent argumentation: Nothing must be judged—let alone this passionately!—before it can be perceived in its entirety. The emphasis of this short warning is not primarily on the act of cursing itself, but on the unwise bearing of a person who makes his final judgment before being able to comprehend a matter in its wholeness. *Nothing* must be decided on the basis of a fragmentary knowledge, since the beginning and the end of any aspect of reality belong together.[22]

6.81 (3)

א[ף] תאתה על בלך
כזי בכל אתר ע[יני]הם ואדניהם
לו[ת] פמך אשתמר לך
אל יהוה טרפי[הם]

(a) Moreover, let it come into your mind,[23]
(b) that in every place are their eyes and their ears!
(c) As regards[24] your mouth: Watch yourself!
(d) Let it not be their prey!

22. A similar phenomenon can be observed in Old Testament Wisdom literature, cf. Prov. 27.1; Eccl. 11.6; Ecclus 11.26.

23. The evaluation of its syntax constitutes the decisive element in the interpretation of this saying. The traditional reconstruction of אל in (a) directs interpretation towards an initial prohibition. However, this cannot be correct. By no means can (a) exhort the addressee not to be overanxious ('let it not come into your mind...', cf. Porten and Yardeni 1993: 36), whereas the following admonitions warn against the ubiquitous potential slanderer. This would result in an internal contradiction. If one reconstructs אף at the beginning of (a), there is no such problem. The identical introduction of 6, 79 (1) can serve as additional evidence derived from the immediate context.

24. Several problems impair the interpretation of 6.81 (3). Most of the damaged consonants can be restored with a high degree of certainty. Lexically, לות (c) and טרף (d) are the most difficult elements of this saying. לות is easily understood as preposition 'towards, as regards' rather than להן (Lindenberger 1983: 73). The root טרף is problematic, since it lacks sufficient Aramaic documentation. None of the previously proposed interpretations satisfies meaning. Therefore, an analogy to Hebrew טרף as suggested by Porten and Yardeni (1993: 37) seems to be the best alternative.

6.82 (4)

מן כל מנטרה טר פמך
ועל זי ש[אל] הוקר לבב
כי צנפר הי מלה
ומשלחה גבר לא לב[ב]

(a) More than all that is watched, watch your mouth,
(b) and towards him who asks,[25] harden your heart!
(c) For a bird is a word,
(d) and he who releases it is a man without reason.

6.83 (5)

מ[ח]י אחדי פמך
אחרי כן הנפק [מלת]ך בעדדה
כי עזיז ארב פם מן ארב מלחם

(a) Eliminate[26] the pungency[27] of your mouth!
(b) Afterwards, utter your word in its time.[28]
(c) For mightier is ambush of mouth than ambush of battle.

25. Based on the reconstruction of the participle of the root שאל, cf. Porten and Yardeni 1993: 36. The more traditional reading שמע is also a possibility. There is no way to decide between these two proposals with certainty. Both fit the lacuna and yield a satisfactory meaning.

26. The first word of (a) was badly damaged. It lacks its middle consonant. There is no indication for a secure reconstruction. The conjectural reading suggested above rests on the late Aramaic/Hebrew meaning of מחי, 'to remove, eliminate'.

27. Several different interpretations have been proposed for the construct chain אחדי פמך. Sachau (1911: I, 164) related אחדי to late Aramaic/Syriac אחדא, 'bolt, peg'. Lindenberger (1983: 77) and many others decided for the Syriac *'whdt'* 'secret'. However, there is a more adequate interpretation that rests on Ezek. 21.21. There, the text contains an exhortation directed towards YHWH's sword to התאחדי, 'sharpen itself'. Clearly, the reference is to the Hebrew root חדד = אחד, which Zimmerli (1979: 472 n. 21) regards as a 'syrianising' Aramaic equivalent to Hebrew חדד. Considering the military overtone inherent to the motive clause (c), a similar etymology might be implied in the אחדי פמך of 6.83 (a).

28. There is considerable uncertainty about the interpretation of בעדדה. The ambiguity in the writing of the consonants ד/ר allows for two possible explanations. Either the word is to be read as בעדרה, 'to his help', or as suggested above, cf. also Kottsieper 1990: 12 and Porten and Yardeni 1993: 36. In the latter reading the prepositional phrase can be understood easily as a reference to the 'right time' which shall be chosen carefully before a word is uttered. לאחו (Lindenberger 1983: 77) is obsolete on grounds of palaeography.

The first comprehensive unit of column 6 consists of three sayings: 6.81 (3)–6.83 (5). All of them caution against unmindful and careless utterances by pointing out the disastrous consequences it may inflict upon a person. Although they form a self-contained assemblage of admonitions, 6.81 (3)–6.83 (5) at the same time introduce a whole complex of formally and thematically related sayings that are arranged around the unifying topic of controlled speech. All of the three sayings examined here are directed to the reader in the form of warnings and admonitions.

Besides this general congruence in literary form further and more significant analogies between the individual units can be noticed on the level of syntax. After the initial warning, 6.81 (3) contains a nominal clause introduced by כאי. By pointing to the ubiquitous 'eyes and ears' of malign persons, it substantiates the reason of the surrounding admonitions and the final warning given in 6.81 (d). The adjacent sayings reveal a similar, though not identical, structure. Each of them contains two initial admonitions, but no warning. In both sayings a nominal clause follows the paired imperatives. The introductory כי clearly indicates its function. 6.82 (c)-(d) as well as 6.83 (c) use a metaphor to illustrate their point. 6.81 (d), 6.82 (c)-(d) and 6.83 (c) function at the same level, only the actual embedding in a framework of admonitions differs. The closeness in syntax between sayings 6.82 (4) and 6.83 (5) is certainly more obvious than structural similarity between this pair of sayings and the preceding admonition in 6.81 (3). From a structural point of view, the only difference between 6.82 (4) and 6.83 (5) can be distinguished with regard to the elements of the substantiating clause. It consists of two parallel elements in 6.82 (4), whereas a single element suffices in 6.83 (5).

When the structural similarities between these two sayings (4) and (5) are compared, the near congruence of their syntactical cores becomes evident. Both main clauses consist of a verbal predicate (imperative) and a direct object, followed by a subordinate clause that combines the subject with a nominal predicate. Whereas in 6.82 (a)-(b) prepositional phrases precede the syntactic core as facultative elements, they are postponed in 6.83 (b) and (c).[29]

29. S = subject; Pred = nominal predicate; O = object; pO = prepositional phrase; P! = imperative.

| 6.82 (4) | 6.83 (5) |
|---|---|
| (a) pO – P! – O | (a) P! – O |
| (b) pO – P!– O | (b) P! – O – pO |
| (c) Pred – S | (c) Pred – S – pO |
| (d) S – Pred | |

In addition to the parallel arrangement of the syntactical elements in (a) and (b) of both sayings, the chiastic order of the verbless predicates and the subjects in 6.82 (c) and (d) deserves attention. There can be no doubt that these two sayings were arranged as a couplet already because of their very similar sentence structures. In contrast, the internal form of 6.81 (3) is much more complicated and lacks the structural parallelism of its constituents. Still, there obviously were enough common features to suggest an editorial arrangement of 6.81 (3) together with the pair 6.82 (4) and 6.83 (5). Structurally, 6.81 (3) precedes the following two sayings as an introductory unit that announces the topic of the following group in a more general perspective.

The keyword of the entire compositional unit is פם. It appears in each of the three sayings (four times altogether) in 6.81 (c), 6.82 (a), 6.83 (a), (c) and is absent from the rest of the column. Instead מלה takes over in the following sayings. This transition marks the shift from the organ to its 'product', speech itself. All statements about פם are characterized by a dynamic character and are exclusively concerned with taking great care (שמר, נטר מנטרה). שאל in 6.82 (b), מלה in 6.82 (c) and 6.83 (b) also belong to this semantic field. The notion of a word's easy escape dominates each of the three precepts and culminates in נפק מלה in 6.83 (b). Terminology related to human perception represents another consistent feature of this group of sayings, comprising עין and אדן in 6.81 (b), אתה על בל in 6.81 (a), הוקר לבב in 6.82 (b) and גבר לא לבב in 6.82 (d). A slight shift can be noticed in 6.83 (c) where a metaphor taken from the realm of battle and weaponry expresses a general statement about a word's possible treacherousness. It prepares the transition to the next compositional unit where exactly this aspect looms large and is elaborated from different points of view.

One might finally note certain repetitions which affirm the internal structure of the individual sayings or aid in ascertaining explicit relations between them. On a merely phonetic level there is a striking resemblance between טרף at the end of 6.81 (3) and the initial paronomasia מנטרה טר פמך of 6.82 (4). Within 6.82 (4) the repetition of the lexeme לבב in (b) and (d) not only strengthens the bonds between the admonition of (b) and the argumentation of (d), but also relates the addressee's reaction ('harden the heart') to the contrasting attitude of the fool ('a man without reason'). A similar internal accentuation is created by the repetition of ארב with two different constructed elements in 6.83 (c) (מלחם / פם). In addition, the reference to battle and weaponry in 6.83 (5) refers the reader back to טרף of 6.81 (3). Hence, a dense semantic reference system coincides with far-reaching syntactic similarities, thus creating a very homogenous group of sayings.

6.84 (6)–6.89 (12) almost entirely deal with the problem of a king's commanding word and a person's utterances in the presence of a ruler. Thus, the entire complex serves as an elucidation of the first group's topic with a more specific accentuation. The setting is definitely less general within this assemblage than in the previous one. It envisages a specific situation that does not affect every possible addressee, but concentrates on the problems and hardships of a person moving about at the royal court where he is permanently confronted with the changing countenance of the ruler. Even if the greater context opened by 6.81 (3) remains predominant, the following group of sayings focuses on a different milieu.

As far as form and syntax are concerned, 6.84 (6)–6.89 (12) as a whole do not constitute a homogeneous block of text. Statements, admonitions, warnings and questions appear beside each other or in combination. The seemingly disordered mixture of elements insinuates a lack of a consistent editorial concept and betrays most of the close affinities between certain sayings. In its macrostructure, only a rather diffuse common theme becomes visible as a unifier for the whole unit, while substantial aspects easily escape the attention of the reader.

The first and most important compositional device which can be distinguished within this group of sayings is a set of few very densely knit semantic fields. These are carefully interwoven and span the entire ensemble of text. The most prominent among them is again that of human utterance, indicating the continuation of the previous context and at the same time expressing the most important concern of this assemblage. Repetitions of מלה and its derivations constitute a high degree of semantic coherence: מלת מלך in 6.84 (a), 6.87 (a), 6.88 (g) (cf. ממלל מלך in 6.84 [a]) being the most frequently used among them. Also לשן מלך in 6.89 (a), אמר in 6.86 (e) and, less closely, פקיד in 6.87 (b), form part of the same semantic field.

The second important keyword in this unit is מלך, appearing seven times in near identical distribution. מלך also serves as a kind of anchor linking the larger unit with its surrounding context. It resumes מלכותא from 6.79 (b) (1) and is also repeated once in each of the following pairs of sayings in 6.91 (14)–6.92 (15) where it appears attached to the heavenly sphere (שמש, אל) as in 6.79 (1) (בעל קדשן, אלהן). The association between the realm of the gods and the court of a king rests therefore totally on the combination of מלך within two different contexts. Statements about the gods and the king are thus connected at an important strategic section of column 6. Hence, they function as a framework around the whole column of text in whose centre sayings about speech are arranged.

A high concentration of terminology related to weaponry and death constitutes another significant compositional element in this section of column 6. This does not come as a total surprise, since already the exhortation טר מנטרה and טרף in 6.82 (4) as well as אחדי and ארב in 6.83 (5) had introduced this semantic field. Here, however, the density of related terminology is even higher. Around the most explicit term מות in 6.90 (c) a whole net of pertaining expressions is spun: ותהך [ו]לא ביומיך in 6.86 (f) and עלעי תנין יתבר in 6.90 (b) are poetic variations which express the simple fact of potential deadliness. סכין in 6.84 (b) and 6.88 (b) also contributes to the same imagery. In a wider sense this is also true for the natural hazards to life, אשה יקדה in 6.87 (c), אשה in 6.88 (a) and ברק in 6.85 (c).[30]

6.84 (6)

אל תכסה מלת מלך
רפאה תהוי [ללב]בך

(a) Do not cover a word of a king!
(b) Let it be healing[32] for your heart!

30. Other repetitions or components of further semantic fields are of a limited importance for composition, i.e. mainly כסי in 6.84 (a) and 6.87 (f), used in two different contexts: the royal command in 6.84 (a) and the reaction of the courtier in 6.87 (f). Whereas the expression כסי מלה is easily understood here, this is not the case for כסי in 6.87 (f), 'to cover one's palms'.

31. Early commentators read תכבה instead of תכסה, cf. Lindenberger (1983: 79); Kottsieper (1990: 12). However fitting this etymology might be in a context where 'fire' and 'lightning' are mentioned, the repetition of the expression כסי מלה in 6.93 (16) favours a similar reading in 6.84 (a). Palaeographic evidence supports this decision.

The first saying of the section is in the form of a simple combination of an initial warning, followed by an admonition. In terms of form, it continues the series of similar admonitions that precede it, though its formulation is much more concise and shorter, echoing the brevity of 6.80 (2). However, despite its brevity 6.84 (6) marks an important thematic transition by introducing the lexeme מלך that dominates the next lines and extends its prevalence almost to the end of the column. The phrase כסי מלה is repeated in connection with לבב at a later point in 6.93 (16), where the meaning is in total contrast to the admonition of 6.84 (6). Still, the repetition as such is meaningful, since it serves as a bracket around a large block of text. The keywords מלה and לבב link 6.84 (6) with the preceding as well as the following. Therefore, this short warning is of strategic importance for compositional continuity. It sets the stage for the sayings to ensue.

6.84 (7)

רכיך ממלל מלך
שדק ועזיז הו מן סכין פמי[ן]

(a) Soft is the speech of a king.
(b) It is sharper and mightier than a double-edged dagger.

6.89-90 (12)

רכיך לשן מ[לך]
ועלעי תנין יתבר
כמותא זי [ל]א מתחזה

(a) Soft is the tongue of a king.
(b) But the ribs of a dragon it breaks
(c) like death which is not seen.

Though separated by a considerable amount of text, 6.84 (7) and 6.89-90 (12) definitely belong together as a proverbial pair. Several indicators ascertain this understanding. On the level of syntax the respective first elements agree totally—a nominal predicate is followed by the

32. Already the scribe corrected the initial writing רפה by the insertion of א between the third and the fourth consonants. There is no doubt about etymology, even though רפה is usually considered as one of the 'canaanisms' within the Aramaic text, cf. Lindenberger (1983: 79); against Kottsieper (1990: 12) (דפאה from the Arabic 'to be hot').

subject, consisting of a construct chain. What may sound a bit far-fetched in this abstraction is immediately evident if the actual wording is considered as well:

רכיך ממלל מלך 6.84 (a)
רכיך לשן מלך 6.89 (a)

Semantics clearly assists in creating structural unity. The first two elements of each saying are linked by the repetition of רכיך that is used in combination with ממלל מלך in 6.84 (a) and לשן מלך in 6.89 (a). The second part of each of the two sayings consists of an element that rests on a paradoxical opposition between the exceptional softness (a) and the absolute deadliness of a king's commands. Each of the two sayings elaborates this concurrent paradox in a different way. Syntactically there is no congruence in this element. Semantically, however, both sayings use grim images of death. 6.84 (7) compares the royal command to a most powerful weapon—ממלל מלך is even stronger than a 'double-edged dagger'. 6.89-90 (12) depicts possible death inflicted by the dagger in mythological imagery.

In their syntactic and semantic symmetry these two sayings through their placement indicate a stylistic strategy. They unmistakably form a pair of sayings which has been separated for compositional reasons, namely to create a framework around a group of sayings concerned with the royal command and the right attitude towards it. 6.84 (7) marks the beginning, 6.89-90 (12) the end of this textual arrangement. The distribution of the semantic fields of 'speech' and 'king' strengthens the argument. לשן מלך in 6.89-90 (12) represents the last intersection of these two semantic elements. Thereafter they are treated separately again, that is, מלך in 6.91 (14), 6.92 (15) and מלה in 6.93 (16). The remainder of the sayings grouped in column 6 partly still elaborate the topic 'king', but accentuate their point differently.

6.85-86 (8)

חזי קדמתך מנדעם קשה
על אנפי מלך אל תקום
זעיר כצפה מן ברק

אנת אשתמר לך
אל יחזנהי על אמריך
ותהך ולא ביומיך

(a) Take heed—before you there is a severe matter.[33]
(b) Against the face of a king do not stand!
(c) His rage is swifter than lightning.
(d) You, watch yourself!
(e) May he not show it because of your words,
(f) lest you die and it is not in your days.

6.87-88 (9)

[חזי מ]לת מלך
הן פקיד לך
אשה יקדה הי
עבק עבדהי
אל תהנשק עליך
ותכסה כפיך
[א]ף מלת מלך
בחמר לבבא

(a) Take heed[34]—a word[35] of a king:
(b) If something is commanded to you,
(c) it is burning fire.
(d) Hurry, do it!
(e) Do not kindle it against you,
(f) and do not cover your palms!
(g) Moreover[36]—a word of a king:
(h) (It is uttered) with fervour[37] of the heart.

33. Although there are no severe problems as far as the preservation of the text is concerned, this saying has been read quite differently. Interpretation depends entirely on the understanding of the syntactic constraints. The position of the prepositional phrase על אנפי מלך (b) has been especially discussed. In the rendering chosen above, it serves as a direct object of the vetitive אל תקום, cf. a similar construction in 6.91 and Lindenberger (1983: 81); Porten and Yardeni (1993: 36). However, the phrase could theoretically also form part of (a), thus implying the meaning a 'severe matter against the king'. Kottsieper (1990: 12) reads ב instead of על and translates the preposition with an adversative meaning: 'Siehe, vor dir liegt etwas Widerborstiges gegen den König.' There is little evidence for such a use of ב.

34. The right margin of the papyrus was severely damaged. The width of the lacuna allows for the restoration of more than a single word. An introductory formula such as חזי fits the context well. Other options like אף, הא, כן (Kottsieper 1990: 12) cannot be excluded.

35. Since Sachau (1911: I, 164) the beginning of the next word has been reconstructed as מ. There is no reason to abandon this reading, especially since מלה serves as one of the keywords of the whole unit (against Kottsieper [1990: 12], חמת; and Porten and Yardeni [1993: 36, טבת]).

There is yet another aspect to this deliberate disposition. One notices that with 6.85-86 (8) and 6.87-88 (9) the most extensive sayings contained in column 6 follow upon each other in an immediate sequence. Again, these two sayings show certain common features which are less clearly distinguishable on the syntactic than on the semantic level. Besides the fact that both elements are more in the form of a small discourse than in that of sayings proper, one might notice that a mixture of admonitions, warnings and nominal elements quoted as evidence to emphasize urgency is characteristic for 6.85-86 (8) and 6.87-88 (9). Also, these two sayings revolve again around the keyword מלך.

The two units begin with a focus marker (חזי) directing the reader's attention to the presentation of the problem. In the case of 6.85 (a) קדמתך מנדעם קשה explicitly states the point of departure by reminding the addressee that the saying is really about a *serious* matter. Similarly, 6.87 (a)-(b)מלת מלך הן פקיד לך asserts the issue of the discourse before elaborating its details. As a second element both sayings contain a metaphor comparing the king's anger with a 'striking' and destructive element of nature, ברק in 6.85 (c), אשה יקדה in 6.87 (c). This metaphor constitutes the core element and appears embedded in a framework of imperatives. A vetitive construction (b) precedes it in (8), whereas a single imperative functions as an introduction in (9). The consecutive imperatives—אנת אשתמר לך 6.85 (d), and עבק עבדהי —6.87 (d)—bear all the emphasis of the respective units.[38] Both in

36. The last two elements of this saying have been a much debated issue. The reading chosen above is that of Sachau (1911: I, 164) and many others, cf. Lindenberger (1983: 84). Again, Kottsieper (1990: 12: 76-77) proposed a new explanation by reconstructing סף, 'execute'. However, this root is not attested in the G-stem elsewhere. In addition, a defective writing would be most uncommon for the orthography of the proverb collection.

37. Again, the ambiguous notation of ד/ר allows for different interpretations. The lexeme may either be understood as חמר, 'fervour, rage, vehemence', or as חמד, 'something valuable'. The latter meaning is poorly attested in Aramaic. In a context which deals with manifestations of the king's rage the former reading is to be preferred. Since there is no verbal predicate, (g)-(h) must be analysed as a nominal clause in which the verb is not explicitly expressed and has to be supplied by the reader.

38. With regard to the greater context it is worth noting a structural analogy between the sequence of imperatives followed by a negative jussive in 6.81 (c)-(d): אשתמר לך אל יהוה טרפיהם and אנת אשתמר לך אל יחזנהי על אמריך in 6.86 (e)-(f).

6.86 (e)-(f) and in 6.88 (e)-(f) vetitive constructions ensue. Each of them warns against disobedience and depicts possible negative results of inadequate behaviour. Because of their 'striking' character, royal ordinances must be carried out as promptly and accurately as possible.

Once more, two adjacent sayings are grouped into a pair by means of related syntactical and semantic structures. Considering these structural elements two proverbial pairs can be isolated within 6.84 (6)–6.89 (12). Their elements are arranged in a chiastic order: 6.84 (7) and 6.89-90 (12) function as the outer elements of the structure; 6.85-86 (8) and 6.87-88 (9) serve as its inner components. Two more elements were interpolated into this elaborately arranged pattern of proverbs, which conceal the structure's refinement: an 'impossible question' in 6.88 (10) and a statement about the bitterness of poverty in 6.89 (11).

6.88 (10)

[מ]ה ישפטון עקן עם אשה
בשר עם סכין
איש עם מ[לך]

(a) Why do [they] dispute: wood with fire,
(b) flesh with knife,
(c) man with king?

6.88 (10) displays strong contextual links on the level of repetition of keywords. Beside yet another reiteration of the noun מלך the most important link is undoubtedly the recurrence of אשה in 6.88 (a). It resumes the catchword אשה from 6.87 (c) and thereby signals the immediate thematic continuation of 6.87-88 (9). Since the striking imagery of this saying revolves totally around the metaphorical use of אשה, its repetition within the first element of the adjacent saying, that is, in 6.88 (a), is even more significant. In addition, yet another resumption of a keyword contextually anchors the tripartite question. 6.88 (b) repeats סכין, first introduced in 6.84 (7) in a rather similar context. There, it expresses the second half of another paradox: The king's command is gentle and soft, yet 'sharper and mightier than a double-edged dagger' (שדק ועזיז הו מן סכין פמין). Here, it comes to stand in the second 'irreconcilable pair' together with בשר, presupposing a negative response. Undoubtedly, the wider context proves very influential for any interpretation of 6.88 (10).

Thus, 6.88 (10) combines two characteristics of a royal command already alluded to in two previous sayings. It resumes אשה and סכין and puts them into a direct equation with the most important element of the final comparison, the king (מלך). Seen from this perspective, 6.88 (10) enumerates three very dangerous elements already known from the context. At the same time it bundles them in a now continuous series of syntactical equivalence (all three are subjects within the nominal clauses they appear in). This new combination results in a series of three most dangerous things, אשה, סכין, מלך, that destroy weaker elements such as עקן, בשר and איש. Since the relationship between the three members of the question is based on the root שפט used in 6.88 (a), it alludes to the possible conflict that might arise at the court of the ruler if a subject opposes his commands. Implicitly 6.88 (10) issues a strong warning against the attitude advised against in 6.85-86 (8). As well, it applies the comparison in 6.87-88 (9): A ruler and his dependent cannot dispute. The weaker part will always lose.

In its simple and formally distinct tripartite structure, 6.88 (10) is firmly attached to its present context, even if one might be tempted to ascribe a greater amount of originality to it than to the complex sayings that precede it.[39] The 'impossible question' bears many characteristics of a condensed abridgment of the preceding sayings. It is an integral means for the accomplishment of textual homogeneity.

6.89 (11)

טעמת אף זעררתא <אף> מררתא
ו[טעמ]א חסין
ולא איתי זי[מ]ריר מן ענוה

(a) I have tasted medlar[40] as well as[41] gall,[42]

39. Does 6.88 (10) echo a riddle (cf. Crenshaw 1995: 265-79)?

40. In אפזעררתא two words were written without intermediate space. In addition, the second consonant of this compound shows a rather unusual shape. זעררתא 'medlar' is well attested. There is no reason to alter the text.

41. No conjunction was preserved between the two nouns. Probably a second אף was lost by haplography. This seems to be even more evident if one acknowledges the strange writing of the preceding אפזעררתא, cf. also Kottsieper 1990: 12.

42. There are anomalies in the writing of מררתא as well. If the reference is to מרר, 'bitter', one would rather expect מריר in accordance with the orthography of the proverb collection. מררתא can be explained more adequately as a substantive signifying something utterly 'bitter'. Traditionally, the lexeme was interpreted as

(b) and the taste[43] was strong.
(c) But there is nothing that is more bitter than poverty.

6.89 (11) remains relatively isolated, since its form as well as its content show no immediate affinity with any of the adjoining sayings. But even in this case a loose thematic association based on the semantic field around לשן and the perception of taste cannot be excluded. It is certainly no coincidence that also 6.89-90 (12) alludes to the *tongue* of the king (לשן מלך) at its beginning. In addition, 6.89 (11) rests on a comparison borrowed from the semantic field of human perception like the surrounding sayings. By referring to the metaphor of 'bitterness', a twofold meaning is implied. 'Bitterness' may either allude to the physical perception of the bitter taste of a substance, or, on the metaphorical level, to the bitter consequences of misdemeanour at the royal court.

The present context presumably favours the metaphorical interpretation. Poverty and the loss of influence are the inescapable outcome of inappropriate behaviour. Here, the contextual attachment of the saying directs interpretation into a direction which might have been secondary at an earlier stage of its individual transmission. Besides this, by taking the form of a biographical statement, 6.89 (11) alludes to the basic conflict of the Ahikar narrative. It perfectly fits the hero's tragic destiny. This might have been a reason relevant for its insertion into the present and final context.[44]

6.90 (13)

בשגיא בנן לבבך אל יחדה
ובזעריהם [אל יאבל]

the name of a plant, *cichorium itybus*. However, the frequent attestations of מררתא in the Aramaic text of Tobit (cf. 4Q196–199.200: [6.4, 5, 7], 9; 11.11) ascertain the meaning 'gall' for the lexeme.

43. Since Cowley (1923: 216, 238), the lacuna has been filled by the restoration of טעמא, 'taste'. This reading fits the width of the broken papyrus very well. Lindenberger (1983: 89), on the contrary, followed Nöldeke (1913: 13) by restoring ואכלת.

44. It is noteworthy that all the later editions of the proverbs of Ahikar, excluding one Armenian recension, group this saying together with the structurally almost identical sayings 11.159 (74) and 11.160 (75). The organization of the Aramaic text therefore forms a rather extraordinary tradition. Undoubtedly the editorial rearrangement of the later versions paid more attention to the structural congruence of these three closely related sayings than the editor of the Aramaic papyrus. However, this different arrangement changed the contextual meaning of 6.89 (11) dramatically.

(a) In an abundance of sons may not your heart rejoice,
(b) and in their scarcity [may it not mourn]![45]

This is even more true for the adjacent saying 6.90 (13). Talking about the restraint the wise man should exercise with regard to his posterity, this twofold admonition takes the reader by surprise. Nothing within the wider context of column 6 indicates a concern about the number of progeny. Besides that, the address 'my son' is unique within this composition, but becomes quite important later in columns 9 and 12.

Syntactically, the two members of 6.90 (13) are arranged in a parallel construction. Semantically, a double pairing of antonyms (בשגיא // בזעריהם; חדי // אבל) reinforces this parallelism. Therefore, the inner structure and style of 6.90 (13) differs markedly from the complex syntax of the sayings about the king which surround it. Neither syntax nor semantics of the admonition reveal explicit contextual links. However, the recurrence of a significant keyword from the context ties even this just remotely related exhortation to the remainder of the section of text into which it was inserted. לבב was introduced in the expression הוקר לבב in 6.82 (b), then repeated once more in 6.82 (d) as גבר לא לבב. Within the phrase רפאה ללבב it was resumed in 6.84 (b) to form part of the prepositional phrase בחמר לבב in 6.88 (h). It will recur again in כסי מלה בלבב, 6.93 (a), to designate the holding back of a matter which should be concealed from public. This massive repetition indicates the great structural importance of לבב, even if one has to distinguish important semantic nuances of the lexeme. As usual, לבב denotes the 'inside' of something as well as emotional reactions (clearly the case in בחמר לבב) or self-control and considerate behaviour (cf. הוקר לבב). The closest semantic affinity is to be observed between לבבך אל יחדה and בחמר לבב, said of the royal command in 6.88 (h).

6.90 (13) can be deemed a further exhortation to exercise prudent and discerning judgment in yet another aspect of reality. Primarily, it does not give advice how to behave if offspring is little or abundant. Its main concern is about cautious conduct under a given circumstance.

45. The end of this saying has been lost by the fracture of the papyrus. There can be no certainty about the original text. However, the parallelism between (a) and (b) and the semantic antonyms שגיא // זעיר suggest a similar relationship between the verbal predicates. The restoration of the word-pair חדי // אבל is a possibility, but remains conjectural. Cf. also Porten and Yardeni (1993: 36).

One should not let oneself delude by appearance. Only cautious judgment and mindful restraint can prevent misfortune. In this, 6.90 (13) makes a similar point to 6.80 (2) by referring to a distinct experience. Furthermore, it echoes the warnings against the potential danger of uncontrolled speech given in 6.81 (3)–6.883 (5). Finally, it is easy to discern a superficial affiliation to the Aramaic narrative where the lack of offspring initiates the dramatic events leading to Ahikar's demise as the king's wise counsellor. These delicate allusions may have facilitated the integration of 6.90 (13) into its present context during the editorial process. The environment of the royal court unites both the biographical reference of the exhortations and the statement about the childless hero of the narrative. Precisely this subtle autobiographical nuance reinforces the coherence between the Aramaic narrative and the ensuing collections of proverbs.

6.91 (14)

מלך כרחמן
אף קלה גבה ה[ו]
מן הו זי יקום קדמוהי
להן זי אל עמה

(a) As a king is merciful,[46]
(b) so his voice is high.[47]

46. There are no major textual problems in 6.91 (14)—the papyrus is well preserved here. Interpretation therefore depends entirely on the description of the complex syntax of this saying. Traditionally, כרחמן has been interpreted as a combination of the comparative particle כ and the divine epithet רחמן, cf. Lindenberger (1983: 93); Kottsieper (1990: 12). Still, there is a severe problem about this proposal: If רחמן indeed referred to a divine name, either a grammatical determination or the proper name of the god would be needed. Furthermore, this function of רחמן is only attested in late texts. Even if an allusion to the god may not be excluded, the comparative ought to be interpreted primarily in its 'profane' meaning as an adjective describing the mercifulness of a king. Exactly this use is attested in the narrative 4.53, which depicts Esarhaddon as מלכא רחמן הו כמנדע, '[Esarhaddon] the king is merciful as is known'. Besides the verbal congruence, the similarity in syntax (הו!) is worth mentioning. Most fittingly, (a)-(b) ought to be understood as two elements of a comparison as suggested earlier by Grelot (1961: 184; 1972: 438). Cf., however, Lindenberger (1982: 110) for the traditional interpretation.

47. קלה גבה simply means 'high, loud voice'. There can be no doubt about the lexical connotations of גבה. The expression most probably refers to the loud, i.e. commanding voice of the king, thus implying the urgency with which his

(c) Who is he who can stand before him,
(d) but (he) with whom El is?

6.92 (15)

שפיר מלך למחזה כשמש
ויקיר הדרה לדרכי ארקא בניח[ה]

(a) A king is beautiful to look at like the sun,[48]
(b) and impressive is his glory to them that tread the earth in his contentment.[49]

6.91 (14)–6.92 (15) share a common type of language. It is best characterized as a solemn, descriptive nominal style which resembles a

decrees are uttered and have to be fulfilled, cf. Lindenberger 1983: 93. There is a considerable amount of semantic polarity between (a) and (b): The mercifulness of the king (a) must not delude the courtier—his decrees are still uttered with vehemence and do not allow for any delay (b); cf. the similar thought expressed also in 6.88 (9). Totally inappropriately, Kottsieper comments: 'Ja, als seinen Gesandten hat er [der Barmherzige] ihn erhöht' (1990: 12). This reading is based on a twofold conjecture: גבה in the G-stem never displays a causative meaning; the reading קל 'messenger' lacks any Aramaic attestation.

48. Like כרחמן in the previous saying, כשמש (a) has widely been accepted as a comparison between the king and the god שמש, cf. especially Lindenberger (1982: 112-14). Again, this notion cannot be excluded. Nevertheless, the primary meaning implies a different connotation. The likeness between a king and the 'sun' appears as a standard topic in Akkadian texts. For example, Ashurbanipal and other neo-Assyrian kings describe themselves as the *dUTU-šu kiššat niše*, 'sun of entire humankind'; cf. Seux (1967: 283-84, 460) and Weigl (1999: 110). Similar descriptions of mortals can also be found in Ps. 89.37 (David's throne will be unshakeable like 'the sun') and Ecclus 50.5-7. There, the hymnical description of Simon, the High Priest, displays similar solar imagery: 'How glorious he was as he glanced from the tent as he came out of the house of the curtain! Like a star he shone among the clouds [ככוכב אור מבין עבים], like the full moon at the festal season [וכירח מלא מבין בימי מועד], like the sun which is shining on the temple of the King [וכשמש משרקת אל היכל המלך], like the rainbow gleaming in splendid clouds [וכקשת נראתה בענן].'

49. The last word of l. 6.92 lacks its last consonant. Usually, the article is restored. The noun is commonly derived from ניח, 'calmness, serenity, contentment'; cf. Cowley (1923: 238); Lindenberger (1983: 94). Kottsieper (1990: 12) restores the enclitic pronoun instead, thereby strengthening the reference to מלך in (a). A different solution was proposed by Sachau (1911: I, 163). One could also split the expression into two words, reading בני חרן, 'free men' as in the broken text of 14.216. No convincing criteria are available to support this reading here.

hymn. This is particularly so in 6.92 (15). Its two syntactic elements are totally parallel, each consisting of a nominal predicate (adjective) followed by the subject and a prepositional phrase of differing internal structure. The same nominal style prevails in 6.91 (14). There, however, structural symmetry rests upon a combination of two statements with an adjoining ascertaining question. It also is made up of two parts, joined together by להן. Each element contains an embedded relative clause which substitutes the internal predicate.

Both sayings originate in the description of the striking appearance of the king. Their respective first statements concern the incomparability and splendour of the monarch. A comparison appears as the initial constituent in each unit. It equates the sovereign with different realities. Whereas כרחמן in 6.91 (a) evokes a specific royal attribute, כשמש in 6.92 (a) encircles his commanding countenance with a solar milieu. These are the primary and obvious semantics of רחמן and שמש. The wider context nevertheless insinuates the intimate association between the king and the divine. מלך once more functions as keyword. Here, its specific correlation to the realm of the gods may already be implied by the two comparisons. Each of them is open for an expansion of its principal meaning, and inherent polysemy indeed favours a metaphorical interpretation.

This notion is confirmed by the explicit mentioning of the divine name אל within the phrase להן זי אל עמה in 6.91 (d). Furthermore, מלך also recalls the rather distant מלכותא in 6.79 (1), used in a stylistically similar context. In addition, a double meaning is positively conceivable for שמש, designating either the 'sun' or the god 'Šamaš'. This polysemy may signal an intimate semantic correlation to בעל קדשן in 6.79 (d). Clearly the repetition of יקיר in similar contexts in 6.79 (a) and 6.92 (b) transforms the statements about the earthly splendour of the monarch into a decisively divine setting. Common syntax and semantics allow us to comprehend 6.91 (14) and 6.92 (15) as yet another pair of sayings interrelated to the hymnal fragment in 6.79 (1). In conjunction with it, 6.91 (14)–6.92 (15) presumably create a tightly knit framework around the enclosed passage of text.

Other phrases are resumed as well. The expression מן הו זי יקום קדמוהי in 6.91 (c) echoes על אנפי מלך אל תקום in 6.85 (b). Implicitly the resumption states a strong warning not to even try to attempt to resist royal commands. A second significant repetition is that of the of the root חזי, occurring for the first time as participial form

מתחזה in 6.90 (c) and being taken up by the infinitive construct למחזה in 6.92 (a). In contrast, there are no obvious semantic conjoints to the last two sayings of column 6. Rather, 6.91 (14)–6.92 (15) formally conclude the complex of sayings about the king. The repeated references to divinity lend final weight to the admonitions and warnings connected with the sovereign. After this, מלך has fulfilled its semantic duty as keyword and does not re-appear again. As a concluding statement, 6.92 (15) marks the termination of the topic indicated by the pattern of repetitions revolving around מלך.

6.93 (16)

מאן טב כס[ין] מלה בלבבה
והו ז[ין] תביר הנפקה ברא

(a) A good container covered a thing/a word in its inner/heart,
(b) but one which is broken let it go outside.

6.93 (16) takes the form of a simple statement. Only an intact container can keep its contents and prevent leakage. Belying their effortless intelligibility, the saying's two components display a rather sophisticated syntax which partly conceals its clear structure. It is characterized by almost complete syntactic parallelism. The order of constituents is identical in both members. A subject is followed by a verbal predicate, an object and an additional facultative element. However, (a) and (b) differ in the way their subject is expressed—a stylistic trait to avoid identical repetition. Whereas (a) introduces it as a combination of a noun and a postponed attribute, (b) makes use of a personal pronoun followed by an attached relative clause. The deletion of the subject in (b) functions as a powerful means to correlate (a) and (b) syntactically, and thereby strengthen syntactical parallelism. Semantics reinforce parallelism even more by the use of antonymous word-pairs split between the two members: כסי :: נפק; לבב :: ברא; טב :: יתבר.

Precisely this refined mutual reinforcement of syntactic and semantic parallelism also characterizes many of the sayings arranged in some of the ensuing columns, particularly 8–9: for example, 8.123 (39); 8.124 (40); 9.136 (50). Within the immediate context, 6.90 (13) is the only other specimen of this stylistic form. Evidently, these two sayings belong to a radically distinct group. There must have been cogent reasons to place these two sayings at the end of column 6 during the compositional process. With regard to 6.93 (16), the editorial decision was certainly motivated by yet another and final repetition of מלה, the keyword of column 6. Serving as a catchword signalling close affinity with most sayings contained within the preceding assemblage, מלה certainly facilitated the compositional integration of 6.93 (16) into its present and final context.

On the level of semantics, pronounced ties with the sayings about proper conduct at court can be observed. The resumption of the idiom כסי מלה from 6.84 (a) in 6.93 (a) functions as the most important structural element. Whereas the phrase implied a negative meaning in 6.84 (a), that is, 'to cover up a king's word' and therefore 'to refuse to execute a royal command', a shift to the positive characterizes it in 6.93 (a), that is, 'to keep a thing within/a word to oneself'. Also, נפק מלה is familiar already from 6.83 (b) where it designated considerate speech, more specifically, the ability of a person to keep something to himself until the right moment to utter it. Placed in opposition within the two members of the present saying, נפק מלה :: כסי מלה constitute the semantic backbone of 6.93 (16) by alluding to previous usage of these two phrases.

Isolated from its present context, the only conceivable interpretation of 6.93 (16) is a literal one. In this case, כסי מלה :: נפק מלה refer to qualities of a vessel, which is either intact and consequently fulfils its purpose by keeping its contents, or, being broken, leaks the things stored in it—a rather banal statement. However, if coming from the reader's perspective, the polysemy of מלה in conjunction with the wider context directs one's attention in a different direction. Having perceived the importance of considerate speech, repeatedly advised to the reader in previous admonitions, the meaning 'word' for מלה inevitably forces itself upon the addressee.

As a consequence, the container's attributes of 'good' and 'broken' lose their primary meaning. Instead, they become metaphors for certain qualities of a person. מאן טב comes to stand for a 'person of integrity', whereas תביר no longer refers to the leakage of the contents of a vessel alone, but envisions a 'broken' person who cannot keep a word to himself but 'leaks' it to its surrounding. Precisely this notion is also implied by the use of the root תבר in the statement about the power of a royal tongue, capable even of crushing a dragon's bones (עלעי תנין יתבר) in 6.89-90 (b). The shattered pot and the crushed ribs of a dragon might by the usage of תבר both allude to the courtier's bones and wilful resistance, smashed by the commanding authority of a king.

Moreover, the metaphor of a broken vessel that leaks its contents recalls the comparison between a word and a bird which flies away and never returns, used in 6.82 (c)-(d) (cf. there שלח מלה). Hence, by the means of integration into the present context, the obvious meaning of 6.93 (16) is altered dramatically. In its context, this saying now compares a trustworthy and deliberate person with an intact container, whereas it likens the foolish chatterer to a cracked pot. The semantic interdependence between 6.81 (3)–6.83 (5) and 6.93 (16) is quite apparent. By placing these two elements at the two margins of a complex of text dealing with verbal discretion, they came to serve as a kind of framework enclosing the sayings about the king. Through them the intended reader enters and exits the textual core of column 6.

6.94 (17)

אריא אזל קרב
לש[לם חמרא] לם
שלם יהוי לך
ענה חמרא
ואמר לאריא

(a) The lion went and approached
(b) to greet the ass[50] as follows:
(c) 'May it be well with you!'
(d) The ass answered
(e) and said to the lion…

The last saying of column 6 belongs to a literary form entirely different from any unit preceding it. In its form it is neither statement nor admonition. Instead, it takes the form of a dialogue between two protagonists, embedded into a very basic narrative framework. Its fragmentary state of preservation does not allow a final judgment about its aim. Even if the dialogue might have found a remote echo in later

50. After an initial -לש, a fracture of the papyrus led to the loss of a few consonants, most probably belonging to two separate words. Several restorations for the lacuna are possible. Cowley (1923: 126, 238) proposed the reading לשלמה לחמרא and was followed by most commentators; cf., e.g., Lindenberger (1983: 96). As Puech (1988: 590) noted, this restoration hardly fits the width of the lacuna. The shorter reconstruction proposed above is based on a more realistic estimate, cf. also Porten and Yardeni (1993: 36).

traditions,[51] no restoration can claim sufficient certainty. Any attempt to assess compositional criteria must therefore limit itself to the extant text and remains hypothetical.

Unlike most of the other animal proverbs and fables preserved on the Elephantine Papyri, 6.94 (17) was not grouped with a second specimen of the same literary form, but stood by itself from the beginning.[52] Neither the width of the broken text nor the continuation in column 7 allow for a lost second dialogue. Was 6.94 (17) positioned at the end of column 6 merely for scribal considerations, for example, for the availability of space on the papyrus? Since there are no obvious connections with the preceding text on the level of form, syntax and semantics this seems to be the only satisfying explanation in the first place. However, an analysis of the interrelation between context and meaning is able to differentiate this judgement once more.

The encounter between lion and ass confronts two very unequal protagonists. Whereas the lion symbolizes unsurpassed strength and ferocity, the ass personifies vulnerability and weakness. This embodiment of distinct and ultimately also conflicting characteristics underlies the entire dialogue. It is primarily not about lion and ass, but about vigour opposite weakness, ferocity opposite defencelessness. The declared intention of the lion who initiates the dialogue by a seemingly unpretentious greeting ('May it be well with you!') conceals his true motivations. Quite easily one can detect biting irony behind this superficially benevolent gesture—how can a lion greet an ass without considering it as its potential prey? Evidently, hidden motives and outer demeanour ought not always agree—appearance can delude.

Even when read detached from its present context, the encounter of and the discourse between lion and ass provoke the reader to transfer the fundamental metaphors to the human realm. Social metaphors embodied and encoded in stories or sayings about animal behaviour are familiar to the proverb collection.[53] The tension between the strong and

51. Cf. especially the Syriac tradition given by Conybeare, Harris and Lewis (1913: 123-24; p. 68 in the Syriac text) and Nöldeke (1913: 46 n. 9), already quoted by Lindenberger (1983: 96). Particularly the greeting of the lion (*t' bšlm*) shows striking affinities to the Aramaic text (שלם יהוי לך) of column 6.

52. On the contrary, such a pairing can be observed in 11.166-67 (80); 11.168-70 (81); 12.180-81 (90); 12.183-84 (92); 12.184-86 (93); 12.186 (94).

53. Notably the fable of the meeting between a leopard and a goat in 11.166-68

the weak is always characteristic. In one case, an interpretative formula explicitly asserts this transformation by likening beast and man in 12.184: הא כן פגעהם זי אנשא, 'Behold, thus is their meeting—of mankind!' Applied to the dialogue of 6.94 (17) this translates into one essential problem: How can a powerful man express his appreciation for the powerless without regarding him at the same time as a means to increase his power and influence?

Here, the actual wider context of 6.94 (17) gains its interpretative force. Positioned as the conclusion to an extensive textual unit concerned with potential conflicts between a king and a courtier, the dialogue implicitly illustrates the latent antagonism of strength and weakness at the royal household. The king is gentle and his word healing—yet at the same time destructive and harmful and unpredictable as stated by 6.84 (7) and 6.89-90 (12). If the countenance of a king shows itself kind and merciful this does not automatically imply that his reasoning indeed *is*. The courtier is constantly exposed to the threat of kindling hostile reactions as asserted by 6.85-86 (8) and 6.87-88 (9), a potential victim of royal anger. The interpretative relationship between the fable and its present context is twofold. On the one hand, the preceding context facilitates the dissolution of the animal metaphors and their application to the human sphere. On the other hand, the fable interprets the sayings about king and courtier by illustrating them by means of a descriptive narration which is formally distinct from any foregoing saying. This delicate mutual conjunction of context and meaning can hardly be deemed coincidental.

*Column 7*

Column 7 originally contained ten stylistically diverse sayings. However, several of these suffered serious damage when the papyrus broke at its right margin. In most cases it is possible to restore a satisfactory meaning, save for 7.97 (20). No common subject dominates the entire ensemble, nor is it possible to determine an apparent pattern of arrangement right away. At first glance, column 7 bears traits of a disordered compilation. 7.95 (18) opens the context as an anthropological observation in the form of a statement. Three rather obscure and badly mutilated sayings, 7.96 (19)–7.98 (21), ensue. 7.99-100 (22) emphasizes the

(80) and the one between bear and lambs in 11.168-71 (81), but cf. also the fragmentary text of 13.203-204 (109) and the animal proverb in 12.183-84 (92).

discrepancy between the potentially treacherous and misleading outward attitude of a person and the necessity to carefully watch with whom one takes sides, followed in 7.101-102 (23) by a fable about an exchange between a bramble and a pomegranate. Retribution is the topic of 7.103 (24), whereas 7.104 (25) is concerned with the decline of the wicked. An utterly grievous biographical statement in 7.105-106 (26) foreshadows through its implicit reference to the addressee the only admonition of column 7, preserved in 7.107-108 (27).

No specific literary form dominates column 7. However, smaller clusters of sayings consisting of solely two members are distinguishable: for example, 7.95 (18); 7.96 (19); possibly also 7.97 (20); 7.103 (24); 7.104-105 (25). The same is true for a certain prevalence of statements, whereas only the final saying of 7.107-108 (27) comprises an admonition. A few significant repetitions and semantic fields indicate limited compositional activity as well. אנשא/איש, represented no less than five times within column 7—that is, 7.95 (18); 7.96 (19); 7.98 (21); 7.99-100 (22); 7.103 (24)—figures as the most meaningful among them. In all instances, except in 7.98 (a), one of these two lexemes forms part of the grammatical subject of the respective saying. In addition, either איש or אנשא always appear within the first syntactical element. אנשא/איש are only absent from the fable 7.101-102 (23). Furthermore, repetitions cease with 7.103 (24), thus indicating a caesura in content. This pattern of recurrences is positive evidence for a deliberate compositional strategy.

Within the second part of column 7, the opposition between the righteous and the wicked emerges as a unifying topic. This is indicated by the use of a pair of keywords: צדיק :: רשיע. One of them is always placed within the first element of each saying. As two elements of an antonymous word-pair, צדיק and רשיע are split between two adjacent sayings in 7.103 (a) and 7.104 (a). רשיע reappears as the subject of 7.107 (a). 7.105-106 (26) partakes in the contrast between the righteous and the wicked by referring to the addressee's ungratefulness. In a remote sense, the adjective טב, which is repeated four times—cf. 7.95 (a); 7.99 (b); 7.100 (e); 7.101 (c)—in the first part of column 7, participates in this opposition as well. Consequently, the semantic field 'wicked' versus 'righteous' indicates topical coherence.

Besides these two governing semantic fields—the frequent recurrence of לבב, and its remote semantic equivalent גוה—references to the gods and divine names abound within column 7. אלהן is contained in 7.96 (a) and quite possibly also in 7.98 (a); the phrase זי לא אל עמה, already familiar from column 6, is repeated in the otherwise unintelligible saying 7.97 (20); finally, שמש is appealed to in 7.107-108 (27). This otherwise unparalleled accumulation of divine names might also be transparent for assessing relevant compositional criteria.

7.95 (18)

איש שפיר מדדה ולבבה טב
כקר[י]ה חסינה זי מי[ן] בג[וה ]איתי

(a) A man whose stature[54] is beautiful and whose heart is good
(b) is like a fortified city in whose midst there is water.[55]

Saying 7.95 (18) marks a shift in topic. Neither appropriate conduct at court nor considerate speech are envisioned any longer. Instead, the fundamental antithesis between righteous and wicked emerges as the dominating issue. Still, there is no absolute topical caesura between columns 6 and 7. By focusing on the harmony between a person's countenance and his ethical disposition, 7.95 (18) dwells on the contrast also characteristic for 6.93 (16). Similar imagery likens these two sayings. The intact or cracked storage jar and the fortified city which is able to withstand military attacks due to the water reservoir in its midst both refer to the capacity and effectiveness of an object. Both metaphors designate human qualities. Inasmuch as the potential

54. Several different readings have been proposed for מדדה. Again, the writing of ד/ר accounts for most of them. Reading מדרה, 'track, journey', Epstein (1912: 138) understood this expression as a reference to one person's conduct of life, cf. also Kottsieper (1990: 10, 17). Most commentators, however, related מדדה to מדה, 'measure, appearance', cf. Cowley (1923: 218, 244) and Lindenberger (1983: 159). There can be little doubt about the accuracy of this interpretation.

55. The loss of an easily understandable text in the second half of (b) incited a wide range of restorations. Among these, מין, 'water', seems most probable, since 'il doit s'agir d'un élément caractéristique des cités bien défendues' (Grelot 1972: 444); cf. also Porten and Yardeni (1993: 38). Most of the earlier proposals are much too long for the width of the lacuna, cf. Cowley (1923: 218, 244), זי מתנגדה בגבר, '(like a bow) which is bent by a strong man', and Lindenberger (1983: 159), מתבניה בטורא, '... built on a hill' (Mt. 5.14). Kottsieper (1988: 125-33; 1990: 10) restores גמ, 'military troop'. However, this lexeme lacks sufficient lexical attestation and remains highly uncertain.

discrepancy between appearance and inner motivation is of significance, there is also a remote topical affinity to the fable 6.94 (17), and—even more meaningful—to sayings ensuing in column 7, especially 7.99-100 (22).

Modelled as a comparative statement comprising two members, 7.95 (18) reveals a great deal of originality and balancing of its syntactic segments. The two elements of the predication are split between the two lines, each containing an elaborate network of internal relations. In its macrostructure, (a) serves as the subject, and (b) as the nominal predicate of the comparison. An extensive attribute is attached to each of these two elements, consisting itself of a nominal predication. In (a) the twofold elements of the attribute are arranged in a chiastic order (S—Pred // Pred—S). Syntax indicates two matching comparisons, namely the equation between a person's beautiful stature and a fortified city and between his good heart and the water reservoir enabling the inhabitants to survive a long period of siege. In its symmetrical syntactic structure, 7.95 (18) resembles 6.93 (16).

Contextual continuity is once more achieved by means of repetition and continuous semantic fields. Most significantly, איש שפיר echoes שפיר מלך in 6.92 (a). The ensuing expression לבבה טב is reminiscent of מאן טב כסי מלה בלבבה in 6.93 (a). In addition, the repetition of חסין in 7.95 (b) directs the reader's attention back to 6.89 (11) and the bitter taste of poverty. Not unlike the hymnical sayings about the king in 6.91 (14) and 6.92 (15), a comparison (כ) functions as a decisive structural element. 7.95 (18) definitely indicates the commencement of a distinct textual unit. Nevertheless it does not remain without a wider interpretative context.

7.96 (19)

[מה י]שתמר איש עם אלהן
ומה יתנטר על און גוה

(a) How[56] can a man guard himself with the gods,
(b) and how can he watch himself against his inner wickedness?[57]

56. Cowley (1923: 218) reads הן לא, 'if not', cf. also Lindenberger (1983: 161), but the width of the lacuna does not permit the restoration of two words. Judging from analogy, the introductory מה as in (b) seems more appropriate both in terms of available space and content, cf. Epstein 1913b: 231; Porten and Yardeni 1993: 38.

7.96 (19) takes the form of a rhetorical question suggesting a negative answer. Its syntactic pattern closely resembles that of the series of 'impossible questions' in 6.88 (10). There, the sequence מה...איש...עם, 'how [can] a man...', structured a threefold question about irreconcilable things. Here, the arrangement is identical. Minor differences solely concern syntactical traits.[58] Just as in the antecedent saying, a well-balanced harmony between the two members characterizes the inner syntactic structure of 7.96 (19). (a) and (b) are complete predications whose constituents display an almost totally parallel arrangement. An interrogative pronoun followed by a verbal predicate derived as tD-stem serves as the headword of both (a) and (b). A prepositional phrase concludes both segments. In (b) the subject is gapped for the sake of grammatical parallelism. Semantically, both questions use two synonymous roots, שמר and נטר, to formulate their predicate. שמר // נטר were of major importance in 6.81 (3)–6.82 (4) as well. Possibly the resumption of this word-pair creates additional textual cohesion between columns 6 and 7.

Besides close stylistic affinity between the adjacent sayings 7.95 (18) and 7.96 (19), the repetition of two keywords—איש at the head of (a), גוה as conclusion of (b)—firmly attaches 7.96 (19) to the previous saying. This significant resumption of keywords indicates topical unity and proposes a process of mutual interpretation between 7.95 (18) and 7.96 (19). Human behaviour in correlation with inner ethical strength

57. The end of the line contains two words written without a separating space: עלאון. און is not attested elsewhere in Aramaic. It can only be understood from its Hebrew cognate 'sin, iniquity, wickedness', so already Sachau (1911: I, 174); Lindenberger (1983: 161). Considerable confusion was caused by the rather unusual application of the prepositions עם in (a) and על in (b). עם (a) can hardly mean 'against' as proposed by most commentators. On the other hand, על (b) never means 'out of…' but rather 'against', cf. already Stummer (1914a: 30). One might also compare the equivalent usage of the preposition עם, followed by a divine name, in biblical Hebrew in Job 25.4 (מה יצדק אנוש עם אל), cf. also Job 16.21; 27.13; 34.9; 40.2. There can be no doubt about the correct rendering. (a) and (b) shed light on two different aspects of reality—the outward assistance of the gods (a) is opposed by the inner wickedness (b) of a man. Even the gods are powerless if a man is unable to control his intimate motives.

58. Whereas in 6.88 (10) only one predicate is used at the beginning of the sentence, in 7.96 (19) the whole phrase is repeated. 6.88 (10) enumerates three irreconcilable things, 7.96 (19), by contrast, has only two elements and formulates the second half with a different preposition (על).

continues to be the primary issue. An implicit inner antithesis between עם אלהן in 7.96 (a) and על און גוה in 7.96 (b) opposes two conflicting attitudes towards reality. In this way, 7.96 (19) contextually restricts the validity of 7.95 (18): Even a successful wise man cannot achieve anything against the will of the gods. This concern will be further elaborated later in the column.

7.97 (20)

[°°]מן [כב]שי בטן
וזי לא אל עמה
מן יהו°אנהי

(a) [...] [secre]ts[59] of the belly,
(b) but he, with whom El is not,
(c) who will [...] him?

Line 7.97 was severely damaged at both margins. Therefore, it is impossible to determine the content and precise wording of (20). בטן (a) might point to a semantic relation with גוה, used in the previous sayings. (b) contains the only intelligible phrase. It repeats זי אל עמה, familiar already from 6.91 (d), in the form of a negative question. This repetition suggests major structural importance. The same is true for the closely related prepositional phrases עם אלהן 7.96 (a) and אל עמה in 7.97 which undoubtedly relate 7.97 (20) with its immediate context.

7.98 (21)

[ה]נחי[ו אלהן] אנשא
ועממא עבדו בהם
ולא שבקו המו
ולבבהם פתיח

(a) [The gods guided][60] humankind,

59. No certainty can be achieved for any part of this saying. כבשי, 'secrets', was originally proposed by Epstein (1913b: 231) but remains a mere conjecture.

60. The deplorable state of preservation of the right margin of the papyrus causes severe textual problems. From the first statement only אנשא is clearly legible. After an initial break, a fragment contains נ. After it, ח or ה and י are discernible. Directly at the right margin of the lacuna there might be a trace of '&'. The fragmentary state of preservation should caution against far-reaching restorations. The above reading is a possibility, inserting the finite form of the verb נחי, 'to lead, guide', and אלהן as the subject. This definitely remains a conjecture.

(b) and peoples they made their servants.[61]
(c) But they did not leave them behind,[62]
(d) instead, their heart is open.[63]

The fracture of the papyrus also extends to l. 7.98. Ambiguities in the notation of individual consonants and severe lexical problems further complicate an accurate interpretation of 7.98 (21). Consequently, any

However, one might point to comparable statements of Old Testament literature, where the guidance of peoples or individuals by YHWH/God is frequently expressed by נחי, cf. Gen. 24.27, 48; Exod. 13.17, 21; 15.13; 32.34; Deut. 32.12; Ps. 77.21; 78.14, 53, 72; 107.30; Isa. 57.18; 58.11; Neh. 9.12, 19 and others. Cf. especially Ps. 67.5: לאמים בארץ תנחם and Job 12.23: שטח לגיום וינחם.

61. Once more, the ambiguity in the writing of ד/ר allows for two different readings of the verbal predicate. עבר ב is frequently used to describe the partitive aspect of an action. In that case, עבר ב, 'to pass through', would be semantically related to שבק, 'to leave behind', in (c). Then, עממא can only serve as the verb's subject. Another recurrent interpretation of the phrase is 'to set free, to spare', cf. already Sachau (1911: I, 174); Cowley (1923: 225); Lindenberger (1983: 164). However, there is a more apt understanding. If the construction is read עבד ב and עממא is considered as the direct object, only the gods (a) can function as the subject of the predication. In this case עבד ב ought to be interpreted as 'to perform something on someone' or more specifically: 'to enslave someone, to make someone a servant'. This understanding has already been suggested at an early point by Halévy (1912: 71) who pointed to Exod. 1.14; Lev. 25.39, 46; Jer. 34.9, 19. One might add Jer. 22.13 and Isa. 14.3; Jer. 25.14; 27.7; 30.8; Ezek. 34.27; Dan. 4.32. Keeping the different literary setting in mind, one could still use the quoted texts as an example for an analogous expression in biblical Hebrew. Since it enables us to understand (a)-(b) easily, it can be adopted as a provisional working hypothesis.

62. It is not necessary to postulate a special meaning for שבק here. It simply means 'to leave (someone) behind' as in all the other recurrences in the proverb collection. The previous decision to regard the 'gods' as the subject of the whole saying—cf. (a)—enables one to reckon with an effortless continuation of the syntactic pattern without a change of the grammatical subject. The pronoun המו refers to the peoples mentioned in the previous line.

63. Two different readings have been proposed for the last word. Since the first consonant of the word is only partly preserved, it can either be read as נ or as פ. Consequently, the form ought to be derived either from נתח, 'to tear'—'their heart is torn'—or from פתח, 'to open'—'their heart is open'. It is impossible to opt for one of these readings with certainty. Both roots are attested in Aramaic. The latter alternative seems more appropriate in terms of context, cf. Cowley (1923: 225, 245); Grelot (1961: 191, nn. 70-71). Once more, one might point to a Hebrew equivalent, i.e. the supplicant's desire for the 'open eyes of YHWH'; cf. 1 Kgs 8.29, 52; 2 Chron. 6.20, 40; 7.15; Neh. 1.6 (להיות עיניך פתחות).

analysis has to reckon with considerable restrictions and remains hypothetical. Each of the four members takes the form of a descriptive statement. If understood correctly, 7.98 (21) displays a rather plain syntactical structure. All segments are simple verbal clauses, coordinated by a conjunction. Even though (a)-(d) are well balanced in length, they lack developed syntactic parallelism. This corresponds to the semantic level. With regard to the literary form of the saying, no correlation to the context is apparent.

In contrast, repetitions of keywords firmly anchor 7.98 (21) in its present context. This is especially so with regard to אנשא and, most probably, also with regard to [אלהן] in 7.98 (a). איש and אלהן were joined in a similar way in 7.96 (19). Semantically related, עממא 7.98 (b) contributes to the same semantic field. The mentioning of לבב in 7.98 (d) refers back to לבב at the beginning of the column in 7.95 (a) and at the same time foreshadows yet another repetition of the lexeme in the adjacent saying 7.99-100 (22). There, לבב functions as *the* keyword, once more in combination with איש. If the expression לבבהם פתיח in 7.98 (d) is correctly understood as meaning 'their heart is open(ed) (for supplication)', there is a sharp contrast to the opening assertion of the next saying 7.99-100 (22), that 'a man cannot see what is in his colleague's heart [לא חזה איש מה בלבב כנתה]'. In this case the accessible and 'listening' heart of the gods opposes the unintelligible motivations of humankind. A similar discrepancy between divine and human behaviour underlies the relation between the expression לא שבקו המו in 7.98 (c) // אל עמה in 7.97 (20) and the usage of the root שבק in 7.107-108 (27).

In spite of its isolation in terms of literary form, even 7.98 (21) fits the present context of column 7 quite well. Its compositional insertion into column 7 was most probably motivated by association of keywords. As a temporary conclusion of the topic of divine assistance it now forms an integral part of column 7 and interprets all of the previous sayings, especially 7.96 (19) and presumably also 7.97 (20). As well, a statement about the accessibility of the gods is very appropriate in a context which is concerned with the antithesis between the righteous and the wicked.

7.99-100 (22)

[לא חזה] איש מה בלבב כנתה
וכזי [יח]זה גבר טב לגבר לח[יתה]

לא ילוה עמה ב[ארחה]
ובעל אגר לא יהוה לה
גבר טב עם ג[בר לח]ה

(a) A man does not see[64] what is in the heart of his colleague;
(b) but if a good person sees a person of badness,[65]
(c) he shall not join him on his way,[66]
(d) and he shall not be his employer,
(e) a good person with a bad person.

In marked contrast to the simple and easily comprehensible syntax of the antecedent sayings, the disposition of 7.99-100 (22) is more complex, consisting of a network of closely interwoven clauses. The five members of the saying are interrelated by frequent pronominal references and internal repetitions which account for a considerable amount of redundancy. (a), (c) and (d) are modelled as straightforward statements. (b) serves as a circumstantial precision. (e) restates the main opposition of the saying in the syntactic form of an adjunction. The complex syntax of 7.99-100 (22) resembles similar dispositions in 6.85-86 (8) and 6.87-88 (9). The saying lacks any syntactical or semantic parallelism. Instead, argumentation proceeds in the form of a discourse, representing the only example for this kind of debate within column 7.

64. The right margin of the papyrus is missing. The width of the lacuna suggests the loss of either one longer or two shorter words. As one of them a negation is needed for the sake of a consistent syntactic and thematic continuation of the saying. Two restorations are commonly accepted: לא ידע, cf. Cowley (1923: 218, 245); Grelot (1961: 191); Lindenberger (1983: 165); and לא חזה, cf. Kottsieper (1990: 10); Porten and Yardeni (1993: 38). Since the reading יחזה is almost secure for the predicate of (b)—cf. Sachau (1911: I, 174)—לא חזה has to be preferred for the introduction of (a) as well.

65. Of the last word of (b) only the initial consonant was preserved. There are slight traces of the subsequent letter that point to ח. In view of the expression גבר לחה in (e), the restoration of לחה or לחיתה is the most probable, cf. Cowley (1923: 218); Grelot (1961: 191); Lindenberger (1983: 165); Porten and Yardeni (1993: 38). However, there is no room for more text as suggested by most earlier commentators. The reading adopted above is that of Kottsieper (1990: 10).

66. (c) ends with the letter ב. The lacuna can only be filled by a conjectural restoration. Baneth (1914: 351) proposed בארחה. This reading has since been accepted by almost every critic, cf. Cowley (1923: 228, 245); Lindenberger (1983: 165). Kottsieper (1990: 10) voted for בעבדה, 'as his servant', instead. However, in that case the preposition must be regarded as ב *essentiae*, cf. Kottsieper (1990: 192 j).

Once more, the interpolation of a saying into its present context was most likely motivated by the repetition of keywords. איש and לבב are certainly the most representative among these, since they both repeat previously applied terminology. לבב (a) resumes the lexeme from the concluding phrase of 7.98 (21) which immediately precedes it. Association by means of a catchword was definitely relevant for the editorial process, even more so if one considers the semantic polarity between לבב פתיח in 7.98 (d) and the negative statement לא חזה איש מה בלבב כנתה of 7.99 (a).

7.99-100 (22) continues and elaborates the topic of the correlation between the behaviour of a person and his motivations hidden deep inside him. טב refers to 7.95 (18), where it was used as an attribute to לבב. Thus, the sequence טב–לבב–איש is identical with that used in 7.95 (18). Four repetitions of גבר associate 'man' with either טב or לחה. This frequent alternative repetition of טב and לחה insinuates the distinction of the righteous and the wicked without employing the available, more specific terminology which is only to be introduced as צדיק :: רשיע in 7.103 (24)–7.104 (25). Here, גבר טב is endangered directly by the secrecy of גבר לחה, although no criterion is given to specify semantically לחה or לחיתא as opposed to טב. Obviously the necessity to discriminate between a person's appearance and his guiding morale is more important in this saying than a precise ethical qualification of טב :: לחה.

7.101-102 (23)

[סנ]יא שדר לרמנ[א] לם
סניא לרמנא
מה טב שג[י]א כביך
[לפ]גע [אנ]ביך
[אף ענ]ה ר[מ]נא
ואמר לסניא
אנת כלך כבן
עם זי פגע בך

(a) The bramble sent to the pomegranate as follows:
(b) The bramble to the pomegranate:
(c) 'What good is the abundance of your thorns
(d) to one who touches[67] your fruit?'[68]

67. The first consonant of the line has been lost. נגע or פגע represent equally suitable restorations. Due to the semantic affinity of these two roots, any decision is

(e) The pomegranate replied
(f) and said to the bramble:
(g) 'You, all of you are thorns
(h) for him who touches you!'

The current placement of a fable in the midst of sayings concerned with ethical values seems awkward at first. Undoubtedly, 7.101-102 (23) belongs to an entirely different literary genre than the sayings grouped around it. Stylistically the fable is utterly distinct from its vicinity and does not presuppose any context at all. Most probably it had a tradition of its own before having been placed in its final context. It shares most literary traits with the narration about the encounter between lion and ass preserved at the very conclusion of column 6.

Two unequal protagonists enter a dialogue whose outcome is apparent from the outset. Instead of physical force, productivity bears full emphasis. Already the selection of characteristic actors prepares the reader for the fundamental conflict. Bramble and pomegranate serve as prototypes for fruitlessness versus fruitfulness. The dialogue itself is bitterly sarcastic, since the fruitless bramble initiates a dispute which it is bound to lose from the outset. Its proclamation vis-à-vis the pomegranate is entirely disproportionate. Taken for itself, the fable narrates the pomposity of a worthless plant in the face of one of the most valued fruit-trees of the Orient. It implicitly invites the reader to apply its punch to the human sphere without hinting at a particular social environment.

Precisely this openness was altered by the insertion of the fable into its present context. The dialogue between bramble and pomegranate about an outwardly naive exchange of 'touches' is transformed into a poignant statement about the worthless and unproductive wicked opposite the fruitful righteous. The initiative is totally on the part of the bramble, that is, the wicked, who doubts the productivity of the fruit

feasible. The repetition of פגע in (h) clearly favours the same reading in (d).

68. Only three final letters have been preserved of the last word of (d). The context clearly suggests an expression for 'fruit'. אנביך has been accepted almost unanimously, cf. already Sachau (1911: I, 175) and lately Porten and Yardeni (1993: 38). I doubt if there is enough room for the reconstruction of a preposition before אנביך as supposed by Lindenberger (1983: 168) *et al.* Again, Kottsieper (1990: 10) proposes a new reading, i.e. שביך, 'wer dich berührt, verfängt sich ja in dir'. However, there is little evidence for a reflexive meaning of the G-stem of שבך. Kottsieper's reading therefore remains insecure.

tree, that is, the righteous. Instead, the wicked focuses his attention to minor and relatively unimportant attributes of the upright and conceals the latter one's essential virtue. By this process of contextual modification the fable emerges as a dispute about the ethical standards and their effectiveness. Therefore, it not only *re-interprets* the contiguous sayings 7.99-100 (22), 7.103 (24) and 7.104 (25), but at the same time is *re-interpreted* itself by these texts. Like 6.94 (17), the fable illustrates and explains human antagonisms and conflicting attitudes by telling a simple story. Context and meaning prove inseparable once more.

Independent as 7.101-102 (23) may have been before it came to be positioned at the centre of column 7, certain meaningful mechanisms secure its contextual attachment. The only keyword the fable shares with its context is טב. Having served as the semantic centrepiece of the previous discourse, טב re-appears within the opening statement of the bramble in the form of an impudent question: מה טב שגיא כביך? Besides its apparent structural importance one ought also notice a slight semantic shift. Whereas טב in the previous saying alluded to character, its principal connotation now is 'useful'. The repetition of פגע, 'to touch', in 7.101 (d) and 7.102 (h) constitutes a further important semantic component. Although none of the contiguous sayings resumes פגע, at least two of the ensuing predicates use semantically related roots. Within the adjacent saying 7.103 (24), נטח denotes a vehement insult on the just. The concluding precept 7.107-108 (27) describes the offensive act of the wicked (רשיעא) as 'grasping [אחד] the corners of a garment'. Consequently, touching, assaulting and grasping characterize wicked attitudes towards the innocent throughout the remainder of column 7. By their usage of פגע bramble and pomegranate anticipate an important contextual component.

7.103 (24)

צדיק אנשא
בעדדה כל נטחוהי הוין

(a) A just person of humankind [= a just man]:
(b) In his time[69] all who assault him[70] perish.[71]

69. As was the case in 6.83 (b), בעדדה can be read in different ways, either as 'in his time' or 'to his help'. The reading depends totally on the analysis of the syntax. If one regards 7.103 (24) as a statement about the fate of the just man, the

In the preferred syntactic interpretation the initial construct chain צדיק אנשא (a) functions as an extrapolated subject to present emphatically the topic of 7.103 (24). A simple statement about an impending event ensues in (b). This conspicuous syntactic accentuation coincides with a significant semantic variation. 7.103 (a) for the first time introduces צדיק into the context.

A comparison between the syntax of 7.103 (24) and 7.104 (25) reveals a considerable amount of congruence between the adjacent sayings with regard to syntactic constituents:

| | | | |
|---|---|---|---|
| צדיק אנשא | בעדדה | כל נטחוהי | הוין |
| קרית רשיען | ביום רוח | - | תתחלל |

Only כל נטחוהי remains unparalleled within 7.104 (25). This essential syntactic harmony is matched on the level of semantics. Whereas צדיק performs as the headword of 7.103 (24), its semantic antonym רשיע forms part of the construct chain initiating 7.104 (25). The distribution of these antonyms follows a chiastic pattern. צדיק is *nomen regens* in 7.103 (a), רשיע is *nomen rectum* in 7.105 (a). צדיק :: רשיע ought to be regarded as two components of a word-pair which was split to contiguous sayings in order to strengthen textual coherence. If indeed 7.103 (24) promises the righteous to witness the downfall of the wicked, 7.104 (25) exemplifies this assertion: A town of wickedness will not persist in difficult times. Both sayings belong to a pair whose elements interpret each other mutually.

Besides this noteworthy correspondence of two ensuing textual units which is of limited importance for the composition of the column, both צדיק and רשיע extend their sphere of impact to 7.105-106 (26) and 7.107-108 (27) as well. While 7.105-106 (26) circumscribes rectitude

apparent solution is to interpret בעדדה as an indicator of time: The just man will be able to watch the downfall of his aggressors within 'his time', i.e. the span of his life. Most commentators opted for the other possibility, however: cf. Epstein (1912: 137); Cowley (1923: 219, 225, 245); Lindenberger (1983: 170).

70. There has been considerable controversy as to the exact meaning of this form. Most fittingly, it ought to be explained as an active participle of the G-stem of the root נטח, 'to touch (in a hostile way), to assault'—cf. esp. Kottsieper (1990: 170 § 278e, 198, 217).

71. The lexical evidence for the root הוה II, 'to perish', remains sparse. However, there is no satisfying alternative. The derivation from הוה I as proposed by Cowley (1923: 245) is very difficult both in terms of syntax and content, cf. Lindenberger (1983: 170).

opposite immorality in different terms, 7.107 (a) repeats רשיע as a catchword directly at its outset and presupposes that the addressee is among the upright. In addition, the resumption of אנשא in 7.103 (a) establishes an obvious bond with the assemblage of sayings preceding the fable. Were it not for this interpolation, a continuous series of recurrences of איש and אנשא would structure 7.95 (18) to 7.103 (24) like a read thread. The absence of the semantic backbone of column 7 from the fable in turn further substantiates its secondary embedding within its final context.

7.104 (25)

[קרית] רשיען ביום רוח תתחלל
ובשהינן יצעון תרעיה
כי בזיזת [...]

(a) A city[72] of wicked—on the day of wind it will be damaged,[73]
(b) and her gates will incline into ruin;[74]
(c) because it will be despoiled [...?].[75]

72. Again, the right margin of the papyrus has not been preserved. The width of the lacuna allows for the restoration of a single word. Since (b) and (c) clearly presuppose the reference to a city, קריה can be considered an almost certain restoration for the missing word. This reading has been universally accepted, cf. lately also Porten and Yardeni (1993: 38).

73. There are two possible etymologies for the finite form תתחלל at the end of (a). It may either be derived from late Aramaic/Syriac חלל, 'to perforate, to damage; to desecrate', or from late Aramaic/Hebrew חול, 'to turn around, to swirl'. Both roots are only attested in late texts. The former etymology is more specific and suits the context much better. It could either refer to the force of the storm raging against the city or—even more likely—to the destruction of the city wall by digging under it. As a logical consequence, the city-gates will incline (b).

74. Again, an etymology needs clarification. שהינן is easily derived from late Aramaic שהי / שהוה and Syriac *šhy'*, 'ruin, desolation, devastation'. Kottsieper (1990: 34-36 §17) proposed a different analysis by relating Aramaic שהינן to Hebrew שאה, 'to roar, to storm'. His arguments for this rather unusual etymology are not convincing, however, since they are almost exclusively based on grounds of content ('better parallelism').

75. The end of l. 7.104 has been preserved entirely and there would be no need to add an element to (c). Since l. 7.105 contains a separation mark after its broken right margin, one has to account for one more word belonging to 7.104-105 (25). There is no clear indication as for what was lost. Any restoration has to remain conjectural in character. Among the many proposals צדיק was the most influential,

The saying displays a clear and simple syntactic structure, containing three statements about the destiny of a city of wicked persons. All parts of 7.104 (25) assert the city's downfall by references to its destruction. (a) and (b) contain the same number of constituents (subject, predicate, prepositional phrase). (a) introduces the nominal elements as construct chains. This is not the case in (b). The subjects of (a) קרית רשיע and (b) תרעיה come to stand at the extremes of each clause. In combination they form an inclusio around all other syntagmas. The arrangement of the verbal predicate and the prepositional object remains unaltered in both parts. Even though the order of the three syntagmas differs between (a) and (b), highly developed syntactic parallelism between these two elements is evident. Semantics reinforce this correspondence. קריה and תרעיה form a pair of a whole and its part. The two synonyms חלל (a) and צעי (b) both indicate destruction. Consequently, this complete symmetry of syntax and semantics recalls the elaborate organization of 7.95 (18).

In addition, 7.104 (a) resumes קריה as its headword from 7.95 (b). Since this is the only recurrence of this lexeme within the column, it is most revealing. Common imagery conjoins the settings of both sayings: Any defence system is worthless if the interior of the city does not support them. Here, however, the reference is to the fate of the inhabitants and not to an individual. In contrast to the איש שפיר of 7.95 (18), exterior beauty and inner strength are not in harmony at all. As a consequence, fortifications (תרעיה presupposes a city wall!) will fail at the most important moment and expose the wicked city-dwellers to plunder and devastation. In individualized form the point of this saying is identical with that of 7.95 (18): Strength needs moral support, otherwise it will not prevail.

These fundamental traits common to both sayings confirm their intrinsic interdependence. In combination, they present a pair of opposed personalities: the righteous and wise in 7.95 (18) in contrast to the wicked in 7.104 (25). Considering these crucial characteristics, their compositional relevance can be fully appreciated. 7.95 (18) and 7.104 (25) form an inclusio around an extensive block of interpolated sayings ranging from 7.96 (19) to 7.103 (24). Within this entire composition, all of the sub-units take the form of impersonal statements, lack any

cf. Cowley (1923: 218); Kottsieper (1990: 10). Lindenberger (1983: 172) read רשעין תאבד, '(the spoil) of the wicked shall perish'.

reference to the addressee, and are joined together semantically by the constant repetition of אנשא/איש. Only the fable in 7.101-102 (23) evades any of these structural peculiarities.

Commencing with 7.104 (25), the elaborate structural network of repetitions and topical unity begins to break down, however. The two ensuing sayings still partake in a basic thematic unity indicated by the repeated reference to רשיע in 7.107-108 (27). Nevertheless, 7.104 (25) marks a caesura. The next saying, 7.105-106 (26), is stylized as a biographical statement and therefore introduces a new literary form into the wider context. As a consequence, references to the speaker and the addressee prevail within 7.107-108 (27) as well. The latter unit develops a directive out of a given situation, thus representing the only precept within column 7. Repetition of keywords diminishes in importance, as does the tension between a person's appearance and his motivation. The conclusion of column 7 is thus characterized by a further change in form and content.

7.105-106 (26)

עיני זי נטלת עליך
ולבבי זי יהבת לך
בחכמה [הו ?]
[וי]הבת שמי בשרחו[ת]א

(a) My eyes which I lifted up to you,
(b) and my heart which I turned towards you,
(c) (It was) in wisdom.[76]
(d) But you turned my name into foulness.[77]

76. At the end of (c) and the beginning of (d) the papyrus is severely damaged. This fact obscures the relation between the two elements. While the restoration of the initial consonants of (d) is widely accepted, different options have been proposed for (c). Cowley (1923: 218, 246) inserted מאסת, reading 'you detested wisdom', cf. Lindenberger (1983: 173). While this insertion yields a most satisfactory interpretation, there is hardly room for four consonants. An alternative solution might be an interpolation of the personal pronoun functioning as a link between (a)-(b) (subject) and (c) (nominal predicate). But even this ought not be necessary. בחכמה could as well stand isolated, functioning as the postponed nominal predicate of (a)-(b).

77. The best etymology for בשרחותא relates it to late Aramaic סרחו/שרחו 'bad odour, foulness', used metaphorically for 'bad reputation, disrepute' (cf. Lindenberger [1983: 55-56]; Porten and Yardeni [1993: 39]). Another possible cognate is derived from the Syriac root, meaning 'to be unrestrained, to lack self-control' (cf.

All members of this saying refer to the past. There is no evident 'morale'. Syntactically, 7.105-106 (26) demonstrate considerable stylistic skill. (a) and (b) form a complete syntactic parallelism in which all constituents are repeated twice in the same order. (c) adds the nominal predicate that has a strong circumstantial notion, whereas (d) stands as a complete statement without any exceptional stylistic traits.

7.105-106 (26) presupposes the setting of a dialogue. Precisely this biographical style indicates discontinuity in form. Frequent pronominal references to the persons communicating and references to the benevolence of the speaker correlate 7.105-106 (26) with the Ahikar narrative. The essential accusation perfectly fits the conflict between the slandered Ahikar and his ungrateful nephew. Hence, it is almost inconceivable to understand this biographical statement as being separate from the narrative. 7.105-106 (26) presupposes an elementary acquaintance with the plot of the preceding tale. Presumably it gained its present position through editorial activity trying to harmonize story and proverbs.[78]

Still, the statement fits its present context well enough. In combination with the antecedent units, it applies the antagonism between the righteous and the wicked to a given situation. The concluding allegation ויהבת שמי בשרחותא, 'you made my name into foulness', in 7.106 (d) sheds light on the evil deeds of the accused without envisioning any specific act of inflicting disrepute to the speaker. On the level of semantics, only לבב in 7.106 (b) links 7.105-106 (26) to its context. Internally, the repetition of the root יהב between 7.105 (b) and 7.106 (d) intensifies the malignancy of the slander committed.

7.107-108 (27)

הן יאחדן רשיעא בכנפי לבשך
שבק בידה
אחר אדני לשמש

Sachau [1911: I, 161]; Kottsieper [1990: 237]). While both etymologies are probable, the former one is to be preferred on reasons of context. A reference to the speaker's lack of self-control does not make much sense here, since the point is to be sought in the *addressee's* wrongdoing. The problems caused by this etymology are evident in Kottsieper's translation, which in addition demands textual alterations: '... ich habe so *meinen* Name [*sic*] durch *meine* Zügellosigkeit entehrt' (1990: 10).

78. Noted already by Lindenberger (1983: 136-37, 173).

הו [י]לקח זי לה
וינתן לך

(a) If the wicked seize you by the corners of your garment,
(b) leave it in his hand!
(c) Then, approach Šamaš!
(d) He will take what is his,
(e) and give it to you.

The conclusion of column 7 presents the reader with a series of admonitions, which explicitly refer to an addressee and culminate in a concluding admonition. However, in contrast to the preceding statement, 7.107-108 (27) lacks any biographical trait. By elaborating a conditional precept, the saying gives valid advice for a specific situation that could occur at any time. It reveals a very transparent syntactic structure. Only (a) and (c) contain more than the necessary syntagmas. They bear the principal stress. In contrast, both (b) and (e) consist of a verbal predicate and a prepositional phrase in an identical arrangement. Being the only admonition of the column, 7.107-108 (27) is formally distinct from its wider context.

Semantically, the conditional admonition fits its context well. By the repetition of רשיע adopted from 7.104 (25), it further elaborates the prevalent topic of column 7. Like 7.105-106 (26), one easily comprehends the advice as resulting from the theoretical treatment of the antagonism between righteous and wicked. A more developed thematic coherence may be observed between this precept and 7.99-100 (22). Implicitly, the exhortation to avoid companionship of an evil man coincides with the advice to leave one's garment behind in order to avoid becoming the victim oneself. 7.107-108 (27) applies and individualizes the morale of 7.99-100 (22).

Contextual cohesion is affirmed by the repetition of שבק, familiar from 7.98 (21) in the same meaning. Moreover, the referral to שמש as a divine aide secures an essential theological framework which was already characteristic for the first part of column 7. In conjunction with the previous biographical saying, 7.107-108 (27) re-interprets the quintessence of column 7 in a reader-orientated perspective.

*Column 8*

Column 8 is in a much poorer state of preservation than columns 6–7. Its left margin, its centre part and the lines at its bottom were completely destroyed. Consequently, analysis remains restricted to general observations. The preserved fragments of column 8 exhibit scribal annotations in the form of short lines inserted between individual sections of text at its right margin. These lines are fully visible after 8.109 (28); 8.110 (29); 8.114 (31); 8.121 (37); 8.122 (38); 8.123 (39); and 8.124 (40). All of these units demarcate a new saying. Undoubtedly the scribal marks were intended to indicate to the reader syntactic and thematic boundaries. The deliberate and careful organization is apparent especially between ll. 8.111 and 8.112. Both are opened by a headword derived from the root שבק. This identical repetition either unifies a pair of associated sayings or connects two segments of the same unit. Accordingly, no scribal mark was written between these two lines.

In addition, there is a clear predilection for biographical statements within the column. Its initial four lines—8.109-112 as well as 8.122 (38)—repeatedly refer to the speaker by pronominal references and verbal suffixes. On the contrary, no literary form clearly dominates column 8. Most probably 8.109 (28) represents an exhortation, followed in 8.110 (29) by a statement about the decline of the speaker's enemies. 8.111-12 (30) remind the addressee of former benevolent deeds which were not rewarded accordingly. In addition, a few repetitions indicate a once coherent organization of sayings. צדיק recurs in 8.109 (28) and thereby associates the first lines of column 8 with the cluster of sayings concluding the previous column. Moreover, in combination with שנאי, 'my enemies', at the outset of 8.110 (29), it once more forms part of an antonymous word-pair. Possibly the divine name אל in 8.109 (28) is reminiscent of שמש in 7.107-108 (27). The transition between columns 7 and 8 was certainly not meant to function as a topical caesura. Rather, the first part of the new column completed the context opened already by 7.105-106 (25) and 7.106-107 (26).

Most of the second portion of column 8 was mutilated beyond recognition. The recurrence of a few expressions might indicate an original cross-relation between individual sayings. לא ידע, for example, was preserved in ll. 8.113 and 8.122, and נפלת ססא is all that remained from 8.119 and 8.121. Also, שבק in ll. 8.111 and 8.112 suggests another certain association between two sayings. Complete loss of context, however, does not permit any far-reaching conclusions.

8.123 (39) and 8.124 (40)

כפן יהחלה מררותא
[ו]צהוה [...]

(a) Hunger sweetens the bitter,
(b) and thirst […].

ישתבע כעס מן לחם
ותתרוה [...]

(a) An angry one is satiated by bread,
(b) and […] will be sated …

8.123 (39) and 8.124 (40) are sharply distinguished in form from the antecedent sayings. They lack any reference to the speaker. Both take the form of simple statements, consisting of three syntagmas (subject, predicate, [prepositional] object) which were arranged in a different order: S-P-O in 8.123 (39), P-S-pO in 8.124 (40). If understood as a pair of sayings, the subjects and verbal predicates are organized in a chiastic structure, whereas the (prepositional) objects keep their syntactic slot.

Semantically, both units dwell on internal contrasts. Within 8.123 (39) two complementary word-pairs (כפן // צהוה; מררותא // ?) were split between (a) and (b). In addition, antonymous polarity internally structures each line. Both predicates of 8.124 (40) ישתבע // תתרוה form part of a synonymous word-pair. The second element was lost due to the poor state of preservation. However, a similar pairing is to be expected (e.g. לחם // מים?). No certainty can be achieved about the complement of כעס in (b). Internal contrasts may have been less pronounced than in 8.123 (39). Syntactic and semantic parallelism undoubtedly facilitated the compositional arrangement as a pair of sayings.

Only if interpreted in their given context, can the close relation between 8.123 (39) and 8.124 (40) be fully appreciated. כעס in 8.124 (a) is semantically related to מררותא in 8.123 (a). Bitterness and grief are akin to each other. The intrinsic polysemy of מרר allows for a double meaning, referring either to the bitter taste of something edible or to emotional bitterness. The same double polysemy could be noticed already in 6.89 (11). As a consequence, לחם most probably shared this polysemy and originally pertained to more than just food. With the second limb of this pair missing, no certainty can be achieved as to its accurate interpretation.

*Conclusions*

As a result of this study, it is no longer possible to regard the Aramaic sayings of Ahikar as a random and chaotic amalgamation of unrelated proverbial units. Though limited to the first three columns of the Elephantine Papyri, the investigation confirms the existence of a far-ranging and comprehensive editorial concept. The smallest and most frequent compositional unit isolated is a pairing of sayings, paralleled either by similarity of syntax and/or semantic synonymy or antonymy. Repeatedly syntactic and semantic parallelism mutually enforce each other. Sometimes, however, it is their antagonism which creates interdependence. There are also clusters of related sayings which were organized into larger sections by a variety of means, thus creating sizeable coherent units of text.

As could be demonstrated, the formal distinction between statements, admonitions and warnings was of minor importance for the process of composition. In contrast, frequent repetitions of keywords, roots or whole phrases were essential. Association of catchwords certainly was a relevant factor, especially in a number of instances where intrinsic relations between sayings remained rather loose. At some points closely related sayings were separated deliberately in order to create extensive textual units. This is obvious with regard to 6.84 (7) and 6.89-90 (12); 6.79 (1) and 6.91 (14); 6.92 (15); 7.95 (18) and 7.104 (25) where a couple of sayings was disconnected for the purpose of the formation of an inclusio around a block of text.

Refined compositional techniques not only facilitate a continuous reading without harsh thematic breaks, but at the same time they assure a correct interpretation of the individual saying by positioning it within a wider context. Often context re-interprets a saying which would have a different meaning if taken for itself. In turn, many a saying, an admonition or a narration applies or illustrates the morale of previous units. Mutual interpretation is a most substantial factor for the assemblage of proverbs of different provenance. As a consequence, context and meaning prove inseparable. Old Testament research has long acknowledged this. In sharing its insights, any interpretation of the intimately related Ahikar tradition will benefit considerably.

## BIBLIOGRAPHY


Baneth, D.H.

1914 'Bemerkungen zu den Achikarpapyri', *OLZ* 17: 248-52; 295-99; 348-53.

Bjørndalen, A.J.

1970 ' "Form" und "Inhalt" des motivierenden Mahnspruches', *ZAW* 82: 347-61.

Boström, G.

1928 *Paronomasi i den äldere hebraiska Meschallitteraturen: Med särskild hänsyn till Proverbia* (Acta universitatis Lundensis, Section 1. Teologi, juridik och humanistika ämnen 23.8; Lund: C.W.K. Gleerup).

Charles, R.H.

1963 'The Story of Ahikar', in R.H. Charles (ed.), *The Apocrypha and Pseudepigrapha of the Old Testament in English*, II (repr.; Oxford: Clarendon Press): 715-84.

Conrad, J.

1967 'Die innere Gliederung der Proverbien: Zur Frage nach der Systematisierung des Spruchgutes in den älteren Teilsammlungen', *ZAW* 79: 67-76.

Conybeare, F.C., J. Rendel Harris and A. Smith Lewis

1913 *The Story of Aḥiḳar from the Aramaic, Syriac, Arabic, Armenian, Ethiopic, Old Turkish, Greek and Slavonic Versions* (Cambridge: Cambridge University Press, 2nd rev. edn).

Cowley, A.

1923 *Aramaic Papyri of the Fifth Century B.C.* (Oxford: Clarendon Press).

Crenshaw, J.L.

1995 'Impossible Questions, Sayings, and Tasks', in *idem* (ed.), *Urgent Advice and Probing Questions: Collected Writings on Old Testament Wisdom* (Macon, GA: Mercer University Press): 265-79.

Engelken, K.

1996 'Baʿalšamem: Keine Guseinandersetzung mit der monographie H. Niehrs', *ZAW* 108: 233-48; 391-407.

Epstein, J.N.

1912 'Glossen zu den "aramäischen Papyrus und Ostraka" ', *ZAW* 32: 128-38.

1913a 'Nachträge und Berichtigungen zu meinen Glossen im Jahrgang 1912 und 1913', *ZAW* 33: 310-12.

1913b 'Weitere Glossen zu den "aramäischen Papyrus und Ostraka" ', *ZAW* 33: 222-35.

1916 'Eine Nachlese zu den Ahiqarpapyri', *OLZ* 19: 204-209.

Fales, F.M.

1993 'Riflessioni sull'Ahiqar di Elefantina', *Orientis Antiqui Miscellanea* 1: 39-60.

Gianto, A.

1995 'A New Edition of Aramaic Texts from Egypt (Ahiqar, Bar Punesh, Bisitun, Accounts and Lists)', *Bib* 76: 85-92.

Ginsberg, H.L.

1955 'Aramaic Proverbs and Precepts: The Words of Ahiqar', in *ANET*: 427-30.

Goldingay, J.
1994 'The Arrangement of Sayings in Proverbs 10–15', *JSOT* 61: 75-83.
Greenfield, J.C.
1968 'Dialect Traits in Early Aramaic', *Lešonenu* 32: 359-68.
Grelot, P.
1961 'Les proverbes araméens d'Aḥiqar', *RB* 69: 178-94.
1972 'Histoire et sagesse d'Aḥîqar l'Assyrien', in *idem* (ed.), *Documents araméens d'Egypte* (LAPO, 5; Paris: Cerf): 427-52.
Grimme, H.
1911 'Bemerkungen zu den aramäischen Achikarsprüchen', *OLZ* 14: 529-40.
Halévy, J.
1912 'Les nouveaux papyrus d'Eléphantine', *RevSém* 20: 31-78, 153-77.
Heim, K.M.
1999 *Like Grapes of Gold Set in Silver: An Interpretation of Proverbial Clusters in the Book of Proverbs* (BZAW, 273; Berlin: W. de Gruyter).
Hermisson, H.-J.
1968 *Studien zur israelitischen Spruchweisheit* (WMANT, 28; Neukirchen–Vluyn: Neukirchener Verlag).
Hildebrandt, T.A.
1988 'Proverbial Pairs: Compositional Units in Proverbs 10-29', *JBL* 107: 207-24.
1990 'Proverbial Strings: Cohesion in Proverbs 10', *GTJ* 11: 171-85.
Kottsieper, I.
1988 '*mgg*—Krieg führen, kämpfen: Eine bisher übersehene nordwestsemitische Wurzel', *UF* 20: 125-33.
1990 *Die Sprache der Aḥiqarsprüche* (BZAW, 194; Berlin: W. de Gruyter).
1991 'Die Geschichte und die Sprüche des weisen Achiqar', in G. Burkard, I. Kottsieper, I. Shirun-Grumach, H. Sternberg-el Hotabi and H.J. Thissen (eds.), *Texte aus der Umwelt des Alten Testaments*, III/2 (Gütersloh: Gerd Mohn): 320-47.
1992 'Die literarische Aufnahme assyrischer Begebenheiten in frühen aramäischen Texten', in D. Charpin and F. Joannès (eds.), *La circulation des biens, des personnes et des idées dans le Proche-Orient: Actes de la XXXVIII[e] RAI (Paris, 8.-10. 7. 1991)* (Paris: Editions Recherche sur les Civilisations): 283-89.
1997a 'Die alttestamentliche Weisheit im Licht aramäischer Weisheitstraditionen', in B. Janowski (ed.), *Weisheit außerhalb der kanonischen Weisheitsschriften* (Veröffentlichungen der Wissenschaftlichen Gesellschaft für Theologie; Gütersloh: Christian Kaiser): 128-62.
1997b 'El—ferner oder naher Gott? Zur Bedeutung einer semitischen Gottheit in verschiedenen sozialen Kontexten im 1. Jtsd. v. Chr', in R. Albertz (ed.), *Religion und Gesellschaft: Studien zu ihrer Wechselbeziehung in den Kulturen des Antiken Vorderen Orients* (AOAT, 248; Münster: Ugarit Verlag): 25-74.
Krispenz, J.
1989 *Spruchkompositionen im Buch Proverbia* (Europäische Hochschulschriften, 23.349; Frankfurt am Main: Peter Lang).

Krüger, T.

1995 'Komposition und Diskussion in Proverbia 10', *ZTK* 92: 413-33.

Kutscher, E.Y.

1970 'Aramaic', in C.A. Ferguson (ed.), *Linguistics in South West Asia and North Africa* (Current Trends in Linguistics, 6; The Hague: Mouton): 347-412.

Lambert, W.G.L.

1996 *Babylonian Wisdom Literature* (Winona Lake, IN: Eisenbrauns [1960]).

Lindenberger, J.M.

1982 'The Gods of Ahiqar', *UF* 14: 105-117.

1983 *The Aramaic Proverbs of Ahiqar* (Baltimore: The Johns Hopkins University Press).

1985 'Ahiqar: A New Translation and Introduction', in *OTP*, II: 494-507.

McCreesh, T.P.

1991 *Biblical Sound and Sense: Poetic Sound Patterns in Proverbs 10–29* (JSOTSup, 128; Sheffield: JSOT Press).

McKane, W.

1970 *Proverbs: A New Approach* (Old Testament Literature; London: SCM Press).

Meinhold, A.

1991 *Die Sprüche*. I. *Sprüche Kapitel 1-15* (Zürcher Bibelkommentare; Zürich: Theologischer Verlag).

Nau, F.

1909 *Histoire et sagesse d'Aḥikar l'Assyrien: Traduction des versions syriaques avec les principales différences des versions arabes, arménienne, grecque, néo-syriaque, slave et roumaine* (Documents pour l'étude de la Bible; Paris: Letouzey & Ané).

Nel, P.

1982 *The Structure and Ethos of the Wisdom Admonitions in Proverbs* (BZAW, 158; Berlin: W. de Gruyter).

Nöldeke, T.

1913 *Untersuchungen zum Achiqar-Roman* (Abhandlungen der Akademie der Wissenschaften in Göttingen, philologisch-historische Klasse 14.4; Berlin: Weidmann).

Perles, F.

1911 'Zu Sachaus "Aramäischen Papyrus und Ostraka" ', *OLZ* 14: 498-503.

1912 'Zu Sachaus "Aramäischen Papyrus und Ostraka" ', *OLZ* 15: 54-57.

Perry, St.C.

1987 *Structural Patterns in Prov. 10.1-22.16: A Study in Biblical Hebrew Stylistics* (PhD dissertation, University of Texas, Austin; Ann Arbor, MI: University Microfilms).

Plöger, O.

1971 'Zur Auslegung der Sentenzensammlungen des Proverbienbuches', in H.W. Wolff (ed.), *Probleme Biblischer Theologie: Gerhard von Rad zum 70. Geburtstag* (Munich: Chr. Kaiser Verlag), pp. 402-416.

1984 *Sprüche Salomos (Proverbia)* (BKAT, 17; Neukirchen–Vluyn: Neukirchener Verlag).

Pola, T.
1995 'Die Strukture von Proverbia 16, 1-15', *BN* 80: 47-72.

Porten, B., and A. Yardeni
1993 *Textbook of Aramaic Documents from Ancient Egypt.* III. *Literature, Accounts, Lists* (Jerusalem: Hebrew University Press).

Puech, E.
1988 Review of *The Aramaic Proverbs of Ahiqar* (Baltimore: The Johns Hopkins University Press), by J.M. Lindenberger, in *RB* 95: 589-92.

Rad, G. von
1992 *Weisheit in Israel* (Gütersloher Taschenbücher, 1437; Gütersloh: Gerd Mohn [1970]).

Richter, W.
1966 *Recht und Ethos: Versuch einer Ortung des weisheitlichen Mahnspruches* (SANT, 15; Munich: Kösel).

Römheld, K.F.D.
1989 *Wege der Weisheit: Die Lehren Amenemopes und Proverbien 22, 17-24, 22* (BZAW, 184; Berlin: W. de Gruyter).

Sachau, E.
1911 *Aramäische Papyrus und Ostraka aus einer jüdischen Militär-Kolonie zu Elephantine* (2 vols.; Generalverwaltung der königlichen Museen zu Berlin; Leipzig: J.C. Hinrichs).

Scherer, A.
1997a 'Is the Selfish Man Wise? Considerations of Context in Proverbs 10.1–22.16: With Special Regard to Surety, Bribery and Friendship', *JSOT* 76: 59-70.
1997b 'Vielfalt und Ordnung: Komposition in den biblischen Proverbien und in den aramäischen Ahiqarsprüchen', *BN* 90: 28-45.
1999 *Das weise Wort und seine Wirkung: Eine Untersuchung zur Komposition und Redaktion von Proverbia 10, 1-22, 16* (WMANT, 83; Neukirchen–Vluyn: Neukirchener Verlag).

Schmidt, J.
1936 *Studien zur Stilistik der alttestamentlichen Spruchliteratur* (Alttestamentliche Abhandlungen, 13.1; Münster: Aschendorff).

Schmitt, C.
1913–14 'Der weise Achikar der morgenländischen Sage und der Achikar des Buches Tobias nach der Übersetzung der Siebenzig', *Pastor Bonus* 26: 83-98.

Seidel, M.
1912 'Bemerkungen zu den aramäischen Papyrus und Ostraka aus Elephantine', *ZAW* 32: 292-98.

Seux, M.-J.
1967 *Epithètes royales akkadiennes et sumériennes* (Paris: Letouzy & Ané).

Skladny, U.
1962 *Die ältesten Spruchsammlungen in Israel* (Göttingen: Vandenhoeck & Ruprecht).

Skoralick, R.
1995 *Einzelspruch und Sammlung: Komposition im Buch der Sprichwörter Kapitel 10-15* (BZAW, 232; Berlin: W. de Gruyter).

Snell, D.
1993 *Twice-Told Proverbs and the Composition of the Book of Proverbs* (Winona Lake, IN: Eisenbrauns).

Stummer, F.
1914a *Der kritische Wert der altaramäischen Aḫiḳartexte aus Elephantine* (Alttestamentliche Abhandlungen, 5.5; Münster: Aschendorff).
1914b 'Zu den altaramäischen Achikarsentenzen', *OLZ* 17: 252-54.
1915 'Zur Ursprache des Aḫiḳarbuches', *OLZ* 18: 103-105.

Ungnad, A.
1911 *Aramäische Papyrus aus Elephantine* (Leipzig: J.C. Hinrichs).

Van Leeuwen, R.
1988 *Context and Meaning in Proverbs 25-27* (SBLDS, 96; Atlanta: Scholars Press).

Weigl, M.
1999 *'Mein Neffe Achikar (Tob 1, 22)': Die aramäischen Achikar-Sprüche und das Alte Testament* (Habilitationsschrift; Vienna: University of Vienna).

Wensinck, A.J.
1912 'Zu den Achikarsprüchen der Papyri aus Elephantine', *OLZ* 15: 49-54.

Whybray, R.N.
1992 'Thoughts on the Composition of Proverbs 10-29', in E. Ulrich, J.W. Wright, P.R. Davies and R.P. Carroll (eds.), *Priests, Prophets and Scribes: Essays on the Formation and Heritage of Second Temple Judaism in Honour of Joseph Blenkinsopp* (JSOTSup, 149; Sheffield: Sheffield Academic Press).
1994 *The Composition of the Book of Proverbs* (JSOTSup, 168; Sheffield: Sheffield Academic Press).

Wilcke, C.
1989 'Die Emar-Version von "Dattelpalme und Tamariske": Ein Rekonstruktionsversuch', *ZA* 79: 161-90.

Zimmerli, W.
1979 *Ezechiel.* I. *Ezechiel 1-24* (BKAT, 13.1; Neukirchen–Vluyn: Neukirchener Verlag, 2nd edn).

# The Sefire Treaty Stipulations and the Mesopotamian Treaty Tradition

William Morrow

Since the discovery of the Sefire inscriptions, scholars have been interested in comparing their form and contents with other examples of ancient Near Eastern treaties. I take pleasure in dedicating this study to Paul-Eugène Dion from whom I learned many of the disciplines necessary to participate in this discussion.

*Introduction*

Recently, the claim that the Sefire inscriptions show marked affinity with first-millennium neo-Assyrian treaty documents has been accepted by both Aramaicists and Assyriologists. Lemaire and Durand (1984) reached this opinion by noting similarities with neo-Assyrian treaty terminology, the deities guaranteeing the oaths, and stylistic affinities with the treaty of Ashur-nirari V and Mati'el. Van Rooy (1989) has concluded that the overall structure of the Sefire inscriptions resembles that of first-millennium Assyrian treaties. Indeed the evidence for neo-Assyrian influence is so strong that one prominent Assyriologist, S. Parpola (1987: 183), concludes:

> The Sefire Treaty...is in reality nothing but an Assyrian treaty imposed on a defeated adversary, but written in his mother tongue. In some details of its formulation, this treaty may well conform with local traditions, but it is good to keep in mind that these local traditions also had their roots in older practices largely originating in Mesopotamia.

The intent of this essay is to explore the possibility that the Sefire inscriptions represent 'nothing but an Assyrian treaty'. Left out of the discussions cited above are the treaty stipulations of the Sefire inscriptions. Two decades ago the influential discussion of McCarthy (1978)[1] underscored affinities between the stipulations of the Sefire inscriptions and second-millennium treaties imposed on Syrian vassals by Hittite kings. Fitzmyer continues to maintain that the presence of the infinitive absolute construction in Sefire 3 is 'under Canaanite influence' (1995: 212).[2] How are such claims to be assessed in light of new evidence and insights from neo-Assyrian parallels? An opportunity presents itself now because a sizeable collection of neo-Assyrian treaty documents is available for comparison,[3] more than were available to McCarthy and more or less ignored by Fitzmyer.

This study will focus on the two features of the Sefire treaty stipulations just mentioned. First, parallels to the form of the Sefire treaty stipulations will be examined. This will allow for an assessment of the claim made by McCarthy. Secondly, parallels to the presence of the emphatic infinitive constructions in Sefire 3 will be analysed. This will allow for an assessment of the claim made by Fitzmyer. The study will conclude that, though the claims of both Fitzmyer and McCarthy must be qualified, they point to genuine non-Assyrian features in the Sefire inscriptions which must be taken into account in any description of its generic affinities.

## *The Form of the Sefire Treaty Stipulations*

The treaty stipulations from Sefire are arranged in paragraphs which typically end with a version of the following formula: '(and/then) you will have been unfaithful to (all the/the gods of) the/this treaty-oath (which is in this inscription)'.[4]

For the purposes of comparison, this clause will be called the 'repression formula'.[5] This formula organizes the contents of Sefire 1.B.21-23; 23-28; 28-33; 33-37; and 37-38. It is impossible to determine if the

1. Fitzmyer (1995: 165-66) quotes McCarthy with approval in his discussion of the genre of Sefire as vassal treaty.

2. The same opinion also appears in Fitzmyer's first edition (1969: 174).

3. These are now collected in Parpola and Watanabe (1988).

4. The following editions were consulted: For Sefire 1.B, 2.B and 3, Donner and Röllig (1971); Fitzmyer (1995); Lemaire and Durand (1984). For Sefire 3, reference was also made to Gibson (1975). Though reconstructions occasionally vary, all are agreed in finding a form of this formula in the places cited.

5. Cf. the term *clause répressive* in Kestemont (1974: 92).

pattern continues because of the badly preserved state of the text, though it is evident that material in 1.B.39-45 touches on obligations related to military aid and dynastic support, topics which previous paragraphs of the stipulations have also addressed. Though the context is mutilated, Sefire 2.B.5-9; 10-14; and 15-18 show a similar construction. Finally, Sefire 3.1-4; 4-7; 7-9; 9-14; 14-17; 17-19; 19-21; 21-23; and 23-27 are similarly organized.

Comparison with the form of Akkadian treaties in the Mesopotamian treaty tradition needs to take into consideration two features of the paragraphs of stipulations in the Sefire inscriptions. First, there is a need to find treaty stipulations in which the overlord refers to himself in the first person and the vassal is referred to in the second person, a consistent feature of the composition of the treaty stipulations in the Sefire inscriptions. Second, it is necessary to find treaties with free-standing, multiple paragraphs marked by the repression formula.

Two groups of Akkadian treaties can be compared. The first group consists of neo-Assyrian treaties; according to Parpola (1987: 186), there are now 14 extant neo-Assyrian treaties. The formal characteristics of a subset of these treaties have been described by Grayson (1987). Grayson limited himself to eight seventh-century documents which explicitly identified themselves by the use of the term *adê*. Not all of these treaties use the same form for expressing their stipulations. The group that concerns this study is the largest group classified by Grayson: 'Form A'. According to Grayson (1987: 131), 'In these texts the superior party is in the third person and imposes the *adê* upon the inferior party who is in the second person and enjoined under oath to observe various injunctions.'

This group consists of Esarhaddon's vassal treaties (Wiseman 1958), Esarhaddon's treaty with Baal of Tyre (Borger 1956: 107-109), the Akitu Treaty (Parpola 1987: 178-80), text VAT 11534 (Grayson 1987: 133-34), the Zakutu Treaty (Parpola 1987: 165-70), Ashurbanipal's treaty with the Arab tribe of Qedar (Grayson 1987: 147-50), and text A.2409 (Grayson 1987: 154). It is the closest comparative group because the other groups of texts use either the third person or the first person to refer to the inferior partner (Grayson 1987: 131).

The treaty between Ashur-nirari V and Mati'el[6] also identifies itself

6. Editions used include both Weidner (1932–33: 17-23) and the fragments published by Millard (1970: 174).

explicitly as belonging to the *adê* type. It was not considered by Grayson because it was not a seventh-century treaty and is formally distinct from the seventh-century texts. Insofar as treaty stipulations are concerned (though this section is badly damaged), it appears that a curse was invoked after each stipulation whereas the seventh-century treaties typically list all the stipulations before the divine curses are invoked. The vassal is the same Mati'el who is mentioned in the Sefire treaties (Fitzmyer 1995: 60). One paragraph, rev. 5.1-7, mentions the overlord in the first person and the vassal in the second person as at Sefire. But this treaty prefers the third person for both parties, although there is also a broken section of second person references. Since the treaty is atypical in form and is substantially connected to the Sefire context, it will not be used for comparison.

The basis for comparison can be extended if allowance is made for those texts classified by Parpola as treaties, though the word *adê* does not appear. These include the Oath of Loyalty to Esarhaddon (Parpola 1987: 174-75) and the vassal treaty K.4439 (1987: 175-78). Outside of these examples, there are some isolated second-person references in Esarhaddon's Accession Treaty (Parpola 1987: 170-74), though overall the form of this document seems to resemble Grayson's 'Form C' because of references to the vassal in the first person (Parpola 1987: 170-74).[7]

For the purposes of reference the assemblage of treaties just listed will be called the 'neo-Assyrian (NA) comparative group'. By and large, the NA comparative group does not organize its contents in series of free-standing conditional constructions. It prefers to use lists of treaty stipulations which are set in long series of conditionally marked protases, which end in a list of apodoses detailing divine curses. There are three exceptions to this pattern. In the treaty with Baal of Tyre, though the context is somewhat broken, second-person treaty stipulations do not appear as a list of protases before an extended set of curses. They occupy a limited set of self-contained conditional constructions in ll. 6-14. The second exception is found in the structure of Esarhaddon's Vassal Treaties (*VTE*). In this lengthy document, most stipulations are conditional protases anticipating the extensive curses found at the end. Nevertheless, this structure is broken up by other paragraphs in which the stipulations appear with self-contained

7. The shift is noted by Parpola (1987: 173). Cf. Grayson (1987: 131).

apodoses in §§7, 18, 28, 33 and 34.[8] A third pattern appears in text K.4439, which consists of a rather short and broken set of treaty stipulations. Rev. 3.4-9 begins with the particle *šumma* and clearly anticipates an apodosis of divine curses later in the document. But rev. 3.10-17 consists of a series of three unconditional instructions similar to the so-called 'apodictic' form identified in biblical law. Unfortunately neither the date nor the identities of the treaty partners in K.4439 can be determined (Parpola 1987: 163).

As noted, the overlord in the NA comparative group is customarily referred to in the third person. There are exceptions, however, including two treaties using second-person references to the vassal in their stipulations which contain references to the overlord in the first person. They are found in text K.4439 and in Baal of Tyre.

If we compare the NA comparative group with the treaty stipulations in the Sefire inscriptions, the following points appear. First, no text in the NA comparative group marks series of treaty stipulations with a repression formula. Second, free-standing conditional constructions are rare, as are treaty stipulations referring to the overlord in the first person and the vassal in second person. The only treaty that shows the use of both of these features together is Baal of Tyre. The fact that this document is from the western part of the neo-Assyrian empire should not be overlooked.

A second set of treaties with comparative value were written in Akkadian during the Bronze Age. Most were imposed on Syrian vassals by Hittite kings (and in some case were written in both Hittite and Akkadian exemplars), but it would be erroneous simply to call these documents 'Hittite treaties'. The Assyriologist, Wiseman (1982: 311), has insisted on a basic unity in the Mesopotamian treaty tradition and stated the case for deriving the treaties of the Hittite kings from this tradition. Therefore, these treaties will be called the 'Second Millennium (SM) comparative group'. It comprises treaties that use a form of the repression formula as a discourse marker and/or that contain stipulations referring to the overlord in the first person and to the vassal in the second person.

A number of texts contain series of treaty stipulations composed as fully formed sets of conditional instructions which end with a repression formula. Examples include the treaties of Suppiluliumas with Tette

8. Divisions correspond to those in the translation of Borger (1983: 160-76).

(obv. 2.32, 47; rev. 3.32, 40, 52; Weidner 1923: 63, 65-67);[9] Suppiluliumas with Aziru (obv. 18, 21; Weidner 1923: 73); Hattusilis III with Bentešina (rev. 4, 11; Weidner 1923: 133); and Mursilis II with Niqmepa of Ugarit (ll. 60, 69, 72; Kestemont 1974: 95-119). With the exception of Niqmepa of Ugarit (l. 60), the repression formula is found in the third person singular, unlike the second person usages in the Sefire inscriptions. No text in the SM comparative corpus organizes long strings of treaty stipulations using the repression formula. The maximum attested is three paragraphs; compare Sefire 1 (five paragraphs) and Sefire 3 (eight paragraphs).

A number of second-millennium treaties contain paragraphs in which the overlord refers to himself in the first person and the vassal is referred to in the second person. An unconditional example occurs in the treaty of Suppiluliumas with Mattiwaza (obv. 60-62 and rev. 22-23; Weidner 1923: 19-25). The majority of examples are in conditional structures: W3 (obv. 2.16-32); W4 (obv. 10-18); the treaty of Muwatallis with Šunaššura (rev. 4.19-24, 32-39; Weidner 1923: 107-109); W9 (obv. 37-43); the Niqmepa of Ugarit treaty (ll. 9-11; 13; 14-21); and the treaty of Niqmepa of Alalakh with Ir-$^{d}$IM of Tunip (Wiseman 1953: 26-31). In the latter case, there is a striking correspondence with the formulations of Sefire. The Ir-$^{d}$IM treaty contains a long series of conditionally introduced paragraphs that comprise the treaty stipulations. The overlord refers to himself consistently in the first person and the vassal is referred to in the second person. But unlike the stipulations in the Sefire inscriptions, the stipulations of the Ir-$^{d}$IM treaty are not punctuated by a repression formula.

To summarize, there is no treaty in the SM comparative corpus which exactly accords with all the conditions described as pertaining to the form of treaty stipulations in the Sefire inscriptions. Closest appears to be the treaty of Niqmepa of Ugarit in which one can find both multiple uses of the repression formula (including one in the second person singular) and stipulations with the desired grammatical features, though not in the same contexts.

Insofar as this information touches on the provenance of the form of the treaty stipulations in the Sefire inscriptions, the evidence does not lead to the conclusion that their form is a feature of neo-Assyrian treaty

9. In all texts cited here, reference is to unrestored or partially restored contexts only.

composition. It is debatable whether McCarthy is to be followed in insisting on the Hittite provenance of this form; but, at the very least, we must assume that in the composition of its treaty stipulations the scribes of Sefire made use of a non-Assyrian tradition which is best attested in the western part of the fertile crescent. The fact that the Assyrians themselves were aware of such traditions and allowed them to be used is probably indicated by the treaty between Esarhaddon and Baal of Tyre. While neo-Assyrian treaties prefer a different syntax for relating stipulations to treaty curses, they could use self-contained conditional formulations as attested, for example, in Esarhaddon's Vassal Treaties. The fact that only conditional treaty stipulations are found in the neo-Assyrian treaty from the most western point of reference should not be overlooked. In the stipulations of both the treaty with Baal of Tyre and the Sefire inscriptions, formal traditions have been preserved which appear to be native to the greater Syrian milieu and which are also attested by such second-millennium products as the treaty of Niqmepa of Ugarit.

## *Rhetorical Style in the Sefire Treaty Stipulations*

The same body of evidence can also permit a review of the possibility that the treaty stipulations in the Sefire inscriptions use a rhetoric which is not dependent on Akkadian sources. This section will compare emphatic constructions in the Sefire inscriptions' treaty stipulations with both the SM and NA corpora. Its focus will be on occurrences of the infinitive absolute preposed to a finite verb form. There are different ways of describing this construction; the terminology used here will be the 'paronomastic infinitive'. Its typical use is to intensify the force of the verb in its context (Waltke and O'Connor 1990: 584).[10]

Paronomastic infinitive constructions in the Sefire inscriptions are confined to the following contexts.[11] First, in an apodosis contrasting with the negative clause(s) beginning the apodosis: Concerning Sefire 3.2, Gibson (1975), Lemaire and Durand (1984) and Fitzmyer (1995) are agreed that a broken conditional construction starting in Sefire 3.1 begins its apodosis with a negative clause in Sefire 3.2:

10. A similar terminology is used in Akkadian grammar; cf. von Soden (1952: §150a).

11. Unless otherwise noted, the translation and text follow Fitzmeyer (1995).

| | | |
|---|---|---|
| Protasis | … (if anyone rants) | |
| | and utters evil words | *wymll mln lḥyt* |
| | against me | *l‘ly* |
| Apodosis | [you] must [not] accept | *[’t l]tqḥ* |
| | such words from him; | *mly’ mn ydh* |
| | You must hand them over | *hskr thskrhm* |
| | into my hands | *bydy* |

As regards Sefire 3.5-6, the context is relatively secure and undisputed:

| | | |
|---|---|---|
| Protasis | (if someone flees from me) | |
| | and they go to Aleppo, | *wyhkn ḥlb* |
| Apodosis | you must not gi[ve th]em food, | *lts[k l]hm lḥm* |
| | or say to them | *wlt’mr lhm* |
| | ‘Stay quietly in your place’; | *šlw ‘l ’šrkm* |
| | nor turn them from me, | *wlthrm nbšhm mny* |
| | you must placate them | *rqh trqhm* |

Secondly, a variant of this pattern appears in Sefire 3.18 with a second appearance of the phrase *rqh trqh*. In this case, the protasis contains a paronomastic infinitive construction which contrasts with the negative commands in the apodosis of the preceding conditional structure. The context is a conditional construction ending in a negative apodosis in Sefire 3.17-18:

| | | |
|---|---|---|
| Protasis | (or if he usurps his brother) | |
| Apodosis | you shall not interfere with them, | *ltšlḥ lšnk bnyhm* |
| | saying to him | *wt’mr lh* |
| | ‘Kill your brother…’ | *qtl ’ḥk* |
| Protasis | [But] if you really make peace between them, | *[w]hn rqh trqh bnyhm* |
| Apodosis | he will not kill, | *lyqtl* |

Thirdly, as emphatic commands resuming a series of related instructions:

| | |
|---|---|
| Sefire 3.12-13 | *nkh tkwh* |
| Sefire 3.13 | *nkh tkh* |

This reconstruction is agreed on by all major editions, though it is usually allowed that there is an orthographic error in the original

(Gibson 1975: 54; Fitzmyer 1995: 153). The context is a conditional construction which begins in Sefire 3.9 and runs to l. 12. The general sense is that 'if someone succeeds in killing me, you must come and avenge me, your son must come and avenge my son, your grandson my grandson, and your descendants my descendants'. The import of this instruction is reinforced by the two conditional structures following, each containing an emphatic use of the infinitive absolute:

Sefire 3.12-13

| | | |
|---|---|---|
| Protasis | And if it is a city, | *whn qryh h'* |
| Apodosis | you must utterly destroy it with the sword | *nkh tkwh bḥrb* |

Sefire 3.13-14

| | | |
|---|---|---|
| Protasis | (And if it is one my people) you must utterly destroy him ... with the sword | *nkh tkh 'y[t]h ... bḥrb* |

There are no other certain cases of the use of the paronomastic infinitive construction in the Sefire inscriptions. Fitzmyer (1995: 111, 212) suggests the use of *mwt* in Sefire 1.B.30, but the context is too broken to restore the finite verb that must follow. He also identifies the phrase *'gr 'gr* in Sefire 2.C.8 as an 'intensive infinitive' construction, but this context has recently been analysed by van Rooy (1991: 149; also Fitzmyer 1995: 133) who concludes that Aramaic usage here is best understood as a *pe'al* imperfect followed by a passive participle. Lemaire and Durand (1984: 139) suggest that a reading *ṭpp yṭpn* is possible for Sefire 1.B.33. But this reconstruction is not supported by other attempts to make sense of this broken section of the text.

Presumably, Fitzmyer's judgment that the paronomastic infinitive constructions in the Sefire inscriptions are due to Canaanite influence rests in part on the conviction that this arrangement is not native to Old Aramaic, though he does not say so. The Old Aramaic evidence will be re-evaluated below. At this point, it should be noted that there is no a priori reason to suppose that if there was influence from a foreign pattern of syntax, the only candidates are Northwest Semitic languages such as Hebrew, Phoenician and Ugaritic. In fact, a parallel use of the infinitive is well known in Akkadian. But to the best of my knowledge, no one has ever compared Akkadian usage with the texts of the Sefire inscriptions.

Though the paronomastic infinitive construction is described in Akkadian grammars,[12] specialized studies are not common. The most thoroughgoing is the monograph of Aro (1961). His study covers all the major dialects of Akkadian and provides citations of over 70 texts. Conspicuous by its absence is neo-Assyrian where Aro (1961: §§3.134; 4.15) notes that, with the exception of one problematic text, no examples are extant. Evidently, neo-Assyrian was not a dialect of Akkadian that regularly used the paronomastic infinitive. Certainly, there are no examples modifying second-person verb forms in the NA comparative corpus surveyed for this essay. One may conclude that the paronomastic infinitive constructions in Sefire 3 do not appear under the influence of neo-Assyrian usage.

Many examples of the paronomastic infinitive construction can be found in Old Babylonian (including Mari) and Old Assyrian.[13] Similar usages also occur in Middle Babylonian and Middle Assyrian (Aro 1961: §§4.10-11). Though the largest number of examples are from letters, legal texts also are represented. Aro notes that the construction is common in Old Babylonian family law contracts and that it is found in the Laws of Eshnunna A.2.38-40, B.2.3-4 (Aro 1961: §§3.130; 4.7). But no treaty documents are cited. Certainly, the construction is absent in the treaty stipulations of the SM comparative corpus cited above. It does not appear that second-person references in treaties are a typical genre for this grammatical construction; however, caution is required—after all, this amounts to an argument from silence.

The significance of such negative evidence may appear a little stronger when it is recognized that there is another emphatic construction in Sefire 3 which does possess parallels in the SM comparative corpus. The feature has the technical term 'heterosis'. The figure of heterosis involves the exchange of one grammatical form for another for the purposes of emphasis. Heterosis involving the imperative is attested in biblical Hebrew.[14]

12. Von Soden 1952; Delitzsch 1889: §133.

13. Aro 1961: §§3.130-32; 4.6-9; see also the examples in Levy (1946: 410-15).

14. Waltke and O'Connor (1990: §34.4c) point to the following biblical examples: 2 Kgs 19.29; Ps. 110.2; and Isa. 54.14. These citations are outside the confines of extended instructional discourse in the Hebrew Bible. I have not been able to identify a certain example of heterosis in instructional discourse. A possible

As far as Old Aramaic is concerned, a case of heterosis can be found in Sefire 3.6 in the construction *whn ly[šb]n b'rqk rqw šm ʿd 'hk 'nh*. This is the only case of an imperative occurring in the main clause of an apodosis in Sefire 3. Although other imperative constructions occur, they are confined to quoted speech: Sefire 3.5, 7, 18, 21, 22. The syntax of the surrounding treaty stipulations leads the reader to expect a finite verb form in Sefire 3.6. A translation that took the heterosis of *rqw* seriously in this context should be more emphatic that the one offered, for example, by Fitzmyer. The force is not simply 'placate them', but 'placate them at once!'

The unusual position of *rqw* in Sefire 3.6 can be underscored by considering the syntax of the treaty stipulations in Sefire 1 and 2. There are no examples of an imperative mood used in a main clause of a conditional construction in their treaty stipulations. The only possible exception to this judgment, given the current state of the reconstructed text, appears to be in Sefire 1.B.28. The editions read as follows:

| | |
|---|---|
| Donner and Röllig 1971 | *wysbn y'th ḥ[ylk 'ly* |
| Lemaire and Durand 1984 | *wysbbny'th b[kl ḥylk* |
| Fitzmyer 1995 | *wysbn[y] y'th ḥ[ylk 'ly* |

There are no word markers in this text. Both Donner and Röllig and Fitzmyer assume that there has been a haplography of the yod on the suffix of *wysbn*, because they read the next word as a prefixed form. Lemaire and Durand (1984: 138) follow a suggestion of Lipiński and read the extant yod as an indication of the first person suffix. The following three letters are read as the imperative *'th*. The ambiguities are considerable. I follow Fitzmyer and Donner and Röllig at this point because the syntax does not parallel that of the more certain case. The case of heterosis in Sefire 3.6 occurs in the first verb of an apodosis which follows a protasis containing a negative verb. Hence, there is an element of contrast. Contrast is also at work in another emphatic construction in Sefire: the use of the paronomastic infinitives in Sefire

candidate is *ḥzq* in Deut. 12.23, but the imperative mood could be explained there as due to a transformation of the well-known admonitory formula *hšmr pn* which is also in the imperative mood. Another possible candidate is the imperative *šmr* beginning Deut. 12.28. But since Deuteronomy is known for its use of the free infinitive as a predicate in context (cf. Deut. 5.12; 16.1; 25.17), one would have to be certain that the form was not better revocalized as an infinitive absolute.

3.2, 6 and 18. This semantic condition does not occur in Sefire 1.B.28. There *y'th* is the first verb in an apodosis which comes after a protasis of two coordinated verbs both positive in form.

Given the fact that heterosis is an attested rhetorical feature in both biblical Hebrew and Old Aramaic, can it be concluded that this is a native Northwest Semitic usage appearing in the treaty stipulations of Sefire? Though the standard Akkadian reference grammar does not record such a use of the imperative, there seem to be genuine cases of heterosis using the imperative in Akkadian. I have found two in instructional contexts: one involving treaty stipulations, the other in a perfume recipe. The first occurs in W7 (rev. 4.32-39) in a context discussing the reception of messengers from the overlord when there is both a written report on a tablet and an oral report from a messenger.

Here is Weidner's transcription of ll. 34-39 (1923: 109):

34 *šum-ma a-wa-ti šá mâr ši-ip-ri a-na a-wa-*[*ti*]
35 *šá ṭub-bi mi-it-ḫa-ar mâr ši-ip-ra a-nu-me-e-am*
36 *m Šú-na-áš-šú-ra ki-i-ip-šú ù šum-ma a-wa-ti šá p*[*î*]
37 *mâr ši-ip-ri a-na a-wa-ti šá ṭub-bi ú-ul mi-it-ḫa-a*[*r*]
38 *m Šú-na-áš-šú-ra mâr ši-ip-ra lu-ú la ta-ak-ki-ip-šú*
39 *ù i-na a-wa-tim a-nu-um-me-am ma-ši-ik-tam i-na libbi-*[*k*]*a lu-ú la-a ta-az-za-ab-bat.*

If the words of the messenger agree with the words of the tablet, as for this messenger, Sunassura, certainly trust him! If, however, the words from the mouth of the messenger do not agree with the words of the tablet, Sunassura, you must not trust the messenger. And from this word, you must not take anything evil into your heart.

The instruction 'trust' is in the imperative: *ki-i-ip-šú.* The parallel negative instructions are in the negated indicative: *lu-ú la ta-ak-ki-ip-šú* (l. 38); *lu-ú la-a ta-az-za-ab-bat* (l. 39). Verbs in the surrounding context are in the present; compare *ta-at-ta-na-an-din-šú-nu-ti* ('you must provide for them') in W7 (rev. 4.24). The verb form *ki-i-ip-šú* is a heterosis for the expected present tense; therefore it has a certain emphatic value.

A second case occurs in a Middle Assyrian perfume recipe published by E. Ebeling. Instructions throughout these texts are in the so-called *heischendes Präsens* ('instructional present') (Ebeling 1950: 28). But two imperative forms occur in KAR 220.6. In the preceding context, the perfumer had been instructed to prepared various ingredients, and pour them after boiling into a vessel filled with well water. The text then reads:

> *ši-qat-ka an-ni-ú ki-i mê(A) li-q[i?] zu-ú-uz*
>
> *dein Massstab ist dies: Gemäss dem Wasser nimm (und) teile!*
>
> (This is your measuring stick: according to the (amount of) water, take and distribute)

There are no other imperative forms in this text, or the other perfume recipes published by Ebeling. The verb forms here are a heterosis for the expected present tense. The inference seems to be 'you must take and distribute'.

The heterosis in W7 (rev. 4.36) is not the only manner in which emphasis is expressed in the SM comparative group. An example of a different kind of emphatic construction occurs in WI obv. 60-62 where the precative *lu-ú mu-uš-šú-ra-at* ('you shall be permitted') stands as the first of a series of five instructions. But the four commands which follow are all negated. The force of the precative is apparent from its position as well as because of its contrast with the other instructions in the series.

The fact that the SM treaty tradition uses rhetorical effects to draw attention to certain instructions and yet does not use the paronomastic infinitive construction has some significance. For whatever reason, SM treaty language was not a genre which used the emphatic infinitive construction. Therefore, it is unlikely that the examples in Sefire 3 occur due to Akkadian influence.

Does that mean that Fitzmyer is correct to aver Canaanite influence? The point of reference will be instructional discourse in the Hebrew Bible. While paronomastic infinitive constructions also occur in Phoenician and Ugaritic (Hammershaimb 1963: 88), only in biblical Hebrew does there remain extant an extensive corpus of cases in instructional discourse. These occur in legal passages in Exodus–Deuteronomy.

Of the three paronomastic infinitive constructions found in Sefire 3 and described above, biblical examples most clearly concur with the first two: there are many parallels to the first case (see pp. 89-90) in an apodosis contrasting with the negative clause(s) beginning the apodosis, compare Exod. 23.23-24; Deut. 7.18; 13.10; 15.7-8, 13-14; 22.6-7; 24.12-13; analogues to the second case (see p. 90) also are attested, for example, Exod. 22.22, 25.

But cases analogous to the third set (see pp. 90-91), where emphatic commands resume a series of related instructions, are difficult to find. The closest to those in Sefire 3.12-14 occur in Lev. 5.19 and 13.44. In each of these texts, a set of ritual instructions uses a paronomastic infinitive construction in a concluding statement. It is noteworthy, however, that both contexts in Leviticus are in the third person and in that way not directly analogous to the usage in Sefire 3. Just as important is their content: they deal with matters of the cult, not statecraft.

In fact, where biblical language does touch on parallel concerns, the construction is just the opposite of the syntax of Sefire 3.12-14. Compare Deut. 13.16 where the reader is enjoined completely to destroy the inhabitants of the offending city: *hkh tkh ʾt yšby hʿyr hhwʾ*. Here the paronomastic infinitive construction acts not in a resumptive manner but as the head command anticipating the instruction for the ban that follows in Deut. 13.16-19. Evidence like this is not conclusive, but it tends to suggest some distance between biblical instruction language and the paronomastic infinitive usages of Sefire 3.12-14.

These observations add weight to the assumption that the paronomastic infinitive construction can be viewed as a feature native to early Aramaic. In Imperial Aramaic, Segert identifies a possible case in Nêrab 2.6 (Segert 1975: §6.6.5.3). Though this analysis of Nêrab 2.6 has been disputed by Gibson (1975: 98), he also believes the construction occurs in Imperial Aramaic and cites the Assur Ostracon, l. 9 (Gibson 1975: 107). Given the widespread use of this construction in other Semitic languages, its presence in Aramaic is to be expected (Lipiński 1997: §53.4; Hammershaimb 1963: 88).

In my opinion, Fitzmyer's claim is unproven. It is simpler to assume that the paronomastic infinitive uses in Sefire 3 are native to Old Aramaic. Clearly there are analogues with attested uses in Northwest Semitic contexts. Nevertheless, there is one construction which does not have an exact analogue in biblical texts and points to a certain independence in usage. It appears that the emphatic infinitive constructions in Sefire represent a native rhetorical tradition which Old Aramaic shares with Canaanite but which it did not necessarily borrow.

## *Conclusion*

Is the Sefire treaty 'nothing but an Assyrian treaty'? The preceding examination suggests that there remain elements in the Sefire inscriptions which cannot be derived from Assyrian influence. These can be found in features of the form and syntax of the Sefire treaty stipulations. On the one hand, the form of the Sefire stipulations is related to and derived from a western Mesopotamian tradition of treaty making which it shares in common with the Baal of Tyre treaty in the first millennium and which is well attested in the SM comparative corpus. On the other hand, there is evidently a syntactical feature of the rhetoric of the Sefire treaty stipulations which cannot be derived from Akkadian treaty rhetoric. These paronomastic infinitive constructions have analogues to examples in biblical Hebrew, but they are not so exact as to demand that their presence in Sefire 3 be explained as a result of Canaanite cultural influence. Rather, the comparative work undertaken above tends to support the idea that Old Aramaic had the paronomastic infinitive construction as part of its native rhetorical repertoire.

Soon after the publication of Lemaire's and Durand's study of the Sefire inscriptions, Dion (1985: 217) rightly noted that their work nullified 'the only full-scale piece of evidence usually quoted in support of a West Semitic tradition of treaty-making in the world of the Old Testament'. In fact, in the context of imperial politics, documents and even languages showing the effects of several cultural influences are to be expected in the western region of Akkadian influence. According to Izre'el (1991: I, 370), the second-millennium Amurru dialect of Akkadian attests to the influence of no less than four substrate languages including Hittite, Egyptian, Hurrian and Northwest Semitic. When Fleming (1992: 279-80) analysed the religious traditions underlying the installation of Baal's High Priestess at Emar, he was able to detect a local Syrian rite which showed influences from both Mesopotamia and Anatolia. Biblical analogies, especially to the book of Deuteronomy, also suggest themselves. Here again there is a document which shows an interweaving of neo-Assyrian influence, traditions in continuity with second-millennium Syrian treaty forms, and native Hebrew rhetoric (Weinfeld 1972: 65-68).

Despite real scholarly advances in understanding the Sefire inscriptions by comparison with neo-Assyrian parallels, it is important not to give this evidence more than its due. In the final analysis, it is too simple to describe the Sefire inscriptions as witnesses to either an Aramaic or Assyrian treaty in terms of cultural origins. The Sefire inscriptions represent an amalgam of different traditions. While the prestige of the dominant neo-Assyrian culture has plainly left its mark, the result is not an eclipse of other forms of treaty rhetoric so much as a means for their accommodation.

## BIBLIOGRAPHY

Aro, J.
1961 *Die akkadischen Infinitivkonstruktionen* (StudOr, 26; Helsinki: Societas Orientalis Fennica).

Borger, R.
1956 *Die Inschriften Asarhaddons Königs von Assyrien* (Afo Beiheft, 8; Graz: Archiv für Orientforschung).

Borger, R. *et. al.* (eds.)
1983 *Staatsvertrage: Texte aus der Umwelt des Atlen Testaments*, I (Gütersloh: Gerd Mohn).

Delitzsch, F.
1889 *Assyrische Grammatik* (Berlin: Reuther).

Dion, P.-E.
1985 'Deuteronomy and the Gentile World: A Study in Biblical Theology', *Toronto Journal of Theology* 1: 200-21.

Donner, H., and W. Röllig
1971 *Kanaanäische und Aramäische Inschriften* (Wiesbaden: Otto Harrassowitz, 3rd edn).

Ebeling, E.
1950 *Parfümrezepte und kultische Texte aus Assur* (Rome: Pontifical Biblical Institute).

Fitzmyer, J.A.
1995 *The Aramaic Inscriptions of Sefire* (BibOr, 19.A; Rome: Pontifical Biblical Institute, 2nd edn [1969]).

Fleming, D.E.
1992 *The Installation of Baal's High Priestess at Emar* (HSS, 42; Atlanta: Scholars Press).

Gibson, J.C.L.
1975 *Textbook of Syrian Semitic Inscriptions.* II. *Aramaic Inscriptions* (Oxford: Clarendon Press).

Grayson, A.K.
1987 'Akkadian Treaties of the Seventh Century B.C.', *JCS* 39: 127-60.

Hammershaimb, E.
1963 'On the So-called *infinitivus absolutus* in Hebrew', in D.W. Thomas and W.D. McHardy (eds.), *Hebrew and Semitic Studies Presented to Godfrey Rolles Driver* (Oxford: Clarendon Press): 85-94.

Izre'el, S.
1991 *Amurru Akkadian: A Linguistic Study* (2 vols.; HSS, 40; Atlanta: Scholars Press).

Kestemont, G.
1974 'Le traité entre Mursil II de Hatti et Niqmepa d'Ugarit', *UF* 6: 85-127.

Lemaire, A., and J.-M. Durand
1984 *Les inscriptions araméennes de Sfiré, et l'Assyrie de Shamshi-ilu* (Hautes études orientales, 20; Geneva: Droz).

Levy, J.
1946 'Studies in Akkadian Grammar and Onomatology 4: Paronomastic Infinitives in Classic Akkadian', *Or* 15: 410-15.

Lipiński, E.
1997 *Semitic Languages: Outline of a Comparative Grammar* (Orientalia lovaniensia analecta, 80; Leuven: Peeters).

McCarthy, D.J.
1978 *Treaty and Covenant: A Study in Form in the Ancient Oriental Documents and in the Old Testament* (AnBib, 21A; Rome: Pontifical Biblical Institute, 2nd edn [1963]).

Millard, A.R.
1970 'Fragments of Historical Texts from Nineveh: Middle Assyrian and Later Kings', *Iraq* 32: 167-76.

Parpola, S.
1987 'Neo-Assyrian Treaties from the Royal Archives of Nineveh', *JCS* 39: 161-89.

Parpola, S., and K. Watanabe (eds.)
1988 *Neo-Assyrian Treaties and Loyalty Oaths* (SAAS, 2; Helsinki: Helsinki University).

Rooy, H.F. van
1989 'The Structure of the Aramaic Treaties of Sefire', *Journal for Semitics* 1: 133-39.
1991 'A Few Remarks on the Aramaic Treaties from Sefire', *JNSL* 17: 145-49.

Segert, S.
1975 *Altaramäische Grammatik* (Leipzig: VEB).

Soden, W. von
1952 *Grundriss der Akkadischen Grammatik* (AnOr, 33; Rome: Pontifical Biblical Institute).

Waltke, B.K., and M. O'Connor
1990 *An Introduction to Biblical Hebrew Syntax* (Winona Lake, IN: Eisenbrauns).

Weidner, E.F.
1923 *Politische Dokumente aus Kleinasien* (Boghazköi Studien, 8–9; Leipzig: J.C. Hinrichs).
1932–33 'Die Staatsvertrag Aššurnirâris VI. von Assyrien mit Mati'ilu von Bit-Agusi', *AfO* 8: 2-34.

Weinfeld, M.
1972 *Deuteronomy and the Deuteronomic School* (Oxford: Clarendon Press).

Wiseman, D.J.
1953 *The Alalakh Tablets* (London: British Institute of Archaeology at Ankara).
1982 ' "Is It Peace?"—Covenant and Diplomacy', *VT* 32: 311-26.

Wiseman, D.J. (ed.)
1958 *The Vassal Treaties of Esarhaddon* (London: British School of Archaeology in Iraq).

# A NEO-BABYLONIAN TABLET WITH AN ARAMAIC DOCKET AND THE SURETY PHRASE *pūt šēp(i)...našû*

Grant Frame

## *Introduction*

Among the approximately 1400 Neo-Babylonian and Achaemenid legal and administrative texts in the collection of Princeton Theological Seminary are at least four tablets bearing Aramaic dockets. One of these, PTS 2061, records a surety agreement and was composed at the city of Uruk on the twenty-first day of Araḫsamna in the first regnal year of the Neo-Babylonian monarch Amēl-Marduk, 19 November, 561 BCE (Parker and Dubberstein 1956: 28). This study of that document and of other documents employing the same surety phrase found in it—*pūt šēp(i)...našû*, 'to assume guarantee for the foot'—is presented here as a modest token of my esteem for Paul-Eugène Dion, both as a scholar and as a colleague in the Department of Near and Middle Eastern Civilizations (formerly Near Eastern Studies) of the University of Toronto.[1]

1. PTS 2061 is published with the permission of W.O. Harris, Librarian for Archives and Special Collections, Princeton Theological Seminary Library. My thanks must be expressed to him and his staff for their help during my visit to Princeton in 1998. My appreciation must also be extended to D. Applewhite for taking the photographs published with this article, to S.M. Freedman for arranging the photographing of the tablet, and to E. Cussini and J. Teixidor for comments on the Aramaic docket. I am grateful to M. Jursa for several valuable suggestions on this study. My appreciation of the problems involved with our understanding of ancient surety transactions was heightened as a result of attendance at a colloquium of the Society for the Study of Ancient Near Eastern Law on 'Security for Loans in Ancient Near Eastern Law' at the Johns Hopkins University, 19–20 March 1999, organized by R. Westbrook and R. Jasnow. The publication of the proceedings of that conference will include an important overview of security for loans in the Neo-Babylonian period by J. Oelsner.

*The Princeton Theological Seminary Clay Tablet no. 2061*

*Transliteration of the Cuneiform Text*

*pu-ut* GÌR.II *šá* $^{md}$U.GUR-*da-ni*
A-*šú šá* $^{m}$GIN-NUMUN A $^{md}$30-TI-ÉR
$^{m}$*si-lim*-$^{d}$EN A-*šú šá* $^{m}$⸢MU⸣-GIN A $^{m}$*ḫa*-⸢*nab*⸣
*ina* ŠU.II $^{md}$30-MU LÚ *qí-i-pi*
*šá é-an-na na-ši* U$_4$.12[(+)].KÁM *šá* ⸢ITI⸣.ŠE
*ib-ba-kaš-šim-ma a-na* ⸢$^{md}$⸣30-MU
⸢LÚ⸣ *qí-i-pi šá é-an*-⸢*na*⸣ *i-nam-din*
⸢*ki*⸣-*i la i-tab-kám-ma la it-tan-nu*
5 MA.NA KÙ.BABBAR *a-na* $^{md}$30-MU *i-nam-din*
LÚ *mu-kin-nu* $^{md}$EN-*na-din*-A A-*šú šá*
$^{md}$AG-ŠEŠ.MEŠ-*bul-liṭ* A $^{m}$LÚ.ŠEŠ-*ba-ni-i*
$^{m}$*gi-mil-lu* A-*šú šá* $^{m}$NUMUN-*ia*
A $^{m}$⸢*ši-gu*⸣-*ú-a* $^{m}$KAR-$^{d}$EN A-*šú šá* $^{m}$A-*a*
A $^{m}$*ár*-⸢*rab*⸣-*tu*$_4$ $^{m}$[E]N-⸢*šú*⸣-*nu* A-*šú šá*
$^{md}$AG-ŠEŠ.MEŠ-MU A $^{m}$*e-gi-bi*
*u* LÚ.UMBISAG $^{md}$AG-EN-*šú-nu* A-*šú šá*
$^{md}$EN-ŠEŠ-GÁL-*ši* A LÚ-$^{d}$IDIM
UNUG.KI ITI.APIN U$_4$.21.KÁM
MU.1.KÁM LÚ-$^{d}$AMAR.UTU LUGAL TIN.TIR.⸢KI⸣

Parts of ll. 3 and 9 are written over erasures.

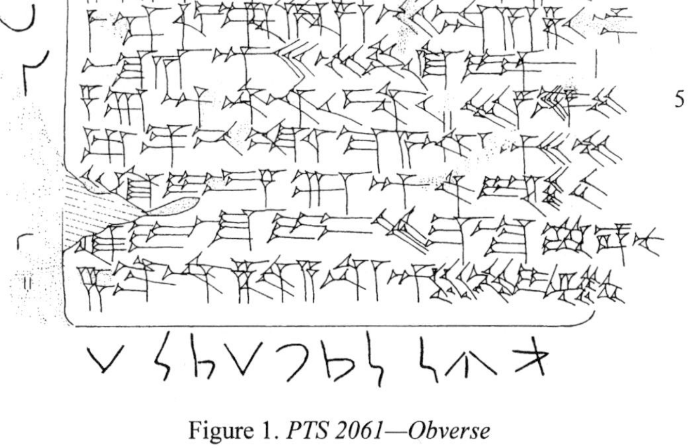

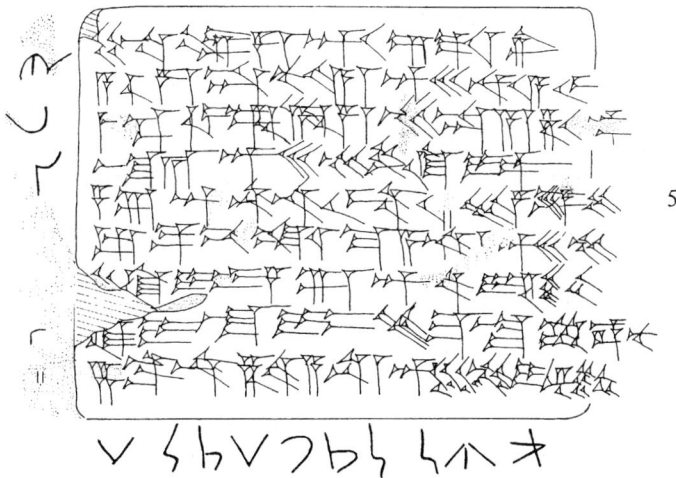

Figure 1. *PTS 2061—Obverse*

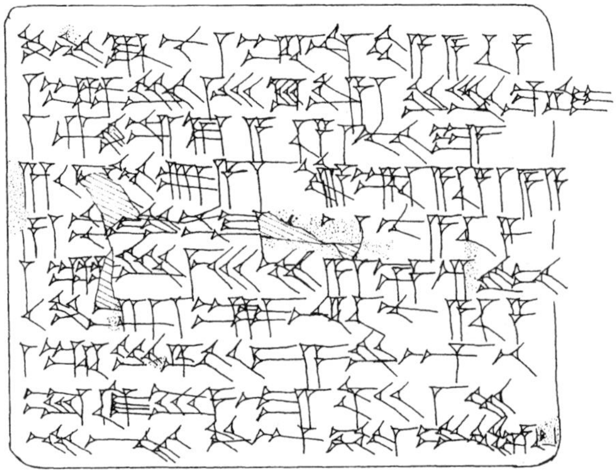

Figure 2. *PTS 2061—Reverse*

## *Translation of the Cuneiform Text*

| | |
|---|---|
| 1-5a | Silim-Bēl, son of Šuma-ukīn (and) descendant of Ḫanab, guarantees the 'foot' of Nergal-dāni, son of Mukīn-zēri (and) descendant of Sîn-leqe-unninnī, to Sîn-iddin, the *qīpu* of Eanna. |
| 5b-7 | He (Silim-Bēl) will bring *him*[2] (Nergal-dāni) on the 12(+)th day of the month of Addaru (XII) and hand (him) over to Sîn-iddin, the *qīpu*[3] of Eanna. |

2. The translation assumes that *ib-ba-kaš-šim-ma* in l. 6 stands for *ibbak* + *am* + *šu*(*m*) + *ma*, with *-šim* written for *-šum* and *-šim/šum* having an otiose *m* (influenced by the following *-ma*). The *-šim* could stand for the dative pronominal suffix -*šum*, '*to him*' (and thus to Sîn-iddin); however, when a pronominal suffix was added to the verb in similar circumstances in YOS 7 no. 170:12 it clearly represented the direct object (*ib-ba-ku-niš-šú-nu-ti-im-ma*). In that case, two persons were to be brought to one official; note the unwanted *-im* between the accusative plural pronominal suffix *-šunūti* and the enclitic particle *-ma*. In addition, in similar circumstances in other surety texts, the name of the person to be brought is sometimes given before the verb *abāku* (e.g. *5R* pl. 67 no. 3:8-9 and YOS 6 no. 119:5). Forms similar to the one in PTS 2061:6 appear in similar surety circumstances in *Nbk*. no. 366:8 (*i-bu-ka-šim-*⸢*ma*⸣) and YOS 6 no. 200:9 (*ib-ba-ka-šim-ma*). Dougherty's translation of the latter text (1930: 90) also considers the *-šim* to represent the direct object and not the indirect object. Cf. also *i-ba-ku-niš-*[*šim-ma*] in GCCI 1 no. 15:8 (following Dougherty 1930: 81); the individual being brought was to be given to two officials and thus if the restoration is correct the *-šim* must refer to the direct object.

3. Bongenaar (1997: 6) suggests that at Sippar we translate the title *qīpu* by 'resident', and *šatammu* (which will appear later in this study) by 'chief administrator'. As he notes, the *šatammu* of Eanna at Uruk corresponds to the *šangû*

| | |
|---|---|
| 8-9 | If he (Silim-Bēl) does not bring (Nergal-dāni) and hand (him) over, he (Silim-Bēl) will give five minas of silver to Sîn-iddin. |
| 10-11 | Witnesses: Bēl-nādin-apli, son of Nabû-aḫḫē-bulliṭ (and) descendant of Aḫu-bani; |
| 12-13a | Gimillu, son of Zēriya (and) descendant of Šigū'a; |
| 13b-14a | Mušēzib-Bēl, son of Aplāya (and) descendant of Arrabtu; |
| 14b-15 | [Bē]lšunu, son of Nabû-aḫḫē-iddin (and) descendant of Egibi; |
| 16-17 | and the scribe, Nabû-bēlšunu, son of Bēl-aḫa-ušabši (and) descendant of Amēl-Ea. |
| 18-19 | Uruk, month of Araḫsamna (VIII), twenty-first day, first year of Amēl-Marduk, king of Babylon. |

*Individuals Appearing in the Cuneiform Text*

*Lines 1-2.* Nergal-dāni (generally with his paternal name but without his family name) appears in several other documents, often with his brother Bēl-lē'i or (more often) his brother's son Nādin. In the texts known to me, he normally appears as debtor or borrower, which might suggest that the reason Silim-Bēl had gone surety for him in PTS 2061 was because he owed five minas of silver to Sîn-iddin, or more likely to the Eanna temple. A document in the City of Birmingham Museums and Art Gallery composed at Uruk on 15-I-year 40 of Nebuchadnezzar II records that Nergal-dāni owed silver and barley to another individual (Jursa 1997: 117, 161 no. 35). The exact understanding of YOS 6 no. 48 (Lasūtu, 27-III-year 6 of Nabonidus) is not clear, but the view that it indicates that Nādin son of Bēl-lē'i had assumed guarantee for dates and silver owed by Nergal-dāni to another individual seems likely (San Nicolò and Petschow 1960: 85)[4]. YOS 6 no. 164 (Lasūtu, 7-XII-year 6 of Nabonidus) records that Nergal-dāni owed six gur of barley. In PTS 3056 (2-VIII-year 7? of Nabonidus), Nergal-dāni and Nādin son of Bēl-lē'i are mentioned as being responsible for a *ḫarrānu*-loan (a partnership arrangement for a business venture); Nergal-dāni's sons Šamaš-aḫa-iddin and Šamaš-rē'ûšunu are also involved in the transaction recorded in the text.[5] Finally, a tablet in the collection of the University

of Sippar, which he translates 'temple administrator'. In this essay, I have preferred to leave most official titles untranslated.

4. The view that Nādin was the one who stood surety in this text might be supported by the fact that he was also scribe of the text. As will be noted below, in several surety texts the person standing surety also served as the scribe recording the surety agreement.

5. I have benefited from discussing the reading of the text of PTS 3056 with Karlheinz Kessler and from seeing his preliminary copy of the tablet.

of Michigan which was composed in the reign of Nebuchadnezzar II (Moore 1939: 34; pl. 52 no. 62) may refer to silver at the disposal(?) of Bēl-lē'i and Nergal-dāni. This text is important in that it informs us that the two were both sons of Mukīn-zēri ($^{md}$EN-DA *u* $^{md}$U.GUR-*da-a-nu* A.ME *šá* $^{m}$GIN-NUMUN, ll. 5-6), that is, they were brothers and not just individuals whose fathers bore the same name. In addition to PTS 2061, two of the aforementioned texts also bear Aramaic dockets: YOS 6 no. 164 and PTS 3056.

Several other documents appear to describe transactions involving both branches of the family. Four of these, dating between the eighth and tenth years of Nabonidus, also involve surety: Snyder (1955: 25-26); TCL 12 no. 96; and YOS 6 nos. 119 and 153. The principals in these texts include Nergal-dāni's son Šamaš-aḫa-iddin and Bēl-lē'i's sons Nādin and Gimillu. The relationship between these four texts has been discussed by Snyder (1955: 27-28). He does not appear to have noted the family relationship between Šamaš-aḫa-iddin, on the one hand, and Nādin and Gimillu, on the other hand, and some of his conclusions are open to discussion. For the well-known family of Sîn-leqe-unninnī, see Kümmel (1979: 79, 132-33, 147) and Lambert (1957).

*Line 3.* Silim-Bēl is also attested in a few texts from Uruk dating to the reign of Nabonidus (YOS 6 nos. 77: 16; 78: 26; 92: 60; and likely 152: 3, 8). In YOS 6 no. 77 (Uruk, 15-III-year 4 of Nabonidus), he was one of several men described as *ērib bīti*, *kinalti*, and *mār banî*, that is, prominent members of the community. For several members of the family of Ḫanab at Uruk, see Kümmel (1979: 23, 27).

*Lines 4-5.* Sîn-iddin was *qīpu* of Eanna from the thirty-fifth year of Nebuchadnezzar II until at least the second year of Amēl-Marduk, and possibly the first year of Neriglissar. See Kümmel (1979: 141) and Sack (1977: 43 n. 4, 52 n. 24; 1994a: 32-33). With regard to Sîn-iddin, note also Sack (1976). He appears in this position accepting surety for one individual from another individual in several texts (e.g. Jursa 1997: 103, 154 no. 7).

*Lines 10-11.* Bēl-nādin-apli appears among other prominent citizens of Uruk in two texts: PTS 2097: 6 (Frame 1991: 39, 47) and YOS 6 no. 77: 4, composed at Uruk in the first and fourth years of Nabonidus respectively.

*Lines 12-15.* Each of the three witnesses—Gimillu, Mušēzib-Bēl and Bēlšunu—is attested in numerous other texts. The three of them appear together on a number of occasions in addition to PTS 2061, for example AUWE 11 no. 213; GCCI 1 no. 262; PTS 3022; W 18213, 25 (see AUWE 11, p. 51 sub commentary to no. 213), and almost certainly TCL 13 no. 220.[6] In most texts, they appear simply as witnesses, but TCL 13 no. 220 is the record of an obligation in which they (and some other men) are said to owe 240 gur of barley.

Gimillu is attested in texts from the sixteenth year of Nebuchadnezzar II to the second year of Nabonidus; see Kümmel (1979: 133, 151), with the addition of Dillard (1975: 55, 243, FLP 1532: 5) (Babylon, 27-XII-year 16 of Nebuchadnezzar II) and Frame (1991: 39: 9, 48). Gimillu appears in the surety agreement PTS 3079 (Uruk, [?]-III-accession year of Lâbâši-Marduk) as one of the individuals (including the *qīpu* and the scribe of Eanna) who accept surety.

Mušēzib-Bēl is attested in texts from the fourteenth year of Nebuchadnezzar II to the first year of Amēl-Marduk; see AUWE 11:63 sub commentary to no. 229 rev. 3, with the addition of PTS 2061 (for attestation in the first year of Amēl-Marduk), and likely GCCI 2 nos. 91: 10 and 385: 16.

Bēlšunu is attested in texts dating from the thirty-fourth year of Nebuchadnezzar II to the sixth year of Nabonidus. See Kümmel (1979: 113, 130), with the addition of Dillard (1975: 80, 248 and FLP 1545: 16-17) (Uruk, [(+)]5-II-year 34 of Nebuchadnezzar II). He appears among the prominent citizens before whom a high official reported a royal command in YOS 6 nos. 71-72:13 (Uruk, 23-VIII-year six of Nabonidus).

*Lines 16-17.* Nabû-bēlšunu is attested in texts from the first year of Amēl-Marduk to the accession year of Cambyses; see Kümmel (1979: 119). Earlier in the same year that PTS 2061 was composed, Nabû-bēlšunu appears as scribe of TCL 12 no. 60, a document which was composed at Babylon (9-I-year 1 of Amēl-Marduk). It is interesting to see Nabû-bēlšunu functioning as scribe at both Uruk and Babylon. Probably he had some association with the Eanna temple and/or its *qīpu*-official and had gone to Babylon on behalf of that temple or

6. On the published copy of TCL 13 no. 220 Bēlšunu's paternal name is given as $^{md}$AG-ŠEŠ.MEŠ-KÁM, i.e. Nabû-aḫḫē-ēreš (l. 4). The KÁM is probably a mistake of either the modern copyist or the ancient scribe for MU.

official. TCL 12 no. 60 states that if a she-ass belonging to Sîn-iddin, the *qīpu* of Eanna, was ever proven to be in the house of a particular individual, that individual was a thief. Nabû-bēlšunu was included among the *mār banî* at Uruk in AnOr 8 no. 47:6 // TCL 13 no. 138:6 and BIN 1 no. 169:6.

In sum, most of the individuals mentioned in PTS 2061 were prominent citizens at the city of Uruk and had connections with the Eanna temple.

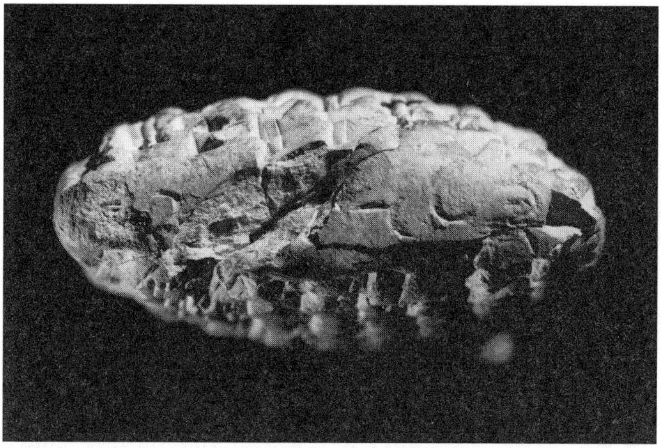

P1.1. *PTS 2061—Left Edge*

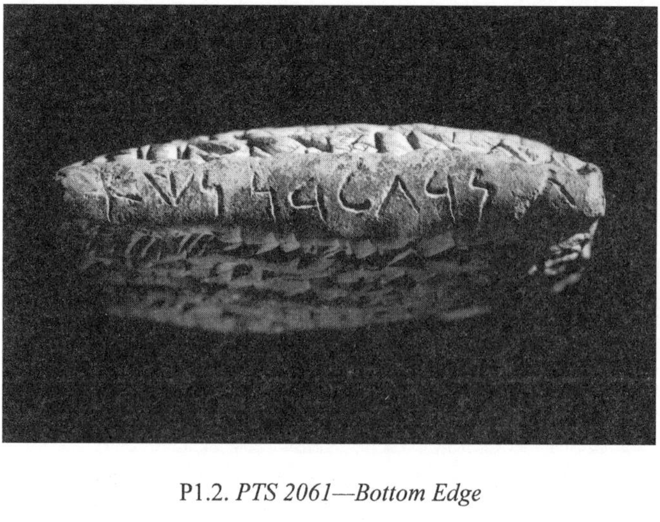

P1.2. *PTS 2061—Bottom Edge*

*The Aramaic Docket*

PTS 2061 is one of a large number of cuneiform tablets from Mesopotamia dating to the Neo-Assyrian, Neo-Babylonian and Achaemenid periods bearing brief notes or summaries which are written in Aramaic and which are commonly referred to as 'dockets', 'endorsements' or 'epigraphs'.[7] A comprehensive study of the Neo-Assyrian dockets has been published by M. Fales (1986) and one of the Neo-Babylonian and Achaemenid ones is currently being prepared by E. Cussini. Fales discusses 61 Neo-Assyrian clay tablets and bullae with dockets and refers to a further 28 unpublished ones. Fitzmyer and Kaufman include over 110 Neo-Babylonian and Achaemenid dockets in their recent bibliography of Aramaic inscriptions (Fitzmyer and Kaufman 1992: nos. B.1.27, B.2.19-20 and 22-24) and numerous others are known to exist.[8] The earliest Neo-Assyrian tablet with an Aramaic docket comes from Nineveh and dates to 687.[9] A Neo-Babylonian tablet with a docket appears to come from 724 (BRM 1 no. 22), but the date of that document has been questioned.[10] Otherwise, the earliest dated neo-Babylonian tablet with such a docket was composed at Babylon in 653 (Brinkman and Kennedy 1983: 32 no. K.99).[11] In Assyria, most of the clay documents with Aramaic dockets are conveyances (documents recording the transfer of ownership of certain kinds of property), but others are contracts (e.g. loans), receipts and judicial documents.[12]

7. Such dockets are also found on a few tablets from Babylonia dating to the Seleucid period (Oelsner 1986: 247-48).

8. Note the additions mentioned in Oelsner (1992: 548-50) and the older list in Vattioni (1970: 493-532; 1979: 139-45). See also Donbaz and Stolper (1997: nos. 38-39, 43-44, 60, 65, 95, 103, and pp. 193-94 Ni. 2844 and Ni. 12928); Jursa (1995: 128-29, 246 no. 38); Joannès and Lemaire (1996: nos. 1, 5 and 7); Weszeli and Baker (1997: no. 10); FLP 1563 (Dillard 1975: 117-19, 256); and the PTS dockets noted below.

9. *ADD* no. 335 = Fales 1986: no. 1 = *SAA* 6 no. 154. The document was composed on 22-V of the eponymy of Sennacherib (687).

10. The tablet was dated according to the years of a Nabû-mukīn-zēri, whose identification with the king Mukīn-zēri is not completely certain; see Brinkman and Kennedy (1983: 65 sub AI.1).

11. The document, 80-B-4, was composed on 5-VIII of the fifteenth year of Šamaš-šuma-ukīn and was found during Iraqi excavations at Babylon.

12. The terminology follows that proposed by Postgate (1976: 4-5, 11-12, 32-33, 55, 58-59) and followed by Fales (1986: 3). As noted by Cussini, with regards to Assyria, the term 'dockets' has been used 'to define a particular type of document,

Only a few non-economic and non-legal Assyrian clay tablets and bullae are known to have dockets: three administrative documents; one extispicy text; and one apotropaic text (Fales 1986: 2). As in Assyria, almost all of the Neo-Babylonian and Achaemenid dockets are found on legal and administrative documents, but a few are found on letters (Oelsner 1992: 549). Although the dockets in both Assyria and Babylonia are mostly found on cuneiform documents which are economic in nature, they do not appear to have had any legal significance and were probably intended to aid in the retrieval of stored documents by individuals more familiar with the Aramaic script than cuneiform. These dockets attest to the growth of Aramaic as the language of the people of Mesopotamia and the decline of both the Akkadian language and the cuneiform script.

The structure of the Babylonian Aramaic dockets is neither fixed nor standardized (Cussini 1995: 23), but they are generally quite short, often comprising no more than one or two words. As noted by Clay almost a century ago, the dockets generally describe the basic nature of the document (e.g. 'Document of Ninurta-uballiṭ son of Mušēzib concerning 15 gur of dates') or give the name of an individual mentioned in the text, usually the person giving up rights or assuming an obligation, that is, a seller or a debtor (e.g. 'Document of Lâbâši') (Clay 1908: 289, 306 no. 19, 309 no. 27). The dockets are either incised onto the tablet or written on it with ink[13] and they may be located either on one of the faces of the tablet or on one or more edges. The docket on PTS 2061 is incised into the left and bottom edges of the tablets and runs continuously from the left edge onto the bottom edge. Thus, the copy of the Aramaic inscription on the bottom edge appears upside down as compared to the cuneiform text on Fig. 1. (Photographs of the docket, oriented for the reading of the Aramaic, are found on Pls. 1, 2.) The inscription reads:

that is "triangular corn loan dockets" recording Akkadian/Aramaic bilingual and Aramaic monolingual contracts'. Such 'triangular-type tablets' are not attested in Babylonia and thus Cussini believes that 'the term "dockets" can still be used in the sense of "abstract, summary" of a document, without clashing with Postgate's and Fales' specific documental classification, which...pertains to the Northern (i.e. Assyrian) sphere only'. See Cussini (1995: 22-23).

13. M. Stolper notes: 'Some of the lightly incised texts are evidently remains of texts which were originally in ink, the remaining marks being the traces left by a hard pen or a stylus dipped in ink' (1985: 12).

left edge: *s*?*l*⌈*m*?⌉[*bl* (x)] xx
bottom edge: *g nrgldn nš'*
'*Silim*-[*Bēl*] *guaran*[*tees the presence of*] Nergal-dāni.'

J. Oelsner laments the fact that 'die Beischriften auf Tontafeln sind... schwer zu deuten bzw. nahezu unleserlich' (1992: 551). The letters on the bottom edge of PTS 2061 are clear, but the identification of the first and third signs on the left edge is not certain. The first sign might better be *y* and the third *d* (thus *yld)*. The tentatively proposed reading of the signs as representing the first part of the Akkadian name Silim-Bēl is based upon the fact that Aramaic dockets generally summarize the basic nature of the cuneiform document and/or give the name of the obligor. In PTS 2061, Silim-Bēl is assuming the obligation to produce Nergal-dāni. Moreover, since the same verbal root is used in both Akkadian (*naši*, l. 5) and Aramaic (*nš'*, bottom edge) and since the subject of that verb in the Akkadian is Silim-Bēl, we might expect him to be the subject of the verb in the Aramaic.

Two other documents using the surety phrase employed in PTS 2061, *pūt šēp*(*i*)...*našû*, also have Aramaic dockets. The first was one of the earliest Neo-Babylonian economic documents ever published (5*R* pl. 67 no. 3 = Vattioni 1970: 503, no. 44; see no. 11 on Table 1 below). This is a standard surety agreement like PTS 2061 and in it a wife guaranteed that her husband would appear before her husband's brother. The docket simply recorded the name of the individual before whom the individual was to appear (*pnbṭm*, Pāni-Nabû-ṭēmu*)*. More important is Ni. 2670 (Donbaz and Stolper 1977: no. 103; see no. 26 on Table 1 below), the latest dated document using this surety phrase and the only one known to come from Nippur. It records an oral request by one person (Nabû-ušēzib) to another (Rīmūt-Ninurta) for the latter to release to him three individuals who were being held in prison and his offer to assume responsibility for their 'foot'. The text concludes with the resulting terms of agreement. The original editors of the text could only read the first two words of the docket, but Jursa, who kindly brought this text to my attention, suggests that the docket reads *šṭr n*⌈*bw*⌉ *'šzb* ⌈*m*⌉*n* ⌈*'*⌉*rdnw/š*⌈*t*⌉ 1+1+1 *nš'*, 'Document of Nabû-ušēzib (who) took three (people) from Arad-Ninurta'.[14] No Arad-Ninurta is mentioned in the

14. In the Murašû dockets, *nwšt* and *'nwšt* are writings for Ninurta and were read Enmaštu by Clay in his studies of the Murašû dockets (e.g. Clay 1908: 304 no. 14).

cuneiform text and this may have been an error for Rīmūt-Ninurta, but see below.

As far as I am aware, the only Aramaic dockets using the verb *nš'* are on PTS 2061 and Ni. 2670 and *nš'* is not normally used in Aramaic in connection with the issuing of guarantees. (For Aramaic contract tablets dealing with surety/guarantee, see Lipiński [1998] and the bibliography presented there.) Thus, its use here might be a Babylonianism, particularly since its placement at the end of the phrases might suggest Babylonian rather than Aramaic word order. In view of our limited knowledge of Aramaic legal terminology in Babylonia at this time, this must, however, remain uncertain. The tentative translation of PTS 2061 assumes that the end of the left edge would have had some word or phrase parallel to the *pūt šēp*(*i*) of the Akkadian (l. 1), but I am unable to suggest any particular reading. The *g* at the beginning of the bottom edge may be the end of a word beginning on the left edge, which would seem to preclude a word for foot (e.g. Aramaic *rgl*). In Ni. 2670, only the verb *nš'* was used in the docket. In that case, it may have been used simply to indicate that the subject (Nabû-ušēzib) had taken away (*nš'*) the three men being held in detention and not to parallel the Akkadian surety phrase *pūt šēp*(*i*)...*našû*. Jursa (private communication) has suggested to me that the docket on PTS 2061 may similarly have stated that Silim-Bēl had taken (*nš'*) Nergal-dāni from some individual whose name is not mentioned in the cuneiform text but is given in the docket (beginning on the left edge and ending with the *g* of the bottom edge). This assumes that Nergal-dāni had been held by the Eanna temple and had been released into Silim-Bēl's custody by his jailer, who was presumably acting under instructions from Sîn-iddin, the *qīpu* of the temple, and as a result of the drawing up of the surety agreement PTS 2061. It would then have been the name of the jailer which was mentioned in the damaged area of the docket.[15] If this was the case, then, in Donbaz and Stolper (1997: no. 103), the Arad-Ninurta of the docket may not be an error for Rīmūt-Ninurta of the cuneiform text, but rather the name of the jailer.[16] While we know that the persons for whom

15. It should be noted that there are not a lot of Akkadian personal names whose final consonant is G.

16. For an Arad-Ninurta appearing in other texts with Rīmūt-Ninurta of the family of Murašû, note in particular Arad-Ninurta son of Enlil-ittannu. TuM 2/3 no. 203 (Nippur, 18-I-year 2 of Darius II) is a document quite similar to Donbaz and Stolper (1997: no. 103) and in it Rīmūt-Ninurta appears with this Arad-Ninurta.

surety was given in that text had been held in detention (*ša ina bīt kīlu...ṣabtū'*, ll. 3-4), there is no direct statement in PTS 2061 that Nergal-dāni was being held in custody. Possibly it did not need to be stated in standard surety agreements since the mere fact that someone had to go surety for an individual may have implied that the latter was being held as distress, whether formally or informally.

As was already mentioned, two other texts involving Nergal-dāni also bear Aramaic dockets: PTS 3056 and YOS 6 no. 164. According to Rosenthal (see San Nicolò and Petschow 1960: 86), the docket on YOS 6 no. 164 is not understandable except for the phrase '5 gur'. As noted by Jursa (private communication), the docket ends with the name Nergal-dāni (*nrgldn*). In addition to PTS 2061 and PTS 3056, at least two other texts in the collection of Princeton Theological Seminary have Aramaic dockets: PTS 2057 (date not preserved); and PTS 3146 (Šīḫu ša Bēlet ša Uruk, 4-I-year 3 of Cyrus). The latter three texts will be published by Kessler.

*Surety and the Phrase* pūt šēp(i)... našû

In addition to PTS 2061, a large number of texts from the Neo-Babylonian and Achaemenid periods refer to one person assuming surety or guarantee for another. According to *Osborn's Concise Law Dictionary*, the term surety can be defined as 'A person who binds himself, usually by deed, to satisfy the obligation of another person, if the latter fails to do so; a guarantor' (Rutherford and Bone 1993: 318). In the Neo-Babylonian and Achaemenid periods, the basic Akkadian phrase used for assuming guarantee or standing surety is *pūt...našû*, but several typical elaborations of this are found in the texts, such as *pūt eṭēri... našû*, 'to guarantee to pay', and *pūt murruqu...našû*, 'to guarantee to clear (property sold) from claims'. The most important study on this topic is Koschaker (1911), but also valuable are Dougherty (1930), San Nicolò (1937), Petschow (1959), and note the more recent overview in Dandamaev (1984: 157-64). A comprehensive examination of the assumption of surety in first-millennium Babylonia which would make use of the numerous relevant documents published since the time the

Rīmūt-Ninurta is again the person accepting surety for distrained individuals and Arad-Ninurta is one of four men offering to stand surety against the flight (*pu-ut la* ZÁḪ-*ši-na ni-iš-šú*, ll. 7-8) of the two women who were being distrained (*ki-la-a'*, l. 6). Note also PBS 2/1 no. 110 (Nipp[ur], 10-XI-year 5 of Darius II) which records a loan of barley from the same Rīmūt-Ninurta to the same Arad-Ninurta.

earlier studies were composed is beyond the scope of the present study and should be written by someone with legal training. Instead, a survey of the texts employing the phrase *pūt šēp*(*i*)...*našû*, 'to assume guarantee for the foot'—the phrase employed in PTS 2061, at least four other unpublished PTS texts known to me, and about 20 previously published documents—will be presented here.[17] (A list of these texts is presented in Table 1.) It is likely that in some/many texts employing this phrase no real legal difference was intended between its use and the use of the more basic phrase *pūt*...*našû*;[18] however, until each phrase is studied independently, this cannot be determined. Thus, in the following study, reference is not normally made to evidence from texts using other surety formulae.

Most of the relevant documents were composed during a period of about 100 years, from 602 to 511 BCE, but one comes from almost a century later (424 BCE). The majority of the texts were drawn up at Uruk or in its immediate area, although some come from northern Babylonia (e.g. Babylon, Opis and Sippar) and one from Nippur. Since many of them come from Uruk, it is not surprising that numerous individuals mentioned in them are connected in some way with its Eanna temple, which had a major role in the economic life of the area and whose archives have been found by archaeologists and illegal diggers. The person for whom surety is given is sometimes a dependant of that temple and the persons to whom surety is given are often officials of that temple. It is frequently clear that the reason an individual needed someone to assume surety for him was that he was in debt to the Eanna temple or had an obligation to that temple which he had not yet fulfilled.

In a standard surety text using the phrase of concern here, the core statement is that one individual (SN) guarantees to another individual (CN) the 'foot' of a third individual (DN): *pūt šēp(i) ša* DN SN *ina qāt* CN *naši*. Instead of following the name of the person for whom surety is given (DN), the name of the person assuming the position of surety (SN) can be placed at the beginning of the sentence (e.g. GCCI 1 no. 260) or immediately before the verb (e.g. YOS 6 no. 119). There are

17. For previous studies of this phrase, see in particular Koschaker (1911: 45-50, 55, 230-31) and Dougherty (1930: 85-90).

18. Note the comment by Dougherty (1930: 89 n. *) suggesting that there may have been a difference.

Table 1. *Texts Employing the Surety Phrase* pūt šēp(i)…našû

1. *'Standard' Surety Agreement Texts*

| No. | Museum no. or excavation no. | Major publication | Date | Location | Sections[i] |
|---|---|---|---|---|---|
| 1 | PTS 3235[ii] | — | [?]-VII-yr 3 Neb. II (602) | Til-Bēltu Ālu-ša-Nabû-ēreš | 'Aa', Cb |
| 2 | YBC 9654 | YOS 17 no. 359 | 9-X-yr 15 Neb. II (589) | Namar-saparrāta | A, Bb, Ca |
| 3 | GCBC 414 | GCCI 1 no. 260 | 9-IX-yr 31 Neb. II (574) | Nēberi-ša-dūri | A, 'Cb' |
| 4 | W 18213,9 * | AUWE 11 no. 222 | 10[(+)]-?-yr [(+)]33 Neb. II (572/571?) | Uruk | A?[ ] |
| 5 | PTS 3426 | — | 2-VI-yr 37 Neb. II (568) | Uruk | A, Ba, Ca |
| 6 | HS 640 | TuM 2/3 no. 196 | 17-XII-yr 38 Neb. II (566) | Ālu-ša-Kurullāya | A, Ba, C |
| 7 | PTS 3233 | — | 9-XII-yr 42 Neb. II (562) | Uruk | A, Ba, C |
| 8 | WHM 1678 | Sack 1994a: no. 100 | 16-[?]-yr 42 Neb. II (563/562) | Uruk | A, 'C' |
| 9 | BM 58505 (82-7-14,2914) * | CT 55 no. 119 | 7?-XII-[yr ?] Neb. II | [(…)] | ⌈A⌉, C, D |
| 10 | PTS 2061 | present article | 21-VIII-yr 1 A-M (561) | Uruk | A, Ba, C |
| 11 | BM 30267[iii] (76-10-16,17) | 5*R* pl. 67 no. 3 | 2-VI-yr 2 Ner. (558) | Opis | Aa, Ba |
| 12 | AO 6851 * | TCL 12 no. 69 | 10-XII-yr 3 Ner. (556) | Uruk | ⌈A⌉, ⌈Bb⌉ |
| 13 | Davenport Public Museum B878 | Snyder 1955: 25-26 | 17-IV-yr 8 Nbn. (548) | Uruk | Aa, 'C' |
| 14 | YBC 3873 | YOS 6 no. 119 | 4-VI-yr 8 Nbn. (548) | Bitqu-ša-Bēl-ēṭir šīḫu ša Bēlet ša Uruk | A, Bb, C |
| 15 | YBC 3717 | YOS 6 no. 200 | 22-V-yr 11 Nbn. (545) | Uruk | A, Ba, C |
| 16 | YBC 3852 | YOS 6 no. 234 | 12[(+1)]-XII-yr 12 Nbn. (543) | Uruk | A, Ba, C, D |

| No. | Museum no. or excavation no. | Major publication | Date | Location | Sections[i] |
|---|---|---|---|---|---|
| 17 | YBC 6847 | YOS 7 no. 1 | 21-X-acc. yr Cyrus (538) | Uruk | A, Bb, C |
| 18 | YBC 6876 | YOS 7 no. 3 | 8-XII-acc. yr Cyrus (538) | Uruk | A, Bb |
| 19 | BM 60740 (82-9-18,714) | *Cyr.* no. 147 | 23-XII-yr 3 Cyrus (535) | Sippar | A, 'C' |

2. *Other Texts*

| | | | | | |
|---|---|---|---|---|---|
| 20 | PTS 3228 | — | 11-VII-yr[iv] 36 Neb. II (569) | Uruk | |
| 21 | BM 30471 (76-11-17,198) | *Nbk.* no. 342 | 26-I-yr 39 Neb. II (566) | — | |
| 22 | BM 31162 (76-11-17,889) | *Nbk.* no. 366 | 23-VIII-yr 40 Neb. II (565) | Opis | |
| 23 | BM 31248 (76-11-17,975) | *Ner.* no. 16 | 1-III-yr 1 Ner. (559) | Babylon | |
| 24 | Smith College 18 * | *SCT* no. 81 | 28-VIII-[yr] 5?[(+)][v] Nbn. | Sippar | |
| 25 | BM 30926 (76-11-17, 653) | *Dar.* no. 296 | 18-I-yr 11 Dar. I (511) | Babylon | |
| 26 | Ni. 2670 | Donbaz and Stolper 1997: no. 103 | 14-VI-yr. 41 Art I (424) | Nippur | |
| 27 | NBC 1146 | BIN 1 no. 19 (letter) | — | — | |

(* = tablet damaged)

i. Some references are given in single quotes, these are discussed below (pp. 118-19).

ii. This text and other unpublished PTS surety texts will be published as part of a future study.

iii. The BM number of this text is erroneously given as BM 30297 in Sack 1994b: 53, 55 and 223 no. 82. The BM number for this text, as well as those for several other texts in the British Museum mentioned in this article, were provided by C.B.F. Walker.

iv. The date of the tablet requires collation.

v. Copy: [M]U 5.KÁM, [M]U [6].KÁM, [MU] 15.KÁM, or [MU] [16].KÁM (551, 550, 541, or 540).

various opinions as to why the word *šēpu* was included in the phrase (see below), but, as indicated by the remainder of the text, SN clearly guarantees that DN would be produced at the required time and place. The word *šēpu* ('foot') is generally written GÌR.II (i.e. with the dual marker), but it is generally thought to have been considered singular in this and similar cases. The logogram GÌR.II is replaced by syllabic writings in two of the texts under consideration: *še-e-pi* in 5*R* pl. 67 no. 3: 4 and *še-pi-šú* in *Nbk.* no. 366: 6. It has sometimes been thought that the basic phrase *pūt*...*našû*, literally 'to lift up the forehead', reflected a formal symbolic act, the actual lifting of the forehead of a person from the hand of the creditor, but Malul feels that it is 'a legal figure of speech on the spoken/written level which does not reflect a formal symbolic act', in part because of such related formulae as *pūt šēp*(*i*)...*našû* and *pūt eṭēru našû* (Malul 1988: 272-76).

In addition to a list of witnesses and a concluding date formula, a standard surety agreement involving the phrase *pūt šēp*(*i*)...*našû* (texts 1–19 in Table 1) might have four sections:

A. SN guarantees to CN the 'foot' of DN.
    Aa. Addition of a fixed date (or temporal clause).[19]
B. SN will produce DN (to CN).
    Ba. Addition of a fixed date (or temporal clause).
    Bb. Addition of a fixed date (or temporal clause) and place.
C. If SN does not produce DN (to CN), SN/DN will pay silver/agricultural produce (to CN/temple/deity).
    Ca. Addition of a fixed date in the conditional clause.
    Cb. Addition of a fixed place in the conditional clause.
D. (In the case of more than one SN), they (SNs) bear guarantee for each other.[20]

In addition to a section A, each of these texts has at least either a section B or a section C.

The essential information contained in the texts in Table 1 for a study of the surety phrase *pūt šēp*(*i*)...*našû* and the documents employing it may be summarized as follows:[21]

19. By a 'temporal clause' is meant a phrase such as 'until CN comes (back)'.

20. With regard to this guarantee of mutual responsibility, note in particular San Nicolò (1937: 33-34).

21. In sections a-e below, emphasis is on texts 1–19 (the 'standard' surety texts),

*Individuals Involved in the Texts*

1. DN is 'related' to SN or CN: nos. 11 (husband of SN and brother of CN); 13 (cousin of CN);[22] 14 (cousin of CN);[23] 16 (daughter of one SN); 19 (father of SN); and 21 (brother-in-law/son-in-law of SN). Compare nos. 6 (possibly son of CN; name of father of DN same as name of CN), 7 (slave of Bēlšunu; one of two SNs is a son of a Bēlšunu), and 8 (possibly son of CN; name of father of DN same as name of CN).[24]

2. DN or SN is a slave or 'dependant': nos. 5 (DN, *zakītu* of the Lady of Uruk); 7 (DN, *qallu*); 9 (DN, *qallu* [passage damaged]); 17 (DN, *širku* of the Lady of Uruk); and 26 (SN, *ardu* of person to whom DNs are in debt). Compare no. 4 (passage badly damaged, but DN possibly associated with the Lady of [Uruk]).

3. SN is also scribe of text: nos. 1, 6 and 15.

4. CN(s) is(are) official(s): nos. 1 (*mār šipri* of the king); 2 (*rab qannāta*); 3 (*ṭupšarru* of Eanna); 10 (*qīpu* of Eanna); 12 (*qīpu* of Eanna); 15 (*qīpu* of Eanna); 16 (*šatammu* of Eanna and scribes); 17 (*šatammu* of Eanna and *ša rēš šarri bēl piqitti* [of Eanna]); and 18 (*šatammu* of Eanna and [*ša rē*]*š šarri bēl piqitti* of Eanna). Compare nos. 5 (CN not known to be an official, but SN to pay Eanna if he does not produce DN), 7 ($CN_1$ and LÚ.EN.MEŠ *pi-iq-né-e-tú*; $CN_1$ later known to be governor of Uruk), 13 (CN same person as in 14, but without citation of position; the two texts were composed two months apart), 14 (*mār šipri* of *ša rēš šarri bēl piqitti* of Eanna), 19 (CN known to have been *ša muḫḫi ešrî* in the following year; see Bongenaar [1997: 430-31]), and 20 (DN to be produced when the *qīpu* and *rab būlim* summon him).

5. Females: nos. 5 (DN); 11 (SN); 16 (DN); 19 (SN); 21 (SN); 23 (SN); and 26 (one of DNs).

but information from texts 20–27 is included where it has been thought useful. For details on texts 20–27, see section f. In sections a-d, the texts will be cited only by their number in Table 1.

22. The fact that the two—Gimillu son of Bēl-lē'i and Šamaš-aḫa-iddin son of Nergal-dāni—were cousins is not obvious from the text, but see the earlier comments on the career of Nergal-dāni, the DN in PTS 2061.

23. Nādin son of Bēl-lē'i and Šamaš-aḫa-iddin son of Nergal-dāni; see the earlier comments on the career of Nergal-dāni.

24. In addition to nos. 13 and 14, it is possible that there are other family relationships between DN, SN and CN which are not made clear in the texts themselves, but which are known from other documents not noted by me.

6. More than one SN: nos. 1 (three); 7 (two); 9 (damaged); 15 (two); 16 (two); and 18 (two). Compare no. 25.

7. More than one DN: no. 26 (three); and compare no. 25 (two).

8. More than one CN: nos. 7; 16; 17 (two); and 18 (two).

*Fixed/Relative Time and/or Place for End of Period of Suretyship/ Handover of DN*

1. Period of suretyship to end: nos. 1 (20-VIII [following month]); 11 (when CN 'crosses over from the other side'); 13 (22?-II [10 months later]); 21 (10-II [following month]); and 26 (28-VI [after 14 days]). Compare no. 24 (IX [following month]).

2. DN to be produced by a stated date: nos. 2 (20-X [11 days later]); 3 (I [4 months later] if DN does not do some specified duties); 5 (1-VII [one month later]); 7 (20?-XII [11? days later]); 10 (12[(+)]-XII [4 months later]); 12 (3[(+)-?]); 14 (1-VII [following month]); 17 (22-X [following day]); and 26 (28-VII [after 14 days]).

3. DN to be produced when CN comes/requests/summons: *alāku*: no. 6; *ebēru*: no. 11; *erēšu*: no. 16; and *rēšu* + *našû*: nos. 15, 18 and 20.

4. DN to be produced at a stated place: nos. 1 (Babylon), 2 (Uruk), 3 (Babylon), 12 (Uruk), 14 (Uruk), 17 (*bīt karê* in Eanna), and 18 (Babylon).

*Verbs Employed for the Handover of DN by SN*

1. *abāku* ('lead/bring') + *nadānu* ('give'): nos. 1?; 2; 5; 7; 9 (partially restored); 10-11; 13-16; 17 (partially restored); 18; 20; and 26. Compare nos. 3 and 22.

2. *nadānu* ('give'): nos. 3 and 12 (passage damaged).

3. *šuzuzzu* ('cause to stand/appear'): no. 6.

*Payment of 'Debt'/'Obligation' if DN not Produced*

1. SN to pay:[25] nos. 1–2; 5; 7–8; 10; 14–17; 19; and 26. Compare 9?

2. DN to pay: nos. 6 and 13.

3. 'Debt'/'obligation' defined: nos. 5 (*mandattu* of DN); 6 (*ilku* of DN); 13 (*rašûtu*); and 26 (*rašûtu* of DNs). See also the discussion of nos. 1, 3, 20, 22–23 and 25 below.

4. 'Debt'/'obligation' is a sum of silver: nos. 1 (one half-mina); 2 (one mina); 5 (five? shekels); 6 (six shekels); 7 (one mina); 8 (five

25. It is assumed here that if no other individual is named it was SN who had to pay.

shekels a month); 10 (five minas); 14 (one half-mina); 15 (five[(+)] m[inas?]); 16 (two minas); and 17 (one mina).

5. 'Debt'/'obligation' is an amount of dates: nos. 9 (ten gur); and 19 (twenty?-five gur).

6. 'Debt'/'obligation' paid to temple or deity: nos. 5 (Eanna); 16 (Eanna); and 17 (Lady of Uruk).

*Miscellaneous*

1. PTS 3235 (no. 1). In first section of the text, DN is described as being detained by CN: DN *šá* CN *ku-um* LÚ.x.KI-*ú-tu šá* $^{d}$GAŠAN *šá* UNUG.KI *ú-ku-ul-la* (ll. 2-4). The sign following LÚ is somewhat similar to NIMGIR.

2. GCCI 1 no. 260 (no. 3). DN has to hand over an amount of dates as his *imittu* (the estimated share of the yield of a field or garden due to its owner by his tenant) to a previously unmentioned individual (i.e. owner of the property?) and to bring another individual to the aforementioned. Only if DN does not do these, does SN have to produce DN to CN. (See Dougherty [1930: 87] for an edition of the text.)

3. Sack 1994a: no. 100 (no. 8). The published edition has ⸢*xx*⸣ ANŠE (beginning of l. 1) and *na-din* (beginning of l. 6), but examination of the published photographs would allow [*p*]*u*-⸢*ut*⸣ GÌR.II and *na-ši*! respectively. At the beginning of l. 3, immediately before the name of the SN, is an unwanted *šá*. The end of that line was erased by the scribe, who probably neglected to erase the *šá* as well when he realized that he had made a mistake. After the basic surety statement (ll. 1-6a), the tablet states that if DN 'has gone off to another place' SN has to pay 5 shekels of silver to CN per month. Presumably SN could stop paying the silver when he was able to produce DN to CN. The five shekels per month might represent what CN stood to lose by being deprived of DN's labour; this would, however, represent an extremely high monthly wage (see Dandamaev 1984: 115). This text was brought to my attention by Jursa.

4. Snyder 1955: 25-26 (no. 13). According to Snyder's edition of the text, if SN does not hand DN over to CN *ra-šu-tu-šú ul i-<dib>-bu-ub* $^{m}$*Gi-mil-lu i-nam-din*, 'of his claim he shall not be free; Gimillu [= DN] will pay' (ll. 7-8). His exact understanding of the first phrase is open to question and his copy has BI, not UB. The transaction may be related to three other surety texts; see Snyder (1955: 27-28) for a discussion of the texts.

5. YOS 7 no. 1 (no. 17). If DN is not produced by SN, CNs are to search (*ú-ba-mu-ú*) for DN. (See Dougherty [1930: 87-88] for an edition of the text.)

6. *Cyr.* no. 147 (no. 19). SN is to give agricultural produce to CN if DN 'has gone off to another place' (cf. Sack 1994a: no. 100 and see below). (See Koschaker [1911: 48] for an edition of the text.)

*Other Texts (nos. 20–27)*

1. PTS 3228 (no. 20). The document records when and by whom an amount of dates belonging to the Lady of Uruk which were remaining due were to be repaid. It then states that one individual has guaranteed the 'foot' of another and that the guarantor will produce (*abāku* + *nadānu*) him when the *qīpu* and *rab būlim* summon (*rēšu* + *našû*) him.

2. *Nbk.* no. 342 (no. 21). The text is a memorandum listing the witnesses before whom a surety agreement was made: *annûtu mukinnē ša ina pānīšunu* SN *pūt šēp*(*i*) *ša* DN *ḫatānīšu adi* $U_4$.10.KÁM *ša* ITI.$GU_4$ *ina qāt* CN *taššû* (*ta-áš-*<*šú*>*-ú*), ll. 1-4.[26]

3. *Nbk.* no. 366 (no. 22). DN is to produce in Opis by the beginning of the following month (1-IX, a few days later) witnesses who will confirm to CN that SN, who had guaranteed the 'foot' of DN to CN, has handed over (*abāku* + *nadānu*) to CN at the correct time DN's wife(?). If witnesses do not confirm this, DN has to pay CN the barley owed by him and its interest in accordance with their promissory note (*u'iltu*). DN's wife may have been intended to work for CN until the debt is paid. The interpretation of the text is not completely certain; see Koschaker (1911: 46-48) and Kohler and Peiser (1890: I, 12-13).

4. *Ner.* no. 16 (no. 23). The text records a debt or obligation of five shekels of silver which is to be paid four months after the date of the text. SN guarantees the 'foot' of the borrower (DN). Collation by M.J. Geller has shown that l. 5 of the text has *pu-ut* GÌR.II, as recognized by Marx (1902: 59), and against *CAD* (N/2: 106a) and Sack (1994b: 154) which read *immēri*/ANŠE instead of GÌR.II.[27]

5. *SCT* no. 81 (no. 24). The tablet records a promissory note (*u'iltu*) in which it appears to be stated that someone assumed guarantee for the 'foot' of another individual, presumably the debtor, until the following month: ...*šá* SN *pu-ut* GÌR!.II! *šá* DN *a-na* ITI.GAN *ina*! ŠU!.II CN *n*[*a*!?-*šú*?-*ú*?] (ll. 3-7). The text may say that SN had handed over (*it-*

26. See Kohler and Peiser (1890: I, 12) for a translation of the text.

27. For an edition of the text, see Sack (1994b: 154-55 no. 16).

*t*[*an*?-*nu*?]) someone to CN (ll. 8-9); reference is also made to an agreement (*riksu*, l. 10). The tablet is damaged and the published copy is likely misleading at several places; for example, the GÌR.II is copied as an 'I' sign (Assyrian form).[28]

6. *Dar*. no. 296 (no. 25). The text describes a dispute about grain and cress (the yield of a field) received by two men. The men acknowledge that they had received the produce and it is stated that they will return it by a particular date (about one month after the text was composed). At the end of the text $SN_1$ guarantees the 'foot' of $DN_1$ and $SN_2$ guarantees the 'foot' of $DN_2$.[29]

7. Donbaz and Stolper (1997: no. 103) (no. 26). One individual (SN) speaks to another individual (CN), asking the latter to release to him for 14 days—from 14-VI of year 41 (of Artaxerxes I) to 28-VI of the same year—three individuals (DNs) who were being held in prison (*ina bīt kīlu*) because they owed agricultural produce (*kūm rēḫtu ebūri*) and saying that he would assume responsibility for their 'foot' (*pūt šēpīšunu luššu*). It is stated that SN will hand the DNs over (*abāku* + *nadānu*) to CN by 28-VI. If he has not done so, he will pay any recorded sum owed by DNs to CN (*mimma rašûtu gabbi ša ina šaṭārīša* CN *ina muḫḫīšunu illâ'*). In this text, SN is a servant/slave (*ardu*) of the person who is actually owed the produce; the person acting as CN was the latter's brother, although this is not explicitly stated in the text (see Donbaz and Stolper 1997: 177). (For a similar document involving the same CN and the surety statement *pūt lā ḫalāqīšunu niššu*, 'we will assume guarantee that they do not flee', see TuM 2/3 no. 204 and Dandamaev 1984: 163-64.) The Aramaic docket on this tablet has been discussed earlier.

8. BIN 1 no. 19 (no. 27). The author of this letter requests of three individuals that someone give surety for an individual who is held in a storehouse: *šá ina* É.GUR$_7$.MEŠ *ṣab-tu*$_4$ *1-en man-ma pu-ut* GÌR.II-*šú liš-ši* (ll. 20-22). (See Ebeling [1930–34: 172-73 no. 219] for an edition of the text.)

9. The phrase *pūt šēp*(*i*)...*naši* was once thought to be found in *Ner*. no. 58 (= Strassmaier 1885: no. 122); see Koschaker (1911: 55 n. 10) and *CAD* Š/2 p. 305. Collation of the text by Sack (1994b: 197 no. 58) indicates that this exact phrase is not present.

28. This text was brought to my attention by Jursa.

29. See Kohler and Peiser (1898: IV, 56-57) for a translation of the text.

Before going on to discuss some aspects of these surety agreements, it must be stressed that the arrangement of sections found in these texts is not unique to surety agreements employing the particular phrase of interest here. This arrangement is often found in texts using the basic formula *pūt…našû*. In addition, both groups of texts employ many of the same operative words and phrases. For example, YOS 6 no. 230 (Uruk, 28-XII$_2$-year 12 of Nabonidus), which has the simpler surety phrase (*pūt* DN SNs *adi* date *ina qāt* CNs *našû*) would have sections Aa, Ba, C and D. Except for the fact that it does not include the word *šēp*(*i*), YOS 6 no. 230 is basically indistinguishable from the texts under consideration in this study.

## *Discussion*

The phrase *pūt šēp*(*i*)…*našû* means literally 'to lift up the foreside of the foot'. Kohler and Peiser (1890: I, 12) thought that this indicated that SN removed DN's foot from being seized by CN ('der Garant bringt den Fuss des Schuldners aus der Verhaftung des Gläubigers, er löst ihn'), but the general opinion (e.g. Oppert 1888: 19; Koschaker 1911: 49; and Dougherty 1930: 85) has been that this meant that one person (SN) guaranteed that another person (DN) would not use his feet to run away and thus not appear at the appointed time. *CAD* Š/2: 303-305, translates the phrase as 'to guarantee a person's presence at some future time' and treats it with usage of *šēpu* meaning 'access, approach, attack'. Thus, *CAD* appears to consider 'foot' to be used in the phrase with the sense of coming forward rather than going away (i.e. a guarantee for DN using his foot to come forward and appear at the appointed time, as opposed to a guarantee against DN using his foot to run away and avoid appearing). Following *CAD*'s understanding of the phrase, Donbaz and Stolper (1997: 150-51) contrast the guarantee for an individual's presence in the one text from the Murašû archive which uses this phrase with guarantees against an individual's flight found in some similar texts from that archive which use different surety phrases.[30] In the texts using the phrase of interest here, the concern that DN might intentionally not appear at the appointed time is indicated somewhat more explicitly in *Cyr.* no. 147 (as noted in Koschaker 1911: 48) and in Sack (1994a: no. 100):

30. See, e.g., Stolper (1985: no. 102: 8-11, *pu-ut la ḫa-la-qu…na-šu-u*, 'they guarantee the non-flight of…').

*Cyr*. no. 147

4 …*ki-i a-na a-šar*
5 *šá-nam-ma it-tal-ka*
6 25? GUR ZÚ.LUM.MA [f]*di-di-*[*i-tu*$_4$]
7 *a-na* [[m]ŠU-[d]UTU] *ta-nam-din*

4-7 If he (DN) goes off to another place, Did[ītu] (SN) will give *twenty-five* gur of dates to [Gimil-Šamaš (DN)].

Sack (1994a: no. 100)

6 …*ki-i a-šar*
7 *šá-nam-ma pa-ni*
8 [md]AG-ŠEŠ.MEŠ-GI
9 *it-tal-ku* ITI 5 GÍN KÙ.BABBAR
10 *a-na* [md]AG-ŠEŠ.MEŠ-GI
11 *i-nam-din*…

6-11 If he (DN) goes off to another place, *away from*[31] Nabû-aḫḫē-šullim (CN), he (SN) will give Nabû-aḫḫē-šullim five shekels of silver per month.

See Koschaker (1911: 49) for two further similar cases, but without the use of *šēp*(*i*) following *pūt* in the initial statement indicating the assumption of surety.[32] Several texts connect the issuing of surety explicitly with the idea (concern) that the individual for whom surety is given might (or did) flee by employing the verb *ḫalāqu*, 'to flee/ disappear', although it must be noted that none of these uses the specific phrase of interest here. Four examples of this will be described briefly. In YOS 17 no. 29, a standard suretyship-document composed on 2-VIII of the accession year of Nebuchadnezzar II, one person stands surety for another to two officials of the Eanna temple and immediately following this is stated what will happen if DN flees (*kī* DN *ḫalqū*, l. 5). UET 4 no. 112 (composed at Borsippa on 15-VIII of year 3 of Nabopolassar) describes what will happen if an individual for whom two men have stood surety flees (*ina ūmu* DN *iḫtelqū*, l. 5, and

31. Possibly read <*ul-tu*> *pa-ni* since *pāni* does not normally have a meaning 'from' when used with *alāku*. See *CAD* A/1: 317-18 for the normal meanings of *pānu* + *alāku* (e.g., 'to lead' or 'to go to meet').

32. Koschaker only cites two cases which have a clause dealing with what would happen if DN 'goes off to another place,' but other cases are attested (e.g., Lutz 1927: 33-34, 81-82 no. 2). See also San Nicolò (1937: 16-17).

*ina ūmu* DN *lā iḫtelqū*, l. 9). A Neo-Babylonian letter, BIN 1 no. 49, states that after several persons had given surety for one another (*gabbi nâšu pūt aḫāmeš kī niššû*, ll. 5-6) two of the individuals had fled (*iḫtelqū*, l. 10). Later in the text they are said to have fled to another land (*ana mātu šanītamma iḫtelqū*, ll. 13-15). Finally, PBS 2/1 no. 23, a letter composed at Nippur on 2-XI-year 1 of Darius II, records:

3 … $^{\text{md}}$MAŠ-TIN-*iṭ* A *šá* $^{\text{md}}$EN.LÍL-BA-*šá šá ina* É *ki-lu*
4 *ṣa-ab-ti ina* IGI-*i-ni muš-šìr-ma pu-ut la* [Z]ÁḪ-*šú*
5 *šá a-na a-šar šá-nam-ma la i-ḫal-li-qu ni-iš-ši*

3-5 Release to us Ninurta-uballiṭ son of Enlil-iqīša who is being held in prison! We assume guarantee that he does not flee, making off to another place.

Note the association of *ana mātu šanītamma/ašar šanâmma* and *ḫalāqu* in both BIN 1 no. 49 and PBS 2/1 no. 23 and the use of (*ana*) *ašar šanâmma* in both *Cyr*. no. 147 and Sack (1994a: no. 100). Thus, when there appears to have been concern that DN might disappear, going off to another land, sometimes the basic phrase *pūt…našû* was employed, sometimes the explicit phrase *pūt lā ḫalāqi…našû*, and sometimes the phrase *pūt šēp*(*i*)…*našû*, a phrase which by the inclusion of the word 'foot' may (Oppert, Koschaker, and Dougherty) or may not (*CAD*) indicate a fear that DN might use his feet to run away.

A concern that DN might disappear would be indicated in those instances in which DN was initially being held in custody, as in PBS 2.1 no. 23.[33] In PTS 3235, CN had been holding (*ú-ku-ul-la*) DN; in Donbaz and Stolper (1997: no. 103), the DNs had been kept in prison (*ina* É ⌈*ki*⌉-*lu*…*ṣab-tu-u'*); and in BIN 1 no. 19, the individual was being held in a storehouse (*šá ina* É.GUR$_7$.MEŠ *ṣab-tu*$_4$). As indicated earlier, the docket on PTS 2061 might have suggested that the DN in that text had also been held in custody, but due to the damaged state of the inscription, this remains mere speculation. Possibly DN was being held as distress in every case, although undoubtedly the form of detention would have been more formal and strict on some occasions than on others. The *bīt kīli*, 'prison', in which the individuals in Donbaz and Stolper (1997: no. 103) (and PBS 2/1 no. 23) were held, may have been in effect a workhouse in which debtors laboured to work off their indebtedness to their creditors, either under the supervision of their

33. With regard to the practice of debtors being held in prison, note the comments of Dandamaev (1984: 159-63).

creditors or under that of their creditors' agents (e.g. Dandamaev 1984: 159-60).

It is, however, not absolutely certain that in some or many cases it was thought that DN might run away to avoid appearing at the appointed place and time, and to avoid paying whatever was owed by him to CN or whatever was the subject of a legal dispute between the two. Instead, the surety agreements may simply have been intended to facilitate DN carrying out his daily business affairs. R.P. Dougherty has argued that since contracts and engagements could not always be concluded immediately, detention of the debtor (or one under obligation) until restitution was made 'was out of the question, as men could best discharge their obligations if allowed to pursue their ordinary occupations'. Thus the practice of giving of security or surety was employed (Dougherty 1930: 74) and DN could continue to work and acquire money to pay off his debt or obligation to CN. If this is correct, in *Cyr*. no. 147, for example, SN may have stood as surety for DN (her father) so that the latter could go about his ordinary business affairs, which might involve him leaving the city for a time. If he should be detained or delayed elsewhere in the course of his affairs, his daughter was then legally responsible for his debt or obligation and CN did not have to be afraid of not receiving it. Dandamaev (1984: 157) states that 'creditors frequently granted loans only upon the condition that someone would stand as guarantor for the debtor'. If so, a surety agreement would presumably have been drawn up at the time a loan was given. *Ner*. no. 16 might represent one such case. The text first records that a debt exists and will be repaid in four months, and then gives the surety statement: SN *pūt šēp*(*i*) *ša* DN *našâta* (ll. 5-6). Otherwise, surety agreements may have been drawn up after a person had missed the original date the loan or obligation was due and were intended to allow the release of the distrained individual (e.g. Donbaz and Stolper 1997: no. 103) or to prevent DN being held in detention. Dandamaev (1984: 163) suggests that the Murašû family may have hired out individuals whom it had distrained for debt and uses as evidence for this TuM 2/3 no. 203, a document which is quite similar to Donbaz and Stolper (1997: no. 103).

Nevertheless, assuming surety for someone was a hazardous act, since the person doing so might end up having to pay the other's debt or obligation. As might be expected, in several texts in addition to *Cyr*. no. 147, SN was related to DN. One can easily understand why a daughter would stand surety for her father (*Cyr.* no. 147), a wife for her husband (5*R* pl. 67 no. 3), or a woman for her son-in-law or brother-in-law (*Nbk.* no. 342). In a few texts, DN was related to CN, either as a cousin (Snyder 1955: 25-28 and YOS 6 no. 119), a brother (5*R* pl. 67 no. 3), or, possibly, a son (see the earlier comments on TuM 2/3 no. 196 and Sack [1994a: no. 100]). Perhaps it was felt that even in the case of intra-family debts it was wise to contract a formal agreement to avoid potential problems. As numerous modern instances can demonstrate, intra-family disputes can become vicious, particularly if financial relationships are not clearly and legally defined. In some cases SN may have been a business partner of DN, but this would often be difficult to prove. Although assuming surety involved a risk for the guarantor, this did not stop individuals from doing so on more than one occasion. For example, Balāṭu son of Kiribtu and descendant of Bābūtu acted as SN on at least three occasions (AnOr 8 no. 52 and YOS 7 nos. 1 and 176), although only once was the phrase of concern here used in the surety agreement (YOS 7 no. 1). In one of these cases, Balāṭu was actually acting as back-up surety to another person; he assumed surety for an individual who had just assumed surety for three other individuals (AnOr 8 no. 52).[34] In none of these cases does Balāṭu seem to have been related to DN.

Exactly why Nergal-dāni required Silim-Bēl to stand surety for him in PTS 2061 is not known, but some of the other texts do provide information as to the reason DN was being held as distress and/or required another to go surety for him. In most cases it was because DN owed something (either as a debt or an obligation).[35] In PTS 3426, the sum SN has to pay if he does not produce DN is said to be DN's *mandattu*. DN is a woman who has been freed for service to the goddess Ištar (*zakīti ša Bēlet ša Uruk*) and SN is to pay the sum to the Eanna temple. Thus, the sum that SN has to pay was supposedly the amount owed by DN (or DN's employer) to DN's owner (the temple) as compensation for DN's labour when DN was working elsewhere than for the temple (Dandamaev 1984: 113-14). According to TuM 2/3 no. 196, the sum to be paid is described as DN's *ilku*, thus likely the monetary amount (probably in lieu of agricultural produce) which was

34. For the practice of back-up (or collateral) surety (Nachbürgschaft), see esp. San Nicolò (1937, esp. pp. 4-5) for an edition of this text.

35. See Koschaker (1911: 34-41) for the various reasons and terms mentioned in surety texts indicating the reasons why these agreements were made.

owing as dues for land held by DN.[36] In both PTS 3426 and TuM 2/3 no. 196, the sum that SN was to pay was quite small (5? shekels and 6 shekels of silver respectively) as compared to the amounts mentioned in some other surety texts using the phrase *pūt šēp(i)…našû* (ranging from one half-mina to 5 minas of silver). These smaller amounts would fit well with the idea of them representing, respectively, compensation for the services of an individual and agricultural dues owed by one tenant. The larger amounts, for example, might realistically represent a loan for the purchase of a field or house. In Snyder (1955: 25-26), the reason for the surety arrangement involves DN's *rašûtu* (debt); if DN is not produced it must be paid (by DN). In Donbaz and Stolper (1997: no. 103), the DNs had been held in prison because of agricultural produce owed by them (*kūm rēḫtu ebūri*) to CN's brother; SN has to pay any debt (*mimma rašûtu gabbi*) owed by them for which written records existed.

In PTS 3235, DN was apparently being distrained in connection with some position in the Eanna temple (*ku-um* LÚ.x.KI-*ú-tu* of the Lady of Uruk). Possibly it was as a result of duties in (or the holding of) that position that DN owed the temple the sum of money (or its equivalent) which SN had to pay if DN disappeared. In GCCI 1 no. 260, although it is not stated that SN has to pay anything, DN is required to give the estimated yield due to the owner of the property held by him (*imittu*), as well as to hand over another individual. PTS 3228 deals with dates owed by (*ina muḫḫi*) an individual to the Eanna temple before presenting the surety statement, and *Nbk.* no. 366 refers to the payment of barley and interest according to a promissory note (*u'iltu*). At the beginning of *Ner.* no. 16, it is stated that five shekels of silver were owed by (*ina muḫḫi*) DN and it is clearly for this debt that SN stood guarantee for him. Finally, *Dar.* no. 296 informs us that the DNs have received some agricultural produce (the yield of a field) and that they were required to return it; the SNs thus stood guarantee that DNs would not run away to avoid returning that produce. In sum, in several cases, DN clearly owed, or was under an obligation to hand over to CN, the sum/produce which SN would have to pay if DN fled. Is it possible, however, that in some cases (PTS 3235?) DN and CN were

36. Possibly the two texts discussed below which indicate that SN was to pay agricultural produce to CN if DN was not produced (CT 55 no. 119, 10 gur of dates; and *Cyr.* no. 147, 25? gur of dates) also deal with agricultural dues which DN was required to give CN.

involved in a legal dispute and DN was required to appear so that the matter could be settled? In these cases, might the sum to be paid by SN represent the perceived value of the matter in dispute?

In PTS 2061, Sîn-iddin was likely acting as CN on behalf of the Eanna temple, not on his own account, and any silver given to him was likely intended for the coffers of that temple. The Eanna temple played an important role in the economic life of Uruk and frequently made loans to individuals from its resources or was owed agricultural produce or money by tenants and dependents. In many surety texts, CN is a high official (or a group of officials) of the Eanna temple at Uruk and the fact that they are acting on behalf of that temple is sometimes made clear by the fact that should DN not appear at the appointed time SN was required to pay silver or agricultural produce to that temple or 'to the Lady of Uruk' (i.e. the goddess Ištar worshipped in the Eanna temple), for example, YOS 6 no. 234 and YOS 7 no. 1. That this might be the case in PTS 2061 is suggested by the surety text GCCI 1 no. 66 (Uruk, 5-XI-year 36 of Nebuchadnezzar II). In that document the individual for whom surety is given is also to be brought to Sîn-iddin, the *qīpu* of Eanna (and to the *bēl piq(i)nēti* of Eanna), but the 'penalty' is to be paid to Eanna. Among the Eanna temple officials mentioned as CNs in the surety texts of concern are the *šatammu* (e.g. YOS 6 no. 234), *qīpu* (e.g. PTS 2061), *ṭupšarru*, 'scribe' (e.g. GCCI 1 no. 260), and *ša rēš šarri bēl piqitti* (e.g. YOS 7 no. 1). They sometimes acted alone as CN, sometimes with another temple official, and sometimes with the 'scribes' of Eanna (e.g. YOS 6 no. 234) or (potentially) the *bēl piq(i)nēti*, 'supervisors,' of Eanna (cf. PTS 3223).[37]

According to PTS 2061, Silim-Bēl was required to produce Nergal-dāni after about four months. The length of time between the date of composition of a document and the date DN is to be produced or the date the period of suretyship is to end in the texts of concern here varies from one day (YOS 7 no. 1) to ten months (Snyder 1955: 25-26). In most cases, it is no more than one month. Sometimes, however, the period is an indefinite one, coming to an end when CN summons DN or

37. Actually in none of the documents using the particular phrase of concern do the *bēl piqnēti* appear with one of the aforementioned temple officials. In PTS 3233, they appear with an individual who is later known to be the governor of Uruk. In other surety texts, however, they do appear acting as CNs, either with one of these officials or on their own (e.g. Jursa 1997: 104, 154 n. 8).

when CN returns to the city (e.g. *5R* pl. 67 no. 3, and YOS 6 no. 200). On occasion DN is to be produced in a different location than the one at which the text was drawn up. Generally, these texts were composed at rural settlements in the neighbourhood of Uruk and DN was to be handed over at Uruk (e.g. YOS 6 no. 119). However, YOS 7 no. 3 was composed at Uruk, and DN was to be produced in Babylon. The CNs before whom DN was to be produced in Babylon were the *šatammu* and *ša rēš šarri bēl piqitti* of Eanna. As noted by Dougherty (1930: 89), this would seem to indicate that the duties of these officials sometimes required them to go to Babylon. Possibly they had gone there to report to the king. No penalty is stated for SN in YOS 7 no. 3 if he does not produce DN in Babylon. Is it possible that this is not really a case of dealing with a delinquent debtor, but rather of providing that DN (a prisoner?) was transported safely from Uruk to Babylon?

In PTS 2061 and most of the other 'standard' surety texts employing the phrase of concern here (as well as numerous other surety documents), the verbs *abāku* and *nadānu* are used together to describe what SN is to do with DN. The use of these two verbs emphasizes the fact that SN is required to take an active part in making certain that DN appears at the appointed time and place.[38] SN is to lead/bring DN to CN and to hand him over to CN. According to the legal terminology employed by Koschaker (and other German scholars), these agreements thus deal with Gestellungsbürgschaft (i.e. a guarantee to produce someone), as opposed to Stillesitzbürgschaft (i.e. a guarantee that someone would appear). Koschaker (1911: 50) thought that the expression *pūt šēp*(*i*)...*našû* ('Fußbürgschaft') was especially used for Stillesitzbürgschaft, although noting that it could also be used for Gestellungsbürgschaft. He was aware of far fewer texts employing this phrase than are currently known. In fact, most state that SN had to play an active part in the production of DN to CN. Of the 'standard' surety agreements, only Sack (1994a: no. 100) and *Cyr.* 147 clearly do not have a statement that SN had to be actively involved in the production of DN, and could thus be examples of Stillesitzbürgschaft. As noted by earlier scholars (e.g. Koschaker 1911: 50-57), SN was guaranteeing that he would produce DN to CN, not that DN would pay CN whatever he owed him. As long as SN produced DN, he was free of any claim

38. The same may be said for TuM 2/3 no. 196 which uses the verb *šuzuzzu*, 'to cause to stand/appear', and for GCCI 1 no. 260 and (likely) TCL 12 no. 69, which employ only the verb *nadānu*, 'to give/hand over'.

against him. Only if SN did not produce DN would he have to pay what DN owed CN. If they had wanted to stress that SN was assuming responsibility for the actual payment of DN's debt or obligation to CN, a different formula would have been used, likely *pūt eṭēri...našû.*

In modern times, a person standing surety would have the right to recover from another individual anything he (SN) has had to pay to settle the latter's obligation (Rutherford and Bone 1993: 318). Such a right, however, is not expressly stated in PTS 2061 or in any of the other texts using the phrase *pūt šēp*(*i*)...*našû*, and remains to be proven with respect to these Babylonian texts. While one might understand why a wife would stand surety for her husband, or a son for his father, without such a right, one would not expect unrelated persons to have done so. It is worth noting that a Neo-Assyrian document recording a judicial procedure demonstrates that in Assyria a SN who had had to pay CN could attempt to recover what he had paid from DN (Radner 1997: 129-32 no. 4). In two cases it is stated that it is DN who has to pay something if he is not produced, not SN (TuM 2/3 no. 196 and Snyder 1955: 25-26). One may ask what the whole point of these two documents was if SN did not have to give something to CN if he could not fulfill his part of the agreement and produce DN at the appointed time. In two or three cases (5*R* pl. 67 no. 3, YOS 7 no. 3, and perhaps TCL 12 no. 69 [text damaged]), it is not stated that either SN or DN had to give anything to CN if DN was not produced at the appointed time. Was there then no penalty in these three cases if SN should fail to fulfil his promise? If not, of what value to CN was SN's agreement to stand as surety for DN? In 5*R* pl. 67 no. 3, SN stood surety for her husband to her husband's brother. Possibly no penalty for SN was stated in view of the fact that what was involved was a family matter. However, why go to the trouble of writing up a document to record the agreement if it was not felt that it was necessary to do everything formally and legally? Perhaps it was simply understood that whatever matter or debt existed between DN and CN would be settled by SN, but this could easily lead to a legal dispute if CN claimed that there had been a greater obligation to him on the part of DN than SN was willing to acknowledge he had been aware of when he assumed surety.

Finally, if there were more than one SN, the surety agreement sometimes indicated that they stood guarantee for each other (section D, found in CT 55 no. 119 and YOS 6 no. 234). Thus, if the SNs could not produce DN and one of the SNs was unavailable or unable, the remaining SN(s) had to make good the full debt or obligation owed by DN to CN. In several texts with more than one SN, however, this stipulation is not found (PTS 3235, PTS 3233, YOS 6 no. 200, and YOS 7 no. 3).

## *Conclusion*

The Neo-Babylonian and Achaemenid tablets using the phrase *pūt šēp(i)...našû*, 'to assume guarantee for the foot', are an interesting group of documents which provide light on the practice of surety in Babylonia of the first millennium BCE. By themselves alone, however, they leave unanswered several important questions about this practice. The discovery of further documents using this phrase and comparison with other surety documents will help to clarify matters.

## *Collection Signatures*

| | |
|---|---|
| AO | Collection of Antiquités Orientales of the Musée du Louvre, Paris |
| BM | British Museum, London |
| FLP | John Frederick Lewis collection of the Free Library of Philadelphia |
| GCBC | Goucher College Babylonian Collection |
| HS | Hilprecht collection of Babylonian Antiquities of Fr. Schiller University, Jena |
| NBC | James B. Nies collection of the Yale University Library, New Haven |
| Ni. | Tablets excavated at Nippur, in the collections of the Archaeological Museum of Istanbul |
| PTS | Princeton Theological Seminary |
| W | Excavation numbers of the German excavations at Uruk/Warka |
| WHM | World Heritage Museum, Urbana, Illinois |
| YBC | Babylonian collection of the Yale University Library, New Haven |

## BIBLIOGRAPHY


Bongenaar, A.C.V.M.

1997 *The Neo-Babylonian Ebabbar Temple at Sippar: Its Administration and its Prosopography* (Publications de l'Institut historique-archéologique néerlandais de Stamboul, 80; Leiden: Nederlands Historisch-Archaeologisch Instituut te Istanbul).

Brinkman, J.A., and D.A. Kennedy

1983 'Documentary Evidence for the Economic Base of Early Neo-Babylonian Society: A Survey of Dated Babylonian Economic Texts, 721-626 B.C.', *JCS* 35: 1-90.

Clay, A.T.

1908 'Aramaic Indorsements on the Documents of the Murašû Sons', in R.F. Harper, F. Brown and G.F. Moore (eds.), *Old Testament and Semitic Studies in Memory of William Rainey Harper* (Chicago: University of Chicago Press): 287-321.

Cussini, E.

1995 'A Re-examination of the Berlin Aramaic Dockets', in M.J. Geller, J.C. Greenfield and M.P. Weitzman (eds.), *Studia Aramaica: New Sources and New Approaches* (JSSSup, 4; Oxford: Oxford University Press): 19-30.

Dandamaev, M.A.

1984 *Slavery in Babylonia from Nabopolassar to Alexander the Great (626-331 BC)* (Dekalb, IL: Northern Illinois University).

Dillard, R.B.

1975 'Neo-Babylonian Texts from the John Frederick Lewis Collection of the Free Library of Philadelphia' (PhD dissertation, Dropsie University).

Donbaz , V., and M.W. Stolper

1997 *Istanbul Murašû Texts* (Publications de l'Institut historique-archéologique néerlandais de Stamboul, 79; Leiden: Nederlands Historisch-Archaeologisch Instituut te Istanbul).

Dougherty, R.P.

1930 'The Babylonian Principle of Suretyship as Administered by Temple Law', *AJSL* 46.2: 73-103.

Ebeling, E.

1930–34 *Neubabylonische Briefe aus Uruk* (4 vols.; Berlin: E. Ebeling).

Fales, F.M.

1986 *Aramaic Epigraphs on Clay Tablets of the Neo-Assyrian Period* (Studi Semitici, NS 2; Rome: Università degli Studi 'La Sapienza').

Fitzmyer, J.A., and S.A. Kaufman

1992 *An Aramaic Bibliography*. I. *Old, Official, and Biblical Aramaic* (Baltimore: The Johns Hopkins University Press).

Frame, G.

1991 'Nabonidus, Nabû-šarra-uṣur, and the Eanna Temple', *ZA* 81: 37-86.

Joannès, F., and A. Lemaire

1996 'Contrats babyloniens d'époque achéménide du *bît abî râm* avec une épigraphe araméenne', *RA* 90: 41-60.

Jursa, M.

1995 *Die Landwirtschaft in Sippar in neubabylonischer Zeit* (Archiv für Orientforschung Beiheft, 25; Vienna: Institut für Orientalistik).

1997 'Neu- und spätbabylonische Texte aus den Sammlungen der Birmingham Museums and Art Gallery', *Iraq* 57: 97-174.

1998 *Der Tempelzehnt in Babylonien vom siebenten bis zum dritten Jahrhundert v. Chr.* (AOAT, 254; Münster: Ugarit-Verlag).

Kohler, J., and F.E. Peiser

1890–98 *Aus dem babylonischen Rechtsleben* (4 vols.; Leipzig: Pfeiffer).

Koschaker, P.

1911 *Babylonisch-assyrisches Bürgschaftsrecht: Ein Beitrag zur Lehre von Schuld und Haftung* (Leipzig: Teubner [repr. Aalen: Scientia Verlag, 1966]).

Kümmel, H.M.

1979 *Familie, Beruf und Amt in spätbabylonischen Uruk* (Abhandlungen der Deutschen Orient-Gesellschaft, 20; Berlin: Mann).

Lambert, W.G.

1957 'Ancestors, Authors and Canonicity', *JCS* 11: 1-14.

Lipiński, E.

1998 'Old Aramaic Contracts of Guarantee', in J. Braun *et al.* (eds.), *Written on Clay and Stone: Ancient Near Eastern Studies Presented to Krystyna Szarzynska on the Occasion of her 80th Birthday* (Warsaw: Agade): 39-44.

Lutz, H.F.

1927 'Neo-Babylonian Administrative Documents from Erech, Parts I and II', *University of California Publications in Semitic Philology* 9.1: 1-115.

Malul, M.

1988 *Studies in Mesopotamian Legal Symbolism* (AOAT, 221; Neukirchen–Vluyn: Neukirchener Verlag).

Marx, V.

1902 'Die Stellung der Frauen in Babylonien gemäss den Kontrakten aus der Zeit von Nebukadnezar bis Darius (604-485)', *Beiträge zur Assyriologie und semitischen Sprachwissenschaft* 4: 1-77.

Moore, E.W.

1939 *Neo-Babylonian Documents in the University of Michigan Collection* (Ann Arbor, MI: University of Michigan Press).

Oelsner, J.

1986 *Materialien zur babylonischen Gesellschaft und Kultur in hellenistischer Zeit* (Assyriologia, 7; Budapest: Eötvös Loránd Tudományegyetem).

1992 Review of Fitzmyer and Kaufman 1992, in *OLZ* 87: 547-52.

Oppert, J.

1888 'Une femme gardienne de son mari', *ZA* 3: 17-22.

Parker, R.A., and W.H. Dubberstein

1956 *Babylonian Chronology 626 B.C.-A.D. 75* (Brown University Studies, 19; Providence, RI: Brown University Press).

Petschow, H.

1959 'Zum neubabylonischen Bürgschaftsrecht', *ZA* 53: 241-47.

Postgate, J.N.

1976 *Fifty Neo-Assyrian Legal Documents* (Warminster: Aris & Phillips).

Radner, K.

1997 'Vier neuassyrische Privatrechtsurkunden aus dem Vorderasiatischen Museum, Berlin', *AoF* 24: 115-34.

Rutherford, L., and S. Bone (eds.)

1993 *Osborn's Concise Law Dictionary* (London: Sweet & Maxwell, 8th edn).

Sack, R.H.

1976 'Some Remarks on Sin-Iddina and Zērija, *qīpu* and *šatammu* of Eanna in Erech...562-56 B.C.', *ZA* 66: 280-91.

1977 'The Scribe Nabû-bāni-aḫi, son of Ibnâ, and the Hierarchy of Eanna as seen in the Erech Contracts', *ZA* 67: 42-52.

1994a *Cuneiform Documents from the Chaldean and Persian Periods* (Selinsgrove, PA: Susquehanna University Press).

1994b *Neriglissar: King of Babylon* (AOAT, 236; Neukirchen–Vluyn: Neukirchener Verlag).

San Nicolò, M.

1937 *Zur Nachbürgschaft in den Keilschrifturkunden und in den gräkoägyptischen Papyri* (Munich: Bayerische Akademie der Wissenschaften).

San Nicolò, M., and H. Petschow

1960 *Babylonische Rechtsurkunden aus dem 6. Jahrhundert v. Chr.* (Munich: Bayerische Akademie der Wissenschaften).

Snyder, J.W.

1955 'Babylonian Suretyship Litigation: A Case History', *JCS* 9: 25-28.

Stolper, M.W.

1985 *Entrepreneurs and Empire: The Murašû Archive, the Murašû Firm, and Persian Rule in Babylonia* (Publications de l'Institut historique-archéologique néerlandais de Stamboul, 54; Leiden: Nederlands Historisch-Archaeologisch Instituut te Istanbul).

Strassmaier, J.N.

1885 'Die babylonischen Inschriften im Museum zu Liverpool nebst anderen aus der Zeit von Nebukadnezzar bis Darius', in M.J. de Doeje (ed.), *Actes du sixième congrès international des Orientalistes, tenu en 1883 à Leide*, II/1 (Leiden: E.J. Brill): 569-624, pls. 1-176.

Vattioni, F.

1970 'Epigrafia aramaica', *Augustinianum* 10: 493-532.

1979 Review of *Studies in Aramaic Inscriptions and Onomastics*, I (Orientalia Lovaniensia Analecta, 1; Leuven: Leuven University Press, 1975) by E. Lipiński, in *Or* NS 48: 136-45.

Weszeli, M., and H. Baker

1997 'Eseleien II', *Wiener Zeitschrift für die Kunde des Morgenlandes* 87: 231-47.

# WHAT EVER HAPPENED TO VIDRANGA? A JEWISH LITURGY OF CURSING FROM ELEPHANTINE[*]

James M. Lindenberger

## *Introduction*

The publications of Paul-Eugène Dion include significant contributions in the realms of Aramaic philology, epistolography and, most recently, history. The present study of a difficult passage in one of the Elephantine letters touches on all three areas, and is dedicated to him with great respect and gratitude for his stimulating scholarship over the years.

The Aramaic letters and legal documents from Elephantine allow us to trace in some detail the career of the man who became the bête noire of the Jewish military colony there for a number of years towards the end of the fifth century,[1] a corrupt Persian official named Vidranga. We first meet him in the fourth year of Darius II (420 BCE), in a legal document recording a lawsuit heard before the two local representatives of the Persian government: Ramnadaina, the regional governor (*frataraka*), and Vidranga, who was then military commander (רב חילא) of the Syene garrison (*AP* 20.4-5 [*TAD* B 2.9]).[2]

The earliest signs of Vidranga's taking a more active role in the affairs of the Jewish community appear in two undated letters from

* Cowley 1923: 30.16-17a; 31.15-16a = Porten and Yardeni 1986: 4.7.16-17a; 4.8.15-16a.

1. Several lots of texts have been published by E. Sachau (1911), A. Cowley (1923) and E. Kraeling (1953). The letters and legal documents have recently been re-edited by B. Porten and A. Yardeni (1986, 1989), see also Porten *et al.* (1996). On the history of the colony, see Porten (1968) and P. Grelot (1972).

2. Two similar texts from late 416 also mention Vidranga in his role as local military commandant: *AP* 25.2, 4 (*TAD* B 2.10), in which he is again called רב חילא, and *BMAP* 8.2, 3 (*TAD* B 3.9), where he is given a double title: 'garrison commander of Syene' (רב חילא זי סון), and a Persian title הפתחתפא which apparently means 'Guardian of the Seventh'.

around 410 or a little earlier. *AP* 38.3 (*TAD* A 4.3), written by Mauziah bar Nathan, one of the leaders of the Elephantine Jews, places Vidranga in Abydos, where, under circumstances that are not clear, he had Mauziah arrested on a spurious charge of theft.[3] *AP* 27 (*TAD* A 4.5) dates from about the same time, apparently a little later. Vidranga has by this time been promoted to *frataraka* (l. 4). The author of the letter accuses him of receiving a large bribe from the Khnum priesthood on the island, and then standing idly by while the priests stormed through the Jewish quarter of town, destroying at least one public building, throwing up a barrier wall, stopping up the water system and vandalizing the temple.[4]

Vidranga's most serious offense against the Jewish colony, the act which provoked their fervent hatred, was his role in the destruction of the temple of YHW later in 410.[5] This incident is recounted at some length in the famous petition for rebuilding the shrine, written by

3. We have only Mauziah's own version of the incident. He was subsequently released through the efforts of two Egyptian hustlers who seem to have aided him for political reasons of their own. Whether they bribed Vidranga, or brought some other kind of pressure, is not clear. The evidence is uncertain, but the two Egyptians seem to have ended up in prison themselves. The interpretation of *AP* 38 is to be the subject of a separate study; for the present, see provisionally my translation in Lindenberger (1994: 58-60).

4. The precise locations of the fortress and well are not known; the Egyptian priests, who also lived on the island, must have had their own sources of water.

5. Whether the destruction of the temple related in *AP* 30 is actually the same event as the riot described in *AP* 27 is debatable. Porten (1968: 284-89) identifies the two incidents, arguing that the destruction of the storehouse and building of a wall related in *AP* 27 presuppose the destruction of the temple. Evidence from real estate transactions a few years later seems to support this. Nevertheless, the events as described in the two letters sound rather different, and in a more recent discussion, Porten approaches the question somewhat more cautiously (Porten *et al.* 1996: 135-37).

*AP* 27 speaks of the stopping of a well and relatively minor damage elsewhere in town carried out by Khnum priests living on the island. The last part of this letter is extremely fragmentary. Isolated phrases imply vandalism in the temple, but not necessarily its destruction: '...to bring meal-offer[ing]...to worship [the] G[od] YHW there...except a brazier...they took the furniture for them[selves]...our [...] which they destroyed.' *AP* 30 speaks of soldiers coming over from Syene to burn and sack the temple, describing the action in considerable detail. In any case, the two events took place the same year (410), probably very close to one another in time.

Yedaniah and the priests to the governor of Judah three years after the event. The petition has survived in two slightly differing drafts, *AP* 30 and 31 (*TAD* A 4.7 and 4.8).[6] It relates that the Egyptian priests again prevailed on Vidranga to cooperate with them in taking hostile action against the Jews. The letter does not state that a bribe once more changed hands, but it is likely. (That is probably what is meant by the reference to the property he received in l. 16.)

Vidranga sent word to his son Nefayan, who had succeeded him as commander at Syene, urging him to lead the Egyptian troops under his command in a raid on the temple.[7] Evidently there were two barracks locations in the military complex below the First Cataract. The Egyptians (and some other troops [*AP* 30.8]) were quartered on the east bank of the Nile at Syene (סון, modern Aswan), and the Jewish garrison on the adjacent island of Elephantine (יב).[8]

The attack of Nefayan's men was a more serious matter than the earlier riot of priests; this time the attackers were professional soldiers. They crossed over to the island, entered the Jewish fort, forced their way into the temple and razed it to the ground, burning what would burn, and carrying away the gold and silver vessels as plunder.

6. The left side of *AP* 31 (nearly half the text) is lost, whereas *AP* 30 is complete. But *AP* 30 is less carefully written and has more interlinear corrections, leading to the supposition that *AP* 31 is the final draft.

7. Vidranga was apparently not in Syene, since he had to communicate with his son by letter. He evidently administered a district larger than the immediate Syene/Elephantine area. See Porten (1968: 42-45) on the names and extent of the administrative districts in Upper Egypt at this time.

8. Both Syene and Elephantine are referred to in the texts by the word fortress (בירה), but it seems that the main fortification was at Elephantine. There was presumably a fortified area in each location, but the excavators of Elephantine found no trace of any massive citadel. The relative ease with which the Egyptian soldiers (according to *AP* 30/31) were able to enter Elephantine suggests that it was the presence of the garrison itself, more than the physical fortification works, that made Elephantine a 'fortress'. On the development of this word and related administrative terminology, see Lemaire and Lozachmeur (1995) and Lozachmeur (1995).

The architecture of fifth-century Elephantine is poorly known. The ruins of the Achaemenid and later periods at the ancient site are jumbled, and the hasty excavations were at the beginning of this century, before the advent of modern stratigraphic methods. Only preliminary reports were ever published. New excavations at the site would no doubt clarify its history. For maps, photographs of the site, and reproductions of the excavators' drawings of some of the areas where papyri were found, see Porten (1968, especially pls. 1-8b and Fig. 3).

### *The Problem of the Vidranga Section*

It is the immediate aftermath of this calamity that I propose to examine. The first response of the Jewish community was to gather together—men, women and children—to put on sackcloth, to fast and to pray. That is, the initial response was liturgical.

Directly following the words 'we fasted and prayed to YHW, the lord of heaven',[9] comes a very obscure passage about Vidranga, which has never been satisfactorily explained. In the following discussion, the passage is referred to as the Vidranga section.

The text of the Vidranga section (*AP* 30.16-17a // *AP* 31.15-16a) is as follows, divided into clauses (a-e) and shown in the two parallel versions:

a. (*AP* 30) זי החוין בוידרנג זך
(*AP* 31) [...] חוינא בוידרנג זך

b. (*AP* 30) כלביא הנפקו כבלא מן רגלוהי
(*AP* 31) כלביא הנפקו כבלוהי מן רגלוהי

c. (*AP* 30) וכל נכסן זי קנה אבדו
(*AP* 31) וכל [.............]

d. (*AP* 30) וכל גברין זי בעו באיש לאגורא זך כל קטילו
(*AP* 31) [..........] בעה באיש לאגורא זך כלא קטילו

e. (*AP* 30) וחזין בהום
(*AP* 31) וחזין בהום

One has only to read a sampling of published translations of these lines to sense the perplexity scholars have felt in trying to make sense of them:

> (…and prayed to Y. the Lord of Heaven), who let us see (our desire) upon that Waidrang. The dogs tore off the anklet from his legs, and all the riches he had gained were destroyed, and all the men who had sought to do evil to that temple, all *of them* were killed and we saw (our desire) upon them (Cowley 1923: 113-14).

9. The syntax of the sentence (perfect of הוה governing a series of participles), lit. 'we were fasting and praying…', suggests that they did so repeatedly. See Rosenthal (1963: 55, §177) on the construction. According to ll. 19-20, the community wore sackcloth and fasted, and abstained from sex, from anointing themselves with oil, and from drinking wine for some three years!

(...and prayed to Y. the Lord of Heaven), who has let us see our desire upon that Vidaranag. The dogs took the fetter out of his feet, and any property he had gained was lost; and any men who have sought to do evil to this temple have all been killed and we have seen our desire upon them (Ginsberg 1950: 492).

(et nous avons...prié Y. le Seigneur du ciel), qui nous a donné en spectacle cette canaille[10] de Vidranga: on a enlevé ses anneaux de ses pieds, et tous les biens qu'il avait acquis ont été perdus. Quant aux hommes qui avaient désiré du mal à ce sanctuaire, ils ont tous été tués, et nous les avons eus en spectacle (Grelot 1972: 410).

(...and praying to Y. the Lord of Heaven) who let us gloat over that Vidranga. The *dogs* removed the fetter from his feet and all goods which he had acquired were lost. And all persons who sought evil for that Temple, all (of them), were killed and we gazed upon them (Porten and Yardeni 1986: 71).

(...and praying to Y. the Lord of Heaven) who let us gloat over that Vidranga, the cur. They removed the fetter from his feet and all goods which he had acquired were lost. And all persons who sought evil for that Temple, all (of them), were killed and we gazed upon them (Porten *et al.* 1996: 142).

Note that the translators all agree that the main verbs in the passage are ordinary perfect indicatives, and translate them accordingly as narrative past tense. Despite differences of detail, all of them understand the section to be relating what happened immediately after the destruction of the temple: the disgrace (and apparently the death) of Vidranga, and the death of his followers.

But from the beginning scholars have felt uneasy about the passage.[11] The crux of the difficulty is clause 'b':

כלביא הנפקו כבלא [variant: כבלוהי] מן רגלוהי

The first word can only be a form of the noun 'dog'; most read it simply as the definite plural of the noun: 'the dogs'. The second word

10. 'Il s'agit d'une épithète infâmante (*klby*) formée sur *kalb* "chien"... Pour la traduction, "canaille" est un italianisme qui a remplacé le vx. fr. "chiennaille" (Grelot 1972: 410 n. s). Grelot does not mention it, but this proposal was first put forward by Barth in 1908, and was adopted by Sachau (1911: 16) in the *editio princeps*.

11. In his *editio princeps*, Sachau (1911) considered most of the options sketched here. Cowley's statement that 'the phrase has not yet been satisfactorily explained' (1923: 116) remains true today.

is a *Haph'el* plural form of the verb נפק, whose normal meaning is 'go out' in the *Pe'al*, and 'bring out' in the *Haph'el*.[12]

The third word is especially difficult. Its meaning is uncertain, and it appears in two forms in the two drafts of the letter: definite singular (כבלא) in *AP* 30, and plural with pronominal suffix, 3 masculine singular (כבלוהי) in *AP* 31. It has generally been identified as the word found in Jewish Aramaic as כבלא/כבל, Syriac *keblā'* 'foot-chain, fetter'.[13]

If we follow these commonly held assumptions, the clause, literally translated, would say, 'The dogs took the fetter(s) out of his feet', just as Ginsberg reads it. But that is not really intelligible, and a variety of imaginative but labored explanations have been invented to try to make sense of it.

First, dogs tore chains or fetters off Vidranga's feet. This is the most widely held interpretation. But it implies, rather implausibly, a writer who assumed that his readers, living far away from the events, would understand simply by reading between the lines that Vidranga was arrested and restrained in fetters in a public place, where he was left to be mutilated by dogs.[14] The text does not actually say any such thing.

This explanation also assumes that הנפק, a common Aramaic verb,[15] has a specialized meaning here which it has nowhere else. 'Taking off'

12. The exact form of the verb and its construction in the context is a separate problem, discussed below.

13. Cf. biblical Hebrew כבל, Ps. 105.18, 149.8 'fetter'; similarly 'foot-chain, irons' in post-biblical Hebrew. In the Hebrew Bar Kochba letter PapMur 43 (ll. 3-7) there appear the words, 'I take heaven to witness against me that if a single man of the Galileans who are with you *is released* [?] I will put fetters on your feet [שאני נתן כבלים ברגלכם] as I did to ben Aphlul.' The protasis is not entirely clear; I restore the damaged verb as יפק[ר] (hophal imperfect of פקר 'to declare free' [Jastrow 1903: 1212a]). (For an alternative restoration, see Pardee [1982: 129-30].) The apodosis, with its reference to 'putting fetters on someone's feet' is reminiscent of the Aramaic passage under discussion, but the similarity is only superficial. The Hebrew letter refers to putting fetters on, not taking them off, and the idiom is entirely different.

14. Porten (1968: 288 n. 19), in a long note sketching the history of interpretation of this passage cites a plausible parallel from Herodotus, 9.112, describing the mutilation inflicted by Amestris, Xerxes's wife on another woman: 'She cut off the woman's breasts and threw them to the dogs, and her nose and ears and lips likewise, and cut out her tongue, and sent her home thus poorly used.'

15. In Old Aramaic, it happens to be attested only in the *Pe'al*. In all other periods of the language, it is common in the causative stem as well.

(taking off clothing or jewellery, for example, or in this case, taking a chain or fetter off someone's foot) is not the same thing as 'taking out' (as, for instance, taking someone's foot out of a restraining chain or fetter). It happens that the English verb 'remove' can be used in either sense. But Aramaic הנפק has only the second sense, 'take out'.[16] Since it is the כבלוהי/כבלא that are 'taken out of his feet', not the other way around, we are forced back to Ginsberg's unhappy translation.

Secondly, van Hoonacker (1915: 42) long ago recognized the problem and proposed that the writer intended for the last two nouns in the clause to be taken in reverse order, that is, 'the dogs took the chains out of his feet' really means 'the dogs took his feet out of the chains'. Van Hoonacker's brief comment is somewhat cryptic. He does not explain whether he is proposing an actual emendation (כלביא הנפקו רגלוהי מן כבלא/כבלוהי) or simply an aberrant syntax.[17] In either case the fact that there are two copies of the letter, both showing the 'mistaken' word order, makes the proposal unlikely, to say nothing of the fact that the problem of unstated assumptions mentioned above also remains.

Furthermore, the publication by Kraeling (1953) of the Brooklyn Museum Aramaic papyri raised a fatal objection to both proposals outlined above. They both imply that the events of 410 led to Vidranga's death: either he was mutilated by animals in such a manner that he

16. Semantically, the Aramaic verb נפק (*Haph'el* הנפק) corresponds exactly to Hebrew יצא (hiphil הוציא): 'to go out' in the simple stem, 'to bring out, take out' in the causative. The impossibility of translating הנפק as 'take off', is pointed out already by Sachau (1911: 16).

If 'take off' were what was intended, the most likely verb to have been used would be עדה (*Haph'el*), which is frequently found in the Targums as a translation of Hebrew סור (hiphil). This verb occurs in Imperial Aramaic (in fact, once in *AP* 30.6, though in a different sense); see Hoftijzer and Jongeling (1995: 829) for references. Various other verbs are used in later Aramaic dialects for 'taking off', clothing, armor, etc. Possibilities suggested by usage in the Targums and Pešīṭā include גלה (*Pa'el*), שלח (*Pe'al*, *Pa'el* or *Haph'el*) שקל and עבר (*Haph'el*). Sachau mentions נתש as a possibility.

17. In the body of his translation, he reads 'Les chiens ont arraché les cordons de ses pieds…', adding in a footnote: 'Litt. *fait sortir…*, pour l'inverse: *ont fait sortir ses pieds des cordons*, comme l'hébreu גלה' (van Hoonacker 1915: 42 and n. b; ellipsis in the note is his). That is the full extent of his explanation. Van Hoonacker's proposal is mentioned in passing by both Cowley (1923: 116) and Porten (1968: 288 n. 19); cf. also Ginsberg (1950: 492 n. 14).

would have died or, alternatively, he was executed first and his body afterwards mutilated. But it now appears from *BMAP* 13.7 (*TAD* A 3.9) that Vidranga did not die at all in 410. He was evidently still alive 11 years later in 399.[18]

Thirdly, a more plausible proposal was put forward by Kraeling himself (1953: 105 and n. 15). He understood two key words in the passage in a manner rather different from what we sketched above: he took כבלא as 'anklet', referring not to a fetter, but to a symbol of Vidranga's high position.[19] And he construed כלביא not as *kalbayyā'*, 'dogs', but as *kalbāyā'*, a singular *nisbe* adjective (ending in *-āy*), 'dog-like', or as Kraeling translates it 'son of a dog'. He took this to be an insulting epithet for Vidranga, linked syntactically to the preceding clause.

Thus, following Kraeling's suggestion (though not his exact words), one could translate colloquially if inelegantly, 'We got our revenge on that son-of-a-bitch Vidranga![20] They took the anklet [variant: his anklets] off his feet.' In other words, his Persian superiors demoted him. Grelot (1972) accepts Kraeling's interpretation on this point.

Kraeling's solution may be the best we can do. His explanation of כלביא is consistent with normal patterns of word-formation in Aramaic.

18. The text is rather badly broken, but what remains of the context suggests that Vidranga may have been released from prison at that time. Kraeling, on whom the significance of *BMAP* 13.7 for interpreting *AP* 30 was not lost, reads יפטרו[ן]....ם וידרנג [רב] חיל, and translates 'They loosed....Widrang [the com]-mander (?)...' (Kraeling 1953: 284-85). Porten (1968: 288 and n. 19), who thinks that Vidranga may indeed have died in 410, attempts to explain *BMAP* 13 away, but his argument is unconvincing. Porten later returned to the text (Porten and Yardeni 1986: 46), and offers a reading and translation of *BMAP* 13.7 (*TAD* A 3.9.7) that leave open the question whether Vidranga was alive in 399: יפטרונ]ני על ד[בר וידרנג ] [חיל, 'They will release [*me in the matt*]er of Vidranga [...] force [...]' The restoration ד[ב....] before Vidranga's name fits the traces better than Kraeling's ם. Nevertheless, the most natural reading of the context suggests that Vidranga is referred to as a living individual rather than that an allusion is being made to a ten-year-old affair designated by his name. In any case, no other person of this name is known in the documents.

19. This suggestion was developed further by Tufnell (1958: 37-54). The meaning 'anklets' for כבלא is very rare, but it is attested once in the Mishna, *Šab.* 6.4; Epstein (1912: 128).

20. The syntax of Kraeling's proposed phrase, וידרנג זך כלביא, is unobjectionable. The medial position of the demonstrative is unusual, but the construction is exactly paralleled by the phrase וידרנג זך לחיא in the same letter (*AP* 30.6-7; 31.6). Contrast, however, *AP* 32.6 וידרנג לחיא זך.

Syriac even has such an adjective (*kalbāyā*) 'canine' (see Payne-Smith 1903: 215a; Brockelmann 1928: 328b), though it is not to my knowledge used as an insulting epithet. But even Kraeling's proposal is not without difficulties. The meaning 'anklets' for כבליא is extremely rare. And the supposition that high-ranking Persians wore anklets as a sign of distinction is not so much a known fact as it is an *ad hoc* suggestion made up to explain this text.[21]

Fourthly, in their 1974 handbook, Porten and Greenfield tentatively translate כלביא as 'axes' ('the axes[?] removed the anklet from his feet'). Such a word is indeed attested in later Aramaic.[22] But it does not offer much help in solving the problems in this passage, and Porten has subsequently given it up (Porten and Yardeni 1986: 71; Porten *et al.* 1996: 142).

A fifth proposal was put forth in an article by Fales (1987: 451-69), in which he demonstrates convincingly the influence of neo-Assyrian epistolary style on Imperial Aramaic letters. In an extended appendix on the word כלביא in this letter, Fales proposes identifying it with Akkadian *kallābu/kallāpu*, 'light troops, auxiliaries'.[23] This new pro-

21. Tufnell (1958) argues that there is literary evidence to support the proposal, but this has not met with acceptance by other scholars. She admits that it is not supported by any of the numerous native artistic representations of the Persian court. Long before Tufnell suggested this possibility, it was considered and rejected by Ungnad (1911: 4): '...kaum Spange als Adelszeichen.'

22. For the late Aramaic word, see Sokoloff (1990: 253b, s.v. כולב). The word is thought to be an Akkadian loan (Kaufman 1974: 61).

23. Fales (1987: 468-69). On the Akkadian word, see *AHw* 425b; *CAD* K, 77b-78a. *CAD* defines it as 'member of the light troops (a special military formation)', noting that the word is used in the annals of Esarhaddon and Ashurbanipal. (Von Soden understands the word somewhat differently as 'Meldereiter, Kourier'.) Fales accepts Kraeling's translation of 'anklet(s)' for כבלא / כבלוהי, and his translation of the passage is otherwise similar to those quoted above: '...and prayed to YHW the Lord of Heaven who let us behold (our desires) on that Vidranga. The *klby'* ['auxiliaries'] took away the anklet from his feet, and all the goods which he had acquired were lost. And all the persons who sought evil for that Temple, all (of them) were killed, and we beheld (our desire) upon them.'

Fales proposes the same reading of כלביא in the Aššur Ostracon (l. 7), יהב המו לי מראי מלכא עם כלביא, 'they were placed with *the auxiliary troops*; and the king my lord assigned them to me'. In the context of the Aššur Ostracon, which is dealing with the treatment of prisoners, that translation is a plausible alternative. But given the extensive evidence for a literary *topos* (and an actual military practice) of subjecting the rebellious, living prisoners and the

posal deserves to be taken very seriously, but two points can be argued against it. First, the Akkadian word is a collective singular. If it were borrowed into Aramaic, we would expect to find כלב, not כלביא.[24] Furthermore, changing the subject of the sentence from 'dogs' to 'auxiliaries' does nothing to solve the problem of construing הנפק, discussed above (pp. 139-40).

There is a problem relating to all the proposals cited thus far, which I have not yet mentioned. It is the supposition, common to them all, that the 'Vidranga section' is past-tense narrative. Scholars do not agree as to what happened to Vidranga—he was demoted, he was disgraced, he was mutilated, he was killed. But they do for the most part agree that the intent of these lines is to inform the readers as to what happened to him.[25]

A closer examination of the form of the letter, however, makes that seem unlikely. The long narrative description of the riot that led to the destruction of the temple actually ends several lines before the 'Vidranga section', with the words לקחו ולנפשהום עבדו, 'they took [the gold and silver vessels, etc.] and made them their own' (ll. 12b-13a).[26] After these words, there follow several short paragraphs in quick succession:

1. A historical note indicating that when Egypt was conquered by Cambyses a century earlier, the Jewish temple had been left unharmed (13b-14).
2. A report of the community's liturgical response to the present calamity: prayer and traditional signs of mourning (15-?).

corpses of slain enemies alike, to ravenous dogs and other animals (see pp. 149-52, below), I am still convinced that 'dogs' fits best both here and in the Aššur Ostracon (see Lindenberger 1994: 18-19).

24. Fales (1987: 169) attempts to answer this objection with the *ad hoc* suggestion that the word should 'be viewed as an original collective subjected in Aramaic to a secondary pluralization'. He does not suggest parallels for such a development. Kaufman (1974) does not give any clear examples of such 'secondary pluralization'.

25. The major exception to this statement is Sachau; for details, see n. 48 below. Porten (1968: 288 n. 19) notes that Sprengling (1917: 438) also denied the possibility of construing the verbs in the passage as simple past tense. Otherwise, the agreement is virtually unanimous.

26. Line numbers in this part of the discussion follow *AP* 30, the complete version, without citing parallels from *AP* 31.

(Next comes the debated 'Vidranga section' (16-17a), which I leave aside for the moment.)

3. A reminder of a letter which was sent in 410 to leaders in Jerusalem, but was never answered (17b-19a).
4. A report of a three-year period of mourning (19b-21a).
5. A note that sacrifice has been discontinued for three years (21b-22a).

The remainder of the letter does not concern us. It consists mainly of the actual petition for support in rebuilding and permission to re-institute sacrifice.

Each of the five changes of topic listed above is clearly marked. The first two open with a temporal phrase ('Now during the days of the monarchy of Egypt…', 'Now when this happened…'),[27] and the remaining three begin with the coordinating conjunction אף, 'furthermore, moreover'.[28]

Thus the 'Vidranga section', ll. 16-17a, is separated from the end of the riot narrative by the first two short paragraphs. Unlike the other five short units, the 'Vidranga section' does not begin with any semantic marker suggesting that a new topic is being introduced. On the contrary, the first word in the section is the relative particle זי, which links it syntactically to the previous sentence, '…fasting and praying to YHW the lord of Heaven'. This means that what I have called the 'Vidranga section' is actually part of the second paragraph. It is not an independent paragraph that can stand alone. I will consider below the question as to how the ambiguous relative זי is best to be translated.

## *Grammatical Issues*

I should note at this point that the overall level of ambiguity in the consonantal text of the 'Vidranga section' is unusually high. Before the passage can be translated, three distinct problems must be addressed:

27. ומן יומי מלך מצרין (l. 13); וכזי כזנה עביד (l. 15).

28. Imperial Aramaic scribes do not make any physical separation of their texts into paragraphs. In many cases, there is not even a lexical marker, though the words כעת or כענת often indicate the introduction of a new topic. Thus the syntactic marking of logical 'paragraphs' in this part of *AP* 30 is striking. Neither the use of אף nor the appearance of a temporal phrase is *always* a sign of a new topic. But they do appear to be so in this case. On אף as a coordinating conjunction, see Lindenberger (1983: 54).

(1) the morphology, syntax and rhetorical relationship of the five main verbs in the section; (2) the syntax of זי; and (3) the meaning of the noun כבל (the variant forms כבלוהי and כבלא).

*Main Verbs in the Passage*

Each of the five clauses in the 'Vidranga section' has a main verb: (a) החוין (variant: חוינא); (b) הנפקו; (c) אבדו; (d) קטילו; and (e) חזין. I have already noted that all five verbs have commonly been taken to be perfect indicative, indicating narrative past tense. But it has not been generally observed that all five forms are ambiguous. Taken in isolation, every one of them may be parsed in more than one way.[29]

In their lexical meaning, verbs (a) and (e) are synonyms, both referring to 'seeing', חוה and חזה.[30] Their inflectional forms, both ending in ין-, are also identical, at least in *AP* 30.

Verbs (b), (c) and (d), enclosed between the pair of 'seeing' verbs are also morphologically parallel, all ending in ו-. Thus, whatever may be the precise grammatical analysis of the five verbs, the purely formal

29. (a) החוין may be either *Haph'el* perfect, first person plural or *Haph'el* imperative third masculine singular + pronominal suffix first plural. The variant חוינא could be either of the two corresponding forms of the *Pa'el*, using the longer נא- form of the first-person plural ending in either case.

(b) הנפקו may be either *Haph'el* perfect third person masculine plural or *Haph'el* imperative masculine plural,

(c) אבדו may be either *Pe'al* perfect third person masculine plural or *Pe'al* imperative masculine plural,

(d) קטילו is probably *Pe'al* passive perfect third person masculine plural. Internal passive forms are found in both perfect and imperfect in Imperial Aramaic (see Lindenberger 1983: 133, 258 n. 412), but the imperative is not attested. However, the *'it- /'et-* forms in Jewish Aramaic and Syriac, which absorb the function of the old internal passives, do occur in the imperative.

(e) חזין may be either *Pe'el* imperative third person masculine singular + pronominal suffix first plural or *Pe'al* perfect first person plural. There are still other morphological possibilities, but they do not need to come into consideration here. Porten, who dismisses the translation proposed here with the casual comment, 'Lindenberger's attempt to see this whole section as an actual prayer founders on the past tense of the verbs' (Porten *et al.* 1996: 142 n. 57), seems unaware of this ambiguity.

30. On these verbs and their usage, see Joüon (1933: 117-19). If there is some special nuance lying behind the choice of the two different verbs in *AP* 30/31, it eludes me.

pattern of their endings suggests a small rhetorical unit structured as an *inclusio*:

(a) ־ין
(b) ־ו
(c) ־ו
(d) ־ו
(e) ־ין

The morphology of the verbs permits, and I believe the sense of the passage virtually requires, that all five verbs be taken not as narrative indicatives, but as expressing a wish. Verbs (a) and (e) are to be read as imperatives; and verbs (b), (c) and (d) are to be taken as precative perfects.

(a) החוין in *AP* 30 is *Haph'el* imperative, masculine singular (החוי) plus pronominal suffix, first person plural, 'show us, let us see'.[31] חוינא in the parallel in *AP* 31 is the corresponding *Pa'el* imperative form, with the longer form of the suffix.[32] In both cases, the object, 'our revenge, our desire', or the like, is implied but not stated.[33]

(e) חזין may be read as *Pa'el* imperative with first person plural suffix ('show us, let us see [them/it]').[34]

The suggestion that (b) הנפקו, (c) אבדו and (d) קטילו are precative perfects is new. This construction is not very frequent in Aramaic, but it is attested, and this passage seems to be virtually a textbook case.

31. In Imperial Aramaic, the pronominal suffix of the first person plural (corresponding to BA ־נא) is ordinarily written simply ־ן (as in החוין [*AP* 30.16] and חזין [*AP* 30.17; 31.16]), but occasionally ־נא (as in חוינא [*AP* 31.15]); see Leander (1928: 28-29); Muraoka and Porten (1998: 52).

32. See the preceding note. In Aramaic generally, the *Pa'el* and *Haph'el* / *Aph'el* forms of this verb are virtually interchangeable; see the lexica.

33. This is a special case of the so-called 'doubly transitive' construction; cf. Deut. 5.21 (*Targ. Onq.*), הא אחזינא יי אלהנא ית יקרה; (Pešīṭā) *h' ḥwyn mry' 'lhn šwbḥh*, 'The Lord our God has shown us his glory'. In both cases, the first object ('[to] us') is expressed by the pronominal suffix; the second is 'his glory'. MT has the same construction; cf. also *Targum Pseudo-Jonathan*. The passage in *AP* 30/31 differs from these examples in the fact that the second object is unstated. For further examples and discussion of the construction, see Nöldeke (1904: 232 §290); on its Hebrew counterpart, see Waltke and O'Connor (1990: 173-77).

34. Several other readings of this verb are morphologically possible; see n. 29. But the rhetorical parallel with החוין in clause (a) speaks in favor of reading it as imperative.

Compare the following definition (Waltke and O'Connor 1990: 494) to the usage in the passage:

> A distinctive use of the irreal perfective is the *precative perfective* or perfective of prayer. [The construction]...can be used with reference to situations the speaker prays for and expects to be realized. This use of the perfective form can be recognized by the presence of other unambiguous forms in the context expressing a volitional mood....(It) is known in several of the cognate Semitic languages: in Aramaic, Arabic, [biblical and epigraphic Hebrew], and Ugaritic.[35]

*The Particle* זי

The particle can be construed in three ways: (1) '(...YHW the lord of heaven) *who* has (done something or other)'; (2) '(praying to YHW...) *that* he would (do something or other)'; or (3) introducing direct discourse, '(praying to YHW... [as follows]: "..." '.

The rhetorical structure of the 'Vidranga section' as a whole, in particular the proposed reading of the main verbs as volitive, appears to support the third possibility. If that is so, the words following זי are the words of the prayer itself.

*Meaning of* כבל

The lexical sense of כבל in this text has always been a problem. I noted that such a word is attested in Hebrew, and in Jewish Aramaic and Syriac as 'fetters, chains', possibly also 'anklets'. But it must be pointed out that this word is not found elsewhere in Imperial Aramaic. Thus, while it is possible that this is the word which appears in the 'Vidranga section',[36] it is by no means obvious that this is the case.

35. See Waltke and O'Connor (1990) for further bibliography on the construction in the various languages. One may ask whether there are 'unambiguous forms in the context expressing a volitional mood'. On this point, the textbook definition may be too rigorous. An unvocalized Aramaic text can hardly be 'unambiguous', but there is nothing grammatically difficult or implausible in reading the first and fifth verbs as imperatives. Also, if we assume that the letter was intended to be read aloud at its destination by a courier who understood its contents, such oral delivery would remove much of the ambiguity that plagues us.

The objection of Muraoka and Porten (1998: 195) that Imperial Aramaic 'does not use the perfect with optative force to indicate a wish' begs the question of whether it is so used in this passage. The construction is rare in the other Aramaic dialects in which it occurs.

36. It is impossible to say with certainty whether or not a different word for

I propose rather to read כבלא/כבלוהי as an entirely different word meaning 'innards, entrails', colloquially, 'guts', corresponding to Akkadian *qablu* (on which see *CAD*).[37] The Akkadian cognate, if such it is, has a wide range of meaning: 'hips, waist, trunk, loins, middle, interior', etc., and includes the senses associated with later Aramaic מעין ('bowels, intestines' in Jewish Aramaic and Syriac, cf. Hebrew מעים).

If this is the word in *AP* 30/31, then the clause in question can be freely translated, 'may the dogs tear out his guts from between his legs'.[38] The entire passage is a curse, an imprecatory wish that Vidranga be done to death by vicious animals (eviscerated or perhaps

'fetter' is attested in Imperial Aramaic. אסרן in J.B. Segal (1983) text no. 30a.10 (*TAD* B 8.4.5) may mean 'bonds, fetters'; see Segal (1983: 51), and Porten and Yardeni (1989: 158). However, the passage is too fragmentary to be sure.

Ahiqar 80 seems to use still another word, ארחא, in the sense 'fetter, bar' (cf. possibly also Ahiqar 196), a word which appears also in later Aramaic. But the relevance of Ahiqar for the passage is questionable, since the Ahiqar proverbs are not written in standard Imperial Aramaic. On the meaning of ארחא in Ahiqar 80 (a matter of some debate), see Lindenberger (1983: 47-48), Kottsieper (1990: 190). (Line numbers for Ahiqar are given here in the familiar form popularized by Cowley [1923]; they must now be revised in the light of the recent re-arrangement of the columns by Porten and Yardeni [1993].)

37. This proposal must be considered tentative, given the phonological discrepancy in the initial consonants (*k* in Aramaic and *q* in Akkadian). This incongruity is unusual, but not without parallel; cf. the forms *kalmatu* (Akkadian) and קלמתא (Aramaic), 'louse, vermin', or *kapalu* (Akkadian) and קפל (Aramaic), 'fold up, roll up'. In both of these examples, the linguistic affiliation of the words with the discrepant consonants is the reverse of that in our proposed case: *k* in Akkadian and *q* in Aramaic, but they suffice to show that the standard textbook equivalents do not always apply. (In none of the examples cited here does the well-known dissimilation of etymological *q* to *k* in the presence of another so-called 'emphatic' consonant come into play.) There are also cases in better-attested words such as קובע/כובע (both forms occur in Aramaic, similarly in Hebrew) where the same word is spelled with both consonants within a single language. A forthcoming article will discuss the phonological issues raised by this proposal in greater detail.

38. Literally, 'may the dogs take out his innards from his legs'. It is not clear whether רגל in the plural may be a euphemism for 'pudenda' in Aramaic, as occasionally in biblical Hebrew (Exod. 4.25; Isa. 6.2; 7.20). In all three of those passages, the Pešītā reads *rglwhy*, but that may simply be a Hebraism. In the same passages, the Targums invariably paraphrase or omit the word. I cannot find certain examples of this usage in later Aramaic.

emasculated, depending on how we translate רגלוהי), or alternatively, a wish that his corpse may be devoured by animals. When the text is read this way, the verb הנפק is no longer a problem. It has its normal meaning, literally 'take out, remove'.

## *Ancient Near Eastern and Biblical Parallels*

Such bloodthirsty imprecations belongs to a type well known in the ancient Near East. Among the common varieties of curse found in ancient Near Eastern treaties and related biblical literature are threats of being attacked and killed by ravenous animals and of having one's corpse desecrated by being eaten by such animals.[39]

### *Death by Wild Animals*

The eighth-century Aramaic treaties from Sefire in northern Syria contain the following curse against a would-be rebel: 'May the gods send every sort of devourer against Arpad and against its people! [May the mo]uth of a snake [eat], the mouth of a scorpion, the mouth of a *bear*, the mouth of an *ant*...' (Sefire 1.A.30-31).

Another of the Sefire curse lists threatens with: 'the mouth of a lion, the mouth of a [*wol*]*f*, the mouth of a panther' (Sefire 2.B.9).[40] The Akkadian treaty of Esarhaddon with Baal of Tyre says similarly, 'May Bethel and Anath-Bethel deliver you to a man-eating lion' (rev. IV 6-7; Reiner 1969: 534).

And Ashurbanipal's annals relate that he punished the fugitive Arab king Uaiṯe' I by locking him up in a cage with a dog and a bear (Eph'al 1984: 143-44 and n. 501).

The threat of punishment by devouring animals is well known in

39. On such curses, see further D.R. Hillers (1964: esp. 54-56).

40. The reading and translation of Sefire 1.A.30-31 follow the edition of Fitzmyer (1967: 14-15), except for the last-named creature, which Fitzmyer reads נמרא, 'panther'. If that reading is correct, it would provide an even better parallel for my purposes. But the word should perhaps be read נמלא, 'ant'; see Lemaire and Durand (1984: 114, 122, 134). Lemaire and Durand also follow A. Dupont-Sommer in emending the difficult דבהה (Fitzmyer, '[she-] bear') to דבר!ה 'bee, wasp'.

The correct readings in Sefire 1.A.30-31 and 2.B.9 have been debated at length; see J. Rimbach (1978: 565-66). In 2.B.9, Lemaire and Durand (1984: 141) read the fragmentary noun as [זא]ב.

ancient Israel, both in the legal tradition[41] and in prophetic literature. Jeremiah 5.6 is a particularly close parallel to the treaty-curses:

> Therefore,
> the lion of the forest strikes them down,
> the wolf of the desert ravages them.
> A leopard lies in wait by their towns;
> Whoever leaves them will be torn in pieces.

Compare also Hos. 13.7-8; Isa. 15.9; 56.9; Jer. 4.7; 12.9; Lam. 3.10-11, etc. (Hillers 1964: 55-56).

*Mutilation of Corpses by Animals*

Among the curses in the vassal treaties of Esarhaddon we find several which speak of dogs and other animals consuming the dead bodies of his enemies:

> Let dogs and pigs eat your flesh.
>
> May dogs and pigs drag around in the squares of Ashur the ... of your young women, the...of your young men before your very eyes.
>
> May the earth not receive your body for burial, may the bellies of dogs and pigs be your burial place (Reiner 1969: 538).[42]

In a similar vein, a text of Ashurbanipal threatens: 'Let dogs tear his unburied body',[43] and his annals claim, speaking of his enemies, that 'With their dismembered bodies I fed dogs, swine, jackals, eagles (or vultures), the birds of heaven, and the fish of the deep...' (Weinfeld 1972: 132 and n. 6). The wording of this last clause is evidently based on curse diction.[44]

41. Lev. 26.22, 'I will loose wild beasts against you and then shall bereave you of your children and wipe out your cattle. They shall decimate you, and your roads shall be deserted.' Note also the corresponding blessing in 26.6; cf. Deut. 28.38, 39, 42; 32.24.

42. The first of these curses occurs in §47 (l. 451); the second and third are found together in §56 (ll. 481-84). For the original text, with a different translation of the second curse, see Wiseman (1958: 63-66). The syntax of the final sentence quoted is a matter of some debate; see Weinfeld (1972: 131 n. 6).

43. *ADD* 647 recto 31 and 646 verso 3; cited from *CAD*, 'K', s.v. 'kalbu', 69; see *CAD* K, 68-72 for additional references to devouring dogs.

44. Yet another curse in the Esarhaddon treaties speaks of evisceration and entrails, without mentioning dogs: 'Just as (these) yearlings...are cut open and their entrails (*irrīšunu*) are rolled around their feet, so may the entrails of your sons

In the Hebrew Bible, the stereotyped curse that 'anyone belonging to ...who dies in the town shall be devoured by dogs...' occurs three times in the prophetic oracles in 1 Kings (of Jeroboam 1 in 14.11, of Baasha in 16.4, and of Ahab in 21.24). The curse is developed into a narrative theme in the story of Naboth's vineyard (1 Kgs 21; 2 Kgs 9). Following the judicial murder of Naboth, Elijah says to Ahab: 'Thus says the Lord: In the very place where the dogs lapped up Naboth's blood, the dogs will lap up your blood too... The dogs shall devour Jezebel in the field of Jezreel...' (1 Kgs 21.19, 23).[45]

Subsequently, when Jehu begins his blood bath at Jezreel (2 Kgs 9.30-37), Jezebel is thrown out the window by two of her own attendants, and is trampled to death by the horses of Jehu and his men. When they go to bury her, they find only 'the skull, the feet, and the hands'. The story ends by quoting a variant of Elijah's prophecy: 'The dogs shall devour the flesh of Jezebel in the field of Jezreel; and the carcass of Jezebel shall be like dung on the ground in the field of Jezreel, so that none will be able to say: "This was Jezebel" ' (vv. 36-37).[46]

Reading the 'Vidranga section' of *AP* 30/31 as proposed here enables us to place the post-disaster liturgy of the Elephantine community into a recognizable cultural context. It is a ceremony of lament, to be sure, but a lament of a special sort. It incorporates a ritual of cursing in a manner deeply rooted in the curse-tradition of the ancient Near Eastern world.

In ancient Israel, the association of a lament with a curse on one's enemies is by no means uncommon. The best-known biblical example is Psalm 137 verses 7-9:

and daughters be rolled around your feet' (Vassal Treaties of Esarhaddon, §70, ll. 551-54).

45. The stereotyped form of the curse follows in v. 24.

46. The biblical story is evidently composite: an original prophecy-fulfillment narrative expanded by Deuteronomistic additions. See Weinfeld (1972: 18-21) for a succinct and convincing reconstruction. The biblical curse in the stereotyped form in which it appears in 1 Kgs 14.11, 16.4 and 21.24 has become a specifically Deuteronomic cliché, expressing the deuteronomist's disapproval of the dynasties of Jeroboam and Ahab (Weinfeld 1972: 131-32). But as the Deuteronomic reform and the literature it produced seem to be unknown at Elephantine, we must assume either that the curse was known to the Jews there from non-Israelite (perhaps Assyrian) sources, or that it was pre-Deuteronomic in Israel.

> By the rivers of Babylon,
> there we sat,
> sat and wept,
> as we thought of Zion.
> ....
> Remember, O Lord, against the Edomites
> the day of Jerusalem's fall;
> how they cried, 'Strip her, strip her
> to the very foundations!'
> Fair Babylon, you predator,
> a blessing on him who repays you in kind
> what you have inflicted on us;
> a blessing on him who seizes your babies
> and dashes them against the rocks!

Further examples are Psalms 79 (like Ps. 137, associated directly with the destruction of the Jerusalem temple); 83; 94; 140 (especially vv. 10-11); Lam. 1.21-22; 3.64-66; 4.21.[47]

## *Conclusion*

It was a mistake from the outset to try to read the passage about Vidranga and the dogs in *AP* 30.16-17a // 31.15-16a as a factual narrative concerning his fate, and to try to interpret it against an imaginary background of Persian judicial procedure.[48] All of the clauses in the passage can be read as volitive—as a series of imprecatory wishes.

47. Cf. also Pss. 63.10-11; 64.8; and 139.19-22, where there are similar curses not explicitly linked with lament. Note especially Ps. 62.23, '...that the tongue of your dogs may have its portion of your enemies'.

48. Sachau (1911: 15-17), unlike most of his successors, did not read the text as past narrative, and discussed in some detail the various problems created by attempting to do so. His own solution to the problem was not the one proposed here; he understood the verbs to be perfect indicative, but construed them as future in sense, the so-called 'prophetic perfect'. This enabled him to read the passage as an allusion to a cultic oracle received by the community: 'Wir...fasteten und beteten zu Jaho, dem Herrn des Himmels, welcher uns mit Bezug auf den genannten hündischen(?) Waidereng [durch ein Orakel] kund tat (was folgt): "Man wird die Kette von seinen füssen entfernt haben, und man wird alle Schätze, die er erworben, vernichtet haben..." ' (Sachau 1911: 21). (The words 'durch ein Orakel' are drawn from the slightly different translation in his notes on p. 17.) There are difficulties with Sachau's translation—in particular the translation of הנפקו כבלא—but he appears to have been closer to the truth than most of his successors.

This becomes readily intelligible against the background of the ancient Near Eastern tradition of curses against an enemy, and biblical traditions linking such curses with lament.

In the literature of Babylonia and Assyria, curses appear or are alluded to in several different types of literary setting.[49] But the setting of particular importance for my purposes here is that of the vassal treaties of the neo-Assyrian period. The curses in these treaties served to give divine sanction to threats against anyone who would commit treason or foment rebellion.

Throughout the fifth century, the Jews of Elephantine, unlike their more independence-minded and sometimes rebellious Egyptian neighbours, remained loyal to the Persian crown. From their point of view, Vidranga was more than just a powerful enemy, he was a traitor, worthy of a punishment traditionally meted out to traitors.

The association of communal lament over a national disaster with the cursing of the enemy who contributed to it had already been made in Israel's exilic and pre-exilic traditions. This is clearly attested in the biblical traditions associated with the fall of Jerusalem and the destruction of the temple in 587, and the pattern may go back much earlier into Israel's history than that.[50]

The Jews of Elephantine were in many regards a syncretistic, non-traditional community.[51]

49. Examples from outside the treaty-curse tradition are found in legal proclamations such as the so-called Code of Hammurabi, boundary stones (*kudurrus*), annals, letters, as well as other settings conventionally related to the wisdom genre.

50. Deut. 32 is related to both the lament and the curse, although it does not belong formally to either genre. The disaster which has come upon Israel (vv. 20-26) and the calamity announced on Israel's enemy (vv. 40-42) are described in language echoing the treaty-curse tradition. The date of this poem has been endlessly debated, but I believe it to be pre-exilic, possibly pre-monarchic.

51. The degree to which this is so has been a matter of much debate. The classic study of Vincent (1937) remains fundamental, though revision is now required at many points. A more up-to-date study is that of Porten (1968) and numerous articles written by him since that work. Porten tends strongly—too strongly in my opinion—to downplay the aberrant features of Jewish religious life at Elephantine.

The term 'syncretism' is a loaded one, and recent studies of ancient Israelite religion enter into vigorous debate as to whether and in what sense that term is appropriate. On this question, see Miller, Hanson and McBride (1987), especially the chapters by McCarter and Dever. A much more aggressive attack on traditional ideas about the development of Israelite religion is found in the essays edited in

They called themselves 'Jews', but it is clear from their relaxed attitude towards the worship of other divinities, from their possession of their own local temple, and from their complete innocence of the basic tenets of the Deuteronomic reform that the word meant something rather different to them than it meant to stricter-minded contemporaries such as Ezra and Nehemiah. Indeed the Jews of Elephantine may have had more in common with some of the opponents of Ezra and Nehemiah than with those worthies themselves.

Thus it is all the more striking that their response to the loss of their temple in 410 was such a deeply traditional one. Like their ancestors in the time of Nebuchadnezzar nearly two centuries before, they fasted, they prayed and they called down God's curse on their enemy.

> We with our wives and our children put on sackcloth, and fasted and prayed to YHW the lord of heaven:
> "Show us our revenge on that Vidranga;
> May the dogs tear his guts out from between his legs!
> May all the property he got perish!
> May all the men who plotted evil against that temple—all of them—be killed!
> And may we watch them!"

### *Acknowledgments*

This is the first in a series of studies undertaken in conjunction with the publication of a new translation of ancient Aramaic and Hebrew letters (Lindenberger 1994). Earlier versions of the paper were presented to the University Biblical Colloquium in Vancouver, and to the Oslo meeting of the International Organization of Targumic Studies (July 1998), to whose members I owe thanks for several valuable suggestions. Thanks are also due to the trustees of the H.R. MacMillan Fund (Vancouver) for a generous grant to underwrite the necessary research costs.

Edelman (1995); see especially the contribution of Bolin (1995) on Elephantine religion. While some of the essays in the latter collection take rather extreme positions, it is becoming more and more clear that the idea of a 'normative Yahwism' in ancient Israel is as deceptive as the once-popular notion of a first-century 'normative Judaism'.

## BIBLIOGRAPHY


Barth, J.
1908 'Zu den Papyrusurkunden von Elephantine', *ZA* 21: 188-94.

Bolin, T.M.
1995 'The Temple of יהו at Elephantine and Persian Religious Policy', in D.V. Edelman (ed.), *The Triumph of Elohim* (Grand Rapids: Eerdmans): 127-42.

Brockelmann, K.
1928 *Lexicon syriacum* (Halle: Max Niemeyer; repr. Hildesheim: Olms, 1966).

Cowley, A.E.
1923 *Aramaic Papyri of the Fifth Century B.C.* (Oxford: Clarendon Press; repr. Osnabrück: Zeller, 1967).

Dever, W.G.
1987 'The Contributions of Archaeology to the Study of Canaanite and Early Israelite Religion', in Miller, Hanson and McBride 1987: 209-27.

Edelman, D.V. (ed.)
1995 *The Triumph of Elohi—* (Grand Rapids: Eerdmans).

Eph'al, I.
1984 *The Ancient Arabs* (Jerusalem: Magnes Press).

Epstein, J.W.
1912 'Glossen zu den "aramäischen Papyrus und Ostraka" ', *ZAW* 32: 128-38.

Fales, M.
1987 'Aramaic Letters and Neo-Assyrian Letters: Philological and Methodological Notes', *JAOS* 107: 451-69.

Fitzmyer, J.A.
1967 *The Aramaic Inscriptions of Sefire* (Rome: Pontifical Biblical Institute).

Ginsberg, H.L.
1950 'Aramaic Letters', in *ANET*: 491-92.

Grelot, P.
1972 *Documents araméens d'Egypte* (Paris: Cerf).

Hillers, D.R.
1964 *Treaty-Curses and the Old Testament Prophets* (Rome: Pontifical Biblical Institute).

Hoftijzer, J., and K. Jongeling
1995 *Dictionary of the North-West Semitic Inscriptions* (Handbuch der Orientalistik, 21; Leiden: E.J. Brill).

Hoonacker, A. van
1915 *Une communauté judéo-araméenne à Eléphantine, en Egypte aux VI^e et V^e siècles av. J.-C.* (Schweich Lectures, 1914; London: British Academy).

Jastrow, M.
1903 *A Dictionary of the Targumim, the Talmud Babli and Yerushalmi, and the Midrashic Literature* (New York: Jastrow).

Joüon, P.
1933 'Les verbes "voir" en araméen: *ḥzh, ḥmh, ḥwh*', *Or* NS 2: 117-19.

Kaufman, S.
1974 *Akkadian Influences on Aramaic* (Chicago: University of Chicago Press).

Kottsieper, I.

1990 *Die Sprache der Ahiqarsprüche* (BZAW, 194; Berlin: W. de Gruyter).

Kraeling, E.

1953 *The Brooklyn Museum Aramaic Papyri* (New Haven: Yale University Press).

Leander, P.

1928 *Laut- und Formenlehre des Ägyptisch-Aramäischen* (Göteborgs högskolas Årsskrift, 34.4; Gothenburg: Elander; repr. Hildesheim: Olms, 1966).

Lemaire, A., and J.-M. Durand

1984 *Les inscriptions araméennes de Sfiré et l'Assyrie de Shamshi-Ilu* (Geneva: Droz).

Lemaire, A., and H. Lozachmeur

1995 'La *Birta* en Méditerranée orientale', *Semitica* 43/44: 75-78.

Lindenberger, J.M.

1983 *The Aramaic Proverbs of Ahiqar* (Baltimore: The Johns Hopkins University Press).

1994 *Ancient Aramaic and Hebrew Letters* (SBL Writings from the Ancient World, 4; Atlanta: Scholars Press).

Lozachmeur, H.

1995 'Un example de ville-garnison judéo-araméenne au V$^{e}$ siècle: Yeb, la forteresse', *Semitica* 43/44: 67-74.

McCarter, P.K.

1987 'Aspects of the Religion of the Israelite Monarchy: Biblical and Epigraphic Data', in Miller, Hanson and McBride 1987: 137-55.

Miller, P.D., P. Hanson and D. McBride (eds.)

1987 *Ancient Israelite Religion* (Philadelphia: Fortress Press).

Muraoka, T., and B. Porten

1998 *A Grammar of Egyptian Aramaic* (Handbuch der Orientalistik, 1.32; Leiden: E.J. Brill).

Nöldeke, T.

1904 *Compendious Syriac Grammar* (trans. J.A. Crichton; London: Williams and Northgate).

Pardee, D.

1982 *Handbook of Ancient Hebrew Letters* (SBLSBS, 15; Chico, CA: Scholars Press).

Payne-Smith, J.

1903 *A Compendious Syriac Dictionary* (Oxford: Clarendon Press).

Porten, B.

1968 *Archives from Elephantine* (Berkeley: University of California Press).

Porten, B., and J.C. Greenfield

1974 *Jews of Elephantine and Arameans of Syene* (Hebrew) (Jerusalem: The Hebrew University).

Porten, B., and A. Yardeni

1986 *Textbook of Aramaic Documents from Ancient Egypt*. I. *Letters* (Winona Lake, IN: Eisenbrauns).

1989 *Textbook of Aramaic Documents from Ancient Egypt*. II. *Contracts* (Winona Lake, IN: Eisenbrauns).

1993 *Textbook of Aramaic Documents from Ancient Egypt*. III. *Literature, Accounts, Lists* (Winona Lake, IN: Eisenbrauns).

Porten, B., *et al.*

1996 *The Elephantine Papyri in English: Three Millennia of Cross-Cultural Continuity and Change* (Documenta et monumenta orientis antiqui; Studies in Near Eastern Archaeology and Civilisation, 22; Leiden: E.J. Brill).

Reiner, E.

1969 'Akkadian Treaties from Syria and Assyria', in *ANET*: 531-41.

Rosenthal, F.

1963 *A Grammar of Biblical Aramaic* (Wiesbaden: Otto Harrassowitz).

Rimbach, J.

1978 'Bears or Bees? Sefire I A 31 and Daniel 7', *JBL* 97: 565-66.

Sachau, E.

1911 *Aramäische Papyrus und Ostraca aus einer jüdischen Militärkolonie zu Elephantine* (Leipzig: J.C. Hinrichs).

Segal, J.B.

1983 *Aramaic Texts from North Saqqara* (London: Egypt Exploration Society).

Sokoloff, M.

1990 *A Dictionary of Jewish Palestinian Aramaic* (Ramat-Gan: Bar Ilan University).

Sprengling, M.

1917 'The Aramaic Papyri of Elephantine in English', *AJT* 21: 411-52.

Tufnell, O.

1958 'Anklets in Western Asia', *Bulletin of the Institute of Archaeology* 1: 37-54.

Ungnad, A.

1911 *Aramäische Papyrus aus Elephantine* (Leipzig: J.C. Hinrichs).

Vincent, A.

1937 *La religion des Judéo-Araméens d'Eléphantine* (Paris: Geuthner).

Waltke, B., and M.P. O'Connor

1990 *An Introduction to Biblical Hebrew Syntax* (Winona Lake, IN: Eisenbrauns).

Weinfeld, M.

1972 *Deuteronomy and the Deuteronomistc School* (Oxford: Clarendon Press).

Wiseman, D.J.

1958 'The Vassal Treaties of Esarhaddon', *Iraq* 20: 1-99.

## A PROPOS DE L'INSCRIPTION DE MESHA' DEUX NOTES*

Pierre Bordreuil

A first note bears on the word RḤMT, line 17 of Mesha's inscription. This word forms a group with the masculine-feminine pairs GRN and GRT (probably assimilated foreign residents), and GBRN (free men) and GBRT (mature ladies, probably past child-bearing, cf. Heb. GBYRH). RḤMT stands outside these pairs, apparently without any masculine counterpart of its own. It seems however that RḤMT forms a pair with GBRT, in that it designates young females capable of procreation, as in Judg. 5.30 and a few times in Ugaritic poetry. The second note bears on ...ŠDQ, the last complete word of the same inscription (line 34). H. Michaud's interpretation of this word on the basis of the Arabic verb ṮDQ, which refers to heavy rainfall, is supported by arguments taken from the Israelite campaign in 2 Kgs 3, and from the hydrography of the wadi Ḥasā region, in the south of Mesha's kingdom. It seems indeed that the end of the inscription (which, by the way, probably does not mention the House of David) refers globally to the same events as 2 Kgs 3, which involved sudden flooding out of the heights of Edom.

### *Les RḤMT (=jeunes femmes) de Nébo (l.17)*

Les sept mille habitants de Nébo mis à mort par Mesha' sont désignés aux l.16 s. de la stèle de ce roi par cinq mots différents parmi lesquels deux au masculin: (G[B]⌈RN⌉ et ⌈GRN⌉), sont suivis par leur équivalent féminin (GBRT et [GR]T). Le cinquième mot, qui est de genre féminin (RḤMT), est dépourvu en revanche d'équivalent masculin. La signification de ⌈GRN⌉ et de [GR]T est ambiguë et ils pourraient désigner les 'hôtes résidents,' c'est-à-dire des personnes d'origine étrangère, hommes et femmes. Cette interprétation semble ici la plus probable,

* La lecture de la thèse de doctorat en théologie de Jean-Pierre Sternberger, soutenue le 23 mars 1998 devant la Faculté de Théologie Protestante de l'Université de Strasbourg, a suscité quelques réflexions qui sont à l'origine de la rédaction de ces deux notes.

étant donné que l'hébreu *gēr/gār* comporte cette même connotation sociale bien établie. Plusieurs auteurs ont interprété ⸢GRN⸣ et [GR]T comme 'petits garçons' et 'petites filles' (Lemaire 1987: 207 nn. 17ss.; Sternberger 1998: 47), par analogie avec l'hébreu biblique où ce mot désigne des petits d'animaux, et l'ensemble de la population serait alors réparti dans les deux tranches d'âge que sont l'âge adulte (G[B]⸢RN⸣ et GBRT) et l'âge tendre (GRN⸣ et [GR]T). Cette interprétation s'appuie sur la double inscription phénicienne de Kition (*CIS* 86 A-B; *KAI* 37; *TSSI* 3, 33, et p. 130) où les GRM qu'on pourrait traduire par 'minets'[1] apparaissent (A l.16; B l.10) à côté des KLBM 'chiens' qui étaient vraisemblablement des prostitués sacrés. Or, le contexte du temple de Kition est très différent de celui de l'inscription de Mesha' et on ne peut assimiler purement et simplement les GRM de Chypre aux GRN de Moab.[2] Par ailleurs dans ce dernier texte la traduction 'jeunes garçons', maintes fois reproduite, n'ayant jamais été réellement démontrée, on préférera s'en tenir au premier sens évoqué plus haut. Comme dans la Bible, les GRN de Moab seraient des étrangers circoncis ayant atteint un degré d'assimilation tel qu'on peut participer avec eux aux fêtes religieuses (Exod. 12.48).[3] Quelle que soit la signification de GRN dans l'inscription de Mesha', l'énumération obtenue et la répartition qu'elle implique ne permettent pas d'expliquer ici l'absence d'un équivalent masculin de RḤMT.

G[B]⸢RN⸣ représente vraisemblablement les hommes adultes en général. Dans la Bible, 'il n'y a pas d'âge pour les braves' et ce terme évoque aussi bien l'homme courageux (Jér. 41.16) que l'adulte dans la force de l'âge (Prov. 30.19), sans autre précision.

GBRT, dont la lecture est certaine, est la forme féminine de G[B]⸢RN⸣, mais les rares indications que donne la Bible sur ce mot ne permettent pas d'y voir l'exacte contrepartie féminine de *geber*. Les trois femmes désignées chacune comme *gēbîrâ* sont: (1) Sarah, l'épouse d'Abraham, (Gen. 16.4) qui est présentée comme la maîtresse (*g*$^{e}$*bîrtâ* 'sa maîtresse') de Hagar; (2) Tapenès (1 Rois 11.19), la belle-mère de Hadad le rebelle fuyant Salomon et accueilli par Pharaon; *g*$^{e}$*bîrâ* désigne ici la reine-mère, comme l'ont bien compris les versions syriaque et arabe; (3) Maakah, fille d'Absalom et reine-mère du roi Abiyam (1 Rois 15.13 = 2 Chron. 15.16), elle était l'épouse de

1. Voir Masson et Sznycer (1972: 20-68).
2. Ainsi Guzzo-Amadasi et Karageorghis (1977: 117s).
3. Référence obligeamment communiquée par A. Sérandour.

Roboam (1 Chron. 11.19) et vraisemblablement aïeule d'Asa (1 Rois 15.2 = 2 Chron. 11.20), puisque la mère de ce dernier s'appelait peut-être Ανα, d'après le grec de 1 Rois 15.10. Or, les trois femmes ainsi qualifiées de *g$^e$bîrâ* ont comme caractéristique commune de n'être plus de première jeunesse. Ce sont des matrones, aussi bien Sarah dont la servante Hagar méprise la stérilité apparemment définitive, que Tapenès qui élève ses (petits?) neveux et que Maakah, (grand-) mère du roi Asa.

On voit qu'au moabite GBR correspond l'hébreu *geber* désignant des hommes libres de sexe masculin indépendamment de leur âge. Au contraire, ce qu'on sait de l'hébreu *g$^e$bîrâ* qui signifie selon le cas 'maîtresse' ou 'reine-mère' donne à penser que les GBRT moabites étaient des femmes libres d'âge mûr qui ne sont plus susceptibles de procréer.

Quelle est alors la signification de RḤMT? La Bible hébraïque présente une trentaine d'attestations du mot *reḥem*: 'matrice', organe féminin de procréation (Gen. 49.25). Dans le cas d'Anne, future mère de Samuel, la fermeture de celui-ci dénote une stérilité congénitale d'origine divine (1 Sam. 1.5, *YHWH sāgar raḥmāh*) et son resserrement correspond à une stérilité temporaire de la famille d'Abimelek (Gen. 20.18, *kî 'āṣōr āṣar YHWH b$^e$'ad kol-reḥem l$^e$bēt '$^a$bīmelek*). Inversement, la fécondité accordée à Rachel est exprimée par son ouverture (Gen. 30.22, *wayyišma' 'elêhā 'ĕlōhîm wayyiptaḥ raḥmāh*); tout premier-né humain ou animal en est les prémices (Nb. 3.12 etc., *peṭer reḥem*) et à plusieurs reprises (Isa. 46.3 etc.), *reḥem* est mis en parallèle avec *beṭen*: 'ventre'. Le désespoir du prophète lui inspire le regret que sa mère menant sa grossesse à son terme normal n'ait pas pu être son tombeau (Jér. 20.17, *wat$^e$hî lî 'immî qibrî w$^e$raḥmāh h$^a$rat 'ōlām*).

Laissant de côté l'ensemble des attestations bibliques où les *raḥ$^a$mīm* 'entrailles' représentent le siège d'émotions, de sentiments tels que la compassion,[4] il reste une attestation dans le Cantique de Débora (Jg. 5.30, *raḥam raḥ$^a$mātayim l$^e$rō'š geber*). Au premier hémistiche, la juxtaposition d'un mot apparemment masculin et de son équivalent au duel féminin pluriel est anormale. Au second hémistiche, ces deux mots font partie de ce qui revient à chaque 'tête de guerrier' dans le partage

4. Voir Dhorme ([1923]1963: 134ss.); Cp. *CTA* 1. 16 I 33: Octavie, fille de Kirta est appelée *rḥmt*, c'est-à-dire 'compatissante'. Cp. Os. 1.6 où la fille du prophète est appelée *lō' ruḥāmâ*: 'non aimée' et 2.25, *w$^e$riḥamtī 'et lō' ruḥāmâ...* 'et j'aimerai la "non aimée" '.

du butin. Au premier hémistiche, le syntagme *raḥam raḥ$^{a}$mātayim* (littéralement 'matrice') désigne certainement par métonymie les femmes capturées à l'ennemi.[5] Cette signification, ignorée de la LXX qui garde la connotation morale habituelle: A, φιλιάζων φίλοις B, οἰκτίρμων οἰκτιρήσει, a été proposée par la *Vulgate* qui traite ce syntagme comme un superlatif: *'pulcherrima feminarum'*. La présence du duel féminin pluriel comme *nomen rectum* fait difficulté pour admettre une telle construction; que signifierait en effet 'la plus belle des femmes pour chaque guerrier'? Avec les traductions récentes, on verra là une simple succession dépourvue de copule: 'une *raḥam*, deux *raḥ$^{a}$mātayim.*' Si la forme *raḥam* est inattendue en hébreu, on la trouve à Ougarit dans un texte alphabétique qui désigne la déesse Anat comme *rḥm* (*CTA* 6 II 27)[6] et dans un autre où une divinité appelée *rḥmy* (*CTA* 1. 15 II 6)[7] est mentionnée en compagnie d'Athirat (*CTA* 23 13, 16, 28). Ce parallèle autorise à traduire Jg. 5.30 ainsi: 'une jeune femme,[8] deux jeunes femmes par tête de guerrier'.

Revenant aux l.16s. de l'inscription de Mesha', on constate que la population de Nebo est d'abord répartie par sexes: les G[B]⌈RN⌉, hommes adultes autochtones quel que soit leur âge et les ⌈GRN⌉, hommes adultes d'origine étrangère, puis par âges: les GBRT, femmes adultes autochtones âgées et les [GR]T, femmes adultes âgées d'origine étrangère. A partir de la répartition ainsi obtenue, RḤMT désignerait les femmes nubiles susceptibles de procréer, c'est-à-dire depuis la jeune fille[9] jusqu'à la femme jeune et on proposera la classe d'âge intermédiaire: 'les jeunes femmes.'[10]

5. Lagrange (1903: 103): 'litt. un sein, métaphore employée pour désigner une esclave, un peu comme on compte les hommes par tête...'

6. Voir Caquot *et al.* (1974: 260); del Olmo (1981: 433 n. 15; 443, 448).

7. Voir les discussions dans Hvidberg-Hansen (1979: 73, 136); Day (1986: 390).

8. Voir les références dans Paul (1991: 15 n. 83, 64 nn. 215, 219).

9. Voir *HNE* (368); Galling (1968: 53); *NSI* (3); van Selms (1954: 110s); Kapelrud (1969: 34-37). La traduction 'nubile lass' a été proposée par Deem (1978: 27).

10. La traduction 'femmes enceintes' proposée par Lemaire (1987: 208; 1991: 159), est trop restrictive. Tout d'abord il existe en hébreu le mot *hārâ* qui désigne spécifiquement la femme grosse; c'est lui et non *raḥam* qui est employé à propos des femmes enceintes massacrées dans les récits de 2 Rois 8.12; 15.16; de même à Os. 14.1 et Am. 1.13 qui sont aussi invoqués par Lemaire à l'appui de sa traduction; ensuite Jér 20.17 montre que la matrice (*reḥem*) peut être ou ne pas être grosse (*h$^{a}$rat*) et qu'il n'y a donc pas lieu de confondre femme nubile et femme enceinte;

### *ŠDQ, dernier mot lisible de l'inscription (l.34)*

On sait que l'inscription de Mesha' avait été gravement endommagée au début des tractations compliquées qui préludèrent à son acquisition par Ch. Clermont-Ganneau.[11] La fin de l'inscription est des plus lacunaire, y compris sur l'estampage exécuté par Ya'aqoub Karavaca dans les circonstances rocambolesques que l'on sait, au point qu'on peut se demander si la destruction des dernières lignes ne serait pas antérieure à l'invention elle-même du monument par F.A. Klein. Toutefois la séquence . ŠDQ . se détache très nettement à la l.34. En l'absence de tout vocable complet précédant ou suivant immédiatement ces trois lettres, la plupart des commentateurs les ont transcrites sans essayer de les expliquer.[12]

A ma connaissance, seul Michaud (1958: 42 n. 5) a rapproché ce mot d'un verbe arabe *ṯadaqa* qui signifie 'tomber en abondance', parlant de la pluie.[13] Il propose de mettre ce verbe en rapport avec l'édification de bassins ('ŠWḤ) et de citernes (BR) décrites aux lignes précédentes (l.9, 23ss.). Ce serait une allusion à l'attente des pluies célestes, gage de prospérité, qui doivent les remplir.

En l'absence de tout environnement textuel, il convient de rester prudent à propos de ce mot isolé et on voudrait seulement souligner ici le rapport qu'il permet d'établir avec la description de la campagne militaire de 2 Rois 3. Il est généralement admis que ce qui reste de la dernière partie de l'inscription de Mesha' doit être mis en relation avec cette expédition projetée par Yoram, roi d'Israël et Yosaphat, roi de Juda, alliés à des éléments édomites, avec participation du prophète Elisée pour attaquer Moab par le sud. Les noms de ces deux rois sont absents de l'inscription de Mesha' dans son état actuel, mais on peut supposer qu'ils figuraient dans le texte originel, de même que 'Omri, roi d'Israël et oppresseur de Moab, est cité par son nom dans la première partie de l'inscription (l.7).[14] Grâce à l'amabilité de Béatrice

enfin *raḥam raḥ$^{a}$mātayim* de Jg. 5.30 se comprend mieux s'il s'agit de jeunes femmes que de femmes enceintes.

11. Sur les circonstances de la découverte, voir Graham (1989: 41-67).

12. En dernier lieu Jackson et Dearman (1989: 95) et Jackson (1989: 98).

13. Voir Freytag (1830: 212); Blachère *et al.* (1970: 1159).

14. A la l.31, la mention de la maison de David, proposée par Lemaire (1994a; 1994b), Puech (1994: 227 n. 3), et Na'aman (1994: 27-30), est surprenante et s'accorde mal avec ce qui précède: '...Ḥawronēn habitait là...', comme avec ce qui

André-Salvini et d'Annie Caubet, conservateurs du département des Antiquités Orientales du Musée du Louvre, il a été procédé le 23 mars 1998, en compagnie de Françoise Briquel-Chatonnet, d'Arnaud Sérandour et de Jean Pierre Sternberger à un examen attentif de l'estampage conservé dans les réserves du Musée du Louvre. Celui-ci n'a pas permis de confirmer la lecture B⌈T⌉ [D]W⌈D⌉ et on a pu constater que le second D, proposé par Lidzbarski, n'est pas incontestable.

D'après le texte biblique, les forces coalisées ont contourné la Mer Morte par le sud pour remonter le *naḥal zered*, aujourd'hui *wadi al ḥesā*, marquant la frontière méridionale de Moab et le séparant d'Edom, territoire de statut incertain à l'époque des évènements.[15] L'armée est assoiffée et Elisée ordonne de creuser dans la vallée des fosses qui se rempliront d'eau, sans qu'aucun vent ni pluie visible n'accompagnent cette montée d'eau.

Il est pertinent de constater que le nom arabe moderne du *wadi al ḥesā*, (au pluriel *ḥasā*), désigne des '...vasques invisibles, filets d'eau, glissant silencieusement dans le sous-sol, réserves bienfaisantes d'eau salubre et pure...bien connues des Bédouins, très adroits pour les retrouver...' (Lammens 1914: 33ss). Ce nom a pu être donné dès l'Antiquité à ce cours d'eau en souvenir du *naḥal zered* biblique (Robinson 1841: 555s) et de la mystérieuse montée des eaux décrite à 2 Rois 3.17 ou en référence à un phénomène récurrent d'inondation dû à l'hydrographie particulière de la région. Ce dernier a été observé par des voyageurs orientalistes qui n'ont pas manqué de le rapprocher du texte biblique.[16]

Trois éléments doivent encore être pris en considération: on a vu que le nom arabe du *wadi al ḥesā* évoque bien le creusement de vasques ou

suit: '...Et Kamosh me dit: descend, combat Ḥawronēn...' La maison (BTH) de 'Omri est bien évoquée à la l.4, mais elle désigne une dynastie désormais éteinte.

15. On a noté la contradiction entre d'une part la mention du roi d'Edom parmi les coalisés (2 Rois 3.9, 26) et d'autre part la présence en Edom à l'époque de Yosaphat d'un 'préfet royal' (1 Rois 22.48), ainsi que l'accession au trône d'un roi édomite mentionnée seulement après la révolte qui eut lieu sous Yoram de Juda (2 Rois 8.20ss.). Voir l'exposé de Bartlett (1983: 135-46; 1989: 121). Lemaire (1991: 156) suppose la participation d'un contingent édomite aux côtés des coalisés, ce qui est plausible, mais il suggère de surcroît que le chef supposé de ce contingent, dont le nom n'est pas même pas mentionné, se soit ensuite fait acclamer roi d'Edom, ce qui est bien hypothétique.

16. Gautier (1901: 89-92) décrit une crue de l'Arnon survenue le 19 mars 1899; Schumacher (1913: 314-415); Dalman ([1928] 1964: 201ss).

de fosses (en hébreu *gēbīm*), sortes de puits artésiens destinés à atteindre la nappe phréatique,[17] mais il est précisé au v. 17 que l'eau emplira les fosses sans que les Israélites n'aient vu ni vent ni pluie. L'explication la plus vraisemblable est qu'un fort orage extrêmement localisé, comme il s'en produit fréquemment au Proche-Orient, s'est abattu sur le plateau d'Edom à quelques km du campement israélite. Gonflant les affluents de rive gauche du *naḥal zered* (Reymond 1958: 68) qui dévalent du plateau édomite vers le nord, il a empli en peu de temps des fosses aménagées au préalable pour la collecte des eaux souterraines.

D'autre part, la remarque de 2 Rois 3 sur l'origine édomite des eaux salutaires est peut-être à mettre en rapport avec la collaboration d'éléments édomites dans l'expédition coalisée mais certainement avec l'idée ancienne que le dieu d'Israël est venu d'Edom et qu'il se manifeste avec prédilection dans l'orage (Judg. 5.4).

Enfin, parmi les affluents de rive gauche nés sur le plateau édomite figure le *wadi La'ban* où l'on peut observer encore aujourd'hui des affleurements de 'terra rossa.'[18] De fait, les eaux de couleur rouge du v. 22 sont un phénomène particulier à cette vallée (Musil 1907: 83, 381 n. 2; Glueck 1936: 150 n. 43), qui a été noté par plusieurs exégètes (Montgomery 1951: 361s; de Vaux 1949: 132 note e; Reymond 1958: 84). On constate la convergence des données topographiques: au v. 20, les eaux viennent d'Edom (*midderek ʾᵉdōm*), des données onomastiques: le nom d'Edom est en rapport avec la couleur rouge et enfin des données géologiques: au v. 22, les eaux sont rouges comme du sang (*ʾᵃdummîm kaddām*) mais le texte, attribuant ce phénomène à l'illusion d'optique née du spectacle d'eaux étales se reflétant à la lumière rose du soleil levant, ne manque pas de jouer sur l'adjectif *'ādōm* 'rouge' et sur le toponyme *ʾᵉdōm*.[19]

Puisqu'il est certain que la dernière partie de l'inscription de Mesha' décrivait la version moabite de l'équipée des armées coalisées contre Moab, ne pourrait-on pas considérer que ŠDQ, dernier mot lisible de ce texte, faisait allusion au même phénomène météorologique évoqué *in absentia* par 2 Rois 3.17? Invisible des assaillants coalisés campés dans le ravin, l'orage frappant le plateau édomite était en revanche

17. *Bible du Centenaire* Tome II: Les prophètes, Paris 1947, p. 242, note g.

18. Je remercie de cette information François Villeneuve, Directeur de la mission archéologique de *Khirbet eḍ Dariḥ* qui est située dans les environs immédiats du *wadi La'ban*.

19. Voir Parker (1997: 126).

parfaitement visible des troupes moabites embusquées sur le balcon septentrional du *naḥal zered.* On déplore d'autant plus vivement la destruction quasi complète des dernières lignes de l'inscription de Mesha' que celles-ci auraient pu assurément donner de ce phénomène une interprétation assez différente de celle du récit de 2 Rois 3.

## BIBLIOGRAPHIE


Bartlett, J.R.
1983 'The "United" Campaign against Moab in 2 Kings 3.4-27', dans J.F.A. Sawyer et D.J.A. Clines (éds.), *Midian, Moab and Edom* (Sheffield: JSOT Press): 135-46.
1989 *Edom and the Edomites* (Sheffield: JSOT Press).

Blachère, R., M. Chouémi et C. Denizeau
1970 *Dictionnaire arabe-français-anglais*, II (Paris: G.P. Maisonneuve et Larose).

Caquot, A., M. Sznycer et A. Herdner
1974 *Textes ougaritiques. I. Mythes et légendes* (2 vols.; LAPO, 7; Paris: Éditions du Cerf).

Dalman, G.
1964 *Arbeit und Sitte in Palästina*, I (7 vols.; Gütersloh: Bertelsmann).

Day, J.
1986 'Asherah in the Hebrew Bible and Northwest Semitic Literature', *JBL* 105: 385-408.

Deem, A.
1978 'The Goddess Anath and Some Biblical Hebrew Cruces', *JSS* 23: 25-30.

del Olmo Lete, G.
1981 *Mitos y leyendas de Canaan segun la tradicion de Ugarit: textos, versión y estudio* (Madrid: Ediciones Cristiandad).

Dhorme, E.
1963 *L'emploi métaphorique des noms de parties du corps en hébreu et en akkadien* (Paris: P. Geuthner [1923]).

Freytag, G.W.
1830 *Lexicon arabico-latinum*, I (4 vols.; Halle: C.A. Schwetschke).

Galling, K.
1968 *Textbuch zur Geschichte Israels* (Tübingen: J.C.B. Mohr [Paul Siebeck], 2[e] éd.).

Gautier, L.
1901 *Autour de la Mer Morte* (Genève: Eggimann).

Glueck, N.
1936 'The Boundaries of Edom', *HUCA* 2: 141-57.

Graham, M.P.
1989 'The Discovery and Reconstruction of the Mesha Inscription', dans A. Dearman (éd.), *Studies in the Mesha Inscription and Moab* (Atlanta, GA: Scholars Press): 41-67.

Guzzo-Amadasi, M., et V. Karageorghis
1977 *Inscriptions phéniciennes* (Excavation at Kition, 3; Nicosia: Ministry of Communications and Works, Department of Antiquities).

Hvidberg-Hansen, F.O.
1979 *La déesse TNT: Une étude sur la religion canaanéo-punique*, II (2 vols.; Copenhague: Gad).

Jackson, K.P.
1989 'The Language of the Mesha' Inscription', dans A. Dearman (éd.), *Studies in the Mesha Inscription and Moab* (Atlanta, GA: Scholars Press): 96-130.

Jackson, K.P., et J.A. Dearman
1989 'The Text of the Mesha' Inscription', dans A. Dearman (éd.), *Studies in the Mesha Inscription and Moab* (Atlanta, GA: Scholars Press): 93-95.

Kapelrud, A.S.
1969 *The Violent Goddess Anat in the Ras Shamra Texts* (Oslo: Universitets-forlaget).

Lagrange, M.-J.
1903 *Le livre des Juges* (Paris: Gabalda).

Lammens, H.
1914 *Le berceau de l'Islam: L'Arabic occidentale à la vielle de l'Hégire. 1er volume le climat. Les bédouins* (Rome: Pontificio Istituto Biblico).

Lemaire, A.
1987 'Notes d'épigraphie nord-ouest sémitique. 19. La stèle de Mésha: épigraphie et histoire', *Syria* 64: 205-14.
1991 'La stèle de Mésha et l'histoire d'Israël', dans D. Garrone et F. Israel (éds.), *Storia e tradizioni di Israele* (Scritte in onore di J. Alberto Soggin, Brescia: Paideia): 143-69.
1994a ' "House of David" restored in Moabite Inscription', *BAR* 20.3: 30-37.
1994b 'La dynastie davidique (*byt dwd*) dans deux inscriptions ouest-sémitiques du IXe s. av. J.-C.' *SEL* 11: 17-19.

Masson, O., et M. Sznycer
1972 *Recherches sur les Phéniciens à Chypre* (Paris: Droz).

Michaud, H.
1958 *Sur la pierre et l'argile: inscriptions hébraïques et Ancien Testament. Cahiers d'archéologie biblique* (Cahiers d'archéologie biblique, 10; Neuchâtel: Delachaux et Niestlé).

Montgomery, J.A.
1951 *A Critical and Exegetical Commentary on the Books of the Kings* (ed. H.S. Gehman; ICC; Edinburgh: T. & T. Clark).

Musil, A.
1907 *Arabia Petraea. I. Moab* (Vienna: Alfred Holder).

Na'aman, N.
1994 'The Campaign of Mesha against Horonaïm', *BN* 73: 27-30.

Parker, S.B.
1997 *Studies in Scripture and Inscriptions. Comparative Studies on Narratives in Northwest Semitic Inscriptions and the Hebrew Bible* (Oxford: Oxford University Press).

Paul, S.M.
1991 *Amos* (Hermeneia Commentary; Philadelphia: Fortress Press).

Puech, E.
1994 'La stèle araméenne de Dan: Bar Hadad II et la coalition des Omrides et de la maison de David', *RB* 101-102: 215-41.

Reymond, P.
1958 *L'eau, sa vie et sa signification dans l'Ancien Testamen* (VTSup, 6; Leiden: E.J. Brill).

Robinson, E.
1841 *Biblical Researches in Palestine, Mount Sinaï and Arabia Petraea*, II (3 vols.; Boston: Crocker and Brewster).

Schumacher, G.
1913 'Eine Wetterkatastrophe in Ostjordanland', *ZDPV* 36: 314-415.

Selms, A., van
1954 *Marriage and Family Life in Ugaritic Literature* (Londres: Luzac).

Sternberger, J.-P.
1998 'Aspects cultuels de la fonction guerrière selon la Bible hébraïque' (Faculté de théologie protestante de l'Université de Strasbourg; Thèse inédite).

Vaux, R. de
1949 *Bible de Jérusalem Deuxième livre des Rois* (Paris: Éditions du Cerf).

# TALES ABOUT SENNACHERIB: THE CONTRIBUTION OF THE SYRIAC SOURCES

Amir Harrak

## *Introduction*

In 681 BCE Sennacherib, the Assyrian 'king of the universe', was assassinated in a family feud.[1] The basic ancient account of this political event is found in the Bible, 2 Kgs 19.36-37, echoed in Isa. 37.36-38 and elsewhere.[2] Here it is said that after lifting the siege of Judah, 'Sennacherib, king of Assyria, returned and resided in Nineveh. And while he was worshipping in Bêth Nisrōk his god, Adrammelek and Shareser killed him with the sword and fled to the land of Arārāṭ.' The core of this biblical account is found in a Babylonian Chronicle: 'On the twentieth day of the month Tebet Sennacherib, king of Assyria, was killed by his son in a rebellion' (Grayson 1975: 81, ll. 34-35).[3] Greek authors also wrote about the assassination with more or less the same details (Berossus; see Schnabel 1923: 269, ll. 24-25),[4] and nothing more is known about this important event.[5]

Nevertheless, a Syriac passage in the story of St Eugene adds new

1. Recent studies about the assassination of Sennacherib include Parpola (1980), Zawadski (1990) and Leichty (1991).

2. Cf. 2 Chron. 32.21-22; Tob. 1.21. Many studies were published about these biblical accounts; see mainly Gonçalves (1986: 119, 331-50 and bibliography). See also Chamaza (1992: 241-42).

3. The Nabonidus Stele (Langdon 1912: 272) and Esarhaddon, son and successor of Sennacherib, also mentioned the event (Luckenbill 1927: 199-201).

4. Jacoby 1957: III C, 386.25-28; Alexander Polyhistor, 270.19-21; 404.11-14 (Jacoby 1957: III C, 404.11-14, Abydenos).

5. The importance of the event lies in the fact that Sennacherib devoted most of his reign to military expeditions against many lands, including (mainly) Babylonia and Judah. This explains the interest of the various sources reporting the event, some with strong feelings.

and intriguing information in that it names the city in which the assassin of Sennacherib supposedly sought refuge. The only scholarly reference to this particular passage was made more than a century ago in a footnote by Budge (Thomas of Margâ 1893: cxxviii n. 1). This scholar passively noted that a monastery was built near the village 'whither Sharezer fled when he had slain his father Sennacherib'. It is worthwhile to have a fresh and close look at this seemingly unique claim. The new information about the assassination of Sennacherib, if valid, would be a rather extraordinary element to add to the biblical and other accounts dealing with this event. If the claim in question is dubious it is worth explaining the reasons for not accepting the statement and avoiding Budge's passive acceptance of it.

The passage in the story of St Eugene that deals with the assassination of Sennacherib is offered first, and is then followed by an analysis and evaluation of its contents.

## *The Syriac Text*

The Syriac story of St Eugene (Bedjan 1892: III, 376-479; esp. 446) revolves around one person, a hero so to speak, named Awgen (Eugene). Eugene was an Egyptian monk, native of the 'island' of Clysma (*Qulzum* of the Arab sources; Yāqūt 1979: IV, 387).[6] He is said to have travelled throughout Syria and northern Mesopotamia during the fourth century in order to introduce the monastic rules of Sts Anthony and Pachomius. In this context of religious piety, details about the assassination of Sennacherib that occurred one and a half millennia earlier are unexpected. The following is the Syriac passage of interest (Bedjan 1892: III, 446) in transliteration and translation:

> *wšry dntkrk bqwr̈y' dqrdw wdn'md ḥnp̈' wdn'qwr byt<ÿ> ptkr̈' w't' qdm'yt lqryt' dbšwply ṭwr' wl' pryq' sgy mn kwl' wšmh srgwg' hy dbh ytb hw' šr'ṣr br snḥrb kd 'rq mn nynw' mdynt' wbn' bh byt ptkr̈' d'bwhy wsgd hw' lh wnṭyr hw' zr'h dhn' wywblh 'dm' lzbn' hw dbh qdyš' mn' ltmn.*

> And he [Eugene] began to go around in the villages of Qardū, baptizing pagans and destroying temple(s). So he first came to a village at the foot of the mountain not too far from the Ark, the name of which was Sargūgā. In it Šar-uṣur son of Sennacherib had settled when he fled from the city of Nineveh. And in it he built his father's temple and worshipped

6. The Red Sea was called 'the sea of Qulzum' by the early arabs.

(in) it, and the offspring and progeny of this one was preserved until the time in which the holy man [Eugene] arrived there.

### *Analysis of the Syriac Text*

The above passage from the story of St Eugene adds new detail to the biblical account about the assassination of Sennacherib. It mentions the city in which the assassin sought refuge. To highlight this new detail the Syriac text will be analysed in the light of the biblical account.

#### *The Villages of Qardū*

The first contradictory element that exists between the biblical account and the Syriac text is the name of the land in which the assassin of Sennacherib is said to have taken refuge. 2 Kings 19.37 names the land Arārāṭ, whereas the Syriac text called it Qardū. The Syriac version of the Bible, the Pešītā, however, suggests that these toponyms are synonymous. Although Arārāṭ is mentioned in both the Pešītā and the Hebrew Bible in 2 Kgs 19.37,[7] in Gen. 8.3 Noah's ark is said to have rested on the 'mountains of Qardū' in the Pešītā and on the 'mountains of Arārāṭ' in the Hebrew Bible.

The identification of Arārāṭ as Qardū is by no means restricted to the Pešītā version of the Bible. At least in this particular passage, the Pešītā follows a long-standing Jewish tradition of associating *qrdw* or *qrdwn* with Arārāṭ. Josephus (first century CE) wrote that the ark of Noah had rested not on the mountains of Arārāṭ as in the Hebrew Bible, but on the mountains 'of the Cordyaeans', τῶν Κορδυαίων (Josephus, *Ant.* 1.3.5-6). Elsewhere he wrote that the remains of the ark were to be found at Καρρῶν 'Carron' (spelled elsewhere in Josephus as Καιρῶν and Καρεῶν) where curious people could see them (Josephus, *Ant.* 20.24-25). Since the mountain where the ark had rested was identified as being in more than one place, one might think that 'Carron' is Carrhae, the Latin name of 'Ḥarrān', a city south east of Edessa. But for palaeographical reasons (among others),[8] 'Carron' should be associated

7. In the Pešītā, Araraṭ is erroneously spelled 'RTD—the Syriac letters R and D are often confused in manuscripts.

8. Ḥarrān is located on a plain and does not fit as a landing-place for Noah's ark. The closest mountain to Ḥarrān is Ğabal Tektek to the east; the foothills of this mountain are 12 km away from Ḥarrān. Edessa, which is located at the foot of the Anatolian massif to the north of Ḥarrān, is some 30 km away from this city.

with the familiar Qardōn. Josephus must have been misled by a corrupt Hebrew or Aramaic transcription of the name *qrdwn* in which the ד was confused with the ר as follows: Καρρῶν < קררון < *קרדון = קרדו.[9]

Biblical Arārāṭ is identified with Qardū in rabbinic and targumic traditions 'with unusual accord' (Ginzberg 1925: 186). *Targum Pseudo-Jonathan* commented on Gen. 8.4 by saying: 'And the ark rested in the seventh month, which is the month of Nisan, on the seventeenth day of the month, upon the mountains of Qardon. The name of one mountain is Qardonia, and the name of the other mountain is Armenia' (Clarke 1984: 9). The name Qardōn is also mentioned in *Targum Onkelos* and *Gen. R.* 33.4 dealing with the flood, and in *Targum Tosefta* dealing with the assassination of Sennacherib (2 Kgs 19.37).[10] It is not difficult to see the dependence of the Pešītā on one of the Targums in this particular case. As a consequence, Syriac as well as talmudic sources[11] normally called the region northeast of the Tigris Qardū, and the inhabitants of that region Qardians (*Qardwāyē*).

It seems that this Judaeo-Christian tradition of calling biblical Arārāṭ Qardū passed on to Islam. To be sure, the Koran, which offers its own version of the story of the flood, called the mountain upon which the ark rested '(Jabal) al-Jūdī', *wastawat 'alā al-Jūdī* ('and it rested upon [mount] al-Jūdī'; *sūrat al-Hūd* 44). This name has survived up until the present time since Muslims, Christians and Yezidis call the mountain upon which the ark had rested by its Arabic name, *Jabal Jūdī*, and or by its Turkish name *Cudi Dağ*. Current scholarly studies (Fiey 1965: 574) as well as mediaeval Arabic sources (Yāqūt 1986: II, 180) identify Koranic Jūdī with a mountain in Arabia and suggest that the Prophet of Islam referred to this mountain when he talked about the flood and Noah. This might well be the case, since other nations identified one of their mountains as the one on which the ark of Noah is said to have rested (see below). Such a suggestion means that in Arabia before

9. Καρρῶν must have been reduced to Καρῶν from which other forms (Καιρῶν and Καρεῶν) were derived. All these forms refer to Qardū (Marquart 1903: 289-90 n. 4).

10. The passage in the story of St Eugene dealing with the murder of Sennacherib is not based on this Targum. Qardū is synonymous with biblical Arārāṭ in Syriac and targumic sources; the story of St Eugene and *Targum Tosefta* referred to it independently.

11. In *Yeb.* 16a: *qrdwyyn*, 'people of Qardū'.

Islam there was 'a story of Noah' that was circulating orally, and that one of its highest mountains, al-Jūdī, was designated as the one on which the ark had rested.[12] The name al-Jūdī was then applied to Mount Qardū perhaps at the beginning of the Arab conquest.[13]

The story of the flood in the Koran, including the name of its hero Noah (Arabic *nūḥ*), is essentially biblical. The many biblical details of the story had probably been conveyed through Jewish and or Christian channels; Arabia at the time of the Prophet was inhabited by large Jewish and Christian communities (Hitti 1985: 60-62). One wonders why biblical Arārāṭ, or Judaeo-Christian Qardū, was not transmitted to the Koran along with the story and its many other details. In other words, could Jūdī be a name derived from Qardū or Qurdī, as the Arab sources spell it? At least one scholar thought about this association. Several decades ago Obermeyer (1929: 132) wrote that Jūdī is simply 'verballhornt von Kardu Kurdī = Jūdī' (Jūdī is a misrepresentation of Kardu Kurdī).

With due reservation, one may support the suggestion by Obermeyer that Jūdī was a deformation of Qardū. In both Syriac and Arabic sources Qardū is written as Qurdī (see above). Aṭ-Ṭabarī (ninth century; 1987, I, 189) and Ibn Khordādhbeh (ninth to tenth centuries; 1889: 76) wrote that the ark of Noah had rested 'upon the mount of al-Jūdī in Qurdī'. Jūdī and Qurdī are a pair of words similar to such other artificial rhythmic pairs as Hārūt and Mārūt, Jūj and Mājūj, Jannes and Jambres, etc. The pair Jūdī-Qurdī may have circulated orally both before the arrival of Islam and during the early Islamic period, hence the phrase 'Jūdī bi-Qurdī' in aṭ-Ṭabarī and Ibn Khordādhbeh.

Thanks to Josephus, we know the origin of the identification of Arārāṭ with Qardū. He himself quoted Berossus, the fourth to third centuries BCE Hellenized Babylonian priest, as saying: 'a portion of the vessel still survives in Armenia on the mountain of the Cordyaeans, and [...] persons carry off pieces of the bitumen which they use as talismans' (Josephus, *Ant.* 1.3.5-6). Jerome the Egyptian, Mnaseas 'and

12. The apologist Theophylus (*Ad Autolycum* 3.C.91) mentions that the remains of the ark were to be seen in Arabia (Eisl. III.574).

13. It has even been suggested that the ethnonym Guteans (Assyrian *Qutu*) attested in cuneiform sources had favoured the transference of Koranic Ǧūdī to Qardū (Eisl. III.574). But this is hardly possible; the Guteans, as the Lullumu, were a vanished people when well-versed scribes of Assyria named them in the royal inscriptions in an almost epic manner.

many others' made the same association according to Josephus. The sources of Berossus are unknown. He may have relied on local Jewish or cuneiform sources, and if this were the case, both sources may not be earlier than the neo-Babylonian period. The country of Urartu, Arārāt of the Bible, collapsed soon after the downfall of Assyria at the beginning of the sixth century BCE and disintegrated, falling under the control of various unsubmissive tribes. Its name also disappeared little by little to be replaced by the name Armina (Armenia), among others. Xenophon, the Greek general and historian who was deeply involved militarily in Asia Minor at the very end of the fifth century BCE, named several mountainous tribes, which were warlike and unsubmissive to the Persian king, among whom were the Χαλδαῖοι, 'Khaldians' (worshippers of the Urartian god Khaldi = Urartians)[14] and the Κορδοῦχοι 'Corduchians' (Xenophon, *Anabasis* III v 15-17; IV ii 8-11, iii 1-30; iv 1; V v 17).

Apparently, the tribe of the Corduchians dominated the southeastern portion of former Urartu and gave its name to the land.[15] Xenophon specified Armenia as the place where the mountain of the Cordyaeans and presumably the Cordyaeans themselves were found (Josephus, *Ant.* 1.93). As for the Khaldians, they seem to have settled in the region between the sources of the Tigris and the Euphrates. Syriac sources dating between the fifth and eighth centuries locate their territory to the north of Amida, as far as the eastern bank of the Euphrates, where their chief city, Enzīte (Syriac and Arabic Hanzīṭ), was located. Strabo (*Geography* 7.231) has a list of cities located in Gorduene, among which were Sareisa, Satalka and Pinaka. Pinaka is the Phenek of the Syriac sources, a city located in Bēt-Zabday (Zabdicene of Ammianus Marcellinus). Bēt-Zabday was the province located between Qardū and Bēt-'Arbāyē. The fame of Mount Qardū has given this name to other places located near the mount. This is the case of a village called Qarday, which is said to have been located near Thamānūn, not far from Mount Qardū itself (Yāqūt 1979: IV, 322). One Syriac bishopric see was called Šahr-Qart (or Šahr-Grd, Arabic Šahr-Qard), Persian

14. The 'Khaldians' were presumably the same people as the ones called 'wr̈ṭy' in Syriac sources and in Arabic sources أرطان (derived from 'Urartians'; Harrak 1993: 43).

15. Some scholars tend to think that the Cordyaeans were the ancestors of the present day 'Kurds'. This association has generated controversy in modern scholarship (Nikitine 1956: 2-5).

'city of Qardy'; it was located somewhere near the Lower Zāb. Qardelabad (Syriac Šennā, Arabic al-Sinn), a city located near the junction of the Lower Zāb with the Tigris, may reflect the toponym Qardū.

The story of the flood struck the imagination of people so much that they designated more than one location as the spot on which the ark landed. The Babylonian original, from which the biblical version derives, mentioned Niṣir as the mountain upon which the ark rested (Borger 1963: III, 64, 141-44).[16] Berossus mentioned the remains of the ark πρὸς τῷ ὄρει τῶν Κορδυαίων, 'on the mountains of the Cordyaeans' (Josephus, *Ant.* 1.93). Nicolas of Damascus, whom Josephus quoted, specified 'a great mountain called Baris' in Armenia, on the summit of which 'one man, transported upon an ark', had landed (Josephus, *Ant.* 1.95). Arabia has already been mentioned as one place where the ark is also said to have landed. Armenian sources dating before the tenth century repeated the general belief that the ark had come to rest in Qardū (Armenian Kordukh). Armenian sources after that date claimed that the ark was found in Armenia proper, namely on 'Mount Arārāṭ', despite the fact that the Bible did not specify any particular mountain. Biblical 'Arārāṭ' had referred to a land, the Assyrian Urartu, not a particular mountain. As a consequence, beginning in the tenth century, the highest and best known mountain of Armenia Mount Masis became known as the place where the ark had rested. The mountain, now known as Büyük Ağri Daği, is located in eastern Turkey, near the frontier of the former Soviet Union with Iran. Not only did Mount Masis acquire a new identity, many places around it took roles traditionally given to places around Mount Qardū (see below). Thus Arnoítn became the place at which Noah came out of the ark; another place (Akori, modern Agori) was designated as the vineyard which he planted; a parallel to the village Thamānūn was created to commemorate the 8 of 80 survivors of the flood; and yet another place (Nakhichevan, now in Azerbaijan) was made to contain the remains of Noah, whereas his wife was put to rest in Marand (also in Azerbaijan; Peeters 1920: 326-28).

Nonetheless, Qardū, now better known as al-Jūdī, is widely accepted as the mountain on which the ark of Noah rested. According to the

16. The spelling of Niṣir is not beyond doubt. Niṣir/Nimuš is identified as Pir Omar Gudrun (Lambert 1980: 185-86).

story of Eugene, a special monument was built on its summit, the ruins of which have probably survived to the present day, as the following section suggests.

### *The Ark*

The story of Eugene claims that the assassin of Sennacherib had settled in a village in Qardū not far from the 'ark' (of Noah). The Syriac term for ark is *k'wl'* or *kwl'* (kēwēlā), known in the name: *Dayrā dbēth kēwēlā d'al tūray Qardū* ('Monastery of Bēth Kēwēlā which is on the mountains of Qardū'). Yāqūt (1986: II, 504) named it, *Dayr al-Jūdī*, 'Monastery of al-Jūdī', and wrote that some believed that it had been built in the time of Noah! Another Syriac term for ark is *qībūthā* (Greek κιβωτός), also found in the Arabic name of a different monastery, called *Dayr al-qībūth* ('Monastery of al-Qibūth [the Ark]').[17] Despite its name that refers to the ark, the monastery was not located in Qardū but at Gurgil (Hoffmann 1966: 175).

People have endeavoured to find traces of the ark since the time of Berossus, either out of curiosity or for religious purposes. Searching for and discovering the ark became a literary motif to describe people with exceptional holiness. In the story of Eugene (Bedjan 1892: 435-37), the literary motif of the ark is applied to James of Nisibis, and not Eugene. James is said to have searched for the ark and when he exhumed a board of it he built a monastery on the spot. Conversely, the role of Eugene is retained since he had exhorted James to find the ark. The story goes on by saying that James gave to Eugene a board of the ark and the latter made it into a cross which he installed in his cell.

Although this literary motif is propagandistic, as shall be seen later, the 'Monastery of the Ark' on Mount Qardū is not the product of imagination. The monastery is attested as early as the fifth century when the Easy Syrian Catholicos Dādīšō' sought refuge there (Vööbus 1958: I, 305). The eighth-century Chronicle of Zuqnīn (also known as Pseudo-Dionysius of Tell-Mahre) describes the total destruction of the monastery by lightning in 765–766. More than 700 or 800 persons had assembled to celebrate the feast of the Ark on 15 November of that year 'in the place where the Ark came to rest'. But lightning occurred in the sky and destroyed both the temple and the pilgrims. The

17. See Mārī in *Akhbār* (Gismondi 1899: 36).

Chronicler noted the irony of this destruction which had happened in the very place where people had once been saved from the deluge (Harrak 1999: 204-205). As noted earlier, Yāqūt mentioned the monastery that 'had built on the summit of the mountain', but that had not been rebuilt up until his time.

Jewish sources do not seem to refer to a monument commemorating the ark on the place where it landed. The Babylonian Talmud mentions Qardū not in reference to Noah but in reference to Abraham. In *B. Bat.* 91a it is said that Abraham was imprisoned in Qardū for seven years and in Kūtha for three years.[18] Rabbi Benjamin of Toledo, who visited Jazīrat ibn-'Umar between 1160 and 1173, attributed the discovery of the ark to Caliph 'Umar ibn al-Khaṭṭāb (634–644). He added that the latter dismantled the ark and used its wood to build a mosque on the spot (Asher 1840: 90-91). Yāqūt (1986: II, 179-80) wrote about this mosque which was still standing at the time of his writing (thirteenth century). Lately, a monument, *mazār*, seems to exist on Mount Jūdī, and is visited by Christians, Muslims and Yezidis in the month of August every year. Gertrude Bell visited the ruins during the first decades of this century, and there is no doubt that they were the remains of a sanctuary, or perhaps an East Syriac monastery.

Jabal Jūdī contains more than the supposed remains of the ark and a monument. A village named Thamānūn ('eighty' in Arabic), located at the foot of that mountain, commemorates the 80 people who were saved from the flood. These, however, are said to have died soon after because of a plague, although Noah again survived (Yāqūt 1986: II, 84). Moses of Khoren translated Armenian T'ĕmnis as 'eight souls', and correctly added that this detail derives from Syriac sources (Budge 1886: 32). On the plain of Mount Jūdī, many villages and towns claim to have some connection with Noah. Bespīn (Syriac *Bēth spintā*?) means 'the place of the ark'; Jam'ah (supposedly from the Arabic √JM') is the place where Noah and his family gathered; Dadar is the place from which the water sprang or the place from which Noah came out of the ark; Dōrnākh is 'the house of Noah'; there is also a place where the 'vineyard of Noah' is located and where festivities take place every year on 14 September; and finally Dēr Abūn, 'the convent of our father', contains the grave of Noah (Yāqūt 1986: II, 496), although

18. The קרטיגני in the Talmud (*Baba Kama* 114b) can hardly be the Carducene of the classical sources, see Obermeyer (1929: 134), since no such transcription dealing with Qardū is attested. The term most probably refers to Carthage.

other locations also claim the privilege of having his remains (Fiey 1965: 750-51).

Other places were also given a role to play in the story of the flood, a fact which again stresses the influence of the story upon many nations. Ibn Khordādhbeh (1889: 76) stated that the mountains of Lebanon were the place where the ark was boarded, or the place where it began to move. The ark of Noah is reported to have hit Mount Sinjār in its course, a reason for which Noah is reported to have said, *sinnu jabalin jāra 'alaynā*, 'the tip of a mountain hit us'. Even Nahavand (near Hamadhān; al-Qazwīnī 1960: 471) has been interpreted as 'Noah had placed', but this is a folk etymology.

### *Sargūgā, the Refuge of Šar-uṣur*

According to the story of Eugene, Sargūgā is a village at the foot of Mount Qardū in which the assassin of Sennacherib sought refuge and settled with his family. Sargūgā as such seems not to be attested in Greek, Latin and Semitic (including cuneiform) sources. The toponym may be a deformation of *Sargūg; Syriac authors normally added the emphatic ending -ā to personal names and toponyms of foreign origin. *Sargūg, in turn, reminds one of other toponyms that also end with -ūg, such as Mabbūg (Manbij of Arab sources), Sarūg (Sarugu of cuneiform sources, Sarūj of Arab sources), and Sarbūg (in the *Acts of Thomas*). Two of these toponyms, Mabbūg and Sarūg, are attested in historical sources. Sarbūg is not attested elsewhere. Burkitt (1903: 125-27) associated it with the ancient Mesopotamian city of Shuruppak (the scene of the flood in cuneiform sources), but this association is unlikely. Shuruppak did not survive the Old Babylonian period (first half of the second millennium BCE), and its name must have sank in oblivion. Sargūgā may have been a historical city of this name, as Sargūg and Mabbūg are. It may also be a misspelled name[19] of a historical city, or simply a fabrication made by the author of the story of Eugene, to make it sound like the historical city of Sarūg or that of Mabbūg.

With regard to the personal name of Šar-uṣur, it is attested in this

19. Misspelling of toponyms and personal names is a common weakness of ancient and mediaeval authors. Syriac chronicles spelled the name of Qūnā, the bishop who laid the foundation of the church in Edessa, as Qūrā, Yūnā and Nūnā; see Witakowski (1984–86: 492).

specific form in the Pešītā version of 2 Kgs 19.37, on which the story of Eugene must have relied. The Hebrew counterpart of the name is *sareser* (שראצר) and both are shortened forms of Assyrian Aššur-šarra-uṣur, '(God) Aššur, protect the king'. The Hebrew Bible mentions a second assassin, Adrammelech, whereas Berossus names only this latter one, in the form Adramelos or Ardumuzan. Although the Syriac text mentions only one assassin, it relied on the Pešītā both for the spelling of his name and for the identity of Šar-uṣur as the 'son of Sennacherib'. The reason it dropped the name of Adrammelech is not clear but it seems that his mention was not deemed crucial to the story as a whole.

### *Evaluation of the Passage about the Murder of Sennacherib*

Although no final word can be said about Sargūgā, there is room for doubting the claim of the story of Eugene that Šar-uṣur sought refuge in it. The following reasons support this cautious attitude.

#### *The Bible as the Basis for the Syriac Account of the Assassination on Sennacherib*

In mentioning the assassination of Sennacherib, the writer of the story of Eugene seems to have relied uniquely on biblical tradition dealing with the same event. First, nowhere outside the Bible is it said that the assassin(s) of Sennacherib took refuge in Urartu/Arārāṭ. Second, the names of both the victim and the assassin are spelled according to the Pešītā version of the Bible. Although 2 Kgs 19.37 does not say that the assassin fled from Nineveh, the Syriac account making this claim probably assumed this from the statement in 2 Kings that Sennacherib returned to Nineveh after his expedition against Judah. Although the phrase 'he fled from Nineveh' in the story of Eugene suggests that the murder took place in that city, there is no indication in ancient sources that this was the case.

There is also a brief Latin parallel to the Syriac account. In a source dated to the thirteenth century, it is stated that the Franciscan Guillaume de Ruysbroeck, ambassador of Louis IX to the Khan of Tartar, arrived at Nakhichevan (in modern Azerbaijan) on Christmas Day, 1253. There he met Armenian clerics who talked to him about the role of Mount Masis in the story of the flood, and he became aware that he was in the land in which the assassin of Sennacherib had taken refuge:

> (...) Arārāt, que est ipsa Armenia: unde in libro regum dicitur de filii(s) Cenacherip, quod interfecto patre fugerunt in terram Armenorum; et in Ysaya autem dicitur quod fugerent in terram Arārāt (Peeters 1920: 330-31).
>
> (...) Arārāt, which is Armenia: since the book of Kings states that the son(s) of Sennacherib, after they had killed their father, fled to the land of the Armenians; however, Isaiah mentions that they fled to the land of Arārāt.[20]

It is not difficult to see in both accounts harmonizing exegesis of biblical passages.

*The Literary Motif of Finding the Ark*

I noted earlier that the task of searching and finding the ark was attributed to certain people of special status, such as the Caliph ‘Umar ibn al-Khaṭṭāb. The story of Eugene states that James of Nisibis also searched for and found the ark, although upon exhortation of Eugene. According to the same story, James even gave a board of the ark to Eugene who made a cross out of it and placed it in his cell. Afterwards, James built the Monastery of the Ark on the spot where the remains of the ark were found on Mount Qardū. Eugene and his disciples were invited to the inauguration of the monastery.

It seems that in Christian hagiographic literature the motif of the ark was normally associated with James of Nisibis (Fiey 1977: 288-29). At any rate, the motif in connection with James of Nisibis was known at least as early as the fifth century, as Peeters has shown (1920: 291, 312-18); it was inserted (and adapted) into the *History of Armenia* by Pseudo-Faustus of Byzantium.[21] The passage about Sennacherib is, however, not included in the motif of the ark found in hagiographic sources. The passage, which is a mere expansion of the biblical account dealing with Sennacherib, must have been added to the story of Eugene

20. Both the Vulgate and Septuagint (Isa. 37.38) mention ‘Armenia’ as the land of refuge.

21. Garsoïan (1989: Book III, chapter x: 77-80). The origin of the story of James and the wood of the ark is a problem. This literary motif exists only in Pseudo-Faustos and Eugene, but the story of Eugene cannot be original since it is a late composition. It is possible that Pseudo-Faustos borrowed a Syriac original version of James and the Ark, and later Syriac authors borrowed (and manipulated) the Armenian translation; for other views, see Garsoïan (1989: Book III, chapter x: 252 n. 1).

(perhaps as late as the ninth century) for propagandistic reasons, as shall be seen later in this study.

*Questionable Reliability of the Story of St Eugene*

I noted earlier that Budge passively accepted the claim of the Syriac text that Šar-uṣur had sought refuge in Mount Qardū. Budge simply accepted the story of Eugene as it was, except for some extraordinary events which he rejected. After initially sharing this passive attitude, Labourt (1904: 302-15) published a critical study of the story of Eugene at the beginning of this century and discredited most of its claims. Other scholars followed suit and stressed the lack of reliability of the story of Eugene.[22]

Thus the claim in the story of Eugene that monasticism was introduced into Persia by the Egyptian Eugene near the middle of the fourth century was challenged. One main reason was the fact that early sources dealing with monasticism on Persia are totally mute about Eugene and his supposed role in early monasticism. He does not appear among the early Syriac holy men and Fathers, nor was his name borne by early Syriac Christians. The story as a whole was not known before the ninth century, a fact which casts doubt about his role in Persian monasticism. Most of his disciples—he is said to have had 70 or more—cannot be fully identified, nor are the monasteries that they supposedly founded known. With regard to the known disciples, cycles were formed about them after the thirteenth century, which were then inserted in the story of Eugene (Scher 1913: 37).

The story also includes accounts about famous personalities of the past, so as to enhance the reputation of the seemingly little known person of Eugene. He is made the contemporary and associate of James of Nisibis, the martyr Miles, and the Persian king Sapor II (all fourth century). The supposed relationship between Eugene and James of Nisibis, of interest to this essay, may be described as follows: While Eugene was settled in the mountain of Nisibis with his 70 disciples, the people of Nisibis elected James as their bishop in 309 on the basis of Eugene's advice. When Nisibis fell under Persian hegemony in 363, the Persian king Sapor is said to have permitted Eugene to travel throughout Persia to spread monasticism there. The fictitious relation-

22. See, among others, Peeters (1920: 339-41); Vööbus (1958: I, 217-20); Fiey (1970: 100-102); and Brock (1985: 108).

ship which the lesser-known Eugene had with the famous and holy man James was intended to give legitimacy to Eugene in the field of monastical and religious expansion in Persia.

There are other reasons for taking the story of Eugene as unreliable. First, it is filled with extraordinary events that invite scholarly scepticism. Eugene is said to have been a thaumaturge during his early career in Egypt, and some of his miracles, such as reviving someone devoured by a lion or walking on the water of the Tigris, are attributed to both Eugene and his disciples (Bedjan 1892: III, 437, 448; 1890: I, 446-51, 512; Scher 1913: 37). Round numbers are also found, such as the 70 disciples of Eugene, corresponding to the 70 disciples of Christ, according to the Pešītā (Lk. 10.1). Anachronisms abound. Mani (third century) is made the contemporary of Eugene (fourth century); Sapor I (third century) is confused with Sapor II (fourth century). The story also mentions several disciples who lived as late as the seventh century (John of Daylam, Babay the scribe) and the tenth century (Joseph Busnāyā, John bar Kaldūn). The cycles of stories about Eugene's disciples, which were inserted in the wider literary frame of the saint, cannot withstand historical criticism.

The exact context in which the account of Sennacherib is inserted also suggests that this account is not reliable. Missionary activities of St Eugene in the pagan region of Qardū are described as though no one had done mission work there before him. His activities consisted of baptizing pagans and destroying their temples (*byt<ÿ> ptkr̈'*). To stress the paganism of this area (and the missionary work of Eugene), the author of the story inserted the biblical account of the assassination of Sennacherib and the fleeing of the assassin to Arārāṭ, the Qardū of the Pešītā. The story wants us to believe that the paganism of the Assyrians (known through the Bible, among other sources) had continued through the Assyrian temple (*byt ptkr̈'*) built by Šar-uṣur as well as throughout the time of his successors and had supposedly survived 'until the time the holy man arrived there'. The story goes on to say that the entire city was baptized and a church was built over the old temple. The paganism of the mountain is further stressed through the person of Sennacherib, as seen in the following section.

### *Sennacherib in Later Sources*

The memory of some Assyrian rulers survived in the land of Mesopotamia centuries before Assyriology brought them to life once more through art and literature. This is, for example, the case of Sargon II. The ruins of his capital city Dūr-Sharrukīn, under its mediaeval name Khurustābādh (modern Khorsabad), was correctly identified by the thirteenth-century Arab geographer Yāqūt (1986: II, 358) as 'the ruins of Ṣar'ūn'.[23] About 2000 years separated the Arab geographer from the time when the Assyrian empire collapsed, ending Assyria as a political entity once and for all. The famous geographer must have gathered this information from the natives of the Assyrian heartland, his contemporaries, who were also aware that Athūr[24] was the ancient name of Mosul (Yāqūt 1979: I, 92) where the ruins of ancient Nineveh are found.

Nonetheless, Sennacherib is the only Assyrian ruler who stimulated the imagination of the later inhabitants of Mesopotamia. He appears in Syriac literature as a pagan ruler whose sons converted to Christianity;[25] and as a consequence of his paganism, they were killed for their faith. This is the case of mār Behnam, a Persian prince and son of 'Sennacherib, the great king of Assyria, who was a Magian',[26] who is said to have lived at the time of Julian the Apostate (fourth century). According to legend, Behnam converted from Zoroastrianism to Christianity at the hand of a disciple of Eugene living in the heartland of Assyria. When Behnam refused to worship Assyrian deities for whom Sennacherib had made a great feast, the latter killed him. Behnam's martyrium (called *gubbā*, the 'pit') is located near the monastery of the same name between Nineveh (Mosul) and Kalaḥ (Nimrod). A popular tradition claims that the martyrium contains a tunnel leading to the (Assyrian)

23. It is quite possible that the Arabic name of the Assyrian king is a garbled transcription of a Syriac original. East Syriac *gamal* (of Sargūn) is often confused with the *'ayn* (hence Ṣar'ūn). It is also possible that Arabic *'ayn* was originally a *ġayn* (both are distinguishable only by a dot), of such a spelling as Ṣarġūn, again a possible Syriac reading of a royal name. The shifting of the *sīn* to a *ṣād* in Arabic is understandable since both are voiceless dental fricatives, the second being the emphatic of the first.

24. *Athūr* is the Aramaic rendering of the Assyrian toponym Ashur 'Assyria'.

25. Other martyrs are said to have been sons and daughters of other kings. This is the case of Dauchtenshah (Persian for 'daughter of the king' of Ahwaz); see Marī in Gismondi (1899: 18-19); Gūbarlāhā was the son of Shapur (Bedjan 1892: IV, 141-63); and Adhurproy was the son of the king in Bēt Garmay (Bedjan 1890: I).

26. See the story of mār Behnam in Bedjan (1891: II, 397-441). A literary analysis of this and similar Syriac hagiographic legends is badly needed. For the time being, see Hoffmann (1966: 17-19); and Scher (1913: 88-93).

city of Nimrod, but there is no archaeological evidence for this.[27]

The story of the Persian martyr Qardāġ (Bedjan 1891: II, 442-506) also claims that this holy man was related to the 'house of Sennacherib through his mother' while he was connected to the 'house of Nimrod through his father'. Both parents of Qardāġ were Zoroastrians, as was their son, but when the latter converted to Christianity he was killed at the order of Sapor the king. Thus Sennacherib seems to have represented paganism that was to be confronted by the power of Christianity. There are many other literary motifs shared by these and other stories of holy men and martyrs, a fact which underlines their didactic character. The connection of Sennacherib with Mount Qardū seems to be a popular tradition that goes beyond the story of St Eugene. Traces of this tradition are apparently found as late as the nineteenth century in the region of Qardū. During the middle of that century a traveller named Israel Joseph Benjamin II visited northern Mesopotamia and encountered a Kurdish tribe that used to climb Mount Arārāṭ three times a year for worship. According to Benjamin, members of this tribe claimed to have been the offspring of the royal family of Sennacherib (Nikitine 1956: 26 n. 2).[28] The Armenians were also called 'Sennacheribians' in Syriac sources much earlier than the time of Benjamin (Bar Hebraeus 1932: 179).

The popular fascination with Sennacherib seems to be based, at least partially, on the Bible.[29] Here the Assyrians are seen as pagans, though used by God to achieve his divine will (Isa. 10.5-6). Sennacherib is remembered as the one who besieged the holy city of Jerusalem, and the irony of his cruel death while worshipping his god must have struck the religious sentiments of members of the three main religions, Judaism, Christianity and Islam. This is certainly true in 2 Kgs 19.36-7 and Isa. 37.36-38. Even the Babylonians realized this irony, since by destroying Babylon, Sennacherib attracted the anger of the Babylonian

27. See Abu aṣ-Ṣuf (1990: 139-41; English abstract on p. 280[5]).

28. How ancient this claim of the local Kurdish tribes is, is not known. In the middle of the nineteenth century they may have learned about Sennacherib through European travellers and archaeologists. Sennacherib left many rock inscriptions and reliefs on Mount Nibur/Nimuš (=Jabal al-Jūdī).

29. The negative representation of Sennacherib in biblical and Syriac sources contrasts sharply with the innovative achievements of this king in art, architecture, religion and politics; see Pešírková (1993: 1-10).

god Marduk.[30] Syriac authors, natives of the Assyrian heartland, were also familiar with Assyrian ‘idols’ through the many rock reliefs still standing at Khinis (Syriac: Ḥinis), Bavian and Ma‘althāiā (Parrot 1969: 73, fig. 81). Rows of anthropomorphic deities, rulers and many symbols depicted in the reliefs must have left spectators in wonder.

At any rate, the Assyrian reliefs in question were marks of paganism *par excellence* as far as the Syriac monks and authors are concerned. Thomas, bishop of Marga (ninth century), wrote about the cells carved by pioneering monks *bṭrn’ l’ mš‘bd l’sṭm’*, ‘in rocks not subjected to steel’ (Bedjan 1901: 347.13) as opposed to those that were carved with Assyrian tools. It is speculated that the caves cut in virgin rocks by monks were considered fit to become graves for deceased monks, whereas the rocks ‘manipulated’ by the ancient Assyrians (as in Khinis) were considered spoiled by paganism. They were, therefore, not fit to become the final resting place for monks unless the latter ‘purified’ them by cutting caves in them and living inside them (Fiey 1965: 788-89; Abūnā 1966: 258 n. 1). Thomas of Marga named one recluse who cut his cell into the Assyrian relief at Khinis, Ḥbīšā by name, literally ‘Recluse’. He was a native of Roman Syria but was exiled, and as a result he landed in the Assyrian heartland sometime during the fourth century CE. His cells bear Syrian architectural features, such as the pillars seen at their entrances. The remains of the recluse and those of his peers were uncovered inside one cave during the time of Thomas of Marga, who visited them (Bedjan 1901: 347).

In the light of what has just been stated, it is safe to say that the account about Sennacherib, including the detail about the parricide said to have settled on or near Mount Qardū, is an expansion of 2 Kgs 19.36-37.

### *The Legendary Character of Mount Qardū*

Perhaps the strongest reason for doubting the claim of the story of St Eugene that Šar-uṣur took refuge in Sargūgā, ‘the village at the foot of the mount not too far from the ark’, is the fact that Mount Qardū, where Sargūgā was supposedly located, is the focus of many legends and the aforementioned claim can be just one of them.

It goes without saying that the reputation of Qardū is based on the story of the flood. Since Sumerian times people had been fascinated

30. See the stela of Nabonidus (555–539 BCE) in *ANET*: 308-309.

with the story of the flood and its hero Noah (or his counterparts). Qardū was identified since the time of Berossus (if not earlier) with the mountain on the top of which the ark is said to have rested, Many places around Mount Qardū were given names related to various aspects of Noah's life as depicted in the biblical story; most of these names have survived to this day. On the basis of this same story, other mountains, such as Arārāṭ (=Ağri dağ), have also been identified as the ones that welcomed the ark of Noah, contradicting a tradition, which is at least one and a half thousand years older, that had opted for Qardū (= Jūdī). Even today, archaeologists and amateurs, fascinated by the story of the flood and misled by conflicting identifications of the mountain of Noah, are still searching for traces of the ark on Arārāṭ. All these details underline the legendary character of Mount Qardū, and by the same token discredit the claim of the story of Eugene that it became the refuge of Šar-uṣur.

### *Conclusion*

The relatively late Syriac writer (ninth century) of the account of St Eugene was aware of the importance of Qardū. He knew also that in the Pešītā the Qardū of Gen. 8.3 was the Arārāṭ of 2 Kgs 19.37; this explains why he mentioned the ark and the assassination of Sennacherib in one and the same passage. But he also knew how to manipulate an early tradition (fifth century) about James of Nisibis that associates him with the ark, by including Eugene in its main details. He projected on his hero, Eugene, a role that he never played, namely that of converting the people living around Mount Qardū, where supposedly the assassin of Sennacherib sought refuge.

The account of the assassination of Sennacherib in the story of Eugene is a mixture of legends (Qardū and the ark, James and the ark), manipulation (connection between James of Nisibis and Eugene), and imagination (Eugene's conversion of pagans and the introduction of monasticism into Persia). The detail about Sennacherib and Šar-uṣur is one among many historical-sounding elements used to add credibility to the fallacious claim that Eugene introduced monasticism into Persia.

## BIBLIOGRAPHY


Abu aṣ-Ṣūf

1990 ''Aḍwā' 'alā 'aṯariyyat dayr mār Bihnām wa-ḍarīḥihi' ('Light on the Archaeology of the Monastery of St Bihnām and its Mausoleum'), in Ǧ. Cas-Mūsā (ed.), *Dayr mār Bihnām aš-šahīd: Kitāb al-yūbīl al-mi'awī as-sādis 'ašar (Monastery of Mār Bihnām the Martyr: The Sixteen Hundred Years Jubilee Book)* (Baghdad: al-Dīwān Press): 139-44.

Abūnā, A.

1966 *Kitāb ar-ru'asā' (Book of Superiors)* (Mosul: al-'Aṣrīyyā Press).

Asher, A. (trans.)

1840 *The Itinerary of Rabbi Benjamin of Tudela I* (New York: 'Hakesheth' Publishing).

Aṭ-Ṭabarī

1987 *Tarikh ar-rusul wal-mulūk*, I (History of the Prophets and the Kings) (ed. M. Ibrahim; Cairo: Dār al-Ma'ārif).

Bar Hebraeus

1932 *The Chronography of Gregory Abû'l Faraj the son of Aaron, the Hebrew Physician Commonly Known as Bar Hebraeus Being the First Part of his History of the World*, II (trans. E.A.W. Budge; Oxford: Oxford University Press).

Bedjan, P.

1890 *Acta martyrum et sanctorum syriace*, I (repr. 1968; Paris: Harrassowitz).

1891 *Acta martyrum et sanctorum syriace*, II (repr. 1968; Paris: Harrassowitz).

1892 *Acta martyrum et sanctorum syriace*, III (repr. 1968; Paris: Harrassowitz).

1894 *Acta martyrum et sanctorum syriace*, IV (repr. 1968; Paris: Harrassowitz).

1901 *Liber Superiorum seu historia monastica coenobii Beth-Abensis autore Thoma, Episcopo Margensi* (Leipzig: Otto Harrassowitz).

Borger, R.

1963 *Babylonisch-Assyrische Lesestücke* (3 vols.; Rome: Pontificio Istituto Biblic.).

Brock, S.

1985 *Luminous Eye: The Spiritual World Vision of St. Ephrem* (Rome: Center for Indian and Inter-religious Studies).

Budge, E.W. (trans.)

1886 *The Book of the Bee* (Oxford: Clarendon Press).

Burkitt, F.C.

1903 'Sarbôg, Shuruppak', *JTS* 4: 125-27.

Chamaza, G.W.V.

1992 'Sanheribs letzte Ruhestätte', *BZ* 36: 241-49.

Clarke, E.G.

1984 *Targum Pseudo-Jonathan of the Pentateuch: Text and Concordance* (Hoboken, NJ: Ktav Publication House Inc.).

Fiey, J.
1965 *Assyrie Chrétienne: Contribution à l'étude de l'histoire et de la géographie ecclésiastiques et monastiques du nord de l'Iraq*, II (Beirouth: Imprimerie catholique).
1970 *Jalons pour une histoire de l'église en Iraq* (Louvain: Secrétariat du CSCO).
1977 *Nisibe métropole syriaque et ses suffragants des origines à nos jours* (Louvain: Secrétariat du CSCO).

Garsoïan, N. G.
1989 *The Epic Histories* (Buzandaran Patmut'iwnk') (Cambridge, MA: Harvard University Press).

Ginzberg, L.
1925 *The Legends of the Jews*, V (Philadelphia: Jewish Publication Society of America).

Gismondi, H. (ed.)
1899 *Akhbār fatarika kursī al-mashriq min kitab al-majdal Mārī ibn Sulayman* (Rome: C. De Luiggi).

Gonçalves, F.J.
1986 *L'expédition de Sennachérib en Palestine dans la littérature Hébraïque ancienne* (Louvain-la-Neuve: Université catholique de Louvain, Institut orientaliste).

Grayson, A.K.
1975 *Assyrian and Babylonian Chronicles* (Texts from Cuneiform Sources, 5; Locust Valley, NY: J.J. Augustin).

Harrak, A.
1993 'The Survival of the Urartian People', *Bulletin of the Canadian Society for Mesopotamian Studies* 25: 43-49.
1999 *The Chronicle of Zuqnīn, Parts III and IV, AD 488–775, translated from the Syriac, with Notes and Introduction* (Mediaeval Sources in Translation, 36; Toronto: Pontifical Institute of Mediaeval Studies).

Hitti, P.K.
1985 *History of the Arabs* (London: Macmillan, 10th edn).

Hoffmann, G.
1966 *Auszüge aus syrischen Akten persischer Märtyrer* (Liechtenstein: Nendeln Kraus).

Ibn Khordādhbeh
1889 *Kitâb al-Masâlik wa'l-Mamâlik* (ed. M.J. De Goege; Leiden: E.J. Brill).

Jacoby, F.
1957 *Die Fragmente der griechischen Historiker*, III (Leiden: E.J. Brill).

Labourt, J.
1904 *Le Christianisme dans l'empire perse sous la dynastie sassanide* (Paris: Librairie Victor Lecoffre).

Lambert, W.G.
1980 'Nisir or Nimuš', *RA* 80: 185-86.

Langdon, H.
1912 *Die neubabylonischen Königsinschriften* (Vorderasiastische Bibliothek, 4; Leipszig: J.C. Hinrichs).

Leichty, E.
1991 'Esarhaddon's "Letter to the Gods" ', in M. Cogan and I. Eph'al (eds.), *Ah, Assyria...:Studies in Assyrian History and Ancient Near Eastern Historiography Presented to Hayim Tadmor* (Scripta Hierosolymitana, 33; Jerusalem: Magnes Press).

Luckenbill, D.D.
1927 *Ancient Records of Assyria and Babylonia*, II (Chicago: University of Chicago Press).

Marquart, J.
1903 *Osteuropäische und ostasiatische Streifzüge: Ethnologische und historisch-topographische Studien zur Geschichte des 9. und 10. Jahrhunderts (ca 840–940)* (Leipzig: T. Weichen; repr. Hildesheim: G. Olms, 1961).

Nikitine, B.
1956 *Les Kurdes: Etude sociologique et historique* (Paris: Imprimerie nationale).

Obermeyer, J.
1929 *Die Landschaft babylonien im Zeitalter des Talmuds und des Gaonats* (Frankfurt am Main: I. Kauffmann Verlag).

Parpola, S.
1980 'The Murderer of Sennacherib', in B. Alster (ed.), *Death in Mesopotamia* (XXVI Rencontre Assyriologique Internationale [Mesopotamia 8]; Copenhagen: Akademisk Forlag): 171-82.

Parrot, A.
1969 *Assur* (Paris: Editions Gallimard).

Peeters, P.
1920 'La légende de saint Jacques de Nisibe', *Analecta Bollandiana* 38: 285-373.

Pešírková, J.
1993 'Assyria under Sennacherib', *ArOr* 61: 1-10.

Qazwīnī, al-
1960 *Āthār al-Bilād wa'akhbār al-'Ibād* (Beirut: Dār Ṣādir).

Scher, A.
1913 *Kaldū wa-Āthūr*, II (Beirut).

Schnabel, P.
1923 *Berossos und die babylonisch-hellenistische Literatur* (Leipzig: Teubner).

Strabo
1930 *The Geography of Strabo* (LCL, 7; trans. H.L. Jones; repr. 1966; Cambridge, MA: Harvard University Press).

Thomas of Margâ
1893 *The Book of Governors: The Historia Monastica of Thomas Bishop of Margâ AD 840* (trans. E.A.W. Budge; London: Oxford University Press).

Vööbus, A.
1958 *History of Asceticism in the Syrian Orient: A Contribution to the History of Culture in the Near East*, I–III (CSCO, 14, 17, 81; Louvain: Secrétariat du CSCO).

Witakowski, W.
1984–86 'Chronicles of Edessa', *OrSuec* 33-35: 487-98.

Wüstenfeld, H.F. (ed.)
1866–73 *Jacuts Geographisches Wörterbuch* (6 vols.; Leipzig: F.A. Brokhhaus).
Yāqūt al-Ḥamawi
1979–86 *Mu'jam al-Buldān (Dictionary of Countries)* (4 vols.; Beirut: Dar Ṣādir).
Zawadzki, S.
1990 'Oriental and Greek Traditions about the Death of Sennacherib', *SAA Bulletin* 4.1: 69-72.

# PHOENICIAN INSCRIPTIONS FROM TELL EL-MASKHUTA

R. Theodore Lutz

## *Excavation History*

Tell el-Maskhuta is located about 15 kilometres west of Ismailia in the eastern delta of Egypt. The *tell* lies on the valley floor of an extinct branch of the Nile which once drained eastwards into the marshy area halfway between Port Said and Suez. The valley is today called the wadi Tumilat, and contains a sweet-water canal which flows towards Lake Timsa, now a part of the modern Suez canal system.

Excavations at Tell el-Maskhuta constitute the major component of the Wadi Tumilat Project (hereafter WTP), a regional survey of the entire wadi. Dr J.S. Holladay, Jr, of the University of Toronto, is principal investigator of the Project, and the Director of Excavations.[1] An introductory survey and feasibility study of the site in 1977 was followed by five major seasons of excavation between 1978 and 1985, in which the most rigorous excavation techniques and methodology currently practised were applied.[2] Dr C. Redmount, then of the University

1. I am pleased here to acknowledge my indebtedness and thanks to Dr Holladay, not only for the intellectual stimulation he has provided by word and deed both in the field and in the corridors and offices of academia, and for permission to make public the following information, but also for his willingness to assist in the production of this essay. I would like to thank also the laboratory staff of the WTP, without whose careful work nothing would be disseminated. I especially would like to express my gratitude to Patricia Paice, whose knowledge of things related to the WTP and whose judgment in matters of ceramics and stratigraphy are second only to the Director's. Ms Paice has cheerfully supplied me with data beyond what was ultimately considered relevant for this essay and has read an earlier draft of it. What failings remain are to be attributed to me alone.

2. The WTP was funded in the early years by the Smithsonian Institution of Washington, DC, since 1981 by the Social Sciences and Humanities Research Council of Canada, and has been significantly assisted by the Society for the Study of Egyptian Antiquities. It is sponsored by the University of Toronto, the American

of Chicago, now at Berkeley, conducted an extensive surface survey of the whole wadi in 1983.

Of utmost concern to the Director and his corps of excavators was that extreme care be taken to ensure absolute control over the stratigraphy (Holladay 1982: 10-11). Considerable stratigraphical analysis has been done in the years since excavations ceased, and some results now seem assured. The site was occupied for about a century during the Second Intermediate period (in Syro-Palestinian archaeological terms, Middle Bronze IIA and B), then completely abandoned for over 1000 years until a town was built there in the time of Necho II, about 610 BCE, and fortified within a few years. Evidence of continuous habitation for the next two centuries, through the Saite dynasty and early Persian period before Egyptian independence in 404 BCE, is abundant. A third period of occupation occurred during Ptolemaic times, and, finally, a fourth during the rule of the Roman emperors Trajan and Hadrian (Holladay 1992: 588-90).

## *The Inscribed Sherds*

While actual excavations were in progress, the archaeological team and support staff were housed in the local school attached to the village situated on the edge of the *tell*. After the first season a major extension to the school was constructed—a gift to the school from the WTP—in one specially secured room of which all objects of any significance, by whatever definition, were stored. At the completion of excavations in 1985, all the major finds and the Egyptian Antiquities Department's share of minor finds were removed from the storeroom, crated and transported to Cairo. Among all the other artefacts that were shipped to the Cairo Museum in August 1985 was a box marked 'ostraca', containing 289 carefully packed sherds, each of which had one or more marks on it which were thought to be letters. Fifty-eight of them seemed sufficiently significant to be separately packaged and labelled 'Study Collection'.

Photographs of each of the sherds had been taken within days of its recovery from the ground.[3] A team of artists, when time permitted, took

Schools of Oriental Research, the American Research Center in Egypt, and is affiliated with the Canadian Institute in Egypt.

3. The WTP was fortunate to have D. Loggie present in the field for the 1979 season, and J. Peacock for the 1981, 1983 and 1985 seasons. Both were gifted

turns at attempting to sketch what they thought they saw on the sherd. These laboratory drawings, by artists with good eyes and obedient hands, but no knowledge of ancient languages, provide an independent interpretation of what is/was actually on the jar or sherd and afford some control over (or verification of) an epigrapher's reading. When, in August 1986, I spent four days in the Cairo Museum, handling each sherd in the study collection, making a careful eye inspection and taking notes, it turned out that the photographs I had brought with me—in the majority of cases—revealed more information than the actual sherd. Some letters were already so faint that without the eye inspection at the time the sherd came out of the ground, it would be easy to believe that, in fact, no marking was on the sherd at all.

The reason for this was that salts in the soil in which the sherds had been buried for more than 2000 years had, under pressure, penetrated the sherd. Now that the pressure was removed, the salt was all too quickly coming to the surface and spreading out over it. The process of removing the salt also risked removing the ink. When sherds recovered in 1978 and 1979 were again examined in 1986, the deterioration was so extensive that virtually nothing was gained by a re-investigation of the original sherd.[4]

Another problem even before the salt appeared was the presence of manganese deposits on the surface of the sherds. Matters were made worse by the fact that the colour of the ink and the manganese are identical.[5] In an illegible text, there were times when no one on the pottery-reading team could tell whether it was ink or not.

Photographs of all 289 sherds that might be ostraca or possibly contain an inscription were studied by a team, one member of which—Professor R.J. Williams of the University of Toronto—was knowledgeable in all languages of the ancient Near East and a recognized authority in those from Egypt. As might be expected from excavating in the sands of Egypt, in layers from the second half of the first millennium

professional photographers, and their photographs have proven to be immensely valuable.

4. Mr Peacock re-photographed in 1981 some of the sherds that had already been photographed in 1978 and 1979. Superior photographer though he was, the 'better' photograph revealed fewer legible features than the earlier one.

5. As but one example, and by no means the worst in terms of quantity, on the right hand side of the sherd M79-125 the colour of the ink is identical to the colour of the manganese on the left.

BCE, the majority and most legible of the writings turned out to be Demotic.

Clearly Egyptian texts, mostly Demotic[6] but a few Hieratic,[7] were assigned to Williams for further study, whereas alphabetic writing[8] was assigned to me. After intense scrutiny of the photographs, the divisions were further culled to produce two collections of sherds that might profit by further investigation—the larger of Egyptian inscriptions, the smaller of alphabetic ones consisting of a maximum of 50 ostraca to be discussed here. A few Greek,[9] and possibly one or two Latin,[10] texts are as yet unassigned, as well as those that may be Coptic.[11] In spite of our apparent confidence in assigning almost two-thirds of these sherds to a specific language designation, the fact is that all are to one degree or another difficult to decipher. We have no sure markers by which to classify the remaining 100 or so sherds in our initial collection. About a third (or 10% of the total collection) has turned out to contain no writing after all,[12] or to be drawings[13] or potter's marks.[14] That still

6. There could be as many as 118 sherds containing Demotic letters.

7. As many as eight sherds may contain Hieratic letters, with another four possibilities from the sherds identified as more likely Demotic. In addition, Williams labelled another 12 'Egyptian' without determining further whether the script might be Demotic, Hieratic or cursive Hieroglyphic. Apart from Hieroglyphic inscriptions on limestone, not included among the collection of sherd inscriptions, M78-045 and M78-101 seem to contain Hieroglyphic writing.

8. In attempting to categorize the various scripts, in virtually all cases extremely fragmentary, we termed those that were not Egyptian or Coptic/Greek/Latin 'alphabetic' (17 sherds). Where we could not make out the letters well enough to differentiate languages we simply called them 'Semitic' (6 sherds). Sherds containing Phoenician letters were classified according to maybe (11), possible (6) or probable (9). At least one sherd contains Aramaic letters, see n. 18 below. See the section 'Phoenician Ostraca by Registry Number' below for details.

9. M78-027, M78-029, M78-099, M78-128, M78-135, M78-152, M78-176, M78-398, M79-193, M81-837, M81-853, M85-440, M85-452, M85-463, M85-464. In all cases only a very few letters remain; it is possible on one or two sherds that the inscription is Coptic rather than Greek, and in at least one, M78-176, Latin is a possibility.

10. M81-852 is a probable candidate as a carrier of Latin letters, and M79-420 a possible one, as well as M78-176 mentioned in the previous note.

11. M78-009 and M78-623, and possibly M78-029, M78-135 and M78-176 listed among the Greek fragments in n. 9 above.

12. M78-464, M79-208a, M79-332, M83-181, M85-248. Almost surely more belong to this category than are here listed.

leaves somewhat more than a quarter that are so illegible as to be unamenable to any deciphering, apart from the tantalizing feeling that what is there is some part of a language.[15]

Several sherds have only one mark, and if it is encircled in space, the likelihood is that some of them may merely be a potter's mark or some other symbol. If it lies at the edge of the sherd, the possibility exists that it may be a letter of the alphabet. A few sherds contain marks which appear to represent numbers.[16]

Forty-five (90%) of the writings identified as alphabetic were found on sherds from imported amphora jars. Six (12%) of these were of Thasian ware, a ceramic particularly suited as a writing medium and used even more frequently on which to write Demotic texts. Thirty-six (72%) turned out to be written on Phoenician storage jar sherds,[17] and three others (6%) from the Levantine coast. Only five (10%) were of 'Egyptian' origin, though even these probably were manufactured somewhere other than at Tell el-Maskhuta. It is possible that none of these texts was written at Maskhuta, but the probability is that 25% or more were not written in the Phoenician homeland. At least some had to have been written somewhere along the commercial route for which the Phoenicians were so famous. These texts may be notes or receipts with ephemeral value. As such, one would expect them to have been produced where they were found. As many as 75%, but more likely

13. M78-212, M78-401, M78-466, M78-605, M79-153b, M79-154a, M79-209, M79-364, M79-417, M79-575, M79-739, M81-334, M81-588, M81-562, M85-176, M85-250, M85-275. Some of the markings on the above sherds look like identifiable objects, or may be part of an object, but they are not obviously letters in any script known from the ancient Near East.

14. M78-206, M79-183, M79-585, M81-275, M81-276, M81-842, M83-040. It may be that none of these sherds contains potter's markings, but the impressions on them seem to be isolated, unrelated to any other markings and unrecognizable as letters.

15. It may be only a figment of our imagination that some markings look like they might have been made in modern times, such as notes from Naville's excavations (M78-477), Arabic (M78-533, M79-575, M79-663, M81-207), compass points (M81-422), or be the doodling of an ancient schoolboy (M81-526).

16. Half a dozen sherds (M79-137, M79-235c, M79-364, M81-190, M85-276, M85-285) consist only of short vertical strokes, which might be Hieratic numbers that could result from the efforts of individuals conversant in any one or more of several ancient languages from this region.

17. See the section 'Ceramic Ware of the Phoenician Ostraca' below for details.

much less, may be remnants of labels such as the one published by Naveh (1987: 27).

Thus, in spite of the famous Maskhuta silver bowls with an engraved Aramaic dedication (Rabinowitz 1956, 1959; Dumbrell 1971), we came to believe our inscriptions were not Aramaic, but Phoenician. Most of the deciphering is still to be carried out, but this working assumption has not yet been decisively negated by the evidence.[18] Patricia Paice, of the University of Toronto, has undertaken a detailed study of the typology of the Phoenician storage jars found at Maskhuta. Her results, as far as their relevance for this study is concerned, are presented in the section 'Ceramic Ware of the Phoenician Ostraca' below.

Whether we were looking at fragments of inscriptions inked onto the jar at the time shortly after manufacture or at an actual ostracon—that is, the secondary use of a sherd for writing purposes—is not always easy to determine. It proves easier to rule out the possibility of a text being an 'inscription' than it does to establish it. An inscription related to the content or ownership of the jar would be meant to be read when the jar was upright. Each sherd was, therefore, noted as to the direction of the lines relative to the plane of the jar. Much spalling had taken place in many cases, but a significant number were sufficiently intact to establish where the horizontal plane was. In spite of the shape of the sherd now, most were found to have inscribed lines parallel with the horizontal finger striations on the interior. Those lines of writing inscribed not on the horizontal plane of the jar were presumed to be ostraca. For example, the writing on M85-178 (Fig 3d) is 45$^{\circ}$ off the horizontal of the jar from which the sherd came, suggesting rather strongly that the text is an ostracon rather than an inscription from the time of the jar's manufacture or first use. This conclusion may be confirmed by the apparent completeness of the text—space to the left and apparently a lamedh at the beginning, though a letter or part of a letter may be missing at the beginning of the second line.

If the horizontal plane could not be determined by finger striation, there was the possibility that a feature such as a rim or shoulder would establish where 'up' was. Sherd M85-84 was spalled on the interior,

18. Professor Philip C. Schmitz, of Eastern Michigan University, Ypsilanti, has kindly undertaken the arduous task of deciphering these fragments, and has supplied a reading and interpretation of M81-226. He has also identified at least one of the inscriptions (M81-336a) as Aramaic, so this statement is no longer absolutely accurate.

but the remnant of a shoulder in one corner shows that the inscription, relative to the shoulder, was clearly written after the jar had become a sherd, and thus was an ostracon.

Another method of determining whether a text was an inscription or not was to match the ceramic ware of the sherd with the script. A Phoenician inscription on a Phoenician amphora is expected, but a Phoenician inscription on a non-Phoenician ceramic ware is not expected. The presence of Phoenician writing on what for a Phoenician merchant(?) would be a foreign object suggests a secondary use of the object. By this criterion, the sherd M79-161, as small a piece as it is, and though the text (written on the exterior) is brief, has to be an ostracon. The writing, even if it turns out not to be Phoenician, is *not* Greek—but the sherd is a part of a jar whose life began on the Greek island of Thasos! Another text is written on this same sherd, but *on the interior*, and that text obviously is also an ostracon. Regrettably, it has been fragmented again after being inscribed.

Jars or ostraca are found with bilingual texts, though in too fragmentary a state for us to know whether each language is conveying the same information. In the large fragment M78-513, pieced together from seven smaller fragments, the top three lines are Phoenician, while the bottom two are Demotic. This particular jar even had a drawing of a human, though it is far enough removed from the writing not likely to be related to it. The sherds come from a particularly good locus, which can be dated to c. 600 BCE.

We even have a palimpsest ostracon, M79-148, with an earlier Demotic text—once again on a Thasian sherd!—being overwritten by what might be a Phoenician one. There are important implications if one accepts this interpretation, however, since, if correct, it would seem to indicate the presence of Phoenicians at Maskhuta.

If we can rely on the 'basket' dates[19] provided by the pottery-reading team and the stratigraphical analysis,[20] we have at least two sherds from as early as before 600 BCE, though only by a few years. At the

19. The basket number has not been given among the details of each Phoenician ostracon, but a 'translation' into a more meaningful date has. Some are only generally assigned to the Saite, Persian, Hellenistic or Roman periods. Others are delineated by centuries or partial centuries. A few, found in well-articulated (usually destruction) levels, have bravely been supplied with precise dates, even so with a c. before it.

20. See Locus Descriptions below for details.

other end, we have texts from after 400 BCE, and possibly as late as the second or first century BCE. Every period in between is represented. There could be up to eight ostraca from the Saite period, as many as 25 from the Persian period, possibly three to five from the years of Egyptian independence, and the remainder from the Hellenistic or Ptolemaic period. It has always been known that the Phoenicians were active traders throughout the Mediterranean during the first millennium. It comes as no surprise to see evidence of their activity, if not actually their presence, in Egypt during the Persian period, when they were normally allies of the Persian government. To see indications of their activity in the Saite and Ptolemaic centuries as well speaks volumes about their attitude to commerce.

Quantity alone makes the Maskhuta Phoenician texts significant. When analysis of these texts is complete, it may be possible to fill in some of the gaps in our palaeographic charts. Once we know what the texts say, we may be in a more knowledgeable position about the movement of goods and people along the Levantine coast.

*Ceramic Ware of the Phoenician Ostraca*[21]

The Phoenician ostraca discovered at Tell el-Maskhuta are almost invariably sherds (49/50) from large container-amphorae and mostly imported. Some could be labels or dockets on trade amphorae, the rest are ostraca written on the sherd after the vessel was broken into tablet-size pieces. In all cases the ware is hard and presents a smooth surface (with the exception of 4j), making it easy to write on. The light-coloured surface easily enables the writing to be seen.

*Phoenician Wares (4a: 1/50; 4c: 3/50; 4e: 32/50)*

Most of the corpus consists of ceramic wares of Phoenician origin. These sherds are all of the type known as 'crisp-ware' from Patricia Bikai's description of the storage-jars excavated at Tyre. These wares are all very hard, dense and well fired, with either no core or a pale coloured core. A significant amount of limestone is always present as an inclusion in the clay and also some iron oxide. The differences between the three wares are largely a matter of fabric and surface colour, probably due to variations in firing and variations in the proportions of limestone and iron oxide present.

21. This section was initially written by P. Paice, but the format has been altered by the author (and editors).

Plate 1a M77-001

Plate 1b M79-142

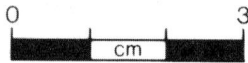

Plate 2 M78-513

Plate 3c M81-336a

Plate 3a M79-716

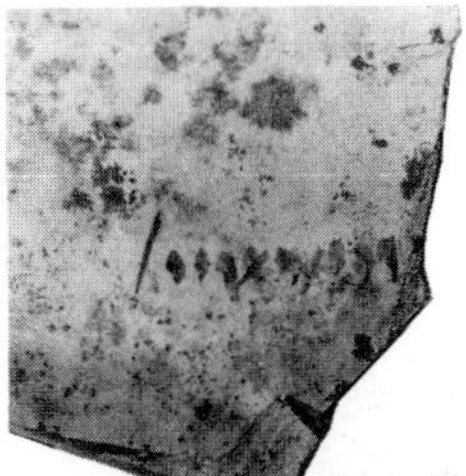

Plate 3d M85-178

Plate 3b M81-226

Plate 3e M85-247

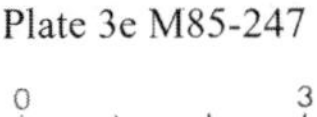

*Phoenician Ostraca by Registry Number*

| Reg. Num | Locus<br>Remarks | Ware | Basket Date[1] | Script | Preserved |
|---|---|---|---|---|---|
| M77-001 | surface find | Phoenician[2] | unknown | Semitic | 5 or 6 letters |
| | Aramaic/Phoenician. The letters appear to be positioned upside down on the storage-jar sherd, thus evidence of secondary rather than original writing (Pl. 1a). | | | | |
| M78-114 | H1: 1001 | Ashdod[3] | late Hellenistic | Semitic | 4 or 5 letters |
| | The letters are illegible, partially worn away, but are not Demotic or Greek. | | | | |
| M78-465 | L2: 2004 | Thasian[4] | sixth/fifth cent. | alphabetic | 3 lines |
| | The forms are peculiar. The script may be mixed; it is not Egyptian. | | | | |
| M78-467 | H1: 1001 | Egyptian-10g[5] | unknown | alphabetic | 1 line |
| | The writing is largely illegible; the possibility of Hieratic cannot be eliminated. | | | | |
| M78-468 | L2: 2004 | Phoenician | second/first cent. | alphabetic | 3 lines |

1. The basket date is not necessarily the date of a specific sherd, nor is it the date of the script based on palaeography.
2. The default Phoenician ware is 4e (32/50=32 out of 50 ostraca). Other Phoenician sherds have -4a (1/50) or -4c (3/50) attached to distinguish which ware type the sherd is. See the following section for a description of ware types.
3. There is only one sherd of the type 4j, but the Levantine type 12a (2/50) may also come from the Ashdod region.
4. There are six sherds of ware type 7k. Since there is no other Thasian type, it is unmarked.
5. The term 'Egyptian' signifies a ware that comes from off-site, but is North African in origin rather than Aegean or Syria-Palestinian. There are four sherds classified in this way, two of type 10g, one each of 10j and 11.

| Reg. Num | Locus<br>Remarks | Ware | Basket Date | Script | Preserved |
|---|---|---|---|---|---|
| | At the apex are two lines of small, neat, separate characters. At the base is one line of large, flowing characters from a different hand. In both cases, letters are only partially extant, indicating that the sherd has been broken (again?) after it was used as an ostracon. | | | | |
| M78-469 | L2: 2004 | Thasian | Persian/Hellenistic | Semitic?[6] | 2 lines |
| | About a dozen signs are clustered together, not well 'lined' up. There are as many as four signs placed under six or seven others. | | | | |
| M78-513b | L2: 2037 | Phoenician | sixth cent. | Phoenician![7] | 3 lines |
| | M78-513b consists of three sherds which join (Pl. 2). This three-piece sherd was then joined to the left edge of 513a, also made up of three sherds. To the upper right of 513a another sherd, 513c, joins. 513a carries a two-line Demotic(?) inscription, the top line of which seems to continue into the bottom piece of 513b which contains four lines of script, the top three Phoenician, the bottom one apparently the continuation of the Demotic of 513a. 513c has on it a drawing of the head of what appears to be a warrior. His nose is completed in 513a, and his body missing, presumably on sherds never recovered. Drawing and both inscriptions are all on the horizontal plane of the jar, thus were inscribed while the jar was still intact, but not at the time of manufacture. | | | | |
| M79-087a | L2: 2102 | Phoenician | c. 450–405 | alphabetic | 2 lines |
| | Nothing is legible any longer, even on the photographs. | | | | |

6. A question mark (?) indicates 'only possible'.
7. An exclamation mark (!) indicates 'probable'.

| Reg. Num | Locus<br>Remarks | Ware | Basket Date | Script | Preserved |
|---|---|---|---|---|---|
| M79-088 | L3: 3008 | Phoenician | c. 400 | Phoenician? | 2 lines |
| | The bottom line consists of three short, slightly curved vertical strokes. They may represent the numeral '3', while the top line states what the jar contains. | | | | |
| M79-096a | L2: 2102 | Phoenician | c. 405, Hell./Rom. | alphabetic | 3 letters |
| | Vertical strokes; possibly numbers. | | | | |
| M79-125 | L2: 2102 | Levantine | Persian, Hell./Rom. | Phoenician! | 4 letters |
| | The letters are written perpendicular to the horizontal plane of the jar. | | | | |
| M79-142 | L2: 2101 | Phoenician | late Saite, Persian | Phoenician! | 1 line + |
| | A complete mouth, rim and shoulder of a Phoenician storage jar. A line of about ten letters, only five or six of which are at all legible, is inscribed 4 cm below the shoulder. To the right of them, about 2 cm higher, is a single large character. This inscription may well indicate the contents of the jar (Pl. 1b). | | | | |
| M79-148 | L2: 2102 | Thasian | Saite, Pers. Hell./Rom. | Phoenician? | 2 lines |
| | A small sherd (6 cm × 5 cm) filled with letters. Dark, carefully executed letters of a formal style (Semitic) seem to be written over lighter, more flowing letters (Demotic), giving the impression of a palimpsest. No letters flow off the edges of the irregularly shaped sherd, suggesting that the inscription is complete. | | | | |
| M79-149a | L2: 2102 | Phoenician | late Saite, Hell./Rom. | Phoenician | 1 sign |
| | One clear mark is evident, but no other ink marks are present. | | | | |
| M79-161 | L2: 2102 | Thasian | Saite, Pers., Hell./Rom. | alphabetic | 3 and 2 lines |

| Reg. Num | Locus<br>Remarks | Ware | Basket Date | Script | Preserved |
|---|---|---|---|---|---|
| | Inscribed on both sides, three lines of 12 letters on the interior and two lines of five or six letters on the exterior. The sherd is small (less than 4 cm × 4 cm) and the letters crowd the edges. The inscription(s) is/are probably incomplete. | | | | |
| M79-201 | L2: 2102 | Phoenician | Saite, Pers., Hell./Rom. | Semitic! | 1 sign |
| | One clear mark is evident, but no other ink marks are present. | | | | |
| M79-236 | L3: 3027 | Thasian | c. 568 | alphabetic | 2 lines |
| | There appear to be three letters on each line. Nothing can be made of the bottom group, but the top looks more like an alphabetic script. | | | | |
| M79-237 | E20: 20002 | Egyptian-11 | late Hell./early Rom. | alphabetic | 1 line |
| | Up to four smudged letters on an Egyptian amphora. | | | | |
| M79-259 | E20: 20002 | Egyptian-10g | late Hell./early Rom. | alphabetic? | 3 letters |
| | Three or four letters moving to the left edge; the text is probably incomplete. | | | | |
| M79-384 | H8: 8049 | Phoenician | slightly pre-601 | alphabetic! | 2 lines |
| | Five letters in the first line, six in the second, and a single letter or two below the second. | | | | |
| M79-578 | L2: 2102 | Phoenician | Persian, Hell./Rom. | Semitic | 3 letters |
| | Three faint but visible large letters, with enough space for another letter between each. The third one goes off the sherd, indicating that the text is definitely incomplete. | | | | |

| Reg. Num | Locus<br>Remarks | Ware | Basket Date | Script | Preserved |
|---|---|---|---|---|---|
| M79-661 | L3: 3112 | Phoenician | c. 525 or later | alphabetic | 3 letters |
| | A fourth letter appears to be partially visible at the left edge of the sherd. The letters are written on the horizontal plane of the sherd. | | | | |
| M79-675 | L2: 2159 | Phoenician | c. 568 | Phoenician? | 2 lines |
| | Three legible letters on the top line, about five illegible ones on a lower line, both inscribed on the horizontal plane about 2.5 cm below the shoulder. The beginning of the top line is missing. The inscription may be a label indicating the contents of the jar. | | | | |
| M79-716 | L2: 2154 | Phoenician | slightly pre-601 | Phoenician | 3 lines |
| | Five or six letters inscribed on the horizontal plane about 1.5 cm below the shoulder. The inscription is incomplete, but probably indicates the original contents of the jar (Pl. 3a). | | | | |
| M81-117 | Q2: 2027 | Phoenician | c. 550 | Phoenician! | 2 lines |
| | The lines, not quite parallel to one another, are separated by 2 cm of space. There are two signs on the first line, five or six on the second; possibly a label. | | | | |
| M81-190 | Q2: 2042 | Phoenician | second cent. | alphabetic | 2 lines |
| | The top line, in parallel with the lower one, has only two or three characters. Parts of the tops of five letters are visible, along with three complete, short and slightly curved vertical strokes, possibly numbers. | | | | |
| M81-226 | S1: 1011 | Phoenician | sixth/fifth cent. | Phoenician! | 1 line |

| Reg. Num | Locus<br>Remarks | Ware | Basket Date | Script | Preserved |
|---|---|---|---|---|---|
| | Ten clear letters in a straight line. There is no other writing above, below or to the right, but the break begins immediately at the right (Pl. 3b). Schmitz reads the letters as (*m*)*sprnm 'rb bn* and interprets them to mean 'I will increase their number in it'.[8] | | | | |
| M81-288 | S1: 1011 | Thasian | second cent. | alphabetic | 2 lines |
| | Two letters in the top line, four in the bottom, but the sherd is narrow (1.2 cm) and the sherd has been broken on the top and right side, cutting off the inscription. | | | | |
| M81-336a | Q4: 4020 | Levantine[9] | c. 525–500 | Aramaic[10] | 2 lines |
| | Ten letters separated by two spaces (3 + 3 + 4) on the top line which, though at a slant on the sherd, are inscribed on the horizontal plane of the original jar. The bottom line now has only parts of three letters, and both lines are cut off at the end (Pl. 3c). | | | | |
| M81-404 | Q2: 2006 | Phoenician | fifth cent. | Phoenician! | 1 letter |
| | One isolated mark, inscribed perpendicular to the horizontal plane. It looks like a daleth of an earlier era! | | | | |
| M81-499a | Q3: 3048 | Phoenician | c. 525, third/second cent. | Phoenician? | 2 lines |

8. Private communication; also mentioned in a paper delivered on 22 November 1999 at the Annual Meeting of the Society of Biblical Literature in Boston, MA.

9. The original call on this sherd by the pottery reading team was Phoenician, but was later changed to Levantine. Recent examination of a colour slide of this sherd was not conclusive in settling the question of why the change was made, and it is possible that the original call should still stand.

10. Identified as Imperial Aramaic by Schmitz, and confirmed by C.R. Krahmalkov.

| Reg. Num | Locus<br>Remarks | Ware | Basket Date | Script | Preserved |
|---|---|---|---|---|---|
| | Top line appears to have about ten letters, inscribed on the horizontal plane. The bottom characters, possibly four, may be Demotic. | | | | |
| M81-534 | S2: 2026 | Phoenician-4a | sixth cent. | Phoenician! | 1 line |
| | Six letters in a straight line, running up to the left edge. Ink on the edge suggests that the inscription continues into the broken off part. | | | | |
| M81-538 | Q4: 4010 | Phoenician | c. 525 | Phoenician! | 1 line |
| | A large complete Phoenician storage jar, with one sign and one line (about 9.5 cm below the shoulder) of six letters between the handles. Regrettably, the writing is faint and almost invisible. | | | | |
| M81-606 | S2: 2028 | Phoenician | c. 525 | Semitic! | 1 letter |
| | One clear sign on the right edge of the sherd; possibly another fainter one above it. | | | | |
| M85-056 | Q2: 2149 | Phoenician | fourth cent. | Phoenician? | 2 letters |
| | There may be two other very faint signs. | | | | |
| M85-072 | Q4: 4086 | Phoenician | c. 450–400 | Phoenician | 1 letter |
| | The letter is incomplete, broken at the edge of the sherd. | | | | |
| M85-084 | Q5: 5054 | Phoenician | fifth cent. | Phoenician? | 1 line |
| | The left-hand corner of the sherd is the tip of the shoulder of the storage-jar. Relative to the shoulder the inscription, a line of about a dozen letters, is inscribed on the horizontal plane, but upside down! | | | | |
| M85-111 | Q3: 3099 | Phoenician | early fifth cent. | Phoenician! | 2 lines |

| Reg. Num | Locus<br>Remarks | Ware | Basket Date | Script | Preserved |
|---|---|---|---|---|---|
| | A body sherd in which the horizontal is not definable. The inscription consists of two lines that contain more than a dozen letters each, though very difficult to read. The inscription runs from edge to edge, so may be incomplete. | | | | |
| M85-171 | Q4: 4151 | Phoenician-4c | late fifth/<br>early fourth cent. | Phoenician | 3 letters |
| | There are faint traces of letters on the top of the shoulder of a storage-jar, but precisely which letters cannot be determined. | | | | |
| M85-178 | Q4: 4151 | Phoenician | late fifth/<br>early fourth cent. | Phoenician? | 2 lines |
| | About ten letters on the top(?) line, six on the bottom. They are not written on the horizontal plane of the sherd. There is space to the left of both lines, but none to the right; the inscription may be incomplete (Pl. 3d). | | | | |
| M85-190 | Q5: 5122 | Phoenician | fifth cent.? | Phoenician? | 2(?) lines |
| | Among the manganese spots there appear to be ink markings that resemble alphabetic type letters. The inscription is on the horizontal plane, but illegible. | | | | |
| M85-240 | L3: 3278 | Phoenician-4c | sixth/fifth cent. | Phoenician? | 3 letters |
| | Very small letters moving into the left edge of the sherd. | | | | |
| M85-247 | Q6: 6007 | Phoenician | fifth/fourth cent. or later | Phoenician? | 1 line |
| | Seven letters inscribed on the horizontal plane (Pl. 3e). | | | | |
| M85-262 | Q4: 4208 | Egyptian-10j | fifth cent. | alphabetic | 2 lines |

| Reg. Num | Locus<br>Remarks | Ware | Basket Date | Script | Preserved |
|---|---|---|---|---|---|
| | There could be as many as 15 letters on the first line, inscribed apparently on the horizontal plane. There appear to be six short vertical strokes after the first two or three letters. The second line, parallel to the first, has as many as six letters. Since the sherd is part of an 'Egyptian' amphora, if the inscription is Phoenician, it may suggest the Phoenicians were present in Maskhuta! | | | | |
| M85-263 | Q4: 4201 | Phoenician | unknown; fifth cent. | alphabetic | 1 line |
| | Three or four letters inscribed on the horizontal plane of a body sherd. | | | | |
| M85-277 | Q5: 5141 | Phoenician-4c | c. 500± | Phoenician | 1 letter |
| | Apparently only one letter is present, but inscribed on the horizontal plane. | | | | |
| M85-284 | Q4: 4208 | local[11] | fifth cent. | Phoenician? | 2 letters |
| | Only two letters just below the rim of what may be a locally made jar. If it is a local product, the sherd would constitute evidence for the presence of Phoenicians at Maskhuta. The inscription is broken off at the edge. | | | | |
| M85-380 | Q3: 3173 | Phoenician | fifth cent. | Phoenician | 1 letter |
| | One faint letter close to the right edge. | | | | |
| M85-442 | L3: 3278 | Phoenician | sixth cent. | alphabetic | 2 letters |
| | Two signs near the bottom of the handle of a Phoenician amphora. | | | | |
| M85-465 | L3: 3278 | Phoenician | sixth/fifth cent. | alphabetic? | 2 letters |
| | Only two letters are visible, but there may be a third before the sherd breaks off. | | | | |

11. Type 34 is the only non-amphora ware. Though the origin is unknown, it was initially thought to be manufactured locally.

4a is a light reddish brown with no core. 4c's colour is redder and the fabric is very hard and possibly even crisper than 4e. 4e is a pink to reddish-yellow marl paste with an occasional very pale brown slip.

Most sherds are of this type, which can be called the standard Phoenician 'crisp-ware'.

*Phoenician-like Wares (4j: 1/50; 12a: 2/50)*

4j consists of a pale yellow calcareous clay with a porous texture and organic inclusions. The fabric is medium to well fired with no core. The sherd comes from an imitation Phoenician storage-jar of unknown origin. It was originally classified as 'Egyptian', like other copies of the Phoenician storage-jar form present at Tell el-Maskhuta, but recently has been reassessed by J.S. Holladay as possibly originating from the Ashdod region.

12a characteristically is very pale in colour, ranging from white to pink or very pale brown. The fabric consists of finely levigated clay, well fired with no core. The sherd is from a Levantine amphora, from the coastal area between Phoenicia and Egypt, possibly Ashdod.

*Thasian Ware (7k: 6/50)*

7k is a pale red to pale orange ware, very hard and very dense marl (almost metallic), and with a very smooth surface—the perfect writing surface. It is from a Greek container-amphora imported from the island of Thasos.

*'Egyptian' Ware (10g: 2/50; 10j: 1/50; 11: 1/50)*

10g, 10j and 11 are very hard, brown to weak red-brown wares with no core. They have been identified as Egyptian amphorae, but may be more regionally classified as North African.

*Local Ware (34: 1/50)*

34 is the only ware which is not normally associated with container-amphorae. The paste colour is light yellowish red with a very pale brown slip on the exterior surface. The clay is finely levigated silt, well fired with no core.

| Locus | Description[22] |
|---|---|
| E20: 20002 | surface clearance |
| H1: 1001 | surface clearance |
| H8: 8049 | occupational build-up of floor surfaces* |
| L2: 2004 | fill |
| L2: 2037 | occupational build-up of floor surfaces, phase 4 to be dated c. 600 BCE* |
| L2: 2101 | surface clearance, phase 10 to be dated 525 BCE or later |
| L2: 2102 | large pit |
| L2: 2154f | foundation trench for wall 2121, phase 3 to be dated pre-600* |
| L2: 2159 | bricky debris* |
| L3: 3008 | wind-laid sand and debris |
| L3: 3027 | floor surface* |
| L3: 3112 | midden pit |
| L3: 3278 | ashy pit |
| Q2: 2006 | pit |
| Q2: 2027 | mud-brick detritus* |
| Q2: 2042 | bricky collapse with pits |
| Q2: 2149 | mud-brick detritus |
| Q3: 3048 | trench |
| Q3: 3099 | probe trench (M85-111 comes from the lower level) |
| Q3: 3173 | pit |
| Q4: 4010 | destruction debris* |
| Q4: 4020 | occupational build-up, courtyard surfaces* |
| Q4: 4086 | fill? ashy layer with charcoal inclusions |
| Q4: 4151 | earth layer; accumulation covering most of west end of courtyard |
| Q4: 4201 | probe |
| Q4: 4208 | occupational build-up; accumulation in room with much pottery* |
| Q5: 5054 | mud-brick detritus* |
| Q5: 5122 | pit fill in ash pit 5120 |
| Q5: 5141 | ashy brick layer* |
| Q6: 6007 | mud-brick detritus above floor 6006, probably collapse of walls |
| S1: 1011 | modern pit |
| S2: 2026 | mud-brick tumble* |
| S2: 2028 | destruction debris |

22. All loci marked with an asterisk are stratigraphically secure.

## BIBLIOGRAPHY

Aharoni, Y.

1966 'The Use of Hieratic Numerals in Hebrew Ostraca and the Shekel Weights', *BASOR* 184: 13-19.

Avigad, N., and J.C. Greenfield

1982 'A Bronze φιαλη with a Phoenician Dedicatory Inscription', *IEJ* 32: 118-28.

Avner, R., and E. Eshel

1996 'A Juglet with a Phoenician Inscription from a Recent Excavation in Jaffa, Israel', *Transeuphratène* 12: 59-63.

Benz, F.L.

1972 *Personal Names in the Phoenician and Punic Inscriptions* (Rome: Biblical Institute Press).

Bikai, P.M.

1978 'The Late Phoenician Pottery Complex and Chronology', *BASOR* 229: 47-56.

Cross, F.M.

1968 'Jar Inscriptions from Shiqmona', *IEJ* 18: 226-33.

1979 'A Recently Published Phoenician Inscription of the Persian Period from Byblos', *IEJ* 29: 40-44.

1979 'Two Offering Dishes with Phoenician Inscriptions from the Sanctuary of Arad', *BASOR* 235: 75-78.

Dothan, M.

1985 'A Phoenician Inscription from 'Akko', *IEJ* 35: 81-94.

Dumbrell, W.J.

1971 'The Tell el-Maskhuta Bowls and the "Kingdom" of Qedar in the Persian Period', *BASOR* 203: 33-44.

Eph'al, I., and J. Naveh

1996 *Aramaic Ostraca of the Fourth Century BC from Idumaea* (Jerusalem: The Hebrew University).

Gibson, J.C.L.

1982 *Textbook of Syrian Semitic Inscriptions*. III. *Phoenician Inscriptions* (Oxford: Clarendon Press).

Glueck, N.

1941 'Ostraca from Elath', *BASOR* 82: 7-11.

Healey, J.P.

1974 'The Kition Tariffs and the Phoenician Cursive Series', *BASOR* 216: 53-60.

Holladay, J.S., Jr

1982 *Cities of the Delta, Part III. Tell el-Maskhuta, Preliminary Report on the Wadi Tumilat Project 1978-1979* (American Research Center in Egypt Reports, 6; Malibu: Undena).

1992 'Maskhuta, Tell el-', in *ABD*: 588-92.

Lipiński, É. (ed.)

1992 *Dictionnaire de la civilisation phénicienne et punique* (Paris: Brepols).

Moscati, S.
1968 *The World of the Phoenicians* (London: Weidenfeld & Nicolson).
Moscati, S. (ed.)
1988 *The Phoenicians* (New York: Abbeville Press).
Naveh, J.
1966 'The Scripts of Two Ostraca from Elat', *BASOR* 183: 27-28.
1987 'Unpublished Phoenician Inscriptions from Palestine', *IEJ* 37: 25-30.
1995 'Phoenician Ostraca from Tel Dor', in Z. Zevit, S. Gitin and M. Sokoloff (eds.), *Solving Riddles and Untying Knots* (Winona Lake, IN: Eisenbrauns): 459-64.
Paice, P.
1986–87 'A Preliminary Analysis on Some Elements of the Saite and Persian Pottery at Tell el-Maskhuta', *Bulletin of the Egyptological Seminar* 8: 95-107.
Peckham, J.B.
1966 'An Inscribed Jar from Bat-Yam', *IEJ* 16: 11-17.
1968 *The Development of the Late Phoenician Scripts* (HSS, 20; Cambridge, MA: Harvard University Press).
Rabinowitz, I.
1956 'Aramaic Inscriptions of the Fifth Century B.C.E. from a North-Arab Shrine in Egypt', *JNES* 15: 1-9.
1959 'Another Aramaic Record of the North-Arabian Goddess Han-'Ilat', *JNES* 18: 154-55.
Segert, S.
1976 *A Grammar of Phoenician and Punic* (Munich: Beck).
Tomback, R.S.
1978 *A Comparative Semitic Lexicon of the Phoenician and Punic Languages* (SBLDS, 32; Missoula, MT: Scholars Press).
Vanel, A.
1967 'Six "ostraca" phéniciens trouvés au temple d'Echmoun, près de Saïda', *Bulletin du Musée de Beyrouth* 20: 45-95.
1969 'Le septième ostracon phénicien trouvé au temple d'Echmoun, près de Saïda', *Mélanges de l'Université Saint-Joseph* 45: 345-64.

# DIALEKTVIELFALT UND SPRACHWANDEL IM FRÜHEN ARAMÄISCHEN SOZIOLINGUISTISCHE ÜBERLEGUNGEN

Josef Tropper

This paper discusses the linguistic differences and the diachronic development of early Aramaic dialects. The first section emphasizes the dialectological diversity of Aramaic in the 9th and 8th centuries BC. With the help of a sociolinguistic model (nomadic versus urban dialects), the second section discusses why Aramaic underwent such fundamental linguistic changes in the first half of the 1st millennium BC and why linguistic changes in Aramaic and Canaanite did not proceed synchronically.

Der vorliegende Beitrag diskutiert linguistische Differenzen und diachronische Entwicklungen der aramäischen Sprachwelt in der ersten Hälfte des 1. Jahrtausends v. Chr. Im Zentrum des Interesses steht dabei die älteste schriftlich bezeugte Sprachperiode des Aramäischen, die hier als 'frühes Aramäisch' bezeichnet werden soll. Dieser Begriff umfaßt die aramäischen Texte des 9. und 8. Jahrhunderts v. Chr. *Terminus ante quem* ist das ungefähre Datum 700, das Degen (1969) als untere zeitliche Grenze seiner 'altaramäischen' Periode angesetzt hat. Im Gegensatz zu Degen ziehe ich in meine Erörterungen alle nordwestsemitischen Dialekte des 9. und 8. Jahrhunderts ein, die nicht eindeutig kanaanäisch sind, unter anderem den Dialekt der Bileam-Inschrift aus Tell Deir 'Allā und das sogenannte Sam'alische, um dessen grammatische Erforschung und Klassifikation sich der Jubilar P.-E. Dion (1974) hochverdient gemacht hat.

Der in der wissenschaftlichen Literatur gängige Begriff 'alt-aramäisch' für die früheste(n) bekannte(n) Sprachperiode(n) des Aramäischen wird hier bewußt gemieden, weil er in der Forschungsgeschichte ganz unterschiedlich definiert wurde.[1] Bekanntlich zählte Rosenthal (1939) hierzu alle aramäischen Textzeugnisse bis zum

1. Zur Diskussion siehe insbesondere Fitzmyer (1979).

Untergang Palmyras (272 n. Chr.), Segert (1975) das Aramäische bis zum Ende der reichsaramäischen Epoche, Beyer (1984) nur das Aramäische der vorreichsaramäischen Zeit und Degen (1969) gar ausschließlich die Inschriften des 9. und 8. Jahrhunderts v. Chr. (ohne Sam'alisch).

Im Laufe der jüngeren Forschungsgeschichte hat sich unser Bild vom frühen Aramäischen ganz erheblich gewandelt. Ging man früher von einer relativ homogenen Sprache aus,[2] so zeigten neuere Inschriftenfunde in aller Deutlichkeit, daß bereits zur Zeit der ältesten aramäischen Inschriften eine erstaunlich breite Palette unterschiedlicher aramäischer Dialekte existierte. Der Befund ist so komplex, daß ihm eine simple Zweiteilung in West- und Ostaramäisch nicht gerecht wird.

Der augenblicklichen Beleglage zufolge lassen sich grob vier Dialektgruppen voneinander trennen:

1. Eine Gruppe von zumindest relativ einheitlichen Dialekten in Zentralsyrien.
2. Das Aramäische der Steleninschrift aus Tell Fekherye (Mitte 9. Jh.).
3. Das Deir-'Allā-Aramäische, der Dialekt der Bileam-Inschrift aus Tell Deir 'Allā (um 800).
4. Das Sam'alische,[3] der lokale Dialekt von Sam'al/Zincirli (8. Jh.)

Die zentralsyrische Dialektgruppe (1), die ich im folgenden als 'frühes Zentralaramäisch' bezeichnen möchte, ist von allen genannten Gruppen am besten bezeugt und kann deshalb als linguistische Hauptbezugsgröße dienen. Zu dieser Gruppe zählen alle Texte, die in der Grammatik von Degen (1969) beschrieben werden.[4]

Das Fekherye-Aramäische (2) kann als ein früher Vertreter eines spezifisch ostaramäischen Sprachzweigs gelten und weicht deutlich vom frühen Zentralaramäischen ab. Hervorzuheben ist, daß das Fekherye-Aramäische orthographische und sprachliche Neuerungen

2. Siehe insbesondere Rosenthal (1939: 1-2), der das gesamte aramäische Textkorpus bis zum 3. Jh. n. Chr. als sprachlich homogen betrachtete.

3. Früher meist 'jaudisch' genannt.

4. Hinsichtlich ihrer Zuordnung umstritten sind lediglich die von Degen (1969) ebenfalls hierher gestellten Inschriften des Königs Barrākib von Sam'al (730-20). Sie könnten alternativ als 'Frühreichsaramäisch' zu klassifizieren sein (siehe Tropper 1993: 297-300).

aufweist, die im frühen Zentralaramäischen noch nicht begegnen, die wir aber später im Reichsaramäischen sowie in jüngeren ost-aramäischen Dialekten wiederfinden.

Das Deir-'Allā-Aramäische (3) weicht noch entschiedener vom frühen Zentralaramäischen ab als das Fekherye-Aramäische und weist zugleich Übereinstimmungen mit kanaanäischen Sprachen auf, insbesondere mit dem Hebräischen. Aus diesem Grund gibt es eine noch immer nicht beendete kontroverse Diskussion darüber, ob dieser Dialekt überhaupt aramäisch ist. Zwar wird eine aramäische Klassifikation dieses Dialektes von einer immer größeren Zahl von Autoren befürwortet. Daneben wurde aber auch eine Zuordnung zum Kanaanäischen erwogen,[5] und schließlich vertraten einige Autoren sogar die Ansicht, daß es sich dabei um ein noch nicht in Kanaanäisch und Aramäisch differenziertes Nordwestsemitisch (Müller 1991: 3) oder einen eigenständigen nordwestsemitischen Sprachzweig neben Kanaanäisch und Aramäisch handle (Huehnergard 1991: 293). Ich habe mich in Tropper (1993: 301-306) mit Nachdruck für die Zuordung des Deir-'Allā-Dialekts zum Aramäischen ausgesprochen. Die inzwischen neu entdeckte Tell-Dan-Inschrift,[6] die sich dem frühen Zentralaramäischen (3) zuordnen läßt, gibt m. E. den letzten Ausschlag für diese These. Sie entkräftet nämlich das wichtigste Gegenargument, das in dem Hinweis auf die Bezeugung der *wyqtl*-Kategorie mit narrativer Funktion (vgl. hebr. *wayyiqol*) bestand. Da diese Kategorie auch in der Zakkūr-Inschrift (Āfis) und der Tell-Dan-Inschrift begegnet, ist sie als Argument gegen eine aramäische Klassifikation des Deir-'Allā-Dialekts untauglich.

Die größten Differenzen zum frühen Zentralaramäischen weist aber das Sam'alische (4) auf. Es steht innerhalb der zeitgenössischen aramäischen Dialekte isoliert da und zeichnet sich vor allem durch betont konservative Merkmale aus. Hervorzuheben ist zum einen die Bewahrung der altsemitischen nominalen Kasusflexion im maskulinen Plural (Nominativ *-ū*, Obliquus *-ī*), zum anderen die Tatsache, daß das Sam'alische das in allen anderen aramäischen Dialekten (an pluralischen und dualischen Nominalformen) bezeugte Pronominalsuffix 3.m.sg. *-wh* = /-awhi/ nicht kennt und stattdessen das altsemitische Suffix *-(y)h* /-(ay)hV/[7] verwendet. Trotz dieser Besonderheiten ist das

5. Insbesondere Hackett (1984a) und (1984b).
6. Publiziert von Biran-Naveh (1993 und 1995).
7. Obliquus *-yh* = /-ayhV/, Nominativ *-h* = /-ūhV/ (siehe Tropper 1993: 190-91).

Sam'alische aber ein aramäischer Dialekt.[8] Ein wichtiges Argument, das bisher gegen eine aramäische Klassifizierung des Sam'alischen angeführt wurde, nämlich das Fehlen des bestimmten Artikels, ist inzwischen nicht mehr stichhaltig, da auch der Deir-'Allā-Dialekt (noch) artikellos ist.[9]

Die beschriebene dialektale Vielfalt des Aramäischen im 9. und 8. Jh. verwundert im übrigen nicht angesichts der politischen und ökonomischen Uneinheitlichkeit Syriens zu jener Zeit, die neuerdings vom Jubilar (Dion 1997) umfassend dargestellt wurde. Sie läßt sich gleichwohl damit allein nicht erklären. Das Ausmaß der sprachlichen Differenzen setzt voraus, daß die Aramäer auch in vorliterarischer Zeit und damit auch in der Zeit vor ihrer Seßhaftwerdung keine einheitliche Volksgruppe gebildet haben. Es ist vielmehr mit einer Mehrzahl unabhängig voneinander agierender Stämme mit verwandten, aber nichtsdestoweniger unterschiedlichen Dialekten zu rechnen.[10]

8. Zur Argumentation siehe Dion (1974: 319-43) und Tropper (1993: 289-97). Zu anderen Klassifikationsvorschlägen, die zunehmend weniger Zuspruch finden, siehe Tropper (1993: 287-89).

9. Aufgrund erheblichen Differenzen zwischen dem Deir-'Allā-Dialekt und dem Sam'alischen einerseits und dem Restaramäischen andererseits hat Huehnergard (1995: 281-82) neuerdings für eine engere Definition des Begriffs 'Aramäisch' plädiert. Nach Huehnergard sind der Deir-'Allā-Dialekt und das Sam'alische nicht als 'aramäisch' zu klassifizieren. Er operierte versuchsweise mit zwei neuen Termini, 'Proto-Aramoid' und 'Proto-Syrian', und verwendete den ersteren als Oberbegriff über 'Proto-Aramaic' und Deir-'Allā-Dialekt, des letzteren als Oberbegriff über 'Proto-Aramoid' und Sam'alisch. Huehnergards Argumentation steht und fällt mit den von ihm postulierten (drei) spezifischen Merkmalen des Protoaramäischen, nämlich (a) 'a definite article represented by final -' ' (b) 'the loss of the N stem' und (c) 'feminine pl. forms in *-ān*' (S. 282). Keines dieser Merkmale ist aber frei von Problemen. Die Aufgabe des N-Stamms (b) ist nicht signifikant und begegnet bekanntlich auch im Äthiopischen. Außerdem gilt hierbei zu beachten, daß die Existenz eines N-Stamms in Deir 'Allā und Sam'al nicht sicher bewiesen ist. Das Merkmal (c) kann nur für Substantive geltend gemacht werden. Adjektive im Altaramäischen von Sfīre weisen bekanntlich (noch) eine fem. Pluralendung *-āt* anstelle der im späteren Aramäischen bezeugten Endung *-ān* auf. Beim bestimmten Artikel (a) schließlich handelt es sich um eine sehr rezente Erscheinung, die sich ab etwa 1000 v. Chr. areal im gesamten zentralsemitischen Raum ausgebreitet hat. Somit sind die genannten Merkmale (a-c) keine geeigneten Kriterien für eine genetische Klassifikation.

10. Man vergleiche etwa die sprachliche Situation nomadischer Ethnien im heutigen Zagros-Gebiet, die Schwartz (1989: 284) wie folgt beschreibt: 'Linguistic

Die ober beschriebene Dialektvielfalt des frühen Aramäischen hat weitreichende Implikationen für das sogenannte Protoaramäische, den größten gemeinsamen rekonstruierbaren Nenner der beschriebenen Einzeldialekte. Auf der Basis des dialektgeographischen Befunds ist festzuhalten, daß eine ganze Reihe von Merkmalen, die traditionell als dem gesamten aramäischen Sprachzweig eigen und damit als spezifisch aramäisch betrachtet werden, in Wirklichkeit erst nach-protoaramäische Innovationen sind. Dazu zählen etwa folgende fünf Merkmale (Tropper 1993: 309):

1. Das Pronominalsuffix der 3. Person m.sg. *-wh* = /-awhi/ ist nicht protoaramäisch, da es im Sam'alischen noch nicht bezeugt ist.
2. Der postponierte bestimmte Artikel (-' = /-ā/) ist ebenfalls nicht protoaramäisch. Bisher sind zwei frühe aramäische Dialekte bekannt, die noch artikellos sind (Sam'alisch und Deir-'Allā-Dialekt).
3. Der Etp$^{e}$'el-Verbalstamm ist in dieser Form, d. h. mit präfigiertem *t-*, sekundär. Protoaramäisch wurde der betreffende Verbalstamm noch mit infigiertem *-t-* gebildet, wie in den meisten anderen semitischen Sprachen. Er ist noch im Fekherye-Aramäischen (Z. 23: *ygtzr* 'er soll entfernt werden') und wahrscheinlich auch im Sam'alischen[11] belegt.
4. Das Protoaramäische kannte wahrscheinlich noch einen N-Stamm. Er dürfte erst später obsolet geworden sein. Mögliche (aber unsichere) N-Belege bieten das Sam'alische[12] und das Deir-'Allā-Aramäische.[13]
5. Der Infinitiv des Grundstamms lautete im Protoaramäischen noch *qtl* = /qatāl/ und nicht *mqtl* = /miqtal/. Die *mqtl*-Bildung stellt eine ostaramäische Innovation dar. Sie ist zum ersten

diversity in nomadic pastoralist ethnic groups is observable in the Iranian Zagros, for example, where Kurds, Lurs and Bakhtiari each speak their own dialects which are interrelated but not identical.'

11. *ytmr* < **y'tmr* 'es wurde (gewöhnlich) befohlen' (Hadad Inschrift, Z. 10); siehe Tropper (1993: 183-84).

12. *nḥšb* 'er wurde geschätzt' (Panamuwa-Inschrift, Z. 10 [Lesung allerdings unsicher]); siehe Tropper (1993: 212).

13. In Frage kommen die Formen *nṣbw* (I:6) und *n'nḥ* (II:12 [2x]); zur Diskussion siehe Tropper (1993: 302).

Mal im Fekherye-Aramäischen[14] belegt und hat sich später, via Reichsaramäisch, ausgebreitet.

Wenn Merkmale dieser Art, die früher als spezifisch aramäisch angesehen wurden, erst sekundär entstanden sind, so folgt daraus zum einen, daß sich das Protoaramäische durch einen betont archaischen Sprachzustand auszeichnet, zum anderen, daß das Protoaramäische dem Protoakanaanäischem sprachlich weit näher steht, als älteren Darstellungen der Thematik es suggerieren.

Vergleicht man das zu rekonstruierende Protokanaanäische und dieses Protoaramäische typologisch miteinander, dann zeigt sich relativ überraschend, daß das Protoaramäische durchweg konservativer ist als das Protokanaanäische. Das Protoaramäische zeichnet sich in phonologischer Hinsicht durch die Bewahrung (wahrscheinlich) aller 29 protosemitischen konsonantischen Phoneme sowie der Diphthonge aus.[15] Daneben weist das Protoaramäische aber auch konservative Züge im morphologischen Bereich auf (Tropper 1993: 309f.). So hat das Aramäische das (ursemitische) Pronominalsuffix 1.c.pl. *-na* bewahrt (gegenüber kanaanäisch *-nū*). Es hat die nominale Nunation im Dual und Plural des Status absolutus beibehalten (gegenüber Mimation im Kanaanäischen). Es weist im Einklang mit dem Klassischen Arabisch für die Präfixkonjugation 3.f.pl. die Form *yaqtulna* auf (gegenüber kanaanäisch *taqtulna*).[16] Und schließlich gilt im Protoaramäischen —wie etwa im Klassischen Arabisch—das sogenannte 'Barthsche Gesetz' (feste Korrelation zwischen Präfix- und Themavokal in der Präfixkonjugation) noch nicht.

Diese typologischen Differenzen zwischen dem Protokanaanäischen und dem Protoaramäischen wurden bisher weder gebührend beachtetet noch erklärt. Im folgenden möchte ich den Versuch wagen, diesen Befund durch soziolinguistische Überlegungen zu beleuchten. Ich greife dabei zurück auf ein Beschreibungsmodell, das sich im Rahmen der arabischen Dialektologie bewährt hat. Dort wird grundlegend unterschieden zwischen Beduinendialekten einerseits, gemeint sind Dialekte von nomadischen Sprechern, und sogenannten Ansässigendialekten andererseits, die sich wieder in Stadt- und Dorfdialekte untergliedern lassen (vgl. Holes 1996). Es läßt sich zumindest im

14. *lm'rk* (Z. 7.14); *lmld* (Z. 9); *lmlqḥ* (Z. 10), *lmšm'* (Z. 9).

15. Siehe Kottsieper (1990: 27-28); vgl. ferner Degen (1969: 30-39).

16. Siehe Huehnergard (1987) und Muraoka-Porten (1998: 105-106).

Gebiet des fruchtbaren Halbmonds eindeutig beobachten, daß erstere, die ich als Nomadendialekte bezeichnen möchte, im Vergleich zu letzteren, die ich hier vereinfachend Stadtdialekte nenne, in praktisch allen Bereichen der Sprache konservativer sind. In der Regel nehmen Sprachveränderungen nämlich in den städtischen Zentren ihren Ausgang, strahlen von dort in die Umgebung aus und erreichen die Nomadendialekte nicht oder erst mit erheblicher Verzögerung.

Wenn wir dieses stark schematisierte Modell auf Sprecher des Nordwestsemitischen etwa zur Zeit der Mitte des 2. Jahrtausends v. Chr. übertragen, ergibt sich folgendes Bild: In Westsyrien, im Libanon und in weiten Bereichen Palästinas stoßen wir auf eine seßhafte Bevölkerung mit städtische Kulturen und damit auf sogenannte Stadtdialekte. Weiter im Landesinnern, im syrischen Steppenbereich, überwog demgegenüber die nomadische oder halbnomadische Lebensweise (von Viehhirten). Das erstere Gebiet ist im wesentlichen der Lebensbereich der früh seßhaft gewordenen Kanaanäer, während als Lebensbereich der Aramäer zu jener Zeit nur das letztere Gebiet in Frage kommt. Folglich kann man—unter Vorbehalt—das Kanaanäische jener Zeit mit nordwestsemitischen Stadtdialekten und das Aramäische jener Zeit mit nordwestsemitischen Nomadendialekten gleichsetzen. Letztlich könnte dies bedeuten, daß die Sprachdifferenzierung zwischen Kanaanäisch und Aramäisch maßgeblich überhaupt erst durch die frühe Seßhaftwerdung *eines* Teils der Nordwestsemiten, nämlich der sogenannten Kanaanäer, zustande kam.

Dieses Modell, wonach die aramäische Dialektgruppe mit Nomadendialekten, das Kanaanäische aber mit Stadt- und Dorfdialekten gleichzusetzen ist, kann natürlich nur solange angewendet werden, solange es mit den realen Gegebenheiten im Einklang steht. Bekanntlich änderte sich die Lebensweise der Aramäer etwa ab dem 12. Jahrhundert v. Chr. radikal. Die Aramäer wurden in relativ kurzer Zeit weitgehend seßhaft, und es entstanden schnell ausgeprägte aramäische Stadtkulturen. Diese Veränderungen hatten unmittelbare Auswirkungen auf die nachfolgende Sprachentwicklung des Aramäischen. Hinfort—und nicht erst, nachdem das Aramäische zur *lingua franca* des Vorderen Orients geworden war—entwickelte sich das Aramäische in einer rasanten Weise sprachlich weiter.

Die tiefgreifenden sprachlichen Veränderungen des Aramäischen in der 1. Hälfte des 1. Jahrtausends erklären zum einen, warum das Verhältnis zwischen Kanaanäisch und Aramäisch um etwa 500 v. Chr.

völlig anders geartet ist als etwa um 1000: Jetzt ist das Aramäische der eindeutig modernere Sprachzweig des Nordwestsemitischen. Es hat das sich gleichmäßer, aber insgesamt langsamer entwickelnde Kanaanäische in der Zwischenzeit sprachtypologisch überholt und weit hinter sich gelassen. Zweitens erklärt die schnelle Entwicklung des Aramäischen aber auch, warum einige, vor allem geographisch isolierte aramäische Dialekte wie etwa das Sam'alische oder das Deir-'Allā-Aramäische, an der rasanten aramäischen Sprachentwicklung nicht in der gleichen Weise teilhatten. Dies schlägt sich in der großen Dialektstreuung nieder, die wir in den ältesten aramäischen Inschriften fassen können.

Nebenbei sei erwähnt, daß die enormen sprachlichen Veränderungen des Aramäischen in der ersten Hälfte des 1. Jahrtausends v. Chr. eine interessante typologische Parallele in der Schriftentwicklung haben. Die aramäische Schrift veränderte sich bekanntlich ab dem 8. Jh. v. Chr. weitaus schneller als die phönizische Schrift, von der sie ursprünglich abstammt, oder gar die überaus konservative althebräische Schrift, was sich etwa in den erheblichen formalen Differenzen zwischen der althebräischen Schrift einerseits und der auf einem aramäischen Schriftzweig beruhenden hebräischen Quadratschrift andererseits niederschlägt.[17]

Das genannte Modell—Aramäisch gleich Nomadendialekte versus Kanaanäisch gleich Stadt- und Dorfdialekte—ist natürlich eine sehr vereinfachte Darstellung der soziolinguistischen Realität. Es gab im Alten Orient natürlich zu keiner Zeit eine strikte und ausschließliche Dichotomie von Nomaden und Seßhaften. Und ferner vollzog sich die sogenannte Seßhaftwerdung ja nachweislich nicht bei allen zu Kanaanäern bzw. Aramäern gezählten Gruppierungen jeweils zur gleichen Zeit. Das Modell als solches wird aber durch diese notwendigen Modifikationen im Detail nicht falsifiziert. Im Gegenteil: Mit Hilfe des Modells lassen sich zum einen sprachtypologische Differenzen innerhalb des Kanaanäischen überzeugender als bisher erklären, etwa die Tatsache, daß einige kanaanäische Dialekte (etwa das Moabitische) deutlich konservativer sind als zeitgenössische andere (etwa das Phönizische).[18] Zum anderen liefert das Modell aber auch eine Erklärung dafür, warum ostaramäische Dialekte wie etwa der Fekherye-Dialekt im Vergleich zu anderen frühen aramäischen

17. Siehe Naveh (1970, bes. 66) und (1982: 78-89, 97-100).

18. Zu den wichtigsten diesbezüglichen Differenzen siehe Friedrich-Röllig (1970: 4).

Dialekten betont innovativ sind. Tatsächlich scheint ja—auch wenn wir von der betreffenden Entwicklung bisher nur ungenügend unterrichtet sind[19]—der Prozeß der Seßhaftwerdung der Aramäer in Nordostsyrien früher eingesetzt zu haben als in anderen Gebieten. Ferner dürfte ins Gewicht fallen, daß die Aramäer dort in engem Kontakt mit den fortschrittlichen Stadtkulturen Mesopotamiens standen. Diese Gegebenheiten führten dazu, daß die dort beheimateten aramäischen Dialekte innovationsfreudiger waren als andere aramäische Dialekte ihrer Zeit. Viele sprachliche Neuerungen des Aramäischen nahmen dort ihren Ausgang und breiteten sich später—nicht zuletzt via Reichsaramäisch—auf das gesamte aramäische Sprachgebiet aus.

## BIBLIOGRAPHY

Beyer, K.
1984 *Die aramäischen Texte vom Toten Meer* (Göttingen: Vandenhoeck & Ruprecht).

Biran, A., und J. Naveh
1993 'An Aramaic Stele Fragment from Tel Dan', *IEJ* 43: 81-98.
1995 'The Tel Dan Inscription. A New Fragment', *IEJ* 45: 1-18.

Degen, R.
1969 *Altaramäische Grammatik der Inschriften den 10.-8. Jh. v. Christus* (Wiesbaden: Deutsche Morgenländische Gesellschaft).

Dion, P.-E.
1974 *La langue de Ya'udi. Description et classement de l'ancien parler de Zencirli dans le cadre des langues sémitiques du nord-ouest* (Waterloo, ON: Wilfrid Laurier Press).
1997 *Les Araméens à l'âge du fer: histoire politique et structures sociales* (Ebib, N.S. 34; Paris: Gabalda).

Fitzmyer, J.A.
1979 *A Wandering Aramean. Collected Aramaic Essays* (SBLMS, 25; Missoula, MA: Scholars Press).

Friedrich, J., und W. Röllig
1970 *Phönizisch–Punische Grammatik* (AnOr, 46; Roma: Pontificum Institutum Biblicum).

Hackett, J.A.
1984a *The Balaam Text form Deir 'Allā* (HSM, 31; Chico, CA: Scholars Press).
1984b 'The Dialect of the Plaster Text from Tell Deir 'Allā', *Or* 53: 57-65.

Holes, C.
1996 'The Arabic Dialects of South Eastern Arabia in a Socio-Historical Perspective', *Zeitschrift für Arabische Linguistik* 31: 34-56.

19. Zur Problematik siehe Schwartz (1989).

Huehnergard, J.

1987 'The Feminine Plural Jussive in Old Aramaic', *ZDMG* 137: 266-77.

1991 'Remarks on the Classification of the Northwest Semitic Languages', in J. Hoftijzer und G. van der Kooij (eds.), *The Balaam Text from Deir 'Alla Re-evaluated. Proceedings of the International Symposium Held at Leiden 21-24 August 1989* (Leiden: E.J. Brill): 283-93.

1995 'What is Aramaic?', *ARAM* 7: 261-82.

Kottsieper, I.

1990 *Die Sprache der Aḥiqarsprüche* (Beihefte zur Zeitschrift für die Alttestamentliche Wissenschaft, 194; Berlin: W. de Gruyter).

Müller, H.-P.

1991 'Die Sprache der Texte von Tell Deir 'Allā im Kontext der nordwestsemitischen Sprachen mit einigen Erwägungen zum Zusammenhang der schwachen Verbklassen', *Zeitschrift für Althebraistik* 4: 1-31.

Muraoka, T., und B. Porten

1998 *A Grammar of Egyptian Aramaic* (Handbuch der Orientalistik; I/32 (Leiden: E.J. Brill).

Naveh, J.

1970 *The Development of the Aramaic Script* (Jerusalem: Israel Academy of Sciences and Humanities).

1982 *Early History of the Alphabet: An Introduction to West Semitic Epigraphy and Palaeography* (Jerusalem: Magnes Press, Hebrew University).

Rosenthal, F.

1939 *Die aramäistische Forschung seit Theodor Nöldeke's Veröffentlichungen* (Leiden: E.J. Brill).

Schwartz, G.M.

1989 'The Origins of the Aramaeans in Syria and Northern Mesopotamia: Research Problems and Potential Strategies', in O.M.C. Haex, H.H. Curvers und P.M.M.G. Akkermans (eds.), *To The Euphrates and Beyond. Archaeological Studies in Honour of Maurits N. van Loon* (Rotterdam/ Brookfield, VT: A. A. Balkema): 275-91.

Segert, S.

1975 *Altaramäische Grammatik mit Bibliographie, Chrestomathie und Glossar* (Leipzig: Verlag Enzyklopädie).

Tropper, J.

1993 *Die Inschriften von Zincirli. Neue Edition und vergleichende Grammatik des phönizischen, sam'alischen und aramäischen Textkorpus* (Abhandlungen zur Literatur Altsyrien-Palästinas, 6; Münster: Ugarit-Verlag).

## UGARITIC SCIENCE*

Dennis Pardee

### *Introduction*

The purpose of this essay is to provide as complete an overview as is possible in a short space of the extant Ugaritic texts that reflect what the Ugaritians considered to be compendia of knowledge.[1] It should be clear from this formulation that I am using 'science' in the broad sense

* A preliminary version of this essay was presented at the Annual Meeting of the Society of Biblical Literature, Philadelphia, 20 November 1995. The texts discussed here and provided in the appendix will all appear in my new edition of the Ugaritic ritual texts: Pardee 2000. Several have already appeared in English translations; this information is supplied in footnotes in the appendix. A full epigraphic, philological and literary commentary will usually only be found, however, in the French edition.

1. The following categories of texts correspond more closely to what other speakers at the original session, entitled 'Magic and Divination in the Ancient Near East', described as 'magic':

a. Ritual texts: The Ugaritic ritual texts have to do with the sacrificial cult in honor of the deities; the only one that might be qualified as 'magical' in a more narrow sense is RS 34.126, the Ugaritic funerary ritual (see Pardee 1993: esp. 208-210). That text is certainly not necromantic but it does constitute the written version of the liturgical vehicle which enabled the deceased king to join his ancestors; to the extent that the joining depended on the rite, the latter is perhaps 'magical'.

b. Two clear incantations are known in Ugaritic, RIH 78/20 and RS 92.2014 (my English renditions may be seen, respectively, in Pardee 1993: 211-13 and 1997. Other less well-preserved texts have been identified as incantations by other scholars; cf., e.g., the treatments of RS 15.134, RS 16.266 and RS 19.054 by de Moor (1987) and by Caquot (1989).

c. Some of the texts that I have dubbed 'para-mythological' may represent 'magical' ceremonies, particularly those dealing with the devenomization of reptiles (English translation with notes of the better preserved one, RS 24.244, in Pardee 1997c: 295-98, text 1.94).

of 'what a given culture considers to be organized, or perhaps listable, knowledge'. This should not obscure the fact that some of these branches of knowledge did develop into what we would consider sciences, such as astronomy or veterinary medicine; lexicography would be closer to a humanities discipline; the divinatory texts might be classed as a branch of metaphysics or as what one may read in certain tabloids. The decision to identify all these categories as 'science' was in no small part based on formal features: the similarity in form between what we classify as divinatory texts and medical texts indicates that the ancients considered that both types of phenomena belonged to the realm of knowledge and that one was no more or less real than the other. Some activities that we could classify as 'mantic' appear, therefore, to be considered no less 'scientific' than veterinary medicine. The exclusion here of other texts having to do with mantic activity, such as incantations (see n. 1), is also largely formal, for the 'scientific' texts are in prose—and very prosaic—while the incantations are poetic[2] and do not take the form of compendia of knowledge.

I am distantly aware of the debate currently going on as to whether Science, with a capital S, was invented in the pre-classical Near East or in Greece, or for that matter in Renaissance Europe, but do not wish to involve myself in the debate except to the extent of saying that all Near Eastern 'science' tended to be of a concrete sort, not involving much theorizing or speculation, at least not in written form; but, at least in some areas, such as mathematics and astronomy, it provided an objective basis for further developments.

My own interest in the Ugaritic scientific texts has more to do with their place in the Near Eastern chain of tradition and, after a description of the textual data, I will briefly discuss that topic.

The following outline provides the major categories and textual references, keyed to the texts and translations provided in the Appendix. The final element of the titles differs more because of current usage than because of differences in ancient practice, for example, the first four categories are all principally divinatory by function, though only one of the four terms ends in '-mancy' (the terms teratomancy, astromancy and splanchnomancy, indicated in parentheses, would be etymologically more precise classifications of most of the texts in the first three sections).

2. As is the prayer to which reference is made below.

1. Teratology (Teratomancy)
   a. Animal fetus omens (RS 24.247$^{+}$)
   b. Human fetus omens (RS 24.302)
2. Astrology (Astromancy)
   a. An astrological report (RS 12.061)
   b. Lunar omens (RIH 78/14)
3. Extispicy (Splanchnomancy)
   a. Inscribed liver models in clay (RS 24.312; 24.323; 24.326; 24.327; 24.654)
   b. Inscribed lung model in clay (RS 24.277)
   c. Inscribed liver models in ivory (nearly 50 texts)
4. Oniromancy (RS 18.041)
5. Hippiatry (RS 5.285$^{+}$; 5.300; 17.120; 23.484)
6. Lexicography
   a. Polyglot vocabularies (RS 20.137, etc.)
   b. Monolingual lists of divine names
      1. RS 1.017 and parallels
      2. RS 26.643 *verso* and parallels

## *Description of Texts*

### *Teratology*

'Teratology' is etymologically the study of monsters, in these cases the science of divining by malformed fetuses of animal or human origin. The structure of both Ugaritic texts is basically that of the protasis and the apodosis: if such-and-such a malformed birth is observed, such-and-such an event may occur. The genre is well known from Mesopotamian literature, where it conventionally goes by the name of the first two words of the protasis, *šumma izbu*, 'if (there is) a malformed birth' or, in the case of human births, *šumma sinništu*, 'if a woman' followed by 'gives birth'. In the Mesopotamian collections of these omens, identical protases can occur followed by a variety of apodoses. This repetition is not attested in any of the Ugaritic omen texts as preserved,[3] though it is found in the hippiatric texts, that is, a given equine ailment may be treated in more than one way. Because of the lack of repetition in the Ugaritic omen texts, I have proposed that they were intended to be reasoned overviews of ominological phenomena, for example, the various possible malformations of the body at birth, rather

3. Cf. Pardee 1986: esp. 142; this point, made with regard to the proper restoration of a single line of the text, has been expanded in the conclusions to my re-edition of this text in Pardee (2000).

than traditional lists of observations of what actually occurred at multiple points in time after such births, which apparently could include hypothetical malformations and possible cooccurring events (Cryer 1994: 150-52). If the Ugaritic texts in their original state did not include repetitions or hypothetical cases in the protases, they represent a departure from the Mesopotamian system. In any case, no single protasis-apodosis set precisely matches any set known from the Mesopotamian, Anatolian or Syrian Akkadian versions, and there are, therefore, no precise data by which to determine the chain of tradition leading to our Ugaritic versions.

*Astrology*

Under 'astrology' I have put two texts, neither of which has anything to do with astrology as the word is used today. The first text, here dubbed 'an astrological report', clearly does not belong to the category of compendia of knowledge but seems to reflect astromantic science in action. It has caused a good deal of ink to flow. One thing that appears quite clear to me is that it has nothing to do with an eclipse of the sun, because the verb *'araba* would not be used for an eclipse and because the phenomenon is described as occurring on six consecutive days. Because there is a reference in a ritual text to the seventh day of a new-moon festival,[4] the first few words of RS 12.061 are best interpreted, it appears to me, in a similar way—that is, the cardinal number 'six' with the noun 'days' in construct with the term for 'new moon' designates the first six days of the month. Because there is some meagre evidence for the divinity *Rašap* being identified with the planet Mars,[5] this text may be taken as describing the visibility of Mars at sunset during the first six days of the month of *Ḫiyyāru* (plausibly the second month of winter, spanning January/February).[6] Though this text is not in protasis-

4. RS 24.256: l. 10 {[b] ⸢š⸣b⸢ʿ⸣ ym ḥdṯ} (this text was first edited by Herdner (1978: 21-26).

5. Nougayrol 1968: 57 n. 3; Sawyer and Stephenson 1970: 467-89, esp. 471; De Jong and van Soldt 1987–88: 65-77, esp. 68; Reiner 1993: 21-22, no. 26. Walker (1989: 204-205) has pointed out how rare is the identification of *Nergal* (the Mesopotamian deity seen in the west as equivalent to *Rašap*) and Mars, and he was kind enough in a personal communication to call to my attention the last edition of the principal texts (Hunger 1992: 72, text 114.8; 278-79, text 502 *recto* 11).

6. There are good reasons, presented in Pardee (2000), for shifting one month forward the identifications of Ugaritic months within the modern solar year proposed by De Jong and van Soldt (1987–88: 71), i.e. *riš yn* would have been the

apodosis form, the texts on the recto and the verso seem to reflect the observation followed by the reaction, though the reading and meaning of the text on the verso are uncertain.

The second astrological text corresponds directly to a class of divinatory texts well known from Mesopotamia, those that indicate a celestial phenomenon in the protasis and an accompanying event on earth in the apodosis. The Ugaritic text corresponds to the series called *Sin* after the name of the Mesopotamian lunar deity, a sub-set of the larger series *Enuma Anu Enlil*, though again there are no specific correspondences between the few protasis-apodosis sets preserved in the Ugaritic text and sets attested in the Mesopotamian tradition.[7] Here, as in the teratological texts, there is no repetition of ominous phenomena, though this text consists of a relatively small fragment and is even more damaged than the animal fetuses text.

*Extispicy*

Extispicy is well attested at Ugarit by a series of clay models of livers and one model of a lung, some inscribed with texts, all inscribed with marks in the clay that represent features of the liver.[8] Also in this case a long Mesopotamian tradition predates the Ugaritic evidence. Most of the Mesopotamian texts are the standard compendia of protasis-apodosis sets ('if the liver has such-and-such a feature, such-and-such an event will occur'). In addition, a number of inscribed livers, some of which served as instructional models, have been found in Mesopotamian sites, notably Mari.[9] The Ugaritic examples, in any case, indicate—wherever the text is clear—the circumstances of a particular consultation, with the answer indicated by the marks on the liver. Thus, according to Meyer (1987: 220; 1990: 269), the consultation recorded on RS 24.312 received a positive response, namely, *'Agapṯarri* was to go ahead and procure the servant-boy.

last month of the lunar year (straddling, therefore, our August–September), rather than the first.

7. For the edition of an Akkadian astromantic fragment from Ras Shamra, see Arnaud (1996a): 7-18.

8. The texts on the inscribed models were published with admirable speed by Dietrich and Loretz (1969), but the correlation of the data from both types of texts took longer: Meyer (1987; 1990: 241-80).

9. On the differences of opinion among scholars as to the literary genres represented by the liver-model texts, cf. Cryer (1994: 173-74 n. 5).

Because of its state of preservation, the interpretation of the texts inscribed on the lung model is difficult. It is clear that they have nothing to do with the technique of lung interpretation, and that they do have to do with sacrifices. But the absence of a link between any of these texts and the object itself, that is, the words 'this lung' are not present, means that there is no explicit connection between the model and any one of the sacrificial victims. Moreover, the inscriptions on side 3 seem to deal with a hypothetical situation, rather than a specific consultation.

Finally, a new province of the study of extispicy at Ugarit has been opened up through the discovery by Jacqueline Gachet (1995: 245-54) of the *Mission de Ras Shamra* that many, probably most, of the ivory objects bearing Ugaritic inscriptions were in fact liver models. Unfortunately, most of the objects are extremely fragmentary and so are the 45 or so inscriptions, to the point that we can gain no clear overall idea of their subject matter.[10] From the few beginnings preserved and from the odd words preserved, it appears clear, however, that the best preserved texts do not deal with circumstances of individual consultations, nor with sacrificial and/or divinatory matters at all, but with broader aspects of personal and corporate security. This makes sense, for all the inscribed ivories were found in the palace, whereas the clay models come from the house of a priest, from a collection of texts including many rituals.

*Oniromantic*

Again because of the state of preservation of the object, the one text classified as oniromantic is of unsure interpretation. The word for 'dream' certainly appears, I believe, in ll. 1 and 28', preceded in l. 1 by the term for 'document', *spr*, usually found in documents with an administrative function, though also present at the beginning of the one hippiatric text of which the first line is preserved (RS 17.120—see below). It is clear that the primary structure of the individual entries is not the protasis-apodosis form characteristic of divinatory texts in general ('if in a dream a man sees such-and-such, then such-and-such an event may occur'; Oppenheim 1956: 179-373). The word *hm*, 'if',

10. See my study (forthcoming) to accompany Gachet's edition of the objects. There I comment on 45 fragments; some bear parts of more than one inscription (i.e. discrete texts on a single object, as in the case of the lung model); I was not able to find two fragments reported to bear inscriptions.

occurs only once in the text as preserved, and then within a paragraph (l. 7). On the other hand, the word *rgm*, 'word', appears after the primary entry in the first and third paragraphs; moreover, the right side of the tablet having suffered the worst damage, it is plausible that this word may have occurred near the end of other paragraphs. Now the word *rgm* is used in the first teratological text (RS 24.247$^{+}$:6, 18) with the word *mṯn*, 'repetition', for a repeated apodosis, and it is plausible to take it in the dream text as introducing the interpretation of the phenomena seen in the dream, that is, the functional apodosis. So an oniromantic interpretation of this text is at least plausible, though one cannot say any more than that. Note, in any case, that it clearly represents a reasoned overview of various concrete entities, animals on the recto, tools, implements and servants on the verso, and that eventualities of action are mentioned (I refer to the horse falling over in l. 7). Many of these entities correspond to entities mentioned in the Mesopotamian dream omen texts and it is, therefore, plausible to hypothesize that this text is oniromantic and that it follows the Ugaritic pattern observed above of giving a reasoned overview of phenomena without repetitions. I note in passing that this is the only omen collection to have parallels in Egypt, but the subject-matter in the protasis is quite different in the two collections (see Cryer 1994: 220-23).

*Hippiatry*

The only branch of medicine presently attested in Ugaritic is hippiatry, the treatment of sick horses. In Mesopotamia, horse remedies are only attested to date as included within human medical texts, though the existence of horse doctors is attested as early as the eighteenth century BCE in Mari (Durand 1988: 55, 570 n. c). Thus, though one may query the assertion that 'Die Geschichte der Pferdeheilkunde beginnt in Ugarit' ('Hippiatry begins at Ugarit') (Schäffer 1987: 502), the earliest attested hippiatric texts are certainly Ugaritic. Given the earlier mention of horse doctors at Mari, I personally would not be surprised if earlier exclusively hippiatric texts were to show up in Mesopotamia or Anatolia, but the primary importance of such a discovery would be literary, proving the earlier existence of the genre to go along with the attested practice of hippiatry. Equally interesting is the later history of the hippiatric tradition, for such texts with the same protasis-apodosis format existed in Greek and Latin, in Punic, in Arabic, and in the modern European languages down to the near past (maybe even to the present). Lack of competence has prevented me from studying the Arabic hippiatric treatises to see whether the structure and vocabulary shows ties with the older Semitic tradition attested by Ugaritic, or if they imitate the classical models—or even if such a distinction is possible given the similarity of form and function of all these texts (cf. Pardee 1992: 154-55; 1996). As regards the Ugaritic texts, we have for the first time the repetition of a given protasis, in this case an ailment of the horse: loud coughing, unnatural whinnying, bulimic eating, and head ailments are all repeated, with different remedies prescribed in these cases of repetition. It is clear, therefore, that the intent of these texts is not to provide a reasoned overview of equine ailments, but a practical manual providing alternatives if one remedy does not work—a feature characteristic of the Classical hippiatric tradition. Finally, because of the absence of early Mesopotamian and Anatolian hippiatric texts, there is even less data available here than in the cases discussed above for possible correlations between the Ugaritic tradition and earlier traditions. It is somewhat ironic, though, that the one sub-genre for which the ancient Mesopotamian literary tradition is as yet unattested is the very one that shows the repetitions of protasis characteristic of the Mesopotamian format and otherwise absent from the Ugaritic format. It is doubtless necessary, however, to see this ironic situation as relatively unimportant: the identity of form of the human and equine medical texts is sufficient to account for the Ugaritic situation.

*Lexicography*

Ugaritic lexicography is certainly beholden to Mesopotamian traditions because the polyglot vocabularies (category 6a) are based directly on monolingual and bilingual Sumero-Akkadian versions. Moreover, this is the place to mention in passing that there are hundreds of tablets from Ugarit that reflect Mesopotamian lexicographical science—not a part of my purview because I am dealing with the data in the Ugaritic language.[11]

11. The 30 texts from the thirty-fourth campaign published by André-Salvini (1991) only provide a small sample of the total. Many of these texts were made available over the years to the authors of *Materials for the Sumerian Lexicon* (1937–), but many remain unpublished in any form. The number can be estimated by perusing the column of 'Remarques' in Bordreuil and Pardee (1989), or in van Soldt (1991: 525-671).

One might dispute the appropriateness of my category 6b as belonging to lexicography because these texts deal exclusively with divine names and because they clearly had a cultic function. I have categorized them thus for three reasons: (1) the Sumero-Akkadian lexical tradition includes divine names (some are present, e.g., in the principal polyglot vocabulary, RS 20.123⁺ (Nougayrol 1968: 240-49, text 137); (2) because the existence of Ugaritic and Sumero-Akkadian versions shows a science of equivalencies or translation values similar to common-name lexicography; (3) because the origin of these lists is still uncertain—though they clearly had a cultic function because a ritual is attested for each list, it would be unwise to conclude at this point that the divinity list is simply an abstraction of the sacrificial list; moreover, the composition of the second list, several entries of which present significant problems of interpretation, makes any decision regarding its origin for the present difficult. In any case, each list constituted a group of deities associated by its title and/or its cultic usage with another entity, the first list with *Ṣapunu*, probably the mountain of that name, the second with the month *Ḫiyyāru* (or another entity, unknown, bearing the same name).[12]

## *Conclusions*

First, two observations with regard to the relationship between these 'scientific' texts and Ugaritic 'religion', a topic that deserves much more extensive treatment. First, note the general absence of explicit divine activity in these texts. They deal with 'objective' phenomena: if the horse coughs, give it a remedy and he may get better; if the rising moon is peculiar, a particular event may occur—not because a deity wills it or effects it but because that's the way it is. Deities only

12. The sacrificial text containing sacrificial rites corresponding to the deity lists contains the following headings for each rite: *dbḥ ṣpn* ('the sacrifices of *Ṣapunu*') in l. 1, corresponding to the heading *'il ṣpn* ('the gods of *Ṣapunu*') of RS 1.017, and *'il ḫyr* ('the gods of *Ḫiyyāru*') in l. 23 (which of course has no correspondence elsewhere because no similar list is attested yet). Note that none of the syllabic lists of which I am aware bears a corresponding heading and that the heading *'il ṣpn* is absent from the second exemplar of the first deity list (RS 24.264⁺). The word *ḫyr* is well attested as a month name (it would correspond to January–February in my understanding of the month correspondences—see n. 6) and very poorly attested as a divine name.

occasionally appear in the apodosis and their activity is presented similarly to human activity. Divinities appear simply as another possible set of actors.

Secondly, in the one ‘prayer’ from Ugarit, preserved as the conclusion to a ritual text, the form is protasis – apodosis, like the ‘scientific’ texts, and the hinge is sacrifice:

| | |
|---|---|
| (26') k gr ʻz . ṯǵ⸢r⸣km .<br>⸢q⸣rd (27') ḥmytkm . | When a strong (foe) attacks your gate,<br>A warrior your walls, |
| ʻ⸢n⸣km . l ⸢b⸣ʻl tšʼun | You shall lift your eyes to *Baʻlu* (and say): |
| (28') y b⸢ʻl⸣m ⸢. -- . t⸣dy<br>ʻz l ⸢ṯ⸣ǵrn(29')y .<br>qrd [l] ḥmytny . | O *Baʻlu*, ⸢if⸣ you drive the strong one from our gate,<br>The warrior from our walls, |
| ʼibr y (30') bʻl . n⸢š⸣qdš .<br>mḏr bʻl (31') nmlʼu [.]<br>[b]kr b⸢ʻl⸣ . nš[q]dš<br>(32') ḥtp bʻ⸢l⸣ [.] ⸢n⸣mlʼu .<br>ʻ⸢šr⸣t . ⸢bʻl⸣ [.] ⸢n⸣[ʻ](33') šr .<br>qdš bʻ⸢l .⸣ nʻl .<br>ntbt b[ʻl] (34') ntlk . | A bull, (O) *Baʻlu*, we shall sanctify,<br>A vow, (O) *Baʻlu*, we shall fulfill;<br>A firstborn, (O) *Baʻlu*, we shall sanctify,<br>A *ḥtp*-offering, (O) *Baʻlu*, we shall fulfill,<br>A *ʻšrt*-feast, (O) *Baʻlu*, we shall offer;<br>To the sanctuary, (O) *Baʻlu*, we shall mount,<br>(That) path, (O) *Baʻlu*, we shall take. |
| w š[mʻ . b]ʻ⸢l .⸣ l ⸢. ṣ⸣l⸢tk⸣ [m] | And *Baʻlu* will hear (your) prayer: |
| (35') ⸢y⸣dy . ʻz l ṯǵ⸢r⸣k[m .<br>qrd] (36') lḥmytk[m ...] | He will drive the strong (foe) from your gate,<br>The warrior from your walls.[13] |

This text actually consists of a double protasis-apodosis structure, that of the text as a whole (*k gr ... w šmʻ...*) and that of the prayer itself (⸢*hm*[14] *t*⸣*dy ... ʼibr y bʻl n*⸢*š*⸣*qdš...*), a double-barreled example of classic *do ut des* religion expressed in circumstantial protasis-apodosis form.[15]

13. Pardee 1993: 213-16.

14. Though not certain, this reading is likely in l. 28'.

15. Note in passing that, when one considers all the divinatory texts, the function of *k* (here in the embedding structure) as opposed to *hm* (here in the embedded prayer) does not seem to express temporality as opposed to conditionality: the cases of a woman bearing and of a horse being sick are introduced by *k* (texts 1b and 5) while that of the moon rising is introduced by *hm* (text 2b). In any case, it is the more ‘temporal’ of the two formulations (*k*) that is used to express the circumstance of the attack and the rescue by the divinity, while the more narrowly conditional formulation is used for the relationship between the requested rescue and the

In this structural feature, the prayer shares what might be called the phenomenological perspective of the scientific texts. This perspective is, by the way, expressed in poetic form in the prayer and it is otherwise absent from the prose ritual texts, which normally consist of prescriptive lists of sacrifices, offerings and other ritual acts.

*The Ugaritic Tradition*

In the course of describing the texts, I have several times observed the absence of specific links with the known Mesopotamian texts. Because of the identity of general form and function between the Ugaritic and Mesopotamian texts, and because of the demonstrated antiquity of several of the sub-genres in Mesopotamia, it has generally been assumed, by myself and by others who have worked on these texts, that the Ugaritic versions are translations of unattested Akkadian originals. As I have worked through all these texts, however, I have been struck not only by the absence of specific correspondences in the attested Akkadian tradition but also by the general purity of the Ugaritic language: there are very few Akkadian loan words and no obvious calques on Akkadian words, expressions or syntactic structures. Where something appears anomalous, for example the predominant SVO (Subject-Verb-Object) word order in the apodoses of the animal fetuses text, it cannot be taken as reflecting an Akkadian *Vorlage* (Pardee 1986: 128-29, 144-45). It appears necessary to conclude that the Ugaritic texts we have reflect an old West Semitic tradition; how old can only be a matter of speculation at this point. The absence of Mesopotamian examples that show the 'general overview' format of some of the Ugaritic texts, in any case, precludes fixing the West Semitic borrowing to a known point in the Mesopotamian stream of tradition. And the general absence in the present archaeological picture of tablets in any language that predate the Late Bronze Age at Ugarit means that there are no local textual data to solve the local problem.[16] The primary feature of the Ugaritic texts that can be cited as a possible indication of date by comparison with the Mesopotamian tradition is the relative simplicity and brevity of the apodoses; the later the text in

subsequent sacrifices—which in form is actually *si dabis dabo*.

16. There may be a slight chink in this chronological wall: Arnaud (1996b, esp. 129) has recently identified a single Old-Babylonian form in an Akkadian text from Ugarit (because the tablet itself does not date to the Old-Babylonian period, it would be a question of an archaism retained in this particular tradition).

the Mesopotamian tradition, the more likely it is that the apodoses will be long and complicated. By this criterion, the Ugaritic tradition should date to the Old Babylonian or perhaps the Kassite period.

While recognizing the impossibility of dating the Ugaritic tradition, I would be remiss if I did not state that the characteristics of the scientific texts that I have cited could well fit into the perception growing in some minds that the early West Semitic contributions to culture have been eclipsed by the preponderance of textual data pouring out of Mesopotamia.[17] Without saying or even wishing to hint that the Amorites invented science, it would not be at all improper for me to hypothesize that their role in the spread of early compendia of knowledge may have been greater than hitherto suspected.[18]

Because of these multiple uncertainties regarding the age, the origin and the place in local thought[19] of these 'scientific' texts, it is as yet difficult to evaluate their place in the intellectual and cultural world of Syria-Palestine. In any case, because of the clear connections with the thought-world of Mesopotamia and the present tenuous state of the evidence for the spread of this 'science' into Palestine,[20] it is difficult to

17. Cf. Jacobsen's identification of the motif of a battle between a weather deity and the sea in the Enuma Elish as of western origin (1968: 104-108; 1976: 168); Bordreuil and Pardee (1993, esp. 69); Malamat (1997).

18. This was the conclusion to a lecture entitled 'La science ougaritique face à la Mésopotamie' that I presented at the Ecole Pratique des Hautes Etudes, Quatrième Section, on 20 November 1992.

19. This uncertainty is owing to our lack of knowledge as to how far the various types of knowledge attested at Ugarit may have spread beyond the intelligentsia who produced the texts. The influence probably varied considerably according to the type of knowledge: anyone with the wherewithal could probably consult a professional diviner and profit from his 'wisdom', or a horse-doctor and profit from his, whereas it is difficult to imagine the circumstances in which a specialist in lexicography would be consulted by a local not belonging to the scribal class. That various scribes were imbued not only with 'science' but with Mesopotamian literary conventions is illustrated by data ranging from high-flown literary compositions (e.g. Nougayrol 1968: 265-321) to epistolary formulae (cf. Arnaud 1982, esp. 107).

20. 'List-wisdom' is explicitly attributed to Solomon (1 Kgs 5.13 [Eng. 4.33]—the root ḤKM appears five times in vv. 9-11), a type of 'wisdom' best attested in the Mesopotamian lexicographic tradition (this observation goes back at least to A. Alt: see Miller [1997, esp. 6]. Scraps of Mesopotamian 'scientific' and literary texts have been found in Palestine, but to date no archive such as those of Ugarit or Emar has been discovered there.

determine to what extent it is valid to cite them as ‘background to the Bible’.

## APPENDIX: TEXTS WITH TRANSLATION[21]

### 1. *Teratology*

a. *Animal Fetus Omens* (*RS 24.247*⁺) Cf. Pardee[22]

*Text*

Recto

| | |
|---|---|
| 1. | ṯ’att ṣ’in ⸢-⸣[- -]⸢-⸣d’at . ’abn . m’adtn tqln b ḥwt |
| 2. | ‘ṣ. hn⸢-⸣[- -(-)]⸢y⸣ ’aṯr yld. bhmth t‘⸢- -⸣[…] |
| 3. | gmš š[ ]n ykn b ḥwt |
| 4. | w⸢’i⸣[n ]ḥwtn tḫlq |
| 5. | ⸢-⸣[ ]rǵbn ykn b ḥwt |
| 6. | [ ]⸢-.⸣ w ẖr ’apm . ḥwt⸢n⸣[----(-)]⸢m⸣ṯn rgm |
| 7. | [w] ⸢’in⸣[ ]⸢m⸣lkn y’iḫd ḥw[t ’ ibh w?] mrḥy mlk ⸢t⸣dlln |
| 8. | [-]⸢-⸣h . m⸢-⸣[- - - -]⸢-m⸣ḫt . bhmtn[-------]⸢-⸣ |
| 9. | ⸢w⸣ ’in šq . [šm’al ] ⸢b⸣h . mlkn ⸢y⸣[- - - - -(-)]⸢’i⸣bh |
| 10. | ⸢w⸣ ’in qṣr[t šm]⸢’a⸣l . mlk⸢n⸣[ - - - - - -(-) ’i]⸢b⸣h |
| 11. | w qrn š’i⸢r⸣ [. b] ⸢p⸣’ith š ⸢m’a⸣[l ]n |
| 12. | ṭḥl . ’in . bh[--]⸢-⸣dn . ⸢-⸣[ ] ⸢m⸣ṯ ⸢n⸣ […] |
| 13. | mlkn . l ypq ⸢š⸣[p]ḥ |
| 14. | [w] ’in ’uškm b⸢h .⸣ḏ ⸢r⸣[‘ ]⸢-⸣ |
| 15. | ⸢w⸣ ’in . kr‘ y⸢d⸣h ⸢-⸣[ ]⸢y⸣ḫlq bhmt [- -]⸢-⸣ |
| 16. | [-]⸢-⸣[-]⸢-⸣[ ] . ’ibn yḫlq bhmt ⸢ḥw⸣t |
| 17. | [ ]⸢-⸣ . ṯnn ‘z y’uḫd ’ib mlk |
| 18. | [ ]ḫlq . mṯn rgm |
| 19. | [ ]rǵb . w tp . mṣq ⸢t⸣ |
| 20. | [ ]⸢y⸣‘zzn |
| 21. | [ ]rn |
| 22. | [ ]bh |
| 23. | [ ]⸢t⸣p ⸢š⸣[…][23] |

21. With regard to the following translations to which a reference to Pardee (1997a-f) is attached, the reader will find in that volume notes on the translation but not the Ugaritic text. For a full defence of readings and interpretations, see Pardee (2000).

22. Pardee 1997a: 287-89, text 1.90.

23. Approximately one-fourth to one-third of the tablet has been lost, and as few as 15 and as many as 30 lines have disappeared.

| | |
|---|---|
| Verso | |
| 24'. | [ ]⌈- . l⌉[…] |
| 25'. | [ ]⌈’i⌉r . lk ⌈-⌉[…] |
| 26'. | w ’in . šq ymn . b ⌈h⌉[…] |
| 27'. | w ’in . ḫrṣp . b k ⌈-⌉[…] |
| 28'. | w ’in . kr‘ . ydh[…] |
| 29'. | l ypq špḥ |
| 30'. | w ’in . ḫr ’apm . kl[…] |
| 31'. | w ’in . lšn bh . r[…] |
| 32'. | špth . tḫyt[24] . k⌈-⌉[…] |
| 33'. | pnh . pn . ’irn . ’u⌈-⌉[ ]⌈-⌉tqṣrn[…] |
| 34'. | ymy . b‘l hn bhm[t …] |
| 35'. | w ’in . ’udn . ymn . ⌈b⌉[h ’ibn y]šdd ḥwt |
| 36'. | [ w y] ḥslnn |
| 37'. | w ’in . ’udn šm’al . ⌈b⌉[h . ]⌈ mlkn⌉[ y]šdd ḥwt ’i ⌈b⌉[h …] |
| 38'. | w yḥslnn |
| 39'. | w qṣrt . p‘nh . b‘ln yġt⌈r⌉ [. ḫ]rd . w ’uḫr |
| 40'. | y . ykly ⌈rš⌉p |
| 41'. | ⌈w⌉ ’a ⌈ph⌉ . k ’ap . ‘ṣr . ’ilm . tb‘⌈rn⌉ . ḥwt |
| 42'. | [ ]⌈-⌉št . w yd’u |
| 43'. | [ ]⌈.⌉ l r’išh . ḏr⌈‘⌉ [.] ⌈m⌉lk hwt |
| 44'. | [-------]⌈ḥ⌉ |
| 45'. | [------]⌈d⌉rh . yṣ’u . špšn . tpšlt . ḥ<br>wt hyt |
| 46'. | [-----]mlkn . yd . ḫrdh . yddll |
| 47'. | [-----]⌈l⌉ . ’ušrh . mrḥy . mlk tnš’an |
| 48'. | [-----]⌈-⌉b . ydh |
| 49'. | [----]⌈-⌉ ’aṯrt . ‘nh . w ‘nh b lṣbh |
| 50'. | [’ibn y]rps ḥwt |
| 51'. | [---]bh . b ph . yṣ’u ’ibn . ysp’u ḥwt |
| 52'. | w [’in] p‘nt . bh . ḫrdn . yhpk . l mlk |
| 53'. | w [- -] lšnh . ḥwtn tprš |
| 54'. | b⌈-⌉[- -]⌈-⌉ḫrh . b p’ith . mlkn . yšlm l ’ibh |
| 55'. | w ’i[n -]⌈k⌉bm . bh . ḏr‘ . ḥwt . hyt yḥsl |
| Upper Edge | |
| 56'. | w ‘⌈-⌉[-] . ’ilm . tb‘rn ḥwt . hyt |
| 57'. | w ‘nh [b] ⌈l⌉ṣbh . mlkn y‘zz ‘l ḫpṯh |
| 58'. | w ḫr . ⌈w -⌉r . bh . mlkn yb‘r ’ibh |
| 59'. | w ’in yd š⌈m’a⌉l bh . ḥwt ’ib ṯḫlq |

24. Read {tḫ<t>yt}.

*Translation*

Recto

1. As for the ewes of the flock, [when t]hey give birth, (if it is a) stone, many will fall in the land.
2. (If it is a piece of) wood, behold [...] in place of the offspring/birth, its cattle will [...].
3. (If the fetus) is smooth, (without) h[air?], there will be [...] in the land.
4. And (if) th[ere is no ...], the land will perish.
5. [...], there will be famine in the land.
6. [...] and (= nor) nostrils, the land [...]; ditto.
7. [And] (if) there is no [...], the king will seize the lan[d of his enemy and] the weapon of the king will lay it (the land) low.
8. [...] [...] cattle [...]
9. And (if) it has no [left] thigh, the king will [...] his enemy.
10. And (if) there is no lower left leg, the king [will ...] his enemy.
11. And (if there is) a horn of flesh [in] its lef[t te]mple, [...].
12. (If) it has no spleen [...] [...]; di[tto;]
13. the king will not obtain offspring.
14. [And] (if) it has no testicles, the (seed-)gra[in ...]
15. And (if) the middle part of its [left?] foreleg is missing, [...] will destroy the cattle of [...].
16. [ ...], the enemy will destroy the cattle of the land.
17. [...], the mighty archers will seize the enemy of the king.
18. [...]perish/destroy; ditto.
19. [...]famine, hard times will disappear.
20. [...]will become strong/strengthen him.
21. [...]
22. [...]
23. [...]

24'. [...] [...]
25'. [...] [...]
26'. And (if) it has no right thigh [...]
27'. And (if) there is no tendon? in [its?] K[...]
28'. And (if) it has no middle part of the [right] foreleg [...]
29'. will not obtain offspring.
30'. And (if) [it has] no nostrils [...]
31'. And (if) it has no tongue [...]
32'. (If) its lower lip (is) like [...]
33'. (If) its face (is) that of a ’IRN, [...] will shorten
34'. the days of the (= our) lord; behold, the catt[le? ...]
35'. And (if) [it] has no right ear, [the enemy will] devastate the land
36'. [... and will] consume it.
37'. And (if) [it] has no left ear, the king [will] devastate the land of [his] enemy

38'. and will consume it.

39'. And (if) its (rear?) legs (are) short, the (= our) lord will confront the *ḫurādu*-troops and

40'. *Rašap* will finish off the posterity.

41'. And (if) its nose (is) like the 'nose' of a bird, the gods will destroy the land

42'. […] and will fly (away?).

43'. […] to/on its head, the (seed-)grain of that king

44'. […]

45'. […] its [-]DR protrudes, the Sun will abase that land.

46'. […], the king will lay low the hand (= power) of the *ḫurādu*-troops.

47'. […] its penis, the weapon of the king will be raised

48'. […] his hand.

49'. […] in place of its eyes and its eyes (are) in its forehead,

50'. [the enemy will] tread the land under.

51'. [And (if)] its [--]B protrudes from its mouth, the enemy will devour the land.

52'. And (if) it has [no] feet, the *ḫurādu*-troops will turn against the king.

53'. And if its tongue is […], the land will be scattered.

54'. (If) its […]ḪR (is/are) in its temples, the king will make peace with his enemy.

55'. And (if) it has n[o] [-]KB, the (seed-)grain of that land will be consumed.

56'. And (if) […], the gods will destroy that land.

57'. And (if) its eyes are [in] (its) forehead, the king will become more powerful than his *ḫupṯu*-troops.

58'. And (if) it has ḪR and [-]R, the king will destroy his enemy.

59'. And (if) it has no left (fore?)leg, the land of the enemy will perish.

b. *Human fetus omens* (RS 24.302)[25]

| *Text* | *Translation* |
|---|---|
| **Recto** | |
| 1. k ⌈t⌉[ld …] | If [a woman] g[ives birth…] |
| 2. ḥw[t …] | the l[and…] |
| 3. k tl ⌈d⌉[…] | If [a woman] gives birth[…] |
| 4. y'zz '⌈l⌉[…] | will become more powerful than[…] |
| **Lower Edge** | |
| 5. k tld ⌈'a⌉[ṯt[…] | If a wo[man] gives birth[…] |
| 6. ḥwt 'ib ⌈t⌉[…] | the land of the enemy will [be destroyed.] |
| **Verso** | |
| 7'. k tld 'a [ṯt…] | If a wo[man] gives birth […] |
| 8'. 'ḏrt tk⌈-⌉[…] | help will be […] |

25. Cf. Pardee 1997a.

| | | |
|---|---|---|
| 9'. | k tld 'a [t̲t...] | If a wo[man] gives birth [...] |
| 10'. | mrḥ⸢y⸣[...] | the weapon of[...] |
| 11'. | l yp[...] | will not ob[tain offspring?...] |
| 12'. | bh⸢-⸣[...] | BH[...] |
| 13'. | t⸢-⸣[...] | will? [...] |
| 14'. | ⸢-⸣[...] | I[f a woman gives birth...] |

## 2. *Astrology*

a. *An Astrological Report* (RS 12.061)[26]

| *Text* | *Translation* |
|---|---|
| Recto | |
| 1. b t̲t̲ . ym . ḥdt̲ | During the six days of the (rituals of) the new moon of |
| 2. ḫyr . 'rbt | (The month of) *Ḫiyyāru*, the sun |
| 3. špš ⸢.⸣ t̲ǵrh | set, her gatekeeper (being) |
| 4. ršp | *Rashap*. |
| Verso | |
| 5'. ⸢w 'a⸣dm ⸢.⸣ tbqrn | The men (?) shall seek out |
| 6'. skn | the prefect. |

b. *Lunar Omens* (RIH 78/14)[27]

*Text*

| | |
|---|---|
| Recto | |
| 1. | ⸢h⸣m . b ḥd[t̲] . y[-] ⸢. -⸣ [-(-)]⸢- - -⸣ šn . ykn |
| 2. | hm . yrḫ . b '⸢l⸣[y]⸢h⸣ . w pḥm |
| 3. | n'mn . y⸢kn⸣ [-]h |
| 4. | [hm .] ⸢yr⸣ḫ b 'lyh . ⸢--⸣q |
| 5. | [ ]⸢b⸣hmtn . tḫlq |
| 6. | [ ]⸢-⸣y ⸢h⸣ . w pḥm |
| 7. | [ ]⸢-⸣ qbṣt |
| Verso[28] | |
| 8'. | [ ]⸢ḫ⸣l ⸢q⸣ |
| 9'. | [ ]⸢-⸣ ḥdt̲ . yrḫ . bnšm |
| 10'. | [ ]⸢.⸣ w thbẓn |
| 11'. | [ ]ym . ⸢y⸣h . yrḫ . kslm . mlkm . tbṣrn |

26. Cf. Pardee and Swerdlow 1993.

27. Cf. Pardee 1997b.

28. If the shape of this tablet was typical, approximately half again as high as it is wide, as many as twenty-five to thirty lines have disappeared.

| | |
|---|---|
| 12'. | [hm .] ṯlṯ . 'id . ynphy . yrḫ . b yrḫ . 'aḫrm |
| 13'. | [- -]lt . mẓrn y⌈l⌉k |
| 14'. | [hm . ] ⌈k⌉bkb . yql . b ṯlṯm . ym . mlkn . ⌈- - -⌉ [...] |

*Translation*

| | |
|---|---|
| 1. | If at the time of the new moon [...], there will be poverty |
| 2. | If the moon, when it rises, is red, |
| 3. | there will be prosperity [during] (that month). |
| 4. | [If] the moon, when it rises, is yellow-green |
| 5. | [ ], the cattle will perish. |
| 6. | [If the moon, when it ri]ses, is red, |
| 7. | [ ] assembly. |
| 8'. | [ will] perish. |
| 9'. | [ ] newness of the moon, the personnel |
| 10'. | [ ] and will be put down. |
| 11'. | [ ]YM YH YRḪ KSLM, the kings will keep an eye on each other. |
| 12'. | [If] three times the moon is seen in the moon/month (and) thereafter |
| 13'. | [...]LT, there will be rain. |
| 14'. | [If] a star falls on the thirtieth day, the king [...]. |

3. *Extispicy*[29]

a. Inscribed Liver models in clay

1. RS 24.312

| *Text* | *Translation* |
|---|---|
| 1. l 'ag⌈pṯ⌉r k yqny ǵzr ⌈d 'a⌉lṯyy | (This liver model is) for *'Agapṯarri* when he was to buy the boy of the *Alashian*. |

2. RS 24.323

| *Text* | *Translation* |
|---|---|
| 1. dbḥt . bṣy . b⌈n⌉ [...] | Sacrificial (consultation) of BṢY, so[n]/ daught[er] of |
| 2. ⌈ṭ⌉ry . l 'ṯṯ⌈r⌉[...] | ṬRY, for the *'Aṯṯaru*[...] |
| 3. d . ⌈b '-tr⌉[...] | who is in *'Aṯṯar*[*tu*]. |

3. RS 24.326

| *Text* | *Translation* |
|---|---|
| 1. kbd . dt ypt | (This is) the liver (pertaining to the consultation on behalf) of YPT, |

29. Cf. Pardee 1997c.

| | |
|---|---|
| 2. bn ykn‘ | son of YKN‘, |
| 3. k ypth̩ . yr⌈h̬⌉ hnd | when this month was about to begin. |

4. RS 24.327

| *Text* | *Translation* |
|---|---|
| 1. [ ]l | […]L |
| 2. d ⌈yb⌉nmlk | of *Yabnimilku* |
| 3. l h̬pṯ | with regard to *h̬pṯ*. |

5. RS 24.654

| *Text* | *Translation* |
|---|---|
| 1. k⌈bd⌉ h̩[…] | (This is) the liver (model) for Ḥ[…] |
| 2. k ymmr[…] | when […] |
| 3. ym š⌈h̩⌉[…] | (on) a/the day of […]. |

b. *Inscribed Lung models in clay* (RS 24.277)

| *Text* | *Translation* |
|---|---|
| Surface 1, Inscription 1 | |
| 1'. dbḥ kl yrh̬ | Sacrifices of the entire month. |
| 2'. ndr | A(n object) vow(ed), |
| 3'. dbḥ | a sacrifice. |
| Surface 1, Inscription 2 | |
| 4'. dt n’at | Those (= the sacrifices) of (= offered by) N’AT |
| 5'. w ytnt | and gifts of (= for) |
| 6'. ṯrmn w | (the deity) *Ṯarrummanni* and |
| 7'. dbḥ kl | a sacrifice of (= offered by) all; |
| 8'. kl ykly | all (will eat this) sacrifice (until) it is gone, |
| 9'. dbḥ k . sprt | in accordance with the writings. |
| Surface 1, Inscription 3 | |
| 10'. dt n’at | Those (= the sacrifices) of (= offered by) N’AT |
| 11'. w qrwn | and *Qurwanu*; |
| 12'. l k dbḥ | (these will be done) like the (preceding) sacrifice. |
| Surface 1, Inscription 4 | |
| 13'. […]⌈r⌉bt | […]RBT |
| 14'. […]bnš | […]personnel. |

| Surface 2, Inscription 5 | |
|---|---|
| 15'. š⸢š⸣[…] | A ram Š[…] |
| 16'. w ⸢-⸣[…] | and […] |
| 17'. d[…] | D[…] |

| Surface 2, Inscription 6 | |
|---|---|
| 18'. ypy[…] | YPY[…] |
| 19'. w s ⸢-⸣[…] | and S[…] |

| Surface 2, Inscription 7 | |
|---|---|
| 20'. ṯr dg ⸢n⸣[…] | A bull of (= for) *Dagan* […] |
| 21'. b bt k . ⸢-⸣[…] | in the house, according to the wr[itings], |
| 22'. w l db⸢ḥ⸣[…] | and to/surely the sacrifice […]. |

| Surface 3, Inscription 8 | |
|---|---|
| 23'. hm qrt t'uḫd . hm mt y'l bnš | If the city is about to be seized, if the man (= warrior) attacks, the (male) personnel (of the city) |

| Surface 3, Inscription 9 | |
|---|---|
| 24'. […]⸢-⸣ 'aṯt yqḥ 'z | […] the women, they will take a goat […] |
| 25'. […]⸢--⸣ | […] |

| Surface 3, Inscription 10 | |
|---|---|
| 26'. bt hn bnš yqḥ 'z | (in) (or: with regard to) the house, the (male) personnel will take a goat |
| 27'. w yḥdy mrḥqm | and see afar. |

c. *Inscribed liver models in ivory*[30]

d. *Oniromancy* (RS 18.041)[31]

| *Text* | | *Translation* |
|---|---|---|
| Recto | | |
| 1. | ⸢s⸣[p]⸢r⸣ [.]ḥlmm . ⸢'a⸣ lp ⸢.⸣ šnt . ⸢w⸣ […] | Document of dreams. A year-old bull and […] |
| 2. | šntm . ⸢'a⸣ lp [.] dkr . rg ⸢m⸣ […] | two years; the mature bull: the word (=interpretation?) […] |
| 3. | 'alp . pr . b'l . ⸢--⸣ . r ⸢b⸣[…] | The bull: the young bull of *Ba'lu* […] |

30. These texts are too fragmentary to be worth providing here *in extenso*; see Pardee (forthcoming).

31. Cf. Pardee 1997d.

| | | |
|---|---|---|
| 4. | w prt . tkt . [ ]⌈-⌉[…] | the heifer (that?) will be slaughtered […] |
| 5. | šnt | (one) year. |
| 6. | s̀sw . ‘ṯtrt . w s̀sw [.] š⌈-⌉[…] | The horse of *‘Aṯtartu* and the horse of Š[…] |
| 7. | w hm . y⌈h⌉pk . s̀sw . rgm .[…] | and if the horse falls over: the word (= interpretation?) […] |
| 8. | d ymǵy . [-] ⌈b⌉nš . ⌈-⌉[…] | that arrives (where) the man (is) […]. |
| 9. | w ḥm⌈r⌉[--]⌈--ḥ⌉mr ⌈.⌉⌈-(-)⌉[…] | And the donkey […] donkey […] |
| 10. | w mṯn[ ]⌈r⌉ [?] ⌈b-⌉[…] | and ditto […] |
| 11. | w bn ⌈-⌉[ ]d ⌈.’a⌉ m ⌈-⌉[…]and BN […] | |
| 12. | l bnš . ḥ⌈mr⌉[ ]d l [?] n ⌈-⌉[…] | to the man, the donkey […] |
| 13. | w d . l mdl . r[ ]⌈-š⌉[…] | and that to the harness […] |
| 14. | w ṣ’in . ‘z . b ⌈-⌉[…] | And the flock: the goat […] |
| 15. | ll’u . bn m ⌈-⌉[…] | the kid, offspring of […] |
| 16. | ’imr . ḫ⌈p?--⌉[…] | the lamb […] |
| 17. | ⌈-⌉n . b ⌈‘l⌉[…] | son(s) of Ba‘lu […][32] |
| Verso | | |
| 18'. | [--]n [.] ’a⌈mt-⌉[…] | […] the servant-girl […] |
| 19'. | ⌈-⌉m[ ]⌈.⌉rḥ ⌈--⌉[…] | […] |
| 20'. | n ⌈’it⌉[--]d . b ⌈n⌉[…] | The *n’it*-tool […] |
| 21'. | ’idk [?] n’it[…] | then the *n’it*-tool […] |
| 22'. | trg[-] [?] ⌈‘b⌉ dk [?] y[…] | SPE[AK], your servant […] |
| 23'. | m‘bd . ḫrm ⌈ṯt⌉ [?] ⌈-⌉[…] | The worker (or: the work) (with) the *ḫrmṯt*-tool […] |
| 24'. | w ks̀t . šqy ⌈-⌉[ ]⌈-⌉[…] | And the cups (of) ŠQYM/T […] |
| 25'. | bn . šqym . ⌈q⌉[…] | the sons of the cup-bearers […] |
| 26'. | kbdt . b ⌈nš⌉[…] | KBDT the personnel […] |
| 27'. | š’inm . n[-]⌈-⌉[--]⌈-⌉[…] | The sandals […] |
| 28'. | b ḥlm . ’a ⌈ṯ⌉[-----(-)]np ⌈-⌉[…] | In a dream […] |
| 29'. | pn ⌈.-⌉[-]⌈-⌉ [?] ⌈y⌉[-]⌈-⌉[-]⌈-⌉[…] | face of […] |
| 30'. | ⌈bnš⌉ m . ’aṯt . ⌈k⌉[--(-)]‘np . ‘[…] | The men (personnel) (and) the women […] |
| 31'. | ⌈š‘⌉rm . ⌈bǵ⌉[----(-)]⌈---⌉’ar .[…] | barley […] |
| 32'. | w ⌈b--⌉[ ]⌈--⌉[ ]⌈-š--⌉[…] | […] |
| 33'. | b m[…] | […] |
| 34'. | ⌈-⌉[…] | […] |

32. Some 15 to 20 lines may have disappeared in the lacuna (to know something closer to the real number, we would have to know the exact shape of the original tablet and whether the lower edge was inscribed or not).

## 5. *Hippiatry*[33]

1. RS 5.285+

| *Text* | *Proposed reconstruction* |
|---|---|
| Recto | |
| 1. [ ] | 1. [spr . n'm . ššwm] |
| | [————————] |
| 2. [ ] | 2. [k . yg'r . ššw . št] |
| 3. [ ] | 3. ['qrbn . ydk . w . ymss] |
| 4. [ ] | 4. [hm . b . mskt . dlḥt . hm] |
| 5. [ ] | 5. [b . mndǵ . w . yṣq . b . 'aph] |
| ———[ ] ] | ———————— |
| 6. k[ ] | 6. k[ . ḫr . ššw . mǵmǵ] |
| 7. w[ ] | 7. w[ . bṣql . 'rgz . ydk] |
| 8. 'a⌈ḥ⌉[ ] | 8. 'a⌈ḥ⌉[dh . wyṣq . b . 'aph] |
| ——[ ] | ———————— |
| 9. k .[ ] | 9. k .[ ḫr . ššw . ḫndrṯ] |
| 10. w . ⌈ṯ⌉[ ] | 10. w . ⌈ṯ⌉[qd . mr . ydk . 'aḥdh] |
| 11. w . y[ ] | 11. w . y[ṣq . b . 'aph] |
| ———[ ] | ———————— |
| 12. k . l . ḫ[ ] | 12. k . l . ḫ[r'a . w . l . yṯtn] |
| 13. mss . [ ] | 13. mss . [št . qlql . w . št] |
| 14. 'rgz[ ] | 14. 'rgz[ . ydk . 'aḥdh] |
| 15. w . yṣq[ ] | 15. w . yṣq[ . b . 'aph] |
| —————[ ] | ———————— |
| 16. k . y'iḫd[ ] | 16. k . y'iḫd[ . 'akl . ššw] |
| 17. št . mkš[ ] | 17. št . mkš[r . grn] |
| 18. w . št . 'aš⌈k⌉[ ] | 18. w . št . 'aš⌈k⌉[rr] |
| 19. w . pr . ḥḏr[ ] | 19. w . pr . ḥḏr[t . ydk] |
| 20. 'aḥdh . w . yṣq[ ] | 20. 'aḥdh . w . yṣq[ . b . 'aph] |
| ————————[ ] | ———————— |
| 21. k . y'iḫd . 'akl . š[ ] | 21. k . y'iḫd . 'akl . š[šw] |
| 22. št . nn'i . št . m ⌈k⌉[ ] | 22. št . nn'i . št . m ⌈k[šr . grn . w] |
| 23. št . 'irǵn . ḥm⌈r⌉[ ] | 23. št . 'irǵn . ḥm⌈r⌉[ . ydk] |
| 24. 'aḥdh . w . yṣq . b[ ] | 24. 'aḥdh . w . yṣq . b[ . 'aph] |
| —————————[ ] | ———————— |

33. Because my edition of these texts (Pardee 1985) contains so many typographical errors, I provide here a cleaner version of all four texts. The structure of the texts is almost identical, and for that reason only the most complete of the four, RS 17.120, is translated. My differences with Cohen's recent presentations of these texts (Cohen 1996; 1997) cannot be addressed here and are in any case of unimportance for the questions of structure and history on which I wish to focus in this presentation.

| | |
|---|---|
| 25. k . yr'aš . s̀s̀w . ⸢š⸣[ ] | 25. k . yr'aš . s̀s̀w . ⸢š⸣[t] |
| 26. bln . qṭ . yṣq . b . ⸢'a⸣[ ] | 26. bln . qṭ . yṣq . b . ⸢'a⸣[ph] |

Lower edge: vacat

Verso

| | |
|---|---|
| 27. k . yg'r[ ] | 27. k . yg'r[ . s̀s̀w . ...] |
| 28. dpr⸢n⸣[ ] | 28. dpr⸢n⸣[ . w . pr . 'ṯrb] |
| 29. dr' .[ ] | 29. dr' .[ w . ṯqd . mr . w] |
| 30. tmṯ⸢l⸣[ ] | 30. tmṯ⸢l⸣[ . gd . w . tmṯl . ṯmrg . w] |
| 31. mǵm⸢ǵ⸣[ ] | 31. mǵm⸢ǵ⸣[ . w . št . nn'i . w . pr . 'bk] |
| 32. w . š[ ] | 32. w . š[t . 'qrb . w .mǵmǵ] |
| 33. w . p⸢r⸣[ ] | 33. w . p⸢r⸣[ . ḥḏrt . w . tmṯl] |
| 34. 'irǵ⸢n⸣[ ] | 34. 'irǵ⸢n⸣[ . ḥmr . ydk] |
| 35. 'aḥd⸢h⸣[ ] | 35. 'aḥd⸢h⸣[ . w. yṣq . b . 'aph] |
| ————[ ] | ———— |
| 36. k . yr⸢'a⸣š . s̀s̀⸢w⸣[ ] | 36. k . yr⸢'a⸣š . s̀s̀⸢w⸣[ . wykhp] |
| 37. m'id . dblt . yṯ[ ] | 37. m'id . dblt . yṯ[nt . w] |
| 38. ṣmq⸢m⸣ . yṯnm . w[ ] | 38. ṣmq⸢m⸣ . yṯnm . w[ . qmḥ . bql] |
| 39. tdkn . 'aḥdh . w[ ] | 39. tdkn . 'aḥdh . w[ . yṣq] |
| 40. b . 'aph | 40. b . 'aph |

2. RS 5.300

| *Text* | *Proposed reconstruction* |
|---|---|
| Recto | |
| 1. [ ] | 1. [spr n'm s̀s̀wm] |
| | [————] |
| 2. [ ]⸢w⸣[ ] | 2. [k yg'r s̀s̀]⸢w⸣ [št 'qrbn] |
| 3. [ ]s̀s̀[ ] | 3. [ydk w ym]s̀s̀[ hm bmskt dlḥt] |
| 4. [ ]⸢w⸣ yṣq b'a[ ] | 4. [hm bmndǵ] ⸢w⸣ yṣq b'a[ph] |
| 5. [ ]s̀w mǵmǵ w b[ ] | 5. [k ḫr s̀]s̀w mǵmǵ w b[ṣql 'rgz] |
| 6. [ ]⸢ḥ⸣dh w yṣq b'aph | 6. [ydk 'a]⸢ḥ⸣dh w yṣq b'aph |
| 7. [ ] s̀s̀w ḫndrṯ w ṯ⸢q⸣[ ]⸢r⸣ | 7. [(w) k ḫr] s̀s̀w ḫndrṯ w ṯ⸢q⸣[d m]⸢r⸣ |
| 8. [ ]⸢ḥ⸣dh w yṣq b'aph | 8. [ydk 'a]⸢ḥ⸣dh w yṣq b'aph |
| 9. [ ]⸢'a w⸣ l yṯtn mss št qlql | 9. [(w) k l ḫr]⸢'a w⸣ l yṯtn mss št qlql |
| 10. [ ]⸢y⸣dk 'aḥdh w yṣq b'aph | 10. [w št 'rgz]⸢y⸣dk 'aḥdh w yṣq b'aph |
| 11. [ ]⸢s̀⸣s̀w št mkšr grn | 11. [(w) k y'iḫd 'akl ]⸢s̀⸣s̀w št mkšr grn |
| 12. [ ]⸢r⸣ ḥ⸢ḏ⸣rt | 12. [w št 'aškrr w p]⸢r⸣ ḥ⸢ḏ⸣rt |
| 13. [ ] | 13. [ydk w yṣq b 'aph] |
| 14. [ ]⸢w š⸣[ ] | 14. [(w) k y'iḫd 'a kl s̀s̀]⸢w š⸣[t nn'i] |
| 15. [ ]⸢ǵn ḥm⸣[ ] | 15. [w št mkšr grn w št 'ir]⸢ǵn ḥm⸣[r] |
| 16. [ ] | 16. [ydk w yṣq b'aph] |
| 17. [ ]⸢ṭ⸣ ydk | 17. [(w) k yr'aš s̀s̀w št bln q]⸢ṭ⸣ ydk |

| | |
|---|---|
| 18. [ ] | 18. [w yṣq b’aph] |
| 19. [ ] | 19. [(w) k yg‘r s̀s̀w --(-) dprn w pr] |
| 20. [ ] | 20. [‘ṯrb dr‘ wṯqd mr w tmṯl] |
| 21. [ ] | 21. [gd w tmṯl ṯmrg w mǵmǵ] |
| 22. [ ]⌈q⌉rb | 22. [w št nn’i w pr ‘bk w št ‘]⌈q⌉rb |
| 23. [ ]⌈l⌉ | 23. [w mǵmǵ w pr ḥd̲rt w tmṯ]⌈l⌉ |
| 24. [ ] | 24. [’irǵn ḥmr ydk] |

| Lower Edge | Lower Edge |
|---|---|
| 25. [ ]⌈q b⌉ [ ]⌈h⌉ | 25. [’aḥdh w yṣ]⌈q b⌉ [’ap]⌈h⌉ |

Verso

| | |
|---|---|
| 26. k yr’aš w ykhp m’id | 26. k yr’aš w ykhp m’id |
| 27. dblt yṯnt w ṣmqm yṯn[ ] | 27. dblt yṯnt w ṣmqm yṯn[m] |
| 28. w qmḥ bql yṣq ’aḥdh | 28. w qmḥ bql yṣq ’aḥdh |
| 29. b ⌈’ap⌉h | 29. b ⌈’ap⌉h |

3. RS 17.120

*Text*

Recto

1. spr . n‘m . s̀s̀wm

---

2. k . yg‘r . s̀s̀w . št . ‘qrbn
3. ydk . w . yms̀ . hm . b . mskt . dlḥt
4. hm . b . mndǵ . w . yṣq . b . ’aph

---

5. k . ḫr . s̀s̀w . mǵmǵ . w . bṣql . ‘rgz
6. ydk . ’aḥdh . w . yṣq . b . ’aph

---

7. w . k . ḫr . s̀s̀w . ḫndrṯ . w . ṯqd . mr
8. ydk . ’aḥdh . w . yṣq . b . ’aph

---

9. w . k . l . yḫr’u . w . l . yṯtn . s̀s̀w
10. [ms]s . št . qlql . w . št . ‘rgz
11. [yd]k . ’aḥdh . w . yṣq . b . ’aph

---

12. [w . k]⌈’a⌉ḫd . ’akl . s̀s̀w . št . mkšr
13. ⌈gr⌉[n .] w . št . ’aškrr
14. w . ⌈pr⌉ . ḥd̲rt . ydk . w . yṣq . b . ’aph

---

15. w . k . ’aḫd . ’akl . s̀s̀w . št . nn’i
16. w . št . mkšr . grn . w . št
17. ’irǵn . ḥmr . ydk . w ⌈. y⌉ṣq . b . ’aph

---

18. w . k . yr’aš . s̀s̀w . št . bln . qṭ
19. ydk . w . ⌈y⌉[ṣ]q . b . ’aph

---

20. w . ⌈k⌉[ ]⌈-⌉bd . s̀s̀w . ⌈g⌉d . ḫlb
21. w . š[ ]⌈-⌉ . ‘l ⌈- . -⌉[ ]
22. ydk[ . ’aḥdh . w. y]⌈ṣq⌉ [. b . ’aph]

23. w . k . y⌈g⌉[‘r . ššw . --(-) . dprn . w]
24. pr . ‘ṯ[rb . dr‘ . w . ṯ]⌈qd⌉[ . mr . w]
25. tmṯl . g⌈d⌉[ . w . tm]ṯl . ṯmrg ⌈.⌉[ w . mǵmǵ]
26. w . št . nn⌈’i⌉ [.] w ⌈.⌉ pr . ‘bk . ⌈w⌉[ . št . ‘qrb . w]
27. mǵmǵ . w . pr . ḥḏrt . w[ . tmṯl]

Lower Edge
28. ’irǵn . ḥmr . ydk . ’a[ḥdh]
29. w . yṣq . b . ’aph

Verso
30. k . yr’aš . w . ykhp . m’i ⌈d⌉
31. dblt . yṯnt . ṣmqm . yṯ[nm]
32. w . qmḥ . bql . yṣq . ’aḥd[h . b . ’aph]

4. RS 23.484

| *Text* | | *Proposed reconstruction* |
|---|---|---|
| Recto | | Recto |
| 1'. | [ ]⌈b⌉[ ] | 1'. [w yṣq .] ⌈b⌉[ ’aph] |
| 2'. | k y’iḫd . ’akl . š⌈š⌉[ ] | 2'. k y’iḫd . ’akl . š⌈š⌉[w . št . nn’i] |
| 3'. | w . št . mkšr . g[ ] | 3'. w . št . mkšr . g[rn . w . št] |
| 4'. | ’arǵn . ḥmr . td[ ] | 4'. ’arǵn . ḥmr . td[k(n) . ’aḥdh] |
| 5'. | w yṣq . b ’aph [ ] | 5'. w yṣq . b ’aph |
| 6'. | k yr’aš . šš⌈w⌉[ ] | 6'. k yr’aš . šš⌈w⌉[ . št . bln . qṭ] |
| 7'. | ydk ⌈. y⌉ṣq . b ⌈’a⌉[ ] | 7'. ydk ⌈. y⌉ṣq . b ⌈’a⌉[ph] |
| 8'. | [ ]⌈-⌉ṣ⌈.⌉šš[ ] | 8'. [---]⌈-⌉ṣ ⌈.⌉šš[w...] |
| Verso | | Verso |
| 9'. | [ ]r ⌈.⌉ ššw[ ] | 9'. [k . yg‘]r ⌈.⌉ ššw[ . --- . dprn . w] |
| 10'. | [ ]‘ṯrb . dr[ ] | 10'. [pr . ]‘ṯrb . dr[‘ . w . ṯqd . mr] |
| 11'. | [ ]tmṯl . gd .[ ] | 11'. [w . ]tmṯl . gd .[ w . tmṯl . ṯmrg . w] |
| 12'. | [ ]⌈w⌉ . št . n[ ] | 12'. [mǵmǵ . ]⌈w⌉ . št . n[n’i . w . pr . ‘bk . w . št] |
| 13'. | [ ]ǵ ⌈.⌉ p⌈r⌉[ ] | 13'. [‘qrb . w . mǵm]ǵ ⌈.⌉ p⌈r⌉[ . ḥḏrt . w . tmṯl] |
| 14'. | [ ]⌈r⌉[ ] | 14'. [’arǵn . ḥm]⌈r⌉[ . ydk ...] |

Translation of RS 17.120[34]

1.1) Document of horse cures.

2.2-4) If the horse has a bad cough, one should bray a ŠT(-measure) of ‘QRBN

34. I have indicated here the paragraph numbers as corresponding to the sections marked on this tablet and in general to those on the others, less well preserved (for the details of the differences, see the studies cited in the preceding note and further references there).

('scorpion-plant') and dissolve it either in a mixture of natural juices or in MNDǴ and administer it through its nostrils.

3.5-6) If the horse whinnies (unnaturally), one should bray MǴMǴ and BṢQL 'RGZ (green walnuts in the hulls?) together and administer it through its nostrils.

4.7-8) If the horse whinnies (unnaturally), one should bray ḪNDRṮ and ṮQD MR (bitter almond) together and administer it through its nostrils.

5.9-11) If the horse does not defecate and does not urinate, a ŠT(-measure) of QLQL (cardamon?) having been reduced to a liquid (or: a powder?), one should then bray it together with a ŠT(-measure?) of 'RGZ (walnuts?) and administer it through its nostrils.

6.12-14) If the horse seizes its food (unnaturally), one should bray a ŠT(-measure) of MKŠR GRN (chopped grain from the threshing floor), a ŠT(-measure) of 'AŠKRR, and the fruit of ḤḎRT and administer it through its nostrils.

7.15-17) If the horse seizes its food (unnaturally), one should bray a ŠT(-measure) of NN'I (ammi), a ŠT(-measure) of MKŠR GRN (chopped grain from the threshing floor), and a ŠT(-measure$^{?}$) of 'IRǴN ḤMR and administer it through its nostrils.

8.18-19) If the horse suffers in the head, one should bray a ŠT(-measure) of BLN from Qaṭi and [...] together and administer it through its nostrils.

9.20-22) If the horse [does X], one should bray GD (coriander) from Aleppo and [...] together and administer it through its nostrils.

10.23-29) If the horse has a bad cough, one should bray [...] of DPRN (juniper), the fruit of 'ṮRB, (i.e. its) seed(s), ṮQD MR (bitter almond), a TMṮL(-vessel/amount) of GD (coriander), a TMṮL(-vessel/amount) of ṮMRG, MǴMǴ, a ŠT(-measure) of NN'I (ammi), the fruit of 'BK, a ŠT(-measure$^{?}$) of 'QRB (a Heliotrope = scorpion?), MǴMǴ, the fruit of ḤḎRT, and a TMṮL(-vessel/amount) of 'IRǴN ḤMR together and administer it through its nostrils.

11.30-32) If the horse suffers in the head and is altogether prostrate, <one should bray> DBLT YṮNT (an old bunch of figs), ṢMQM YṮNM (old raisins), and QMḤ BQL (flour of groats) together and administer it through its nostrils.

6. *Lexicography*

Lexicography at Ugarit is attested in multiple forms, most of them basically Sumero-Akkadian. Ugaritic data appear in two principal forms:

a. As a column in syllabically written polyglot vocabularies published for the most part by Nougayrol;[35] the advantages of these lists are (1) that the polyglot format, with each entry containing the appropriate word in Sumerian, Akkadian, Hurrian and Ugaritic, makes the meaning of the word clear; and (2) that the syllabic writing provides the vowels that are generally unnoted in Ugaritic (e.g. Ugaritic *mlk*, 'king', is shown by the entry *ma-al-ku* [Nougayrol 1968: 244-45] to have been pronounced /malku/);

35. The data for Ugaritic lexicography from the polyglot vocabularies and from random occurrences of Ugaritic words in other syllabically written texts have been assembled and analyzed by Huehnergard (1987).

b. As monolingual lists of divine names attested in Ugaritic and Sumero-Akkadian; two of these lists are presented here, the two for which both alphabetic and syllabic versions exist (though the second is presently only attested in Ugaritic in the corresponding ritual, RS 24.643, not yet in list form).

1. *Deity list (RS 1.017 and parallels)*[36]

| RS 1.017 | | RS 24.264$^{+}$ | | RS 20.024 | | RS 24.643.1-9 | |
|---|---|---|---|---|---|---|---|
| 1. | ’il ṣpn | | | 1. | dbḥ ṣpn | | |
| 2. | ’i⸢l’i⸣b | 1. | ’il’ib | 1. | DINGIR-a-bi | | [’il’ib] |
| 3. | ’i⸢l⸣ | 2. | ’il | 2. | DINGIR$^{lum}$ | 2. | ’il |
| 4. | dg⸢n⸣ | 3. | dgn | 3. | $^{d}$da-gan | | [dgn] |
| 5. | ⸢b⸣‘l ṣpn | 4. | b‘l ṣpn | 4. | $^{d}$IM be-el ḪUR.SAG.ḫa-zi | | [b‘l ṣpn] |
| 6. | b‘lm | 5. | b‘lm | 5. | $^{d}$IM II | 3. | b‘lm |
| 7. | b‘lm | 6. | b‘lm | 6. | $^{d}$IM III | | [b‘lm] |
| 8. | b‘lm | 7. | b‘lm | 7. | $^{d}$IM IV | | [b‘lm] |
| 9. | ⸢b‘⸣lm | 8. | b‘lm | 8. | $^{d}$IM V | 4. | b‘lm |
| 10. | [b]⸢‘⸣lm | 9. | b‘lm | 9. | $^{d}$IM VI | | ⸢b‘l⸣[m] |
| 11. | [b‘l]m | 10. | b‘lm | 10. | $^{d}$IM VII | | [b‘lm] |
| 12. | [’arṣ] w šm⸢m⸣ | 11. | ’arṣ w šmm | 11. | $^{d}$IM ù IDIM | 5. | ’arṣ w šmm |
| 13. | [kṯr]⸢t⸣ | 12. | kṯ⸢r⸣t | 12. | $^{d}$sa-sú-ra-tu$_4$ | | kṯr[t] |
| 14. | […] | 13. | ⸢y⸣r⸢ḫ⸣ | 13. | $^{d}$EN.ZU | | yr⸢ḫ⸣ |
| 15. | […] | 14. | ⸢ṣ⸣pn | 14. | $^{d}$ḪUR.SAG.ḫa-zi | | [‘ṯt]⸢r⸣ (?) |
| 16. | […] | 15. | kṯr | 15. | $^{d}$é-a | 6. | ṣpn |
| 17. | […] | 16. | pdry | 16. | $^{d}$ḫé-bat | | kṯr |
| 18. | […] | 17. | ‘ṯtr | 17. | $^{d}$aš-ta-bi | | pdry |
| 19. | […] | 18. | ǵrm ⸢w⸣[thmt] | 18. | $^{d}$ḪUR.SAG.MEŠ u A$^{mu-ú}$ | | ǵrm ⸢w thm⸣t[37] |
| 20. | […] | 19. | ’a[ṯ]rt | 19. | $^{d}$aš-ra-tu$_4$ | 7. | ’aṯrt |
| 21. | […] | 20. | ‘nt | 20. | $^{d}$a-na-tu$_4$ | | ‘nt |
| 22. | [šp]⸢š⸣ | 21. | špš | 21. | $^{d}$UTU | | špš |
| 23. | [’a]rṣ⸢y⸣ | 22. | ’arṣy | 22. | $^{d}$al-la-tu$_4$ | | ⸢’a⸣rṣy |
| 24. | [’u]šḫr⸢y⸣ | 23. | ’ušrḫry | 23. | $^{d}$iš-ḫa-ra | | ‘ṯtr⸢t⸣ |

36. As the campaign numbers indicate, these texts only became known gradually; moreover, the first attested was the least well preserved and the full original form could only be appreciated as the other texts appeared. The syllabic version was published by J. Nougayrol (1968: 42-64, text 18) and the ritual text RS 24.643 in the same volume by Virolleaud (1968: 580-82, 584, text 9), who only pointed out briefly the similarity with RS 1.017. The second exemplar of the Ugaritic list, RS 24.264$^{+}$, appeared in 1978, published by Herdner.

37. The new readings of RS 20.024.18 (my thanks to D. Arnaud) and RS 24.643.6 were inspired by the new deity list RS 92.2004 and comparison with RS 24.643 verso (see next text).

| | | | |
|---|---|---|---|
| 25. [ʻ]ṯtrt | 24. ʻṯtrt | 24. $^{\text{d}}$EŠDAR$^{\text{iš-tar}}$ | 8. ʼušḫry |
| 26. ʼil tʻḏr bʻl | 25. ʼil tʻḏr bʻl | 25. DINGIR.MEŠ til-la-at $^{\text{d}}$IM | ʼil tʻ⌈ḏ⌉r bʻl |
| 27. ršp | 26. ⌈r⌉[š]p | 26. $^{\text{d}}$GÌR.UNU.GAL | ršp |
| 28. ddmš | 27. ddmš | 27. $^{\text{d}}$dá-ad-mi-iš | ddmš |
| 29. pḫr ʼilm | 28. pḫr ʼi⌈lm⌉ | 28. $^{\text{d}}$pu-ḫur DINGIR.MEŠ | 9. pḫr ʼilm |
| 30. ym | 29. ym | 29. $^{\text{d}}$A.AB.BA | ym |
| 31. ʼuṯḫt | 30. ʼuṯḫ⌈t⌉ | 30. $^{\text{d dug}}$BUR.ZI. NÍG.NA | |
| 32. knr | 31. knr | 31. $^{\text{d giš}}$ki-na-rù | [k]⌈n⌉r |
| 33. mlkm | 32. mlkm | 32. $^{\text{d}}$ma-lik-MEŠ | |
| 34. šlm 33. šlm | 33. $^{\text{d}}$sa-li-mu | | |

2. *Deity list (RS 24.643 verso and parallels)*[38]

| RS 92.2004 | | RS 24.643 *verso* | | RS1.017[39] |
|---|---|---|---|---|
| 1. | DINGIR-a-bi | 23. | ʼilʼib | l. 2 |
| 2. | $^{\text{d}}$KI ù AN | 24. | ʼarṣ w šmm | l. 12 |
| 3. | DINGIR$^{\text{lum}}$ | 25. | ʼil | l. 3 |
| 4. | $^{\text{d}}$NIN.MAḪ | | kṯrt | l. 13 |
| 5. | $^{\text{d}}$KUR | 26. | dgn | l. 4 |
| 6. | $^{\text{d}}$X ḫal-bi | | bʻl ḫlb | absent[40] |
| 7. | $^{\text{d}}$X ḪUR.SAG.ḫa-zi | 27. | bʻl ṣpn | l. 5 |
| 8. | $^{\text{d}}$šar-ra-ši-ya | 28. | ṯrṯy | absent |
| 9. | $^{\text{d}}$XXX | 29. | yrḫ | l. 14 |
| 10. | $^{\text{d}}$ḪUR.SAG.ḫa-zi | | ṣpn | l. 15 |
| 11. | $^{\text{d}}$é-a | 30. | kṯr | l. 16 |
| 12. | $^{\text{d}}$aš-ta-bi | | ʻṯtr | l. 18 |

38. As compared with the previous deity list, which is attested in list form in Ugaritic, in this case the list is found only in syllabic script; but, as in the case with the previous text, the list corresponds in large part to a section of the sacrificial text RS 24.643. The transliteration of RS 92.2004 (currently unpublished) is the one that Arnaud kindly provided for me in November 1995 for my commentary of RS 24.643 (Pardee 2000). Arnaud will undoubtedly propose modifications in his publication of the text; in the meantime, see his re-edition (1994a) of the small fragment RS 26.142, published by Nougayrol (1968: 320-22; 446), which once contained this same list. I was slow to see that the same deities occur in the same order in RS 26.142 and in RS 24.643 verso (1992a: 166-67); it was not until I was endeavoring to determine the genre of RS 92.2004 at Ras Shamra in June 1992 that the correct orientation of RS 26.142 became obvious to me (its recto and verso were inverted in the *editio princeps*) and hence its comparability with RS 24.643 verso.

39. This column is provided to facilitate comparison with the preceding text.

40. *bʻl ḫlb* could, of course, correspond to one of the *bʻlm* in ll. 6-11.

| | | | | |
|---|---|---|---|---|
| 13. | $^{d}$aš-ra-tu$_4$ | 31. | [’a]⌈ṯ⌉rt | l. 20 |
| 14. | $^{d}$ḪAR ù GÌR | | šgr w ’iṯm | absent |
| 15. | $^{d}$UTU | 32. | [šp]š | l. 22 |
| 16. | ⌈$^{d}$x⌉-it-ri-ib-bi | | ršp ’idrp | absent |
| 17. | ⌈$^{d}$xx⌉-nam-ṣa-ri | 33. | [----] ⌈mṣ⌉r | absent |
| 18. | [$^{d}$da-ad-m]i-i š | 34. | [ddmš] | l. 28 |
| 19. | [...] | | [-(-)]mt | absent |
| 20. | [...] | 35. | [...] | |
| 21. | [...] | 36. | [...] | |
| 22. | [$^{d}$iš]-ḫa-ra | 37. | [’ušḫry] | l. 24 |
| 23. | [$^{d}$nin-]urta | 38. | [gṯr?] | absent |
| 24. | [$^{d}$]EŠDAR | | [‘ṯ]⌈tr⌉[t] | l. 25 |
| 25. | $^{d}$SIRIŠ | 39. | [trṯ] | absent |
| 26. | $^{d}$ma-za-ra | | mḏr | absent |
| 27. | DINGIR.MEŠ.URU.KI | 40. | [’il q]⌈r⌉t | absent |
| 28. | DINGIR.NITA.MEŠ ù DINGIR.MUNUS.MEŠ | | ’il m⌈-⌉[...] | absent |
| 29. | $^{d}$ḪUR.SAG.MEŠ ù $^{d}$A.MEŠ | 41. | [ǵr]⌈m⌉ w ⌈t⌉hm | l. 19 |
| 30. | $^{d}$A.AB.BA | | [ym] | l. 30 |
| 31. | $^{d}$E.NI.TU.ma-me-ri | 42. | [--]⌈m⌉mr | absent |
| 32. | $^{d}$su-ra-su-gu-PI | | s⌈r⌉[---] | absent |
| 33. | $^{d}$E.NI.ḪU.RA.UD.ḪI | | [...] | absent |
| 34. | DINGIR.MEŠ da-ad-me-ma | 42-43. | [’il dd]⌈m⌉m | absent |
| 35. | DINGIR.MEŠ la-ab-a-na | 43. | ’il lb[-]⌈n⌉ | absent |
| 36. | $^{d}$DUG.BUR.ZI.NÍG.DIN | | ⌈’u⌉[ṯḫt] | l. 31 |
| 37. | $^{d}$GIŠ.ZA.MÍM | | [(knr)] | l. 32 |
| 38. | $^{d}$X | | [b‘lm] | ll. 6-11 |
| 39. | $^{d}$X | 44. | b‘lm | ll. 6-11 |
| 40. | $^{d}$X | | [b‘lm] | ll. 6-11 |
| 41. | ⌈$^{d}$X⌉ | | [b‘lm] | ll. 6-11 |
| 42. | [$^{d}$ma-l]ik-MEŠ | | absent | l. 33 |
| 43. | [$^{d}$]SILIM | | absent | l. 34 |

## BIBLIOGRAPHY

André-Salvini, B.

1991 'Textes lexicographiques, no. 48-77', in P. Bordreuil (ed.), *Une bibliothèque au sud de la ville* (Ras Shamra–Ougarit, 7; Paris: Editions Recherche sur les Civilisations): 105-26.

Arnaud, D.

1982 'Une lettre du roi de Tyr au roi d'Ougarit: Milieux d'affaires et de culture en Syrie à la fin de l'âge du Bronze Récent', *Syria* 59: 101-107.

1994 'Relecture de la liste sacrificielle RS.26.142', *SMEA* 34: 107-109.

1996a 'L'édition ougaritaine de la série astrologique "Éclipses du dieu-Soleil" ', *Semitica* 45: 7-18.

1996b 'Un exercice scolaire d'hépatoscopie d'Ougarit: RS 22.405', *AuOr* 14: 127-30.

Bordreuil, P., and D. Pardee

1989 *La trouvaille épigraphique de l'Ougarit* (Ras Shamra–Ougarit, 5.1; Paris: Editions Recherche sur les Civilisations).

1993 'Le combat de *Ba'lu* avec *Yammu* d'après les textes ougaritiques', *MARI* 7: 63-70.

Caquot, A.

1989 *Textes ougaritiques*. II. *Textes religieux et rituels, correspondance* (LAPO, 14; Paris: Cerf).

Cohen, C.

1996 'The Ugaritic Hippiatric Texts. Revised Composite Text, Translation and Commentary', *UF* 28: 105-53.

1997 'Hippiatric Texts (1.106)', in Hallo and Younger 1997: 361-62.

Cryer, F.H.

1994 *Divination in Ancient Israel and its Near Eastern Environment: A Socio-Historical Investigation* (JSOTSup, 142; Sheffield: JSOT Press).

De Jong, T., and W.H. van Soldt

1987–88 'Redating an Early Solar Eclipse Record (KTU 1.78): Implications for the Ugaritic Calendar and for the Secular Accelerations of the Earth and Moon', *JEOL* 30: 65-77.

De Moor, J.C.

1997 *An Anthology of Religious Texts from Ugarit* (Nisaba, 16; Leiden: E.J. Brill).

Dietrich, M., and O. Loretz

1969 'Beschriftete Lungen- und Lebermodelle aus Ugarit', in J.C. Courtois (ed.), *Ugaritica*, VI (Paris: Geuthner): 165-79.

1990 *Mantik in Ugarit: Keilalphabetische Textge der Opferschau—Omensammlungen—Nekromantie* (ALASPM, 3; Münster: Ugarit Verlag).

Durand, J.-M.

1988 *Archives épistolaires de Mari*, I/1 (Archives Royales de Mari, 26; Paris: Editions Recherche sur les Civilisations).

Gachet, J.
1995 'Les ivoires inscrits du palais royale', in M. Yon *et al.* (eds.), *Le pays d'Ougarit autour de 1200 av. J.-C., histoire et archéologie* (Ras Shamra–Ougarit, 11; Paris: Editions Recherche sur les Civilisations): 245-54.

Hallo, W.W., and K.L. Younger, Jr. (eds.)
1997 *The Context of Scripture.* I. *Canonical Compositions from the Biblical World* (Leiden: E.J. Brill).

Herdner, A. (ed.)
1978 *Ugaritica*, VII (Paris: Geuthner).

Huehnergard, J.
1987 *Ugaritic Vocabulary in Syllabic Transcription* (HSS, 32; Atlanta: Scholars Press).

Hunger, H.
1992 *Astrological Reports to Assyrian Kings* (SAAS, 8; Helsinki: Helsinki University Press).

Jacobsen, T.
1968 'The Battle of Marduk and Ti'āmat', *JAOS* 88: 104-108.
1976 *The Treasures of Darkness: A History of Mesopotamian Religion* (New Haven: Yale University Press).

Malamat, A.
1997 'The Cultural Impact of the West (Syria-Palestine) on Mesopotamia in the Old Babylonian Period', *Altorientalische Forschungen* 24: 310-19.

Meyer, J.-W.
1987 *Untersuchungen zu den Tonlebermodellen aus dem Alten Orient* (AOAT, 39; Kevelaer: Verlag Butzon & Bercker).
1990 'Zur Interpretation der Leber- und Lungenmodelle aus Ugarit', in Dietrich and Loretz (eds.) 1990: 241-80.

Miller, J.M.
1997 'Separating the Solomon of History from the Solomon of Legend', in L.K. Handy (ed.), *The Age of Solomon: Scholarship at the Turn of the Millennium* (SHANE, 9; Leiden: E.J. Brill): 1-24.

Moor, J.C. de
1987 *An Anthology of Religions Texts from Ugarit* (Nisaba, 16; Leiden: E.J. Brill).

Nougayrol, J.
1968 'Textes suméro-accadiens des archives et bibliothèques privées d'Ugarit', in J.C. Courtois (ed.), *Ugaritica*, V (Paris: Geuthner): 1-446.

Oppenheim, A.L.
1956 *The Interpretation of Dreams in the Ancient Near East, with a Translation of an Assyrian Dream-Book* (Transactions of the American Philosophical Society, NS 46.3; Philadelphia: The American Philosophical Society).

Pardee, D.
1985 *Les textes hippiatriques* (Ras Shamra–Ougarit, 2; Paris: Editions Recherche sur les Civilisations).
1986 'The Ugaritic *šumma izbu* Text', *AfO* 33: 117-47.
1992a 'RS 24.643: Texte et structure', *Syria* 69: 153-70.
1992b 'Some Brief Remarks on Hippiatric Methodology', *AuOr* 10: 154-55.

1993 'Poetry in Ugaritic Ritual Texts', in J.C. Moor and W.G.E. Watson (eds.), *Verse in Ancient Near Eastern Prose* (AOAT, 42; Kevelaer: Verlag Butzon & Bercker): 207-218.

1996 'Quelques remarques relatives à l'étude des textes hippiatriques en langue ougaritique', *Semitica* 45: 19-26.

1997a 'Ugaritic Birth Omens (1.90) (RS 24.247 + RS 24.302)', in Hallo and Younger 1997: 287-89.

1997b 'Ugaritic Lunar Omens (1.91) (RIH 78/14)', in Hallo and Younger 1997: 290-91.

1997c 'Ugaritic Extispicy (1.92) (RS 24.312, RS 24.323, RS 24.326, RS 24.327, RS 24.654, RS 24.277)', in Hallo and Younger 1997: 291-93.

1997d 'Ugaritic Dream Omens (1.93) (RS 18.041)', in Hallo and Younger 1997: 293-94.

1997e 'Ugaritic Liturgy Against Venomous Reptiles (1.94) (RS 24.244)', in Hallo and Younger 1997: 295-98.

1997f 'A Ugaritic Incantation Against Serpents and Sorcerers (1.100) (1992.2014)', in Hallo and Younger 1997: 327-28.

2000 *Les textes rituels* (Ras Shamra–Ougarit, 12; Paris: Editions Recherche sur les Civilisations).

forthcoming *Ivoires inscrits de Ras Shamra–Ougarit, connus et inconnus* (Ras Shamra–Ougarit, 14; Paris: Editions Recherche sur les Civilisations).

Pardee, D., and N. Swerdlow

1993 'Not the Earliest Solar Eclipse', *Nature* 363.6482 (3 June): 406.

Reiner, E.

1993 'Two Babylonian Precursors of Astrology', *NABU* 1.26: 21-22.

Sawyer, J.F.A., and F.R. Stephenson

1970 'Literary and Astronomical Evidence for a Total Eclipse of the Sun Observed in Ancient Ugarit on 3 May 1375 B.C.', *BSO(A)S* 33: 467-89.

Schäffer, J.

1987 Review of *Les textes hippiatriques* (Ras Shamra—Ougarit, 2; Paris: Editions Recherche sur les Civilisations', by D. Pardee, in *BiOr* 44: 501-507.

Van Soldt, W.H.

1991 *Studies in the Akkadian of Ugarit: Dating and Grammar* (AOAT, 40; Kevelaer: Verlag Butzon & Bercker).

Virolleaud, C.

1968 'Les nouveaux textes mythologiques et liturgiques de Ras Shamra (XXIV[e] campagne)', in J.C. Courtois (ed.), *Ugaritica*, V (Paris: Geuthner): 554-606.

Walker, C.B.F.

1989 'Eclipse Seen at Ancient Ugarit', *Nature* 338.6212 (16 March): 204-205.

# OBSERVATIONS ON THE DATE OF THE SYRIAC *CAVE OF TREASURES**

Clemens Leonhard

In this essay I intend to discuss some bits of evidence which suggest a date of the composition of the Syriac *Cave of Treasures* (abbreviated as *SpTh* [*Spelunca Thesaurorum*]). It will not be possible to assign too narrow a date to a text which does not allude to persons or events of history and which reworks many pieces of the old literary heritage of Judaism and Christianity. Nevertheless, I assume that it includes enough material to plead a later date rather than an earlier one.

## *The Status Quaestionis*

The *SpTh* is a summary of the history of salvation from the creation of the world to Pentecost. The translations and adaptations[1] of the text testify to its success in late antiquity and the Middle Ages. It has been analysed as being extant in a West-Syrian and an East-Syrian recension.[2]

* I am indebted to Dr Witold Witakowski for the enrichment of my bibliography and for his invaluable comments to a draft of this essay. I am also grateful to Petra Heldt, Angela Y. Kim and Dr Serge Ruzer for many hours of discussion of the *SpTh* in Jerusalem 1997/98. *SpTh* (*Spelunca Thesaurorum*) is quoted as 1.1, referring to chapters and verses according to Ri (1987a). References to differences between the two recensions are indicated as $1.1^{e}$ for a passage of the eastern recension and $1.1^{w}$ for a passage of the western recension.

1. The text (Kourcikidzé 1993) and translation (Mahé 1992) of the Georgian version and the parallels in a Coptic text (Coquin and Godron 1990) can be added to Ri's list of sources (1987a, trans.: xxiv-xxvi). Götze (1923, 1924) analysed quotations of the *SpTh* in later works, some of which he regarded as witnesses of the text.

2. Ri (1987a, text). The division of *Spth* into two recensions does not explain the history of the text exhaustively. Especially the position of the eastern MSS *A* (British Museum Add. 25875, written 1709/1710 [Götze 1922: 5]) and *F* (Berlin Sachau no. 9, written 1695 [Ri 1987a, text: viii]) in the stemma codicum remains

Götze (1922: 91 §78), who was the first one to devote a thorough study to the text, assumes the fourth century (c. 350)[3] as a date of the compilation of an earlier version, the *Urschatzhöhle*, and a later redaction in the sixth century by an East-Syrian scholar.[4] He mainly relied on Bezold's *editio princeps* (1888)[5] and did not take into account the West-Syrian witnesses.[6] His approach remained normative for subsequent studies.[7]

The assumption of an East-Syrian redaction is supported by two polemic, anti-Monophysite statements. One of them (29.10[e]) refers to 'Cyril, the villain, and Severus' (only MSS *D,F,H*, and *M*). However, this remark replaces the more general term 'the heretics' of the other eastern manuscripts.[8] The unspecified polemic statement is probably

unclear. De Lagarde (1888: 833-39; 1889: 65) observed that the MS *A* versus the other eastern MSS represent two recensions of the text. This has been obscured in Bezold (1888). On the basis of Ri (1987a) it is clear that the MSS *A* and *F* contain material of the West-Syriac MSS, which were not yet available to de Lagarde. The question has yet to be studied. The MSS *A* and *F* may turn out to represent a third recension, etc.

3. The main arguments are: the ideology of the *SpTh* is close to that of the Gnostics and Ebionites; it knows Aprahaṭ's *Demonstrationes*; its chronology presupposes Julius Africanus († after 240); Aprēm did probably not know the *SpTh*.

4. The term 'East-Syrian' replaces the misnomer Nestorian (Brock 1996). Götze's statement about the fourth century (1922: 90 §77) is a typographical error (cf. Götze 1923: 52).

5. De Lagarde (1888, 1889, 1891)] published two scathing review articles about the edition. Nöldeke (1888), too, discussed the edition briefly. His rather positive reaction was severely criticized by de Lagarde (1889: 77-79) in an appendix to the reprint of his earlier piece (1888). De Lagarde's judgment about the edition was blurred by his anti-Jewish resentments against the text and his jealousy of the younger scholar, Bezold (1888), who published a text on which de Lagarde (1891: 6) himself had been working for a long time. Budge (1927) published a translation of the MS *A* reproaching Bezold for not having taken this MS as his textual basis (cf. Budge 1927: xi-xii). His point is well taken, although he does not prove it. Ri's hypothesis (1987a, text: xxiv) that the most comprehensive tradition (MS *A* and *F*) be a conflation of western and eastern elements is not more convincing than the assumption that the shorter recensions independently abbreviated a fuller text.

6. The East-Syrian character of the script of MS *B* (one of the most important witnesses of the eastern recension [Ri 1987a, text: xxiv]) is not beyond doubt (Ri 1987a, text: xii).

7. Cf., e.g., Witakowski (1993: 640; 1990: 101); Bruns (1998).

8. Cf. the second heresiological passage which also speaks about 'the heretics' 21.19[e]. See below, p. 256.

older (Ri 1987b: 190) and Severus's (†538) name should not be taken as an indication for the *terminus a quo* of a redaction of the whole work.[9]

Ri, the editor of the new edition, claims (1987a, trans.: xxii-xxiii; 1987b: 189) that the text should mirror the atmosphere of interfaith discussions in the Caesarea of Origen's time (or Julius Africanus's; Ri 1987b: 190).[10] In an article on the *SpTh* and Aprēm (†373), Ri (1998a: 82-83) concludes his presentation of some parallels with the remark that Aprēm 'knew the *SpTh* by heart' before his full acceptance of Christianity. Aprēm is said to have left out the dangerous Gnostic speculations of the *SpTh*. Ri (1998a: 82-83) basically accepts Götze's (1922) date of 350. Nevertheless, he suggests (on the basis of unspecified parallels to Christian authors of the second and third centuries) that the *SpTh* 'had existed in the form of a *Catechesis* or *Scholium* of ancient Christians (or Jewish Christians) in an environment of hellenized Syrians until Aprēm's time'. This points to an earlier date of the text than 350. In his paper on the prologues of the *SpTh*, Ri (1998b: 150) proposes that the *SpTh* should have been 'a fundamental book of the original Christian communities' of Iran (Ri 1998b: 137) and was replaced later by the spread of the canonical texts together with the dissemination of orthodoxy.

Ri (1987a, 1998b, 1998a) does not refer to Bagatti's and Testa's (1978) theory of the identification of the then newly discovered cavity on the foot of the rock of Calvary/Golgotha in the Church of the Holy Sepulchre as the origin of the legends of the *SpTh*. Bagatti confirms Ri's early date, although he uses different arguments. According to Bagatti (1979) and Bagatti and Testa (1978: 27-30, 34-40), these

9. Nöldeke (1888) assumes the sixth century as a date for the *SpTh*, although he suggests that the anti-Monophysite remarks 21.19 and 29.10 are later additions. For a similar date cf. Baumstark (1922: 95-96), Budge (1927: xi). Apart from these explicit statements one could also refer to 49.19 which allegorizes the difference between the Synoptic Gospels on Christ's two *natures* (*kyānē*)—one *happy and immortal* (*pṣīḥā w-lā māyōtā*) and the other *sad and mortal one of humanity* (*kmīrā w-māyōtā d-nāšūtā*). 49.16-20 may be a later addition, as well as a remark by the author. Cf. also the difference of the *blood and water* running from Christ's side *unmixed*—*lāw gēr ba-ḥdādē ḥlīṭīn (h)wāw*—between 51.19[e] (MSS H and M) and the parallel to this reading in the western recension including the rest of the eastern MSS *mixed*—*kad ḥlīṭīn* (*ḥad b-ḥad*).

10. De Lagarde (1888: 839-43) bases his assumption of a likewise earlier date among other arguments on the anti-Jewish thrust of the text.

legends of the *SpTh* belong to the earliest strata of the Jerusalemite Christians' traditions about Adam's grave in the rock of Golgotha. The theory has, for example, been opposed by Corbo (1982: 101) and Taylor (1993), accepted tentatively by Kretschmar (1987), and ignored in Gibson and Taylor (1994).

The assumption that the *SpTh* was composed in Syriac has never been challenged.[11] This and the theses about its date have to rely on internal observations on the text, because the oldest Syriac manuscript was copied in the sixteenth century and the first manuscript containing parts of the *SpTh* reworked and transferred into Arabic probably goes back to the ninth century (Ri 1998b: 135).[12] De Lagarde (1891) emphasizes that what Bezold published as an Arabic translation of the *SpTh* is in fact Bezold's (1888) extract of one of the branches of the Arabic (Pseudo-) Pseudo-Clementine tradition,[13] which reworks the *SpTh*. It is not a translation of the *SpTh* as an independent work. This has to be borne in mind for the reconstruction of the original shape of the text. The authors of the Arabic and Ethiopic Pseudo-Clementine works changed their *Vorlage* where they wanted and misrepresented its original length.[14] As an additional witness, the fragments of a larger work in Coptic, an *Encomion sur Marie-Madeleine*, which has been influenced by the *SpTh*, were likewise dated to the ninth century.[15] The

11. Bezold (1883: ix-x) assumes a Syriac author, first, because of the statements of Syriac national identity and pride. Secondly, he refers to *nomina portentosa*, e.g. Haikal the daughter of Nâmos (14.3$^{c}$), Noah's wife. Cf. Götze (1922: 38; and section f below, pp. 280-81).

12. Bagatti (1979: 278) took the Arabic text of the *SpTh* 'come il testo più antico della Caverna'. However, a ninth-century MS cannot be taken as a witness for the oldest form of the *SpTh*, even if it was composed in as late a century as the sixth. M.D. Gibson (1901: x) tentatively suggests the ninth century for the (undated) MS Sinai 508 on the basis of paleographic comparisons.

13. This tradition is not a translation of the *Recognitiones*, etc., cf. below. Götze (1922: 23-37) describes the MSS and their relationship. Bezold (1888) had taken the MS the text of which was closest to the Syriac *SpTh*. The MSS of Bezold's (1888) and Gibson's (1901) editions represent two different branches of this Pseudo-Clementine tradition.

14. Thus, the portion of *SpTh* as contained in the Ethiopic Pseudo-Clementine texts is not representative for the original length of the *SpTh*, cf. n. 20.

15. Poirier (1983: 416-17) assumes that the Coptic translator had a Syriac text very much like the extant one at his disposal. The text apparently continued beyond 48.5. The text of the second fragment corresponds to the Syriac text and not to the Arabic version, which ends here (Bezold 1888: 247; cf. Dillmann 1853: 137). The

*SpTh* was quoted in Syriac literature from the seventh century onwards.[16]

A relationship between the *SpTh* and the Pseudo-Clementine literature has been supposed but not studied thoroughly.[17] Parallel concepts in these two works could with due caution be used as indications for the date of the *SpTh*. As F.S. Jones (1992: 239) assumes 380 as a possible date for the translation of the *Recognitiones* into Syriac, the author or compiler of the *SpTh* would have been able to use such a translation in the fifth century. Götze (1922: 60-66) supposes that the *SpTh* and the Pseudo-Clementines used the same much older sources where the stories of the *Life of Adam and Eve* were supplemented with material reaching the time of the patriarchs.[18]

The Arabic and Ethiopic texts of the Pseudo-Clementines (*Qalēmenṭōs*) which were translated by Grébaut (1911–21) as 'littérature éthiopienne pseudo-clémentine' must not be confused with the Pseudo-Clementine *Recognitiones*. Their compiler reworked among other traditions the *Recognitiones* and the *SpTh* (Grébaut 1911: 73)[19] although

*Encomion sur Marie-Madeleine* does not include more material of the last parts of the *SpTh* than the Arabic version in Bezold (1888). It contains the beginning of the *SpTh* (except for Poirier's [1983] material) 2-6.23 (Coquin and Godron 1990 trans.: 206-210). The Hexaemeron of the Syriac *SpTh* is not part of this tradition which starts with Adam's creation. The Coptic tradition is not a witness for the high antiquity of the *Zusatzteil der syrischen Schatzhöhle* (Götze 1922: 85). The designation *les prologues de la 'Caverne des trésors'* (Ri 1998b) for parts of the Arabic and Coptic parallels to the *SpTh* is an inadmissible oversimplification of the literary relationships.

16. Ri (1987a, trans.: xviii) = Götze (1923: 52), who listed it as a quotation from the sixth century. The first major parallels are given in Pseudo-Methodius's apocalypse.

17. Cf. Götze's (1922: 62-65) list of parallels. For the typology of Adam and Christ, the need to interpret false statements of Scripture, etc. (e.g. 42.6-7, see below, p. 261), cf. Drijvers (1990), Götze (1922: 61 §26).

18. One of Götze's (1922: 62 §26) arguments is the neglect or rejection of Adam's sin in the Pseudo-Clementines versus the description of the fall in the *SpTh*. *Recognitiones* 1.28.4 indeed jumps from the creation of man directly to the eighth generation, where sin emerged, 1.29.1 passing over Gen. 3; Frankenberg (1937: 36), Jones (1995: 54-55). However, as Ruzer has shown (in a yet unpublished paper given in Notre Dame, June 1999) the description of the fall in the *SpTh* totally exculpates Adam (cf. Grébaut 1911: 169, = Coquin and Godron 1990: 208-209).

19. Götze (1922: 38 §47) states that this Ethiopic tradition 'kann nur sekundäre Bedeutung besitzen', and he did not re-evaluate it in his studies (Götze 1923, 1924). I am indebted to Witakowski for the reference to the new edition and translation of

he may have had access to another form of the text than that which is extant.[20]

The Georgian version (cf. Mahé 1992: xxi) of the *SpTh* does not represent one of the two recensions as edited by Ri (1987a), although they go back to a single type of text. It was probably translated from an Arabic *Vorlage*, which is not extant and which was different from the Arabic Pseudo-Clementines (Mahé 1992: xxv-xxvi). The Georgian translation contains the whole text of the *SpTh*.[21]

Götze's (1922: 35) opinion about the end of the *Urschatzhöhle* in 44.7 is based on a corruption of the text in all MSS which were available to Bezold (1888) and himself. The Syriac text and the Arabic parallels state that 'their [i.e. the Jews'] books have been burnt in the fire three times', but then only two of the events are enumerated.[22] Nöldeke's (1888: 235) emendation of the passage[23] and his evaluation

the *Qalēmenṭōs* by Bausi (1992) which I could not yet obtain.

20. De Lagarde emphasizes that the use of the Ethiopic MSS be an indispensable prerequisite for the study of the text of the Arabic and hence the Syriac text (1888: 833-39 = 1889: 65-71). Bezold (1883) refers to the results of his study of the *Qalēmenṭōs* in the notes to the translation. He did apparently not use them for textual decisions in the edition (1888). According to Dillmann (1858: 203-205) the *Qalēmenṭōs* was translated from an Arabic original that was composed in the eighth century and the *Gadla Adām* (*The Life of Adam* = Trumpp 1881) was more complete in the parallel passages to the *Qalēmenṭōs* (1858: 213-14). He concludes that both the *Gadla Adām* and the *Qalēmenṭōs* took their material from the *SpTh*. This statement apparently revises his older opinion (1853: 9), that the *Gadla Adām* be the source for the *Qalēmenṭōs*. The parallel to the *SpTh* runs until 37.18 (the reign of Joram) in the MSS of Tübingen and Paris, Dillmann (1858: 191), Grébaut (1911: 74; 1912: 144).

21. The Georgian version (Mahé 1992: 13-14; as a replacement of 6.9-14) and the Arabic Pseudo-Clementine texts (Gibson 1901: text 12-17; trans.: 13-17; Mingana 1931: text 162 fol. 58v.-165 fol. 59v., trans.: 110-15) (a reworked version of the *horarium*) share the addition of the *Testament of Adam* against the *SpTh*. The question of the origins of the *Testament of Adam* cannot be dealt with here. But even if Ri (1990) should be right in his analysis of the *Testament of Adam* as a piece of exegesis of the *SpTh*, there is still enough time between the sixth century and the appearance of the Arabic Pseudo-Clementine texts in order to assume that the *Testament of Adam* was inserted into the *SpTh* before the whole text was used for the composition of the Arabic Pseudo-Clementines.

22. The Georgian translation testifies to the corrupted text indirectly by changing the *three* to *two* (Mahé 1992).

23. Nöldeke's (1888) proposal for an emendation '...zweitens zur Zeit des Herodes, drittens bei der Zerstörung Jerusalems' corresponds to Ri's (1987a) MS *D*

that the textual corruption has to be older than the translations is certainly correct. The work did not end there.

To sum up, Ri and others assume a very high age of the *SpTh* (and especially of the traditions reworked therein) dismissing many passages as later additions. Other scholars took some of these passages in order to reconstruct a late redaction of the work. In order not to build far-reaching conclusions about the date of the *SpTh* on passages which are likely to be such later additions, the next section discusses the literary character of the *SpTh* and addresses the question which parts of it may be classed as additions to an original, basic composition. Only after that can some pieces of evidence for establishing the date of the text be presented.

### *Gradual Growth and/or Redaction?*

In a few cases the differences between the MSS, the versions and the recensions help to establish the history of the text. However, if manuscript evidence such as two versions of a passage is missing, scholars tend to look for stylistic characteristics in order to cut the text into an earlier *Grundschrift* and its later additions (Götze 1922). In other words, one's presuppositions about the features of the genre of a text determine the analysis of its layers and the reconstruction of its history. But what is the genre of the *SpTh*? How much tolerance towards deviant elements were acceptable in a text of this genre? In this section passages which may be classed as later additions are examined.

#### *Gradual Growth of the Text*

Some passages of the *SpTh* have close parallels within the work itself. It is very likely that a part of them was added in the process of the copying of the text—that is, that copyists associated pieces of text read earlier or later and added them at their current spot.[24]

The first one of two remarks (1.4$^{e}$ and 2.2$^{w}$/3$^{e}$) on the Trinity may be a later addition (cf. n. 39). However, the traces of Christianity are

(Beirut), which was not available before Ri's edition. Götze's (1922: 36) arguments for a rupture in the text at this point must be dismissed, because the frequent change of narratives, listings, and explanatory remarks are part of the stylistic repertoire of the whole work.

24. A typical case is 14.15$^{e}$, cf. below. The few longer inclusions of biblical material (Pešīṭā) also belong to this category, cf. n. 84.

deeply rooted in the text. There is, for example, no textual indication that the journey of the ark in the shape of a cross (19.5) should be a secondary addition.[25]

Adam's creation 2[w] is more elaborate than in the eastern MSS. Some of the pluses of the western recension expand motifs which appear in the eastern MSS elsewhere.[26]

Not all the remarks on the 'centre of the earth' belong to the oldest stratum of the text (cf. 4.3, and n. 49). The same suspicion can be held against many similar passages, as the concept of the 'centre of the earth' continued to function as a structuring device beyond the completion of the original text.

The stereotypical reiteration of the antediluvian patriarchs' testaments also invited scribes to introduce subtle changes into the text.[27] There is no trace of a purposeful redaction here.

The branch of MSS *H* and *M* contains a long genealogical piece 11.3[e], which is either a careless inclusion of a marginal note into the main text or an erroneous copy of a disconnected page of the *Vorlage*. The first part, *d-men Ādām l-Šēt* until *w-men Šēm l-Arpakšār w-men Arpakšār*, was inserted after its original continuation, namely, the second part, *l-Šālāḥ w-men Šālāḥ l-'Ābār w-men 'Ābār l-Pālāg* until *wa-'dammā la-zqīpēh da-mšīḥā*. The text appears in MS *M* at this spot, because it is missing in this MS in 52.1-6, where the rest of the eastern MSS contain the genealogical list. Consequently, the fragment of the list 11.3 ends with *Bā'āz*, where the MS *M* begins in 52.6b. The context regarding *Yūbāl* and *Tōbalqīn* continues after the insertion in ch. 11.

Abraham's life is summarized along the biblical text 28.1–29.3. The following paragraphs 29.4-14 have to be classed in several categories.

25. Cf., e.g., Mahé (1992); Gibson (1901, text 28 ll. 13ff.; trans.: 29); Bezold (1888: 99). The description of Malkiṣedeq's offering 28.11 alludes to the eucharist (*d-neštāwtap b-rāzē qaddīšē*) in the part of the text which includes rewritten biblical material; 'Or Melkisedek fit communier Abraham au pain et au vin qui étaient offerts' (Mahé 1992); 'And Malkiṣedeq consecrated an offering of fine bread and drink' (Gibson 1901, text 37 ll. 17-18; trans.: 38). Cf. Bezold (1888: 145); Grébaut (1912: 134).

26. E.g. 2.16[w] (= Gibson 1901, text 6 ll. 6-8; trans.: 6), Adam's creation in the 'centre of the earth' etc.

27. E.g. irrelevant pluses in 8.14[w]: *w-kad emar l-hōn* until *men yāwmā d-qaṭlēh l-Hābēl*; 9.8[e]: *šammeš qdām alāhā b-gāw m'arrat gazzē*; cf. 13.8-10[e] but also the variants to 13.8-10[w]; 22.11[e]; 16.23-28[e] and MSS *d* and *e* par. 22.12[w] par. 23.19-21[e], etc.

Firstly, 29.4-8 accumulates events and notions at the place of Golgotha (the 'centre of the earth')—topics which are typical of the *SpTh* and recall other events and paragraphs. This piece may be understood as a specimen of the internal growth of the text.

Secondly, 29.9-14 discusses the typology of the *Binding of Isaac*. Within this paragraph 29.10-11$^{e}$ contains a badly preserved[28] apology for East-Syrian Christology. The following observations show that 29.10–11$^{w}$ is an abbreviation of the eastern text rather than 29.10$^{e}$ an expansion of a common source with the western text. This explains the fact that the reference to the circumcision 29.10-11$^{w}$ only fits the argument of the eastern recension but not its present context. It is useless there, because only in the eastern texts is Christ's circumcision one of the proofs for the theory that the godhead did not suffer—neither crucifixion nor circumcision.[29] In the Arabic parallels and the Georgian version the traces of the circumcision were deleted together with 29.10-11$^{w}$ (Bezold 1888: 149; Gibson 1901, text 38, ll. 5-17; trans.: 39; Mahé 1992: xxix-xxx, 52). However, a trace such as it is preserved in the Syriac western recension has also been left in the *Gadla Adām* (Trumpp 1881: 150; Dillmann 1853: 122),[30] where it does not fit the context. This piece of evidence from the tradition in Ethiopic, which is based on an Arabic tradition (Trumpp 1881: iv), makes it unlikely that the Arabic Pseudo-Clementines (Bezold 1888; Gibson 1901), where the reference to the circumcision is missing, should represent the oldest reading.[31] Thus, the pointedly East-Syrian recension of 29.10-11

28. The text of this piece seems to be far from established. Bezold's text (1888: 148) differs from Ri's (1987a), whose text (MS *M*) is the *lectio difficilior*. The differences may have been caused by confusion over *b-sāwkāw(hy)—b-hwkw(hy)* (*sic* Ri 1987a)—and *d-bsmwhy* = *da-bsāmāw(hy)*? The MSS *D*, *F*, *H* and *M* seem to contain the worse text.

29. The MS *F* spoiled the point by introducing the topic of 46.15-18$^{e}$ (plus MS *d*), where the theological argument is replaced by the miracle of Christ's circumcision in which 'nothing was cut away from him'.

30. Dillmann (1853: 143 n. 134) was right in his judgment about his text—ultimately based on the Syriac western recension—here: 'diese in [ ] von mir eingeschlossene bemerkung [*sic*] ist hier vollkommen sinnlos.' It can only be understood on the basis of the East-Syrian remark in the *SpTh*.

31. Götze (1922: 34) argued from a comparison of the ideas about Malkiṣedeq that the extant Arabic parallels represent the oldest accessible stratum of the text. This question has to be examined again, taking into account the possibility that the Arabic versions may be abbreviations of their Syriac *Vorlagen*.

precedes the West-Syrian one. It is, therefore, not reasonable to reconstruct a *lectio brevior* as a more original form of the text. The former chief witness for the last and latest redaction[32] according to studies on the *SpTh* emerges as the oldest accessible one.

The concept of the three Pesaḥs in Israel's history may have spread from 43.8 to other places, for example, 40.12.

Ms. *A* (MS *F* is not preserved here) and the western recension contain 44.12-13, a piece of text that summarizes the topics of the *SpTh* as a collection of notions which 'even the ecclesiastical authors were not able' to show 'accurately'.

After the discussion of the significance of Christ's garment, 50.13-19 refers to the 'three gifts' of 'kingdom, priesthood, prophecy'; the 'holy Spirit' and the 'Pesaḥ', which were taken from 'the Jews'. There the text 50.16$^{e}$ (including MS *d* and the parallel notion in 50.16$^{W}$) may be an addition, as it ignores the long allegorical explanation of Christ's purple garment, which is interpreted as a 'royal' sign. The passage presupposes a *priestly* significance of the garment. The contradiction may, however, also have escaped the attention of the author, who liked handy enumerations.

*Possible Redactional Passages*

*Explanations and Controversial Issues*. The *SpTh* is no exegetical text. Therefore, terms such as 'this means' (*hānāw*) hardly ever occur as an introduction to explanatory remarks. Some of the bits of interpretation following, for example, *hānāw* may be later additions, cases of 'gradual growth' of the text (cf. above), or remarks especially where they occur only in one of the recensions.[33] The same is true for other bits of

32. As noted above, the specification of the *hērēṭīqā* (MSS *A, B, C, E, L, O, P, S, U* and *V*) as *Qūrillōs w-Sēwīrā* in MSS *D, H, M* and *F* may be secondary. The East-Syrian redactor may have been the author of the *SpTh* (against Götze 1922: 35 § 40). The parallel statement does, however, not fit its context well, cf. below.

33. Cf., e.g., 1.8$^{e}$ (and MS *e*) the composition of the *rqī'ā* ('firmament). 1.13$^{e}$ *lā mtaqqantā w-lā mṣabbattā* (= *tōhû wā-bōhû*), 1.25$^{W}$ *šabbtā* is being translated. 2.8$^{e}$ explains the four elements (followed by *hānāw* 'that means'). 2.10$^{e}$ (par. 2.11$^{W}$) a rhetorical question is asked: 'Why did God make Adam from these weak elements?' 3.1$^{e}$ 'rebellious rank' (of angels) is explained. 3.18 and 3.20 explain biblical passages. In 4.16$^{e}$ and 16.8, biblical imagery is interpreted briefly. 20.11 explains the sign of the bow of the covenant with Noah. 34.1 specifies *yubbālā da-bnay Isrāyēl*. 52.16$^{e}$ (16$^{W}$: *qārē*) interprets the *šešlātā* ('chains', cf. Ps. 118.27). 52.19$^{e}$

exegetical terminology such as 'by means of that he informs about…' (2.3$^{e}$, 11$^{W}$).

A few passages of the *SpTh* contain parallels to Aprahaṭ's *Demonstrationes* which may be dependent upon this work.[34] Aprahaṭ interpreted Jacob's vision in three ways (Parisot 1894: 144-45 = 4.5-6;= Wright 1869: 63). First, the 'gate of heavens' is said to be Christ (*enā nā tar'ēh da-šmayyā*, cf. Jn 10.9). Secondly, the ladder is interpreted as 'our Savior', because 'the just ones are ascending and descending on it.' Thirdly, the 'ladder is again a symbol for our Savior's cross. It is set up such as a ladder and the Lord is standing above it, because above Christ is the Lord of all' (cf. Parisot 1894: 684; 14.39; = Wright 1869: 288).

The *SpTh* refers to 'our Savior's cross' (31.17), but it interprets the ascending and descending angels (Gen. 28.12) in another way and assigns other roles to God and Christ (against Aprahaṭ).

Thus, the author of the *SpTh* may have known Aprahaṭ's theology, but he does not use it carefully. 31 was probably part of the original text of the *SpTh*.

Aprahaṭ's *Demonstrationes* were certainly used for the technical chapter 33 (Parisot 1907: 45 l. 22-49 l. 14 = 23.15-17 = Wright 1869: 465-66). The material is reworked in the *SpTh* (cf. Götze 1922: 48-76). The discussion is not out of place in the context, because it solves an exegetical problem. It could be learned from Genesis 38 that God prevented the intrusion of Canaanites into Christ's genealogy. However, in the case of the Moabites, he was more lenient. While showing how Boaz was related to Judah (via Pereṣ, 33.3-7) and how Solomon married one of Lot's daughters (*Na'mā*, 33.13), the reason for Ruth's acceptance in the sequence of generations was given as Lot's protection of his guests (Gen. 19). The chapter fits the approach of the

specifies the day of the last judgment (52.19$^{W}$ less explicitly). 54.10 explains the imagery of the sheep in Jn 21.15-17.

34. Götze (1922: 72-76, esp. 76) refers to Bezold (1883: 79 n. 134) who had already given Aprahaṭ as the source of the *SpTh* in its interpretation of Jacob's dream. He noted that this piece was not included in the *Gadla Adām* and hence an 'Interpolation der Urschatzhöhle, da sie im Adam-Buch fehlt, das sonst an Aphraates-Stellen Teil hat'. Cf. for the chapter, Mahé (1992), Gibson (1901: text 40 ll. 19-22; trans.: 42), Bezold (1888: 161-62) and Parisot (1894: 148-49), (Wright 1869: 64) for Aprahaṭ's opinion on Gen. 29 and baptism.

*SpTh.*[35] The probable use of Aprahaṭ († after 345) provides another *terminus a quo* for these texts.

Several times the *SpTh* contains refutations of other sages' opinions.[36] Such remarks interrupt by virtue of their very nature the course of the narrative into which they are inserted. They may fit their contexts better or worse. However, they do not contain motifs or expressions of an ideology which are absent from the rest of the text as a whole. They also do not betray a consistent conception of a planned redaction of the whole book. Many of them contain elements which disprove the thesis of a composition of the text in the first centuries.[37] Hence, it is justified to use these paragraphs for dating the whole text rather than to cut them out to leave an undatable (and therefore presumably early) hypothetical composition.

In many places the *SpTh* includes etymological remarks and etiological stories and digressions[38] from the stream of the rewritten

35. Note that the Moabites and Ammonites are not mentioned in the list of peoples which are hated by God, 33.16.

36. Cf., e.g., *maktbānē ḥakkīmē* in the context of the millennia; regarding Gen. 6 (15.4-8); the 'heretics' of 21.19[e]; and Syriac as the primordial language (n. 37); 26.12-18 against people who misinterpret the previously mentioned *kōkītā d-rūḥā* and mix it up with the flood. Both events have different reasons and designations according to the *SpTh.* 27.18-22 against superstition; 33.1: the reading *myabblīn* of most of the MSS may be secondary against *mbalblīn*, 42-44.

37. Cf. the refutation of Hebrew as primordial language. 24.10-11 is an explanatory remark to the paraphrase of Gen. 11.1 in the Pešītā, quoted in 24.9. See below.

38. Short etymological remarks are, for example (apart from the frequent explanation of a city's name by means of its founder's name): 1.25 *šabbtā*; 3.6 Satan and demons (cf. Coquin and Godron 1990: 207); 17 *'den* and *'ēdtā* (as an etymology?). Malkiṣedeq's name is used to derive his parents' names 22.4, 23.8. 23.15[W] Jerusalem, 23.18 Golgotha etc. including *gpīptā*—not as 'grotto', but the geographical name in Jn 19.13 (Why should a New Testament term be a case of 'spéculations ésotériques des chrétiens primitifs fondées sur une ancienne tradition juive' [Ri 1998b: 148]?); 24.14 (Gen. 10.25) *Pālāg*; 31.10 Jericho 'millstone' *raḥyā* (Bezold 1883: 79 n. 133); 35.17 Palmyre; 46.23 Isa. 7.14 *'Ammannū'ēl*—given by *Pērōzdād* the *mgūšā*. The collection of etiological material includes, for example, the background for the Abraham narrative: 25.8-14 the reason for idolatry; 26.1-10 sacrifices of infants, 26.11 Mesopotamian tells, 27 the Persians' religion, science, incestuous customs, etc. Nöldeke (1888: 234) observed that the names of *Jezdegerd* and *Pêrôz* together with the remarks about the Persian religion presuppose a late Sassanian date for the text—i.e. towards the end of 224–651 (cf. against that de

Bible, which runs through the text. Such passages may be excluded or included in the reconstruction of a basic layer of the text in an arbitrary way only. However, in order to avoid circular argumentation—for example, the conclusion that the oldest stratum of the text be Jewish after the deletion of all references to Christianity (e.g. Bagatti 1979)[39]—the most comprehensive approach is recommendable.

For example, the story of the invention of purple (36.1-8) is certainly part of the original composition. It is attested frequently in antiquity (Nöldeke 1888; Götze 1922: 78). It serves its purpose in the *SpTh* as setting the stage for the understanding of the significance of the royal garment, which was used by the soldiers to mock Jesus.[40]

The long discussion of Jesus' garment has several parts. First, the social meaning of purple is repeated; secondly, the synoptic evidence is allegorized; thirdly, the allegory of Raḥab's thread is added. They fit the style and theology of the *SpTh* (cf. n. 9). 50.1-3 goes on to discuss the significance of the 'crown of thorns'. After that the division of Christ's garments is discussed again (50.4-12).[41]

Lagarde 1888: 840-41 = de Lagarde 1889: 72-73). 30 the building of Jerusalem (by 12 pagan [cf. Mahé 1992: xvi] kings—Jericho by seven 31.7-10); 35.21 Heliopolis (in all kinds of misreadings), 36.1-8 purple; 38.26 = 2 Kgs 17.24-28; 42.4 the origins of the book of Lamentations; 46.3 how and why the *mgūšē* were also 'kings' etc.; 49.11-15 why Jesus's garment was not divided up.

39. In 1.6-7 the *rūḥā* of Gen. 1.2 is read as the holy Spirit (e.g. against Aprēm). Should this be a later addition? In 2.4 'the angels listened to this' (i.e. God's) 'word in awe.' This may imply that the plural in 'let us make man' of Gen. 1.26 was interpreted as a scenario of God talking to the angels in some stage of the tradition. In both recensions the Trinity is connected with this important proof-text in different ways; 2.3[e] 'while he informs by means of that *Nūn* 'instead of an *Ālap* about the glorious hypostases' (*qnōmē šbīḥē*) 'of the Son and the Spirit', 2.2[w] *emar alāhā abā la-brā wa-l-rūḥā qaddīšā* (= Bezold 1888: 11), missing in Gibson (1901: text 5 l. 10-12 trans.: 5), Coquin and Godron (1990: 206) but contained in Grébaut (1911–1921, 1911: 82). The Georgian version relies on both recensions and elaborates the point (Mahé 1992). This indicates that some kind of remark on the Trinity was present in the oldest form of 2.2–4 which can be reached by means of the comparison of MSS.

40. The parallel is even referred to on a literal level. 36.1-8 only gives *pūrpūrōn lbūšā d-malkē* whereas in 49.11-16 *argwānā* is used together with *pūrpūrōn. Pūrpūrōn* is not attested in the New Testament Pešīṭā. The Sinaiticus gives a doublet here *naḥtē da-zḥōrītā w-d-argwānā* (Kiraz 1996, vol. I.434).

41. In the MS *A* (cf. the apparatus to 50.7) the story of the garment culminates in its being sent to Rome in the end.

Throughout the *SpTh* massive doubt is cast on the truth of Scripture as well as the whole of previous world literature (*maktbānē d-'ebrāyē wa-d-yāwnāyē wa-d-sūryāyē*). Instead, *SpJh* promotes its own version of the biblical history, 42.6-7; 43.13-14, 'I am holding the true tradition and I am showing the truth to everybody' (43.14; cf. 4.3[c]). 44.1, the raison d'être of the composition, is given as providing information of paramount importance for the understanding of the biblical history. This is proven in 42-44 leading directly to the longer genealogical list from Adam to Christ (44.21-47) after the shorter one from *Zurbābēl* to Christ (42.8-9; 43.15-25). Apart from these lists the passage contains narratives about the time of the exile[42] and paragraphs of meta-language (42.6-7; 43.8-10, 13-14; 44.1-20, 48-57). in order to give explanations and to address the readers.

The modern reader may be disappointed (such as the scribe of MS *d*) that, for example, the Scriptures are carefully hidden (42.1-3),[43] just to be discovered burned later on (43.2); and if 'Azrā reconstructed this literature in the holy Spirit from its ashes, whence the pathos of the *SpTh* to be the only reliable source of truth (42.6-7)? Despite such objections, 42–44 can be understood as a meaningful piece, which argues in favour of the importance of the whole work. The narrative and the argumentative paragraphs support the same ideology.[44]

The two lists are likewise not doublets, but mirror the evidence of the Gospel—42.8-10, 43.15-25 rework a third of Matthew's genealogi-

42. 42.1-5, 10-22 end with a biblical quotation (Pešīṭā Zach. 4.14) and the remark on the end of the fifth millennium. 43.1-6 *Zurbābēl, Īšō' bar Yōzādāq*, and *'Azrā* restore the scriptures, Adam's triple office of 'king' (or 'teacher' 51.4[w]), 'priest' and 'prophet'; and the Pesaḥ 43.7. The MS *d* has a different account of *'Azrā's* restoration of the Scriptures. Its scribe tried to remove the tensions of the text. Thus, he attributes the last Pesaḥ to 'our Lord' and not to *'Azrā*. For the idea of only five Pesaḥs as having been celebrated in the history of ancient Israel cf. the chronicle of Hippolytus (Bauer and Helm 1955: 116-18).

43. Götze (1923: 83) is too optimistic regarding the reliability of the *Gadla Adām* for textual emendations of the Syriac *SpTh*. There the priest Simon stores only the *ashes* of the books in the cistern. This is not attested in any Syriac MS and may be an adaptation of 42.2 (*w-lā āwqed ennōn*) to 43.3. Cf. also the change of Jeremiah's grave against the rest of the tradition, but agreeing better with the Bible in the *Gadla Adām*.

44. The story about the hiding and finding of the Scriptures is, therefore, not an *Einschub* (cf. Götze 1922: 80). The versions of Mahé (1992) and Gibson (1901) roughly contain the same text in these chapters.

cal table,[45] and 44.21-47 Luke's. Between the lists and the narrative material the author fights for the supremacy of his historical reconstruction. This creates a frame around 44.21-47 in which the same topics are addressed. The author of the *SpTh* did not invent each motif or story by himself, but presented diverse arguments in a coherent way. He does not want to abolish the Bible but to emphasize the relativity of its interpretation against his own approach. He may also show his superiority by explaining why a certain biblical text was written. In 47.1-8[e] [46] the rhetorical question 'where was Christ when the infants were killed?' is asked, and answered, 'he was not present in Judaea'. This explains the raison d'être of the biblical narrative itself. It does not reflect contemporary discussions.

In the dialectic of asserting its own uniqueness against the biblical text on the one hand and of its high dependence upon that text with regard to the material which is reworked on the other hand, the *SpTh* creates an atmosphere of high dignity and antiquity vis-à-vis the Bible. In addition, this procedure creates the following situation. Passages in which the *SpTh* claims to replace the biblical version of the events are 'true' beyond doubt, because they are deeply rooted in the biblical text. However, in many passages where the *SpTh* appears to be just summarizing the Bible, it inserts its own ideology.[47]

*Biblical Proof-Texts.* Some paragraphs interrupt the flow of the renarration of the Bible and refer to other biblical texts as proof or background.

Thus, 1.11[e] alludes to (introduced by *d-emar bar Išay* in a minority[48] of MSS) Pešīṭā Ps. 148.4 for the 'upper water'.

3.17–4.1, 3 discusses issues of the typology of *'den/Pardaysā* and the church.[49] The text resumes the thread of the narration of Satan's

45. Both lists are changed in order to include Joseph and Mary. The shorter list begins with *Yōyākīn* (= *Yōkanyā*) and not with Abraham, because the author of the *SpTh* inserts it into the running narrative at the point where *Yōyākīn* enters the stage.

46. Except for the MS *d* the western recension is unintelligible. The Georgian translator tried to make sense of it without much success (Mahé 1992).

47. Cf. below. Thus, Ri's (1998b) analysis of the work as apocryphon describes the setting of its literary fiction but not its date.

48. The reference is missing in the Georgian (Mahé 1992) and in Gibson (1901: text 4 ll. 9-12; trans.: 4; Bezold 1888: 5-7). It may be secondary.

49. The text was developed with minor differences in the two recensions. The last part of passage 4.2-3 (= Mahé 1992; reworked in Gibson 1901: text 7 l. 23–8

jealousy with a reference to the protoplasts' attire and appearance (*maprgīn*, 3.14; 4.4).

A similar typology is used in 18.3-8 comparing the situation in the ark with the (Paradisiacal) circumstances of the life in the church.[50]

11.12 contains the biblical proof (quoting Pešītā Ps. 82.6 but implying v. 7) for the defence of the designation of *bnay alāhā* for the *sons of Seth*.[51] The question is raised again in 15.4-8 (Mahé 1992; Gibson 1901: text 24 ll. 7-17; trans.: 24-25; Bezold 1888: 79). The opinion of anonymous 'earlier authors' (*maktbānē qadmāyē*) that the *bnay alāhā* were angels is refuted by means of the argument that the nature of the spiritual beings would not allow for sexual relations with women.[52]

A typological and apologetical discussion is contained in the explanation as to why Canaan was cursed by Noah, 21.18-23 (until 'among all the peoples'; cf. Mahé 1992; Gibson 1901: text 30 l. 3-11; trans.: 30-31: Bezold 1888: 109-110; shorter). It begins with the parallels between the drunken Noah and Christ and its proof text, Pešītā Ps. 78.65. Then only 21.19[e] continues to refute the exploitation of the verse as indication that 'God was crucified'. 21.20 elaborates the typology of the Jews and Canaan. However, the basic thread of arguments continues 21.23 by reading the (contemporary) 'Egyptians' as *typos* for 'Canaan'. Thus, 21.18-23 appears as a footnote which was

l. 11; trans.: 8; cf. Coquin and Godron 1990: 207-208) states that the cross stood at the place of the tree of life in the 'centre of the earth'. 4.3[W] quotes Pešītā Gen. 2.15-17. Both recensions share the remark about the location of the cross. This disturbs the geographical system of the *SpTh*, implying that Adam's body was brought to the 'centre of the earth' only after the flood and that Paradise was not located there. 4.2-3 can be classed as a case of internal growth. The power of the 'centre of the earth' to attract events was stronger than the internal coherence of the ideology of the *SpTh*.

50. The other versions (and 18.3-8[W]) are shorter here (Mahé 1992; Gibson 1901: text 27 l. 13-18; trans.: 24; Bezold 1888: 93).

51. The MSS *C* and *S* corrected the *SpTh* to *'lhym* (not exactly the *'lwhym/ Alhōhīm* of Pešītā Gen. 6.2). The passage had apparently become a standard theological *topos*, where Gen. 6 and Ps. 82.6 had been conflated (Mahé 1992: Gibson 1901: text 21 ll. 3-64 trans.: 21: Bezold 1888: 63).

52. Cf. n. 36 for parallels. The remark fits its context stylistically and ideologically. Cf. the remark on 'Seth's sons', 18.15 quoting Pešītā Ps. 82.6 followed by a paraphrase of v. 7; par. (Mahé 1992; Gibson 1901: text 28 ll. 4-8; trans.: 28: Bezold 1888: 97).

badly adapted to its context.[53] It may also be a later addition. As a working hypothesis, it may be assumed that plusses of the eastern recension preserve a more elaborate original text than the western recension; this question has yet to be studied (see above and n. 2).

As the *SpTh* used Malkiṣedeq's parents in its narrative, it became necessary to account for Heb. 7.3, where the fact is exploited that Malkiṣedeq's parents are not named in the Bible.[54] Thus, 30.12-13[w] =17[e] and 30.14-16 refute the idea (against unidentified *hedyōṭē*) that Malkiṣedeq was a divine being, as 'he neither had a beginning nor an end'. One could not ignore the authority of the epistle to the Hebrews. The verse had to be demythologized. The *SpTh* argues that from the fact that there are no data of Malkiṣedeq's life and provenance provided in the tradition (i.e. the genealogical lists of Matthew and Luke), it may not be inferred that he was a divine being.[55] The passage supports narrative elements of the *SpTh* and was not a later redactor's addition.[56]

53. The tension is preserved in the Georgian (Mahé 1992). 21.19-20[e] is missing there. The Arabic Pseudo-Clementine version of the Sinai is tuned much better to the context and avoids the reference to the Egyptians. This is probably not an older version of the original text, as the other branch of the Arabic tradition mentions the Egyptians (*al-aqbāṭ awlād ḥām mutafarriqīn fī l-arḍ kullihā*, etc. [Bezold 1888: 111 l. 2]—translating Syriac *'gbṭy'*). For the same equation (*miṣr malik al-aqbāṭ*) cf. Bezold (1888: 159 l. 2). In 25.1 (Bezold 1888: 129 l. 6) the Arabic version rendered Syr. *meṣrāyē* as *miṣriyyīn* (cf. Trumpp 1881: 145 n. 2); *ahl miṣr* (Gibson 1901: text 33 l. 24), but not the Syriac gloss *hālēn d-ītayhōn 'gbṭy'*, which may belong to the oldest text, as the *Gadla Adām* also explains the name 'Egypt' here; 'and the translation of its name is Mesrīn' (Trumpp 1881: 145 ll. 1-2; Dillmann 1853: 117).

54. Aprēm knew the tradition according to which Malkiṣedeq was identical with Šem (Hidal 1974: 116-18). This idea is not referred to in the *SpTh*. Except for the assumption that both the *SpTh* and Aprēm refuted Gnostic tendencies which interpreted Malkiṣedeq as a divine figure, Ri (1998a: 78-79) could not point to any connection between Aprēm and the *SpTh* in this context.

55. Cf. Simon (1937: 71) to the apocryphal text *sur Malchisédech* of Athanasius, where a similar line of arguments shows Malkiṣedeq *non point sans famille, mais sans généalogie*. Simon's references to the *SpTh* have to be checked carefully. He refers to Budge (1927: 19) for the *SpTh* (1937: 87). However, Budge summarizes a parallel from the *Life of Adam and Eve* there.

56. The paragraph which refutes the 'idiots' and which occurs at different places in the two recensions is an alternative explanation and may be secondary to 30.14-16.

Except for the MSS *A*, *H* and *M*,[57] both recensions lack a passage containing the quotations of Pešītā Isa. 6.3 in 46.22-25, together with the explanation of the significance of the angels' appearance at Christ's birth. 46.22-25 appears to interrupt the flow of the narrative, which continues in 46.26, 'and they prostrated themselves towards him such as towards a lord and a king'.[58] However, 46.22-25 is a speech by *Pērōzdād* (*mgūšā*), who explains the events around Christ's birth to his fellows. Should 45.16-17 (likewise in MSS *A*, *H* and *M* only) and 46.22-25 be later additions? They do not disturb (otherwise smoothly continuing) contexts. Thus, they may have been left out by a copyist. The motive for the omission could have been a copyist's anti-Judaism, as 45.16-17 and 46.22-25 contain the only sympathetic statement about Jews (*'Ebrāyē*) as the teachers of the *mgūšē* in the *SpTh*.

A similar textual situation is 47.3-4[e], quoting Mt. 2.15 and continuing *know!* (*da' lāk*), etc., with a reference to Pešītā Isa. 19.1 in MSS *A*, *H* and *M*.[59] The paragraph may be a later addition as well as a note to the text by its original author.

As the listing of typological correspondences between Adam's existence in Paradise and Christ's death, 48.11-30 is itself a non-narrative text; the quotation of Ps. 22.13 in 48.14 is not necessarily a later addition.

A similar case is the allusion to Isa. 5.1ff. in 51.5-17 which is combined with Deut. 32.32-33. It is a collection of biblical passages associated with the motif of the vinegar in the narration of the Passion.

Thus, most of the passages containing biblical parallels may be read as an author's annotations to his survey of the history of salvation. They let the reader step aside for a moment in order to consider questions which cannot be dealt with in the form of the narrative.

*Lists.* As the raison d'être of the whole book is identified as an apology for Christ's genealogy, and as the importance of an unbroken documen-

57. According to Ri (1987a: text n. ** *ad* 46.22), the other MSS include a *lacune* here. Does he mean a text which was once written in the MSS and is currently missing, or a text which is not included in the tradition of this branch of the stemma?

58. The passage together with 45.16-17 is missing in the Arabic Pseudo-Clementinum (Bezold 1888: 237, 243), and in the Georgian version (Mahé 1992).

59. The verse is not quoted in the New Testament. Except for *'rq*, it is identical with the Pešītā. However, this is only the version of the MS *M* (cf. 47.3, *'raq l-Meṣrēn*). The MSS *A* and *H* read the root *'ll*, as the Pešītā.

tation of the tradition is emphasized, the long lists of the *SpTh* are certainly among its basic components.[60] They interrupt narrative contexts. As indicated above, especially where Golgotha is mentioned, the *SpTh* tends to summarize its contents and to enumerate events which happened there.[61] In such cases it is impossible to tell whether the longer or the shorter form is the older one.

The last long list, 52.3-13, is motivated twice by Pešītā Ps. 118.27, 'bind the feasts by means of chains' (52.1-2, 15)—preceded and followed by the interpretation that the 'feasts of the Jews were handed down until our Lord's cross', where they were taken from the Jews together with 'priesthood, kingdom, prophecy' and 'the Pesaḥ'. A remark on Dan. 9.26 closes the discussion. The list may be understood as a summary of the whole *SpTh*.

*Literary Frames and Connecting Devices*. The chronology of Adam's creation and fall creates a literary connection of the events of the creation (3 and 5.1) with the Passion (48.11-30).[62] In 49.1 it is supported by an allusion to Phil. 2.7, Heb. 2.17, 1 Cor. 15.22 and the like. Both passages are best understood as integral parts of the oldest form of the *SpTh*.

One of the most puzzling features of the *SpTh* is its literary frame as a letter to *Nāmōsāyā*, which only emerges towards the end of the

60. For lists in this context cf. *the* 70 *languages* 24.16-21 (Mahé 1992; Gibson 1901: text 33 l. 9-16; trans.: 34; Bezold 1888: 125-26). The list is based on Gen. 10 (Witakowski 1993: 640-41.). The first genealogical discussion of the *SpTh* addresses the exegetical question of Ruth among Christ's ancestors versus Solomon's aberrations with foreign women, etc. 33–34.1 (Mahé 1992; Gibson 1901: text 43 l. 10-22; trans.: 44-45; Bezold 1888: 166-67).

61. Cf. 49.1-10[e]. The western MSS only give 49.1-3, 9-10, which is of paramount importance for the *SpTh*—cf. the parallel in 51.22. The MSS *H* and *M* even add a prayer 49.10 *w-āwdī* until *wa-b-māwtēh* after the statement of Adam's posthumous baptism. This is the only one of its kind in the *SpTh*.

62. Although it was not part of the *Urschatzhöhle*, Götze (1922: 86-87 § 65) suggested that it emerged from the same Gnostic concepts as the *Urschatzhöhle*. Thekeparampil (1983) (assuming the sixth century as a date for the *SpTh*) wanted to show that this typology in the *Passionssedrē* (some of them attributed to the patriarch *Yōḥannān*, † 648) was dependent upon the *SpTh*. Ri (1998a: 81) suggested that it '*a imprégné toutes les œuvres de Mar Éphrem*', being derived '*au moins... d'une source commune*'—which does not prove that it should antedate Aprēm. It is contained in the Georgian version (Mahé 1992).

book.[63] The work started as a paraphrase of the Bible with many digressions and short discussions. In 33.5[e64] the reader is addressed for the first time: *hā ḥāwwīt lāk*. Several times an addressee, *rāḥem alāhā, aḥūn Nāmōsāyā*, is mentioned (Poirier 1995: 115-16). In the Pseudo-Clementines he may of course be called 'my son Clement' (*yā bnī 'qlymns*), according to the literary framework of a dialogue between Clement and Peter.

Given that the (western?) Syriac *SpTh* was reworked in the Arabic (and Ethiopic) Pseudo-Clementines, etc., and that there is no literary work extant which was itself used as a source in these passages of the *SpTh*, it is clear that its author did not intend to write the whole book in the style of a (fictitious) letter. This may have had didactic reasons. The text starts like a re-narration of the Bible and only gradually becomes a contribution to a polemic dispute. Only as late as in 42–44 is the purpose of the whole work revealed—encompassing its beginning, too. The *SpTh* is designed to guide its readers carefully departing from their own biblical knowledge towards its ideology.

*Literarkritik or Textual History: The Long Omissions.* Both recensions share *grosso modo* the same amount of text until 36.9, where the eastern MSS (except for MSS *A* and *F*) skip the whole period of the divided monarchy joining in as late as 41.11, the time of the exile. This is probably due to a loss of text because of a homoioteleuton.[65] Ri claimed that the passage was a later insertion.[66] In addition to the high

63. Poirier (1995) did not solve the enigma of the name or designation *Nāmōsāyā*, but only explained the origin of its equivalent in the Coptic parallel.

64. This and the following remarks are contained in a chapter, which reworks Aprahaṭ's *Demonstrationes*. This latter work is cast in the form of a letter. The introduction 33.1-3 is left out in the Arabic Pseudo-Clementines (Bezold 1888: 167) beginning with 'and Fārṣ the son of Juda begot Ḥṣrwn' (Gibson 1901; text 43 l. 10; trans.: 44). The other addresses in 33.6, 8 *ḥzāw*, 'see!' *hāšā ḥzī*, 'see now', are partly present in the parallels; *wa-qad 'arraftuka an, fa-nẓur al-ān* (Bezold 1888: 169 ll. 4, 5), *wa-'lam an, fa-nẓur yā bnī 'qlymns* (Gibson 190: text 43, ll. 14-15).

65. Ri (1987b: 185; 1987a, trans.: xix) refers to de Lagarde (1889: 67-68 = 1888: 835-36) and Götze (1922: 8-9) for the assumption of a scribal error. The text as contained in the MSS *A* and *F* is not identical with the western recension in the lacuna. It is not impossible that the MSS *A* and *F* contain the original text of the eastern tradition.

66. Ri (1987b: 185) says that '*après cette lacune continue la légende des Écritures Saintes et du prophète Jérémie, exprimée dans un style littéraire*

probability of a scribal error it is not true that the *SpTh* would not be a *livre de chronique* without the text in the lacunae of 36.9–41.11 and 41.12. On the contrary, the ideology of the rest of the *SpTh* requires a continuous line of tradition through the history until Christ. It is most likely that these passages were part of the original work, because the *SpTh* is also a chronicle—even without these texts.

Moreover, not all MSS of the western recension contain the whole text of the *SpTh*. Thus, the MS *e* stops before Christ's genealogical tree (43.13–44.53 is missing) giving a colophon and the summary of the millennia 48.5-7$^{e}$, which is otherwise not attested in the western MSS.[67] This is also the point where one of the Arabic Pseudo-Clementines stops to rework the *SpTh*.[68] After omitting the story of Ḥiram and the invention of purple, 35.25–36.10, MS *e* continues at the point, where the long lacuna of the eastern MSS begins.

The Ethiopic Pseudo-Clementines continue until 37.18.[69] The *Gadla Adām* goes beyond that passage, ending with a summary of the ascension. The use of the *SpTh* in this literature shows that compilers of new works could dispose of their material freely and did so.

Some differences between versions and manuscripts such as the long lacunae emerged during the history of transmission of the text and are

*fabuleux*'. These observations do not support the claim, as Jeremiah is mentioned (42.4-5) as a figure of the time of the exile in agreement with the course of the biblical narrative. The *SpTh* contains many other paragraphs which also just paraphrase biblical text with little additions. The text also gives, for example, the wives of the kings in accordance with the aim of the whole book, *la-mḥāwwāyū men a(y)k nāsbīn (h)wāw neššē*, cf. 42.7, 44.14. The text of the *lacune* fits perfectly its broader context.

67. It is not unlikely that 48.5-7$^{e}$ is a case of internal growth of the eastern text in an early stage of its transmission, because the following context is likewise a collection of summaries culminating in the typology of Adam's creation and Christ's death. 48.8-10 is an integral part of the narrative, as it summarizes parts of New Testament history which are not elaborated in the *SpTh*. There the last supper is identified as *peṣḥā b-baytēh d-Nīqādīmōs aḥū(h)y d-Yāwsep*, par. 53.17.

68. The Arabic texts include the genealogical list. Bezold (1888: 247) ends with a parallel to 48.1-4; Gibson (1901: text 56 l. 18) with c. 44.53-57 = Bezold (1888: 227 l. 17).

69. 'And Joram, his son, was king after him. And he was 32 years of age when he became king' (Grébaut 1912: 144; Bezold 1888: 187 n.d). The remark about his age is only attested in the eastern MS *A*. It is absent from the *Gadla Adām* (Dillmann 1853: 127; Trumpp 1881: 157).

irrelevant for the reconstruction of the genesis, the genre and the shape of the original.

*A Composite Text?*

In this review, many passages have been collected, which seem to stand out from their contexts, etc. One could discard these paragraphs as later insertions. The resulting cleaned text would be plain re-narration of the Bible. Should this text ever have existed independently as an *Urschatzhöhle*?

The *SpTh* contains both cases of broken coherence[70] and examples of strong continuity of concepts and motifs throughout the whole text. The latter observation may also be taken as an argument in favour of the originality of the last chapters of the *SpTh*.[71] Apart from smaller details, the *SpTh* as a whole may be read as a meaningful composition. The book is characterized by its emphasis on genealogies, seeming chronological accuracy (cf. Mahé 1992: xviii-xix), its basic anti-Jewish,[72] etiological and apologetic thrust, and its paraphrases of the Pešītā, which are sometimes explained in exegetical paragraphs.

*Literarkritik* based on stylistic observations fails in the case of the *SpTh*, as there is, for example, no reason why the chronological framework or the genealogical lists should not have been introduced by the same person who also abbreviated and summarized the Pešītā. The explicative remarks and arguments in the text share the objectives of the whole composition. There is no redactional layer discernible, where somebody attempted to change the orientation of the book. The author did not, of course, invent all his stories, but he also did not rework a coherent text where most of them had already been assembled before him.

70. The importance assigned to the place of the Cave of Treasures in the first chapters and the fact that the *mgūšē* take the three gifts for Christ quasi from nowhere 45.12 (*Nēbō* or *Nō/ūd*, *Nō/ūdā* resp.) shows that the author did not care to continue each narrative thread of the text, see p. 272. Likewise Malkiṣedeq disappears after having been settled on Golgotha. He is mentioned again in 49.2.

71. Cf. 45.11, where the reference to 'Nimrod's revelation' seems to presuppose his esoteric education, 27.6-11. 45.14-15 refers to the three gifts of 5.17. 49.11-16, the purple (garment) recalls 36.1-9. 48.12-30 the chronology of the passion (and its typological significance) expands the notion of 5.1.

72. Concerning this question, which requires a separate treatment, I was allowed to address the Third Syriac Symposium at Notre Dame University, June 1999. A publication of this contribution is planned.

Some marginal developments of the text in its long history of transmission are visible. However, one has to look for a date of the *SpTh in toto*, based on research in the history of the repertoire of its motifs. In the following section, some of these issues are discussed.

### *The Cave of Treasures and its Time*

*Golgotha and the Tradition of Adam's Tomb*

As indicated above, the notion of the *SpTh* that Adam was buried in the rock of Golgotha was used as an argument for its high antiquity. In this section important contributions from Holl (1918) to Taylor (1993) are discussed.

When Holl took it upon himself to determine the date of the poem *Carmen adversus Marcionitas* (cf. Pollmann 1998), which was ascribed to Tertullian, he devoted a long passage of his paper to the sources of the legend of Adam's grave in the rock of Calvary/Golgotha (Holl 1918: 36-47). From this research, 450 emerged as the *terminus a quo* for the work under discussion.[73] Pseudo-Tertullian had a similar repertoire of information on the place of Adam's burial as the *SpTh*. Thus, one could briefly examine Holl's (1918) sources and apply his conclusions to the *SpTh*.

However, as indicated above, Bagatti used the *SpTh* as evidence that the (Jewish) Christians of Jerusalem of the first century assumed that Adam was buried in the rock of Golgotha[74] under the place where Christ had been crucified (Bagatti 1979: 277, 282). In this set of arguments the *SpTh* is of paramount importance, as it is assumed to contain

73. ...*der früheste Ansatz, den man danach für unseren Verfasser wagen darf.* Cf. the recent attribution to c. 420–450 by Pollmann (1998), dated by means of theological parallels to Augustin's works (Pollmann 1991: 33).

74. Kretschmar's (1987: 42 n. 36) and Bagatti's (1977: 5-6) explanation of Greek κρανίον (Mt. 27.33 par.) as referring to Adam's 'skull' is a case of *petitio principii*. It is a later, secondary interpretation (cf. Epiphanius, † 403; Holl and Dummer 1980: 5.6-7 = p. 209) and historically unreliable. Bagatti (1977: 8) explains the fact that Adam's grave was not represented in the architecture of the Constantinian edifices with the employment of architects who were not versed in the local (Jewish) Christian traditions. Based on the assumption that the epistle to the Hebrews (understood by Bagatti as written shortly after 70) already contains the notion that Golgotha replaced the Temple Mount, Bagatti (1979: 280) proposed that the Jews transferred the local tradition of Adam's grave to Hebron after the Christians' transfer of this tradition from Moriah to Golgotha.

traditions of the first century[75] and hence to be the oldest unequivocal witness to the localization of Adam's grave in the—at that time newly discovered—cave in the rock of Golgotha (Katsimbis 1977; Bagatti 1979: 277; Corbo 1982: 95-97).[76]

First, the textual, and secondly, the archaeological evidence, points against Bagatti's hypothesis. First, Bagatti's (1979) assumption that 'the book', namely the *SpTh*, 'does not speak about an ideal cave but about that of Calvary, which has been under the eyes of the first Christian generations' is not justified on the basis of the Syriac text of the *SpTh*. 2 and 3 respond to the geographical setting of Genesis 2 as an exegetical problem. Adam is created from the earth (at the place of Christ's crucifixion, 'the center of the earth' [2.15-16[W]; Gen. 2.7]) and subsequently elevated to Paradise (3.8; Gen. 2.15). The Cave of Treasures is located on the 'Mount of Paradise' (5.15) or 'on top of the mountain', *b-rēš ṭūrā*, near the 'fringes of Paradise', *špōlay Pardaysā* (e.g. 15.1). After Adam's body had been removed from there (17.6),[77] the text presupposes that the place had been destroyed in the flood (cf.

75. Bagatti (1979: 281) uses parallels to Jewish legends as an argument for the high antiquity of the sources of the *SpTh*—apparently presupposing that common traditions with Judaism could only be inherited from a distant past and could not be due to influences at a later date. Kretschmar (1987: 68) likewise postulates ancient roots for alleged parallels between the Gospel of John and rabbinic texts.

76. The literature has been discussed by Kretschmar (1987: 86-99). Belayche (1997) collects and discusses the textual and archaeological sources for the location of the Capitoline temple of Aelia Capitolina. She concludes that it was located at the place of Golgotha (and not on the Temple Mount). The assumption that Hadrian built the Capitol there out of an anti-Christian motivation is refuted (Belayche 1997: 394).

77. In a summary of the *SpTh*, Kretschmar (1987: 90) notices this narrative element and suggests to see there a reflection of the Jewish tradition of Adam's grave in the cave of *Makpelā*. While this cannot be excluded it is also not verifiable. Kretschmar (1987: 90-91) admits the highly hypothetical character of these assumptions. Jeremias (1926: 100 n. 1; cf. Gibson and Taylor 1994: 59) assumes that the traditions of the cave of *Makpelā* were combined with that of the Temple Mount and formed, thus, the pattern for the site of the Cave of Treasures, which could carry the significance of both of them—e.g. being Adam's grave and the entrance to Paradise. As the *SpTh* bypasses the temple and its service, it could well have attracted some of its traditions while implying that the real place was destroyed in the flood—i.e. that the centre of the Jews' worship until 70 had already been entirely meaningless after the flood.

17.9; 19.3-4).[78] It does not play any role after the flood and there is no indication in the text that it should have had any connection with Golgotha. Threads of the narrative which were initiated in these first chapters were not taken up later on. The *SpTh* does not, for example, tell how the three gifts for Jesus came from the ark to Mount Nebo, or *Nōlūd* (*Nōlūdā*) (45.12), whence finally the *mgūšē* took them. There is no indication that the Cave of Treasures should refer to any real place in the world after the flood, according to the author.

Secondly, the interpretation of the archaeological finds at the Rock of Calvary/Golgotha is irrelevant for assigning a date to the *SpTh.*[79] Moerover, as Calvary is not a realistic location for the scenario of an execution (Gibson and Taylor 1994: 59-60; Taylor 1993: 131-32, 141-42) it could not have been at the focus of the early Christians' remembrance of the event.[80]

Holl (1918), Jeremias (1926), Kretschmar (1987) and others discussed these concepts of the *SpTh* within the documents of patristic literature.[81] The localization of Adam's grave in the Rock of Calvary /Golgotha is indeed attested—but in pilgrims' accounts and other sources from the sixth century onwards. The theological assumption that Adam should be buried at the place of Christ's crucifixion can be traced back to the third century.[82] However, it is omitted by Eusebius

78. The question about the fate of Adam's body is raised by the writer's adversaries in the *Encomion copte sur Marie-Madeleine* (Coquin and Godron 1990: 205, 210).

79. Taylor (1993: 132-34) and Gibson and Taylor (1994: 71, 81-83) refute the thesis that the cavity which Bagatti and others had identified with the Cave of Treasures had been of any cultic significance in the Hadrianic structures, let alone before that time. It was obstructed in order to sustain the hollow rock and only opened up after the destruction of the church in 614—probably because Adam's grave was searched there.

80. For the veneration of places in general after Constantine, cf. Markus (1994).

81. Despite Kretschmar's own collections of sources and even against his recurrent indications (1987: 55-56, 86-88, 99-100, 107) that the older theological synthesis of Christ's death and Adam's redemption should not be taken as a proof for the antiquity of the localization of Adam's grave in the Rock of Golgotha, he accepts Bagatti's (1979: 277, 282) idea that Adam's grave in that place be '...die einzige christliche Überlieferung, die mit Sicherheit als echte Ortstradition an der Memorialstätte der Kreuzigung Christi in vornicänische Zeit zurückreicht' (Kretschmar 1987: 107).

82. Kretschmar (1987: 83-85, 97-98, and esp. n. 160). Thus, Origen's interpretation of the Gospel of Matthew (Klostermann and Benz 1941: 226) states that

and refuted by Jerome, whose opinion caused most Western theologians to oppose the concept until the time of the Crusades (Holl 1918). Kretschmar (1987: 85) points out that the tradition is not linked to a certain location in Jerusalem before its broader acceptance in the East after the fourth century. The *SpTh* mirrors a situation where the idea is already taken for granted. In addition, the concentration of Malkiṣedeq's place of worship, the location of the Binding of Isaac, and Abraham's sacrifice at Adam's grave is likewise not attested in sources before the sixth century (Kretschmar 1987: 98-99; Taylor 1993: 131).[83]

To sum up, the *SpTh* fits the concepts which gained broad acceptance only long after the fourth century, even if they existed as hardly attested theological opinions before Constantine. The text would be an exceptional and rare witness for an otherwise suppressed (Bagatti and Testa 1978: 40; cf. n. 76 above) or forgotten (cf. Kretschmar 1987: 53-54, 85 n. 160) tradition. However, if the *SpTh* was written after the fourth century, its motifs and imagery fit their time. Otherwise one has to assume many sub-hypotheses in order to explain why this text preserved such old traditions, which are not attested elsewhere, and why they were suppressed exactly in a time when they would have been expected to gain broad acceptance after the abolition of Hadrian's allegedly intentional profanation of the place.

### *The Biblical Text*

Ri (1987a: trans.: xxii; 1987b: 189) concluded from the observation that the *SpTh* hardly quoted biblical text *verbatim*[84] that these parts—

'*venit enim ad me traditio quaedam talis, quoniam corpus Adae primi hominis ibi sepultum est ubi crucifixus est Christus*' referring to 1 Cor. 15.22. In a Greek fragment, the anonymous informants are identified as *Jews* (Holl 1918: 36 n. 4; Klostermann and Benz 1941: 226 §551; Klostermann, Benz and Treu 1976: 263-65 §126). However, in Origen's time today's Rock of Calvary was not yet a place of worship for Christians, but included in the structures of the Capitol, cf. n. 76. Moreover, even after Constantine the term 'Golgotha' referred to the whole site and only 'during the course of the Byzantine period the term gradually came to apply to the so-called Rock of Calvary alone' (Gibson and Taylor 1994: 59; cf. Taylor 1993: 120-21).

83. The *SpTh* probably ignores the legend of the finding of the cross (cf. 50.20-21; 53.6), which was probably translated in the early fifth century into Syriac (Drijvers and Drijvers 1997: 25), because it seeks to avoid unequivocal historical references to later times in order to remain within the confines of its literary fiction.

84. One branch of the western recension (4.3, 12, $20^{W}$) includes paragraphs of a

that is, the basic layer of the work—were not based on an established (Syriac) biblical text in written form, and that they were consequently composed at a time and in an environment where the Pešītā was not known.

Apart from the fact that the Pešītā may be older than Ri assumed in these articles, his hypothesis is based on three presumptions—two of which are inadmissible. First, it is true that names of persons and places were frequently updated by later copyists, if they did not correspond to their current Bible. Thus, the forms of the names of the Pešītā in the *SpTh* do not prove that the original author knew that version. Secondly, however, all texts which actually paraphrase biblical narratives—to this category belongs a large part of the text[85] of the *SpTh*—would have been copied from the Pešītā if it should have been available to the author. Thirdly, those texts which quote a biblical text which is identical or almost identical with the Pešītā (see above), are later redactors' additions and have to be dismissed (because of presuppositions regarding the properties of the genre).

It may be inferred from a few cases where the *SpTh* and the Pešītā share a translation which is not the obvious one of the Masoretic text (and the Septuagint),[86] that the *SpTh* presupposes the Pešītā also in

text very similar to the Pešītā. They are filling gaps in the re-narration of Gen. 3. It is acceptable to dismiss them as later additions. This may also be inferred from Götze's (1922) observation that the chronology of the *SpTh* presupposes the Septuagint but was revised according to the Pešītā (cf. n. 101). The author used Greek (secondary) sources for his chronology.

85. The presentation of a piece of text which is interpreted subsequently is rare, cf. the Hexaemeron, and, e.g., 31.13-16 interpreted in 17-19; 20-21 interpreted in 23-25; and 26 interpreted in 26-27. In the following chapter (32), the biblical text is summarized only. Nöldeke (1888: 235) observes that the *SpTh* uses the Pešītā of the Old and New Testaments. His only objection is based on the apparent echo of the Septuagint Gen. 1.2 (ἀόρατος και ἀκατασκεύαστος), 1.13, *lā mtaqqantā w-lā mṣabbattā* 'unordered and unadorned'. This text belongs, however, to the interpretative material and not to the paraphrase of Gen. 1. It is apparently a piece of exegesis inherited from a Greek source.

86. Gen. 1.1 (1.3) Hebrew *br'šyt* could also have been translated in another way than Syriac *b-rēšīt*. The Syriac Pseudo-Clementine recapitulation of the biblical history begins with *b-rēšīt*, such as the Pešītā translating ἐν ἀρχῇ (Frankenberg 1937: 34 l. 13 = ch. 27.1). That text continues translating the Greek vorlage, e.g. *'bad* for ἐποίησεν instead of *brā* as in the Pešītā. The *SpTh* 1.25 is at pains to explain *šabbtā* on the basis of *ettnīḥ* = Hebrew *šbt*. Only the Pešītā associates the place of the 'Binding of Isaac' with the *'mry'* (Brock 1981: 3 §3, 7-8). As the *SpTh*

those passages, which belong to the basic biblical re-narration and are, therefore, not a redactor's additions.

What is more, for a book whose purpose is given as attempt to replace and to correct the biblical history, the *SpTh* is remarkably faithful to its source—regarding textual details, but not the overall conception of history.[87] Deviations from the biblical stories are intentional bits of exegesis of well-known texts. They are not signs of the instability of an oral tradition.

Aprēm wrote his commentary on the Diatessaron. The *SpTh* is already based on the Gospels. 30.16 refers to Matthew and Luke as authors of the genealogical lists, which are given in 42–44. The author was, however, not only aware of the differences between the Gospels, but he even used them for exegetical purposes. Thus, the two colors given for Jesus's royal garment had to be explained (49.16, 'one of the Evangelists said'; 49.17, 'and the other one said') after the colour purple was so much emphasized earlier.

As indicated above, the apparent naïveté of many passages of the *SpTh* is part of its approach to the Bible in a form of the Pešīṭā of both Testaments. Where it presents itself as esoteric lore, it follows the text rather closely;[88] and where it seems to summarize the Bible, it introduces its changes.

### *Graves, Relics and Liturgy*

Markus (1994) proposed to interpret the appearance of the notion of 'holy places', which was alien to Christianity before the fourth century, such as the new cult of relics being the young church's attempt to secure the continuity of its identity with the former persecuted church of the martyrs through the massive changes of the Constantinian era. The *SpTh* presupposes the results of this development. Its attitude

does not re-write biblical books with a difficult Hebrew text, the number of such test cases is small.

87. Cf., e.g., as a minor change to the source (apart from many interpretative paragraphs) that Adam alone is created on Friday (1.24). Malkiṣedeq's ancestry requires an interpretation of Hebrews, cf. p. 264. In 1.3 the angels are created before the world—a once hotly debated issue. For the dialectic of changing and copying biblical text, see above.

88. *And thus he made again the tradition of the tribes…I am holding the true tradition* (43.13-14[e]). In the western parallel he refers also to the missing women and priests in the genealogy (from 42.7?). The following lists of 44 are based on the Gospels, just adding the names of the women.

towards relics and graves makes it likely to have been composed after the fourth century. Moreover, the absence of the notion of death-impurity increases the distance between the *SpTh* and rabbinic Judaism.[89]

The embalming and burial of the antediluvian patriarchs is a recurring topic in a large part of the text devoted to their epoch. They are buried in the Cave (of Treasures),[90] where the antediluvian liturgy is taking place. It is one of the offices of the Sethites's leaders, 'that he should serve in front of Adam's body in a pure way' (*da-nšammeš qdām pagrēh d-Ādām zahyā'īt*, 7.20[e]). Before Malkiṣedeq's appearance in the *SpTh* this cult is not explicitly related to the eucharist.[91] From Lamek's testament onwards, Malkiṣedeq's eucharistic office and life-style are described and explained.[92] The place of Malkiṣedeq's worship is over Adam's grave on Golgotha. The service begins with Adam's (second) burial there.

The position of Adam's body in the ark is compared with the situation of a church. However, his grave is at the location of the Bema ('Adam's body is placed like a *bēm* in the middle,' 18.6) and not beneath an altar where the eucharist is celebrated.[93]

The transposition of Adam's remains into the ark and then to his grave in the Rock of Golgotha shows[94] that it was not only the martyr's

89. Ri (1998b: 150) did not prove his claim of a close proximity to Jewish sources.

90. For references to the burial of the antediluvian patriarchs and/or their worship in front of the bodies, cf. 6.21; 7.13, 20; 8.15, 17; 9.1, 8, 10; 10.8, 10; 13.6-7, 9, 11; 14.16-17; 16.12—in the ark, 20.

91. 4.1[e] only Adam's service in Eden is *a(y)k kāhnā b-'ēdtā qaddīštā*, cf. 5.27.

92. 16.22-25[e]; 22.4-5, 12[w]; 23.19-21; 28.11-12. It is emphasized several times that Malkiṣedeq would not sacrifice animals, but 'bread and wine'. The rock of Num. 20/Exod. 17 is used to block the doorway of Jesus' grave (53.8-10), but also identified with the *Mšīḥā* (1 Cor. 10.4 in 53.15). Later it gives 'bread and wine' to the guards of the grave in order to make them sleep, that (54.4) Peter (*Kēpā*) and not the guards be the first one to see him. He reveals himself in that action to the guards later.

93. Apart from the fact that no altar is mentioned in the ark, the situation there not only reflects a typology of the church but also one of the world. Therefore, Adam's body is placed 'in the centre' of that microcosm before being transferred to the same location in the macrocosm.

94. For the first attested transposition of a martyr's remains in 354 (Antioch) cf. Auf der Maur (1994: 108). The inclusion of Veterotestamental persons among the saints (in the *sanctorale*) was an extension of the veneration of martyrs (Auf der Maur 1994: 118). Adam was not among them (Auf der Maur 1994: 118-19).

grave which was venerated but already the saint's relics. Despite the fact that martyrs' graves are attested from the early third century onwards (Auf der Maur 1994: 96), the veneration of martyrs at their tombs begins in the fourth century (1994: 95-99).[95] The acceptance of the transposition of the martyrs' remains under the altars of the churches was the result of a long process which had to overcome the prohibition to bury the dead within the confines of the cities. Even in places where *martyria* were built over the martyrs' graves one would still not transfer relics into the community churches (Kötting 1965).

The situation of Malkiṣedeq's liturgy could reflect the idea of a cult in the martyrium of a saint/martyr. In the situation of the ark the shrine of the martyr's remains had already been transferred into the church of the community. These concepts are widespread in the *SpTh* and reflect a situation well after the fourth century.

*Jeremiah's Death and Burial Place*

The *SpTh* knows Jeremiah's grave to be located in Jerusalem (42.5). The account ignores the biblical story of Jer. 43.7-44.30.[96] The extant parallels differ from each other, but they agree (except for the Georgian version) that Jeremiah died in Samaria and was buried in Jerusalem.[97]

As the *SpTh* occasionally opposes the biblical text, it is not astonishing that it knew about Jeremiah's grave in Jerusalem. However, the probably pseudonymous letter of Cyril of Jerusalem also mentions this location of the grave, 'and we passed the graves of the prophets Isaiah and Jeremiah' (Brock 1977: text 270 §6; trans.: 275). Whether the letter was written by Cyril (Wainwright 1986) or not very much later

95. According to Auf der Maur, tombs of the martyrs were incorporated into the basilicas in the east a little earlier than in the west (sixth–seventh centuries). Rev. 6.9 was interpreted as the earthly (and not the heavenly) altar (beneath which the martyrs are buried) from the fourth century onwards (Kötting 1965: 22).

96. Götze (1923: 83) remarked that the *Gadla Adām* changed the text according to biblical common sense: 'and afterwards this prophet Jeremiah departed to the land of Egypt and he died there' (lit. *in it*) (Trumpp 1881: 161; Dillmann 1853: 130).

97. The basic facts were apparently embellished by the compilators. Thus, e.g., it is added in Gibson (1901: text: 51 l. 20; trans.: 53) that his grave 'was the only building [left] in Jerusalem'. Both the texts of Bezold (1888: 203-205) and of Gibson (1901) did not refer to the prophet's activity of singing lamentations over the destruction of Jerusalem (Ri 1987a; Mahé 1992). Götze (1922: 79) did not know a parallel for the claim that Jeremiah's grave should have been located in Jerusalem.

than the beginning of the fifth century (Brock 1977: 283),[98] the author of the *SpTh* could have learnt this tradition from the fifth century onwards.

*The Concept of the Septimana Mundi and the Chronology of the Cave of Treasures*

Ri (1998b: 147) argues that the *SpTh* had been composed and read by members of early Christianity in an Iranian environment. He claims that the millenarian structure of this text should mirror an ancient Iranian millenarism instead of the later Christian one.[99] However, Gignoux (1999: 225) cast serious doubts on the high antiquity of these motifs in Iranian apocalypticism and dated them in the Sassanian period (1999: 224-651).[100] If paleo-Iranian origins of the chronology of the *SpTh* are doubtful, it has to be read in another context.

The copyists of the *SpTh* understood that the millenarian framework of the *SpTh* was not its most important system of reference and of the organization of the text.[101] This can be inferred from their careless treatment of the motif. The end of the second millennium is not indicated in 14.15[w], except for MS *e*.[102] However, it is evident from the parallel in 17.22[103] that the reference to the millennium in 14.15[e] is a

98. The text is extant in two MSS of 1899 and the sixth-century. There is no proof of a Greek original. For Brock, the mention of Jeremiah's grave is one of the arguments against the authenticity of the letter.

99. He does not prove the claim that the *SpTh* should indeed have been influenced by (authentic?) sources of an 'astrologie irano-babylonienne' (cf. 45.8-19) and 'ésotérico-exégétique' interpretations of Dan. 9.25-26 (Ri 1998b: 148-49).

100. Gignoux (1999: 225) referred to 'conceptions nestoriennes sur la fin du monde qui devait même arriver un peu plus tôt' as a parallel to the Zoroastrian concept of the end of the world. The purpose of his paper is to refute Widengren's theses. Bardaisan's opinion was based on other observations (Witakowski 1990: 100).

101. Götze (1922: 83 §59) observed that the *SpTh* changed the numbers of the Septuagint in order to approach the Pešītā 'and its Jewish numbers' in the genealogical lists of the antediluvian persons. Regarding the third millennium, the *SpTh* gives the numbers of the Pešītā although the result presupposes the count of the Septuagint (Götze 1922: 83-84 §60).

102. The *Vorlage* of Mahé's (1992) text follows 14.15[w]. The reference to the millennium is given at this spot (and not around 17.22) in the Sinaitic Pseudo-Clementine version (Gibson 1901: text: 23 l. 23–24 l. 2; trans.: 24).

103. The Georgian corrected the date of 17.22[w] to 2240, but misinterpreted the reference to the Septuagint.

case of internal growth within the eastern recension, as both recensions share a reference to a millennium in 17.22. The copyist of the prototype of 17.22$^{e}$ remembered that he had already counted the second millennium before and referred to the third one,[104] whereas 17.22$^{w}$ gives the year 2000 *anno mundi* as the date for Noah's entering the ark. In 24.27 both recensions refer to the end of the third millennium. 14.15$^{e}$ is, therefore, an erroneous addition.[105]

The witnesses agree on the beginning of the fourth and fifth millennia (34.16; 42.22 par.; 44.53). Daniel 9.25-26 is given in 44.54 as the scriptural proof for this system and its correspondence to the chronology of Christ's death: 'Behold, our brother, Nāmōsāyā, that the fifth millennium came to an end in the days of Cyrus and until the passion of our savior there were five-hundred years according to the true prophecy of Daniel, who prophesied that after 62 weeks, the Messiah/ Christ (*mšīḥā*) is killed. These weeks are five-thousand and five-hundred years.' The author of the *SpTh* used millenarian traditions such as are attested in Hippolytus's chronicle without paying too much attention to the details.[106] Hippolytus (and probably Julius Africanus before him) had assigned the year 5500 to the annunciation of Christ's birth (or his birth itself) and not to his death.[107] In the *SpTh* the contemporary, commonplace system of current chronology stands in the background only.[108]

The author of the *SpTh* was not interested in the chronology of the world's history after Christ's death.[109] He uses only the pre-Christian

104. The MS *A* refers to the second millennium, together with the western texts.

105. Here and in the mentioning of the second millennium (16.15$^{e}$) most manuscripts refer to the 'seventy wise authors'—i.e. the Septuagint (Götze 1922: 80-85)—as a source for the millennia.

106. The computation is incorrect. Nevertheless, it is not unlikely that the *SpTh* is based on extracts, etc., from this tradition. Hippolytus enumerated all five Pesaḥs of the Veterotestamental history (Bauer and Helm 1955: 116-19 = ch. 8).

107. Ri (1998a: 79) refers to Julius Africanus for the date of 5502 (5500; Witakowski 1990: 97) for Christ's birth as an explanation for the visibility of the star during two years (45.2$^{e}$). The change from the date of Christ's death to that of his birth within a few paragraphs fits the generally free approach to traditional material in the *SpTh* (cf. Witakowski 1990: 102).

108. Götze (1922: 84-85) assumes that the dates of the later millennia in the *SpTh* were not based on actual computations but given as exegesis of Dan. 9.

109. In addition, Dan. 9.25-26 only accounts for the computation of the 500 years (62 weeks) preceding the death of the *mšīḥā*.

part of the larger concept of the *septimana mundi* which was designed to include the whole of past and future history within one system. After the year 500 BCE—that is, 6000 *anno mundi*—had passed, authors had to cope with the fact that nothing had changed. The old system of the end of the sixth millennium either as the end of the world (*Aprahaṭ*) or the beginning of a special era implying the return of Christ (Aprēm), etc., was refurbished (*Īšo'dād* of Merv), rejected (George Bishop of the Arab tribes) or handed down indifferently (*Gīwargīs bar 'Ebrāyā*).[110]

Thus, the chronological framework of the *SpTh* fits the Eastern Christian sources of, for example, the sixth century. The compiler of this text accepted those parts of traditional chronography which did not interfere with contemporary issues and deleted from the system what had become untenable.

*Emphasizing Syriac Identity*

Several passages of the *SpTh* imply its author's high respect for the Syriac language. Rubin (1998) discusses these passages in her paper on the language of creation and the primordial language. 24.11 emphasizes that Syriac was the primordial language[111] and that its writers were on the right side of God on the day of judgment. The missing Syriac version in the inscription of the cross shows that the 'Syrians do not partake in the killing of Christ', 53.22-26. Subsequently, the *SpTh* alludes to the legend of King Abgar, who wanted to destroy Jerusalem because of the crucifixion of Christ (53.26-27).

Witakowski (1993: 641) attributes the invention of *Yōnṭōn* to the author of the Syriac *SpTh.*[112] As *Yōnṭōn* was the teacher of Nimrod, who is drawn very positively in the *SpTh* as the founder (30.19) of Edessa, Nisibis and Ḥaran (besides others, 27.23), it fits the method of the author of the *SpTh* to anchor these achievements almost in the

110. Witakowski (1990) describes the development of the idea in Syriac literature.

111. The notion belongs to the basic form of the *SpTh*. Cf. the Georgian version (Mahé 1992), where the error regarding the direction of writing is corrected. Syriac is also mentioned in the Pseudo-Clementines (Bezold 1888: 123; Gibson 1901: text: 32 l. 24-33 l. 5; trans.: 33-34; Grébaut 1912: 26).

112. Gero argued for a high age of the figure and assumed that the rabbinical interpretation of Gen. 9.24 as castration of Noah was a reaction against the invention of *Yōnṭōn* by a 'branch of Mesopotamian Judaism, which adopted a broadly favorable attitude toward Babylonian astrology, and was receptive to local historical lore' (Gero 1980: 328). From there it was taken over into Christianity. The hypothesis is based on several hardly verifiable assumptions.

antediluvian history. It was probably part of the original work.

The first author who assumed that Syriac was the primordial language was Theodoret († 466; Rubin 1998: 321).[113] The atmosphere in which this opinion emerged is determined by the Syrians' growing awareness about the domination of their cultural expressions and identity by Greek learning. The need to defend Syriac culture may be older, but the *SpTh* and Theodoret are witnesses to the same attempt to promote this point by means of the exegesis of Genesis 11.

## *Conclusion*

In the preceding pages, two main theses have been discussed: first, that the Syriac *SpTh* has to be read as a coherent work and that no layer of an *Urschatzhöhle* can be analysed within it (apart from a few passages which were apparently added to the text after its author had completed it); secondly, the work contains elements which make it very unlikely that it could have been written before the fourth century. On the contrary, a date in the fifth or sixth centuries is very probable. Thus, the work loses its appeal of primordial antiquity and esoteric anticipation of much later concepts, but it becomes a much more meaningful contribution to the exegetical and religious dialogue of its time.

## BIBLIOGRAPHY

Auf der Maur, H.
1994 'Feste und Gedenktage der Heiligen', in P. Harnoncourt and H. Auf der Maur, *Feiern im Rhythmus der Zeit*, II/1 (GDK, 6.1; Regensburg: Verlag Friedrich Pustet): 65-357.

Bagatti, B.
1977 'Note sull'iconografia di "Adamo sotto il Calvario" ', *LA* 27: 5-32.
1979 'Qualche chiarificazione su la "Caverna dei tesori" ', *ED* 32: 277-84.

Bagatti, B., and E. Testa
1978 *Il Golgota e la Croce: Richerche storico-archeologiche* (SBF.CMi, 21; Jerusalem: Franciscan Press).

Bauer, A., and R. Helm
1955 *Hippolytus Werke*. IV. *Die Chronik* (GCS 46 [36]; Berlin: Akademie-Verlag).

113. The opinion is allegedly shared by Aprēm. No direct quotation on this matter is extant (Rubin 1998: 322-23). Theodore of Mopsuestia's opinion is likewise only attested in late, secondary sources.

Baumstark, A.

1922 *Geschichte der syrischen Literatur mit Ausschluß der christlich-palästinensischen Texte* (Bonn: A. Marcus & E. Webers Verlag Dr. jur. Albert Ahn).

Bausi, A.

1992 *Il Qalēmenṭos etiopico: La rivelazione di Pietro a Clemente. I libri 3-7.* (Istituto Universitario Orientale, Studi Africanistici, Serie Etiopica, 2; Naples: Istituto Universitario Orientale).

Belayche, N.

1997 'Du Mont du Temple au Golgotha: Le Capitole de la colonie d'*Aelia Capitolina*', *RHR* 214: 387-413.

Bezold, C.

1883 *Die Schatzhöhle* (translation; Leipzig: J.C. Hinrichs).

1888 *Die Schatzhöhle* (text; Leipzig: J.C. Hinrichs).

Brock, S.P.

1977 'A letter attributed to Cyril of Jerusalem on the rebuilding of the Temple', *BSO(A)S* 40: 267-86.

1981 'Genesis 22 in Syriac tradition', in P. Casetti, *et al.* (eds.), *Mélanges Dominique Barthélemy* (OBO, 38; Göttingen: Vandenhoeck & Ruprecht): 2-30.

1996 'The "Nestorian" Church: A Lamentable Misnomer', *BJRL* 78: 23-35.

Bruns, P.

1998 'Spelunca Thesaurorum/Schatzhöhle', in S. Döpp und W. Geerlings (eds.), *Lexikon der Antiken christlichen Literatur* (Freiburg: Herder): 566.

Budge, E.A.W.

1927 *The Book of the Cave of Treasures: A History of the Patriarchs and the Kings their Successors from the Creation to the Crucifixion of Christ* (London: The Religious Tract Society).

Coquin, R.-G., and G. Godron

1990 'Un encomion copte sur Marie-Madeleine attribué à Cyrille de Jérusalem', *BIFAO* 90: 169-212.

Corbo, V.C.

1982 *Il Santo Sepolcro di Gerusalemme: Aspetti archeologici dalle origini al periodo crociato.* I. *Testo* (SBF.CMa, 29; Jerusalem: Franciscan Press).

Dillmann, A.

1853 *Das christliche Adambuch des Morgenlandes* (Göttingen: Dieterich).

1858 'Bericht über das äthiopische Buch Clementinischer Schriften', *Nachrichten von der G.A. Universität und der Königlichen Gesellschaft der Wissenschaften zu Göttingen* 17-19: 185-226.

Döpp, S., and W. Geerlings (eds.)

1998 *Lexikon der Antiken christlichen Literatur* (Freiburg: Herder).

Drijvers, H.J.W.

1990 'Adam and the True Prophet in the Pseudo-Clementines', in C. Elsas and H.G. Kippenberg (eds.), *Loyalitätskonflikte in der Religionsgeschichte: Festschrift für Carsten Colpe* (Würzburg: Könighausen & Neumann): 314-23.

Drijvers, H.J.W., and J.W. Drijvers
1997 *The Finding of the True Cross: The Judas Kyriakos Legend in Syriac* (CSCO, 565; CSCO.Sub, 93; Louvain: Peeters).

Frankenberg, W.
1937 *Die syrischen Clementinen mit griechischem Paralleltext: Eine Vorarbeit zu dem literargeschichtlichen Problem der Sammlung.* (Texte und Unterzuchungen zur Geschichte der altchristlichen Literatur, 48.3 [4.3.3]; Leipzig: J.C. Hinrichs).

Gero, S.
1980 'The Legend of the Fourth Son of Noah', *HTR* 73: 321-30.

Gibson, M.D.
1901 *Apocrypha Arabica* (Studia Sinaitica, 8; London: Clay and Sons).

Gibson, S., and J.E. Taylor
1994 *Beneath the Church of the Holy Sepulchre Jerusalem: The Archaeology and Early History of Traditional Golgotha* (PEF Monograph; Series Maior, 1; London: Committee of the Palestine Exploration Fund).

Gignoux, P.
1999 'L'apocalyptique iranienne est-elle vraiment ancienne?', *RHR* 216: 213-27.

Götze, A.
1922 *Die Schatzhöhle: Überlieferung und Quellen* (SHAW, 4; Heidelberg: Carl Winter).
1923 'Die Nachwirkung der Schatzhöhle', *ZS* 2: 51-94.
1924 'Die Nachwirkung der Schatzhöhle', *ZS* 3: 53-71, 153-77.

Grébaut, S.
1911-21 'Littérature éthiopienne pseudo-clémentine. III. Traduction du Qalêmentos', *Revue de l'Orient Chrétien* 16 (1911): 72-84, 167-75, 225-33; 17 (1912): 16-31, 133-44, 244-52, 337-46; 18 (1913): 69-78; 19 (1914): 324-30; 20 (1915–17): 33-37, 424-30; 21 (1918–19): 246-52; 22 (1920–21): 22-28, 113-117, 395-400.

Hidal, S.
1974 *Interpretatio Syriaca: Die Kommentare des Heiligen Ephräm des Syrers zu Genesis und Exodus mit besondere [sic] Berücksichtigung ihrer auslegungsgeschichtlichen Stellung* (CBOT, 6; Lund: C.W.K. Gleerup).

Holl, K.
1918 'Ueber Zeit und Heimat des pseudotertullianischen Gedichts *adv. Marcionem*', in *idem*, *Gesammelte Aufsätze zur Kirchengeschichte*, III (Darmstadt: Wissenschaftliche Buchgesellschaft; repr. 1965): 13-53.

Holl, K., and J. Dummer (eds.)
1980 *Panarion haer. 34–64* (GCS; Epiphanius II; Berlin: Akademie-Verlag, 2nd edn).

Jeremias, J.
1926 'Golgotha und der heilige Felsen: Eine Untersuchtung zur Symbolsprache des Neuen Testaments', *Angelos* 2: 74-128.

Jones, F.S.
1992 'Evaluating the Latin and Syriac Translations of the Pseudo-Clementine *Recognitions*', *Apocrypha* 3: 237-57.
1995 *An Ancient Jewish Christian Source on the History of Christianity* (SBLTT Christian Apocrypha Series, 37.2; Atlanta: Scholars Press).

Katsimbis, C.
1977 'The Uncovering of the Eastern Side of the Hill of Calvary and its Base: New Lay-out of the Area of the Canons' Refectory by the Greek Orthodox Patriarchate', *LA* 27: 197-208; Pls. 19-38, and A-C.

Kiraz, G.A.
1996 *Comparative Edition of the Syriac Gospels: Aligning the Sinaiticus, Curetonianus, Pešiṭtā and Ḥarklean Versions*. Vol. 1, *Matthew* (NTTS, 21.1; Leiden: E.J. Brill).

Klostermann, E., and E. Benz (eds.)
1941 *Origenes Matthäuserklärung,* III (GCS; Origenes, XII; Leipzig: J.C. Hinrichs).

Klostermann, E., E. Benz and U. Treu (eds.)
1976 *Origenes Matthäuserklärung.* II. *Die Lateinische Übersetzung der Commentariorum Series* (GCS, 56; Origenes, XI; Berlin: Akademie-Verlag, 2nd edn).

Kötting, B.
1965 *Der frühchristliche Reliquienkult und die Bestattung im Kirchengebäude* (Arbeitsgemeinschaft für Forschung des Landes Nordrhein-Westfalen; Geisteswissenschaften, 123; Cologne-Opladen: Westdeutscher Verlag).

Kourcikidzé, C.
1993 *La caverne des trésors; Version géorgienne* (CSCO, 526; Louvain: Peeters).

Kretschmar, G.
1987 'Festkalender und Memorialstätten Jerusalems in altkirchlicher Zeit', in H. Busse and J. Kretschmar, *Jerusalemer Heiligtumstraditionen in altkirchlicher und frühislamischer Zeit* (Abhandlungen des Deutschen Palästinavereins, 8; Wiesbaden: Otto Harrassowitz): 29-111.

Lagarde, P. de
1888 'Die Schatzhöhle' (review of Bezold 1888), *GGA* 2 (22): 817-44.
1889 'Die Schatzhöhle' (review of Bezold 1888), in *idem*, *Mittheilungen*, III (Göttingen: Dieterich): 49-79.
1891 'Noch einmal Die Schatzhöhle' (review of Bezold 1888), in *idem*, *Mittheilungen.* IV (Göttingen: Dieterich): 6-16.

Lavenant, R. (ed.)
1990 *V Symposium Syriacum 1988* (OrChrA, 236; Rome: Pontificium Institutum Studiorum Orientalium).

Mahé, J.-P.
1992 *La Caverne des Trésors: Version géorgienne* (CSCO, 527; Louvain: Peeters).

Markus, R.A.
1994 'How on Earth Could Places Become Holy? Origins of the Christian idea of Holy Places', *Journal of Early Christian Studies* 2: 257-71.

Mingana, A.
1931 *1. Vision of Theophilus. 2. Apocalypse of Peter* (Woodbrooke Studies, 3; Cambridge: W. Hefer and Sons).

Nöldeke, T.
1888 'Die Schatzhöhle' (review of Bezold 1888), *LZD* 8: 233-36.

Parisot, D.I.
1894 *Aphraatis Sapientis Persae Demonstrationes* (PS, 1.1; Paris: Firmin-Didot).
1907 *Aphraatis Sapientis Persae Demonstratio XXIII de Acino* (PS, 1.2; Paris: Firmin-Didot).

Poirier, P.-H.
1983 'Fragments d'une version copte de la *Caverne des Trésors*', *Or* 52: 415-23.
1995 'Note sur le nom du destinataire des chapitres 44 à 54 de la *Caverne des Trésors*', in J.-M. Rosenstiehl (ed.), *Christianisme d'Egypte: Hommages à René-Georges Coquin* (Cahiers de la Bibliotèque Copte, 9; Paris: Peeters): 115-22.

Pollmann, K.
1991 *Hypomnemata: Das Carmen adversus Marcionitas* (Untersuchungen zur Antike und zu ihren Nachbarn, 96; Göttingen: Vandenhoeck & Ruprecht).
1998 'Gedichte, Anonyme', in Döpp and Geerlings 1998: 246-47.

Ri, A.S.-M.
1987a *La caverne des trésors: Les deux recensions syriaques* (CSCO, 486 [text]; 487 [trans.]; Louvain: Peeters).
1987b 'La caverne des trésors: Problémes d'analyse littéraire', in H.J.W. Drijvers *et al.* (eds.), *IV Symposium Syriacum 1984. Literary Genres in Syriac Literature* (OrChrA, 229; Rome: Pontificium Institutum Studiorum Orientalium): 183-90.
1990 'La Caverne des Trésors et le Testament d'Adam', in R. Lavenant (ed.), *V Symposium Syriacum 1988* (OrChrA, 236; Rome: Pontificium Institutum Studiorum Orientalium): 111-22.
1998a 'La Caverne des Trésors et Mar Ephrem', in R. Lavenant (ed.), *Symposium Syriacum*, VII (OrChrA, 256; Rome: Pontificium Institutum Studiorum Orientalium).
1998b 'Les prologues de la "Caverne des Trésors" et la notion d' "Apocryphe" ', in J.-D. Dubois and B. Roussel (eds.), *Entrer en matiére: Les prologues* (Patrimoines; Religions du Livre; Paris: Cerf): 71-83.

Rubin, M.
1998 'The Language of Creation or the Primordial Language: A Case of Cultural Polemics in Antiquity', *JJS* 49: 306-333.

Simon, M.
1937 'Melchisédech dans la polémique entre juifs et chrétiens et dans la légende', *RHPR* 17: 58-93.

Taylor, J.E.
1993 *Christians and the Holy Places: The Myth of Jewish-Christian Origins* (Oxford: Oxford University Press).

Thekeparampil, J.
1983 'Adam–Christus in den Passionssedrē und in der Schatzhöhle', in R. Lavenant (ed.), *III Symposium Syriacum 1980: Les contacts du monde syriaque avec les autres cultures* (OrChrA, 221; Rome: Pontificium Institutum Studiorum Orientalium): 323-32.

Trumpp, E.
1881 '*Gadla Adām.* Der Kampf Adams (gegen die Versuchungen des Satans), oder: Das christliche Adambuch des Morgenlandes', *Abhandlungen der*

*Philosophisch-Philologischen Classe der Königlich bayerischen Akademie der Wissenschaften* 15./3 (Abt./no. 52, III–XIII): 1-172.

Wainwright, P.
1986 'The Authenticity of the Recently Discovered Letter Attributed to Cyril of Jerusalem', *Vigiliae Christianae* 40: 286-93.

Witakowski, W.
1990 'The Idea of *septimana mundi* and the Millenarian Typology of the Creation Week in Syriac Tradition', in R. Lavenant (ed.), *V Symposium Syriacum 1988* (OrChrA, 236; Rome: Pontificium Institutum Studiorum Orientalium): 93-109.
1993 'The Division of the Earth between the Descendants of Noah in Syriac Tradition', *ARAM* 5: 635-56.

Wright, W.
1869 *The Homilies of Aphraates, the Persian Sage: Edited from Syriac Manuscripts of the Fifth and Sixth Centuries, in the British Museum, with an English Translation.* I. *The Syriac Text* (London: Williams & Norgate).

Isabelle

# BIBLIOGRAPHY OF PAUL-EUGÈNE DION: SCHOLARLY PUBLICATIONS AND LECTURES

## *Refereed Publications*

### *Books*

1974 *La langue de Ya'udi: Description et classement de l'ancien parler de Zencirli dans le cadre des langues sémitiques du nord-ouest* (Waterloo, ON: Wilfrid Laurier University Press).

1975 *Dieu universel et peuple élu: L'universalisme religieux en Israël depuis les origines jusqu'à la veille des luttes maccabéennes* (LD, 83; Paris: Cerf).

1982 *Handbook of Ancient Hebrew Letters* (Sources for Biblical Studies, 15; Chico, CA: Scholars Press) [D. Pardee, P.-E. Dion, J.D. Whitehead and S.D. Sperling].

1997 *Les Araméens à l'âge du fer: Histoire politique et structures sociales* (Ebib NS 34; Paris: J. Gabalda).

### *Chapters in Books*

1981 'Ressemblance et image de Dieu dans l'Ancien Orient et dans l'Ancien Testament', in *DBSup*, X, fasc. 55, col. 365-403.

1984 'The Greek Version of Deut 21:1-9 and its Variants: A Record of Early Exegesis', in A. Pietersma and C. Cox (eds.), *De Septuaginta: Studies in Honour of John William Wevers on his Sixty-Fifth Birthday* (Toronto: Benben): 151-60.

1985 'La bilingue de Tell Fekherye: Le roi de Gozan et son dieu; la phraséologie', in M. Tourgues and G.-D. Maillhiot (eds.), *Mélanges bibliques et orientaux en l'honneur de M. Mathias Delcor* (AOAT, 215; Neukirchen–Vluyn: Neukirchener Verlag): 139-47.

1986 'Israël et l'étranger dans le Deutéronome', in M. Tourgues and G.-D. Maillhiot (eds.), *L'Altérité: Actes du colloque pluridisciplinaire tenu à l'occasion du 75e anniversaire du Collège dominicain de philosophie et de théologie* (Paris: Cerf): 211-33.

1988 'Institutional Model and Poetic Creation: The First Song of the Servant of the Lord and Appointment Ceremonies', in L. Eslinger and G. Taylor (eds.), *Ascribe to the Lord: Biblical and Other Studies in Memory of Peter C. Craigie* (JSOTSup, 67; Sheffield: JSOT Press): 319-39.

1991 'Deuteronomy 13: The Suppression of Alien Religious Propaganda in Israel during the Late Monarchical Era', in B. Halpern and D. Hobson (eds.), *Law and Ideology in Monarchic Israel* (JSOTSup, 124; Sheffield: Sheffield Academic Press): 147-216.

1992 'Letters: Aramaic', in *ABD*, IV: 285-90.

1993 'La procédure d'élimination du fils rebelle (Deut. 21, 18-21): Sens littéral et signes de développement juridique', in Georg Braulik, Walter Gross and Sean McEvenue (eds.), *Biblische Theologie und gesellschaftlicher Wandel: Für Norbert Lohfink, SJ* (Freiburg: Herder): 73-82.

1994 ' "Voici! Yahvé n'a pas de maison comme les dieux, ni de cour comme les fils d'Ashérah": Pourquoi les Israélites jugèrent nécessaire d'élever un temple à leur Dieu', in J.-C. Petit *et al.* (eds.), *Où demeures-tu? (Jn 1,38): La maison dans le monde biblique* (Mélanges Guy Couturier; Montréal: Fides): 139-51.

1995a 'Aramaean Tribes and Nations of First-Millennium Western Asia', in J.M. Sasson (ed.), *Civilizations of the Ancient Near East*, II (New York: Charles Scribner's Sons): 1281-94.

1995b 'Les Araméens du Moyen-Euphrate au VIIIème siècle à la lumière des inscriptions des maîtres de Suhu et de Mari', in *Congress Volume: Paris 1992* (VTSup, 61; Leiden: E.J. Brill): 53-73.

1999 'The Tel Dan Stele and its Historical Significance', in Y. Avishur and R. Deutsch (eds.), *Michael: Historical, Epigraphical and Biblical Studies in Honor of Professor Michael Heltzer* (Tel Aviv: Archaeological Center Publications): 145-56.

in press 'Old Aramaic: Earliest Inscriptional Material', in D. Sperling (ed.), *A Handbook of Aramaic and its Dialects* (Handbuch der Orientalistik; Leiden: E.J. Brill).

*Articles*

1965a 'L'origine du titre de "Paraclet": A propos d'un livre récent', *Sciences Ecclésiastiques* (now *Science et Esprit*) 17: 143-49.

1965b 'La prédestination chez saint Paul', *RSR* 53: 5-43 (condensed ET *Theology Digest* 15 [1967]: 147-49).

1966a 'La notion paulinienne de "richesse de Dieu" et ses sources', *Sciences Ecclésiastiques* 18: 139-48.

1966b 'Quelques traits originaux de la conception johannique du Fils de l'Homme', *Sciences Ecclésiastiques* 19: 49-65.

1967a 'Le genre littéraire sumérien de l'"hymne à soi-même" et quelques passages du Deutéro-Isaïe', *RB* 74: 215-34.

1967b 'The Patriarchal Traditions and the Literary Form of the "Oracle of Salvation" ', *CBQ* 29: 198-206.

1967c 'Yahweh, Dieu de Canaan, et la terre des hommes', *Canadian Journal of Theology* 13: 233-40.

1970a 'Les chants du serviteur de Yahweh et quelques passages apparentés d'Isaïe 40-55', *Bib* 51: 17-38.

1970b 'The "Fear not" Formula and Holy War', *CBQ* 22: 565-70.

1970c 'L'universalisme religieux dans les différentes couches rédactionnelles d'Isaïe 40–55', *Bib* 51: 161-82.

1974a 'Une inscription araméenne en style *awīlum ša* et quelques textes bibliques datant de l'exil', *Bib* 55: 399-403.

1974b 'Réactions à l'exposé du Père R. Bellemare', *Eglise et Théologie* 5: 271-73.

1974c 'Le rôle de la foi yahwiste dans la vie politique d'Israël', *Science et Esprit* 26: 173-203.

1975a 'Deux notes épigraphiques sur Tobit', *Bib* 56: 416-19.

1975b 'Le message moral du prophète Amos s'inspirait-il du "Droit de l'Alliance"?', *Science et Esprit* 27: 5-34.

1975c 'Notes d'épigraphie ammonite', *RB* 82: 24-33.

1976a 'Les deux principales formes de l'angélologie de l'Ancien Testament dans leur cadre oriental', *Science et Esprit* 28: 65-82.

1976b 'Raphaël l'exorciste', *Bib* 57: 399-413.

1977a 'The Hebrew Particle *'t-* in the Paraenetic Part of the "Damascus Document" ', *RQ* 34: 197-212.

1977b 'Synagogues et temples dans l'Egypte hellénistique', *Science et Esprit* 29: 45-75.

1978a 'The Language Spoken in Ancient Sam'al', *JNES* 37: 115-18.

1978b 'An Overview of Ancient Hebrew Epistolography', *JBL* 97: 321-46 [D. Pardee, P.-E. Dion and J.D. Whitehead].

1978c 'Quelques aspects de l'interaction entre religion et politique dans le Deutéronome', *Science et Esprit* 30: 39-55.

1979a 'Le "Rouleau du Temple" et les Douze', *Science et Esprit* 31: 81-83.

1979b 'Les types épistolaires hébréo-araméens jusqu'au temps de Bar-Kokhbah', *RB* 86: 544-79 [P.-E. Dion, D. Pardee and J.D. Whitehead].

1980a 'A Note on the Samaritan Christian Synagogue" in Ramat-Aviv', *JSJ* 11: 217-22 [P.-E. Dion and R. Pummer].

1980b 'Tu feras disparaître le mal du milieu de toi', *RB* 88: 321-49.

1981a 'The Aramaic "Family Letter" and Related Epistolary Forms in Other Oriental Languages and in Hellenistic Greek', *Semeia* 22: 59-76.

1981b 'Aramaic Words for "Letter" ', *Semeia* 22: 77-88.

1981c 'Did Cultic Prostitution Fall into Oblivion during the Post-Exilic Era?: Some Evidence from Chronicles and the Septuagint', *CBQ* 43: 41-48.

1982a 'Deutéronome, 21,1-9, miroir du développement légal et religieux d'Israël', *SR* 11: 13-22.

1982b 'Image et ressemblance en araméen ancien (Tell Fakhariyah)', *Science et Esprit* 34: 151-53.

1982c 'La lettre araméenne passe-partout et ses sous-espèces', RB 89: 528-75 [P.-E. Dion, D. Pardee and J.D. Whitehead].

1983a 'Le Pain des Forts (Ps. 78, 25a) dans un dérivé de la littérature hénochienne', *Science et Esprit* 35: 223-26.

1983b 'Sheshbazzar and Sâsnûrî', *ZAW* 95: 111-12.

1984a 'Dt. 12 et la vision de Pierre à Joppé', *Science et Esprit* 36: 207-210.

1984b 'Un nouvel éclairage sur les malheurs de Job', *VT* 34: 213-15.

1985a 'The Angel with the Drawn Sword (1 Chr 21:16): An Exercise in Restoring the Balance of Text Criticism and Interpretation', *ZAW* 97: 114-17.

1985b 'Deuteronomy and the Gentile World: A Study in Biblical Theology', *Toronto Journal of Theology* 1: 200-21.

1987a 'Despoiling the Egyptians: Thomas Mann, the Sun-Disc Theology, and Nazi Racism', *SR* 16: 389-92.

1987b 'Dt. 12 et la vision de Pierre à Joppé', *Science et Esprit* 36: 207-10.

1987c 'Early Evidence for the Ritual Significance of the Base of the Altar: Around Deut 12: 27 LXX', *JBL* 106: 487-90.

1987d 'Formulaic Language in the Book of Job: International Background and Ironical Distortions', *SR* 16: 187-93.

1987e 'Strophic Boundaries and Rhetorical Structure in Psalm 31', *Eglise et Théologie* 18: 183-92.

1989a 'Medical Personnel in the Ancient Near East: *asû* and *āšipu* in Aramaic Garb', *Aram* 1.2: 206-16.

1989b 'Sennacherib's Expedition to Palestine', *Eglise et Théologie* 20: 5-25 (= *CSMS Bulletin* 48 [1988]: 3-25).

1990 'La rwḥ dans l'Heptateuque: La protestation pour la liberté du prophétisme en Nb 11, 26-29', *Science et Esprit* 42: 167-91.

1991a 'Balaam l'Araméen d'après de nouveaux documents akkadiens du VIIIème siècle', *Eglise et Théologie* 21: 85-87.

1991b 'The Civic-and-Temple Community of Persian Period Judaea: Neglected Insights from Eastern Europe', *JNES* 50: 281-87.

1991c 'Psalm 103: A Meditation on the "Ways" of the Lord', *Eglise et Théologie* 21: 13-31.

1991d 'The Structure of Isaiah 42.10-17 as Approached through Versification and Distribution of Poetic Devices', *JSOT* 49: 113-24.

1991e 'Yhwh as Storm-god and Sun-god: The Double Legacy of Egypt and Canaan as Reflected in Psalm 104', *ZAW* 103: 43-71.

1992 'Les KTYM de Tel Arad: Grecs ou Phéniciens?' (*Centenaire* 1892–1992 = *RB* 99: 70-97).

1993 'Changements sociaux et changements législatifs dans le Deutéronome', *Eglise et Théologie* 24: 343-60.

1994a 'Deut 19:3: Prepare the Way, or Estimate the Distance?', *Eglise et Théologie* 25: 333-41.

1994b 'El, the God of the Ammonites?: The Atef-crowned Head from Tell Jawa, Jordan', ZDPV 110: 158-67 [P.M.M. Daviau and P.-E. Dion].

1995 'Syro-Palestinian Resistance to Shalmaneser III in the Light of New Documents', *ZAW* 107: 482-89.

1999a 'The Horned Prophet (1 Kings XXII 11)', *VT* 49: 259-61.

1999b 'L'incursion d'Aššurnaṣirpal II au Luḫutu', *Or* 69: 133-38.

1999c 'The Seal of Ariyāramna in the Royal Ontario Museum', *JNES* 58: 1-17 [P.-E. Dion and Mark Garrison].

2000 'An Inscribed Incense Altar of Iron Age II at Ḫirbet el-Mudēyine (Jordan)', *ZDPV* 116: 1-13 [P.-E. Dion and P.M.M. Daviau].


## *Non-Refereed Publications*

### *Books*


1988 *Hebrew Poetics* (Mississauga, ON: Benben Publications).

1990 *The Jews during the Persian Period: A Bibliography* (*Newsletter for Targumic and Cognate Studies*, Suppl. 5; Toronto: University of Toronto, Department of Near Eastern Studies).

*Articles*

1961 'L'humilité d'un saint Thomas, plus que jamais nécessaire', *La Revue dominicaine*: 206-210.

1970 'Bible et action sociale', *Liaison: Bulletin des Dominicains canadiens* 8.2: 6-8.

1973 'Bible et libération', *Bulletin of the Canadian Association of Theological Students Supplement*: 1-7.

1975 'Morale et religion dans l'Ancien Testament: Héritage immémorial et commandements divins', *Communauté Chrétienne* 14: 394-405.

1977a 'Une constitution pour le peuple de Dieu: Dt 17–18', *Société Catholique de la Bible, Bulletin Biblique* 3.39: 2.

1977b 'Israël et l'étranger selon le Deutéronome', *Société Catholique de la Bible, Bulletin Biblique* 3.42: 2.

1977c 'A Tentative Classification of Aramaic Letter Types' (SBLSP; Missoula, MO: Scholars Press): 415-41.

1995 'The Syro-Mesopotamian Border in the VIIIth Century BC: The Aramaeans and the Establishment', *CSMS Bulletin* 30: 5-10.

*Unpublished Papers Presented at Meetings and Symposia*

1964 'L'origine et la portée des qualificatifs attribués à Dieu en Israël', ACEBAC Regional Meeting (Montréal, November).

1966 'Proverbes 8 et Ecclésiastique 24: Genres littéraires et modèles', ACEBAC Regional Meeting (Montréal, 11 November).

1971 'The *'asher/she* Compound Conjunctions in the Book of Qoheleth', Canadian Society of Biblical Studies Annual Meeting, St John's (Newfoundland, May).

1975 'Lung and Liver Models from Ras Shamra in Religio-Historical Perspective', The American Oriental Society Annual Meeting (Columbus, OH, April); a shorter version of the same was read at the CSBS Annual Meeting (Edmonton, May).

1982 'Michael O'Connor's Hebrew Verse Structure: A General Introduction', Canadian Society of Biblical Studies Annual Meeting (Ottawa, June).

1984 'The New Stele Found at Sultaniyeköy near Dascyleion', Society of Biblical Literature Annual Meeting (Chicago, December).

1995 'Aramaean Kings: Gods during their Lifetime, or after their Deaths?' at the Symposium ' "Vanished Races", in Celebration of the 150 years of the Department of Near Eastern Studies' (University of Toronto, 22 March).

1996 'Aramaean Courts and Civilian Structures of Authority', at 'Who Were, or Are, the Aramaeans?', Symposium of the ARAM Society for Syro-Mesopotamian Studies (Cambridge, MA, 10 June).

*Invited Lectures*

1973 'Le rôle de la foi yahwiste dans la vie politique d'Israël', Association Catholique des Etudes Bibliques au Canada, Annual Reunion (Spring).

1975 'Les deux principales formes de l'angélologie de l'Ancien Testament dans leur cadre oriental', Association Catholique des Etudes Bibliques au Canada, Annual Reunion (Spring).

1976 'The Language Spoken in Ancient Sam'al', Colloquium on Aramaic Studies, Oriental Institute (University of Chicago, November).

1977 'Quelques aspects de l'interaction entre religion et politique dans le Deutéronome', Société Canadienne de Théologie, Annual Reunion (November).

1982 'La bilingue assyro-araméenne de Tell Fakhariyeh', First Annual Meeting of L'Association des Etudes du Proche-Orient Ancien (Ottawa, June).

1988 'La rwḥ dans l'Heptateuque: La protestation pour la liberté du prophétisme en Nb 11,26-29', Association Catholique des Etudes Bibliques au Canada (Québec, May).

1989 'Yhwh as Storm-god and Sun-god: The Double Legacy of Egypt and Canaan as Reflected in Psalm 104', Biblical Colloquium of Kitchener-Waterloo (April).

1992a 'Les Araméens du Moyen-Euphrate au VIIIème siècle à la lumière des inscriptions des maîtres de Suhu et de Mari', XIVth World Congress of the International Organization for the Study of the Old Testament (Paris, 22 July).

1992b 'Sur l'éthique du Pentateuque', Association Catholique des Etudes Bibliques au Canada (Québec, 31 May).

1994 'The Tel Dan stele fragments and their Historical Implications', lecture given to the Altorientalische Seminar, University of Tübingen (11 June) and to the Curatorial Staff, Aleppo Museum (8 August).

1995 'The Syria-Iraq Border in the VIIIth Century B.C.: The Aramaeans and the Establishment', CSMS lecture (Toronto, 12 April).

1996a 'Le Moyen-Euphrate au VIIIe siècle av. J.-C.: Araméens et Assyro-Babyloniens', Québec, Laval University, Department of History and Faculty of Theology (10 April).

1996b 'Political Structures in the Aramaean Kingdoms: The Court and the Administration', Toronto, Department of Near Eastern Studies, Near Eastern Studies Association (27 March).


## *Book Reviews*


1963a *Die apostolische und nachapostolische Zeit* (Göttingen: Vandenhoeck & Ruprecht, 1962), by L. Goppelt, in *RB* 70: 602-603.

1963b *Der Paraklet* (Leiden: E.J. Brill, 1963), by O. Betz, in *Sciences Ecclésiastiques* 17: 143-49.

1971a *The Burden of Babylon* (Lund: C.W.K. Gleerup, 1970), by S. Erlandsson, in *Bib* 52: 439-42.

1971b *The Psalms* (New York: Alba House, 1969), by L. Sabourin, in *SR* 1: 128-29.

1971c *The Threat of Falsehood* (London: SCM Press, 1970), by T.W. Overholt, in *SR* 1: 129-30.

1980 *Inscriptions hébraïques*. I. *Les Ostraca* (Paris: Cerf, 1977), by A. Lemaire, in *JAOS* 100: 362-63.

1981 *The Aramaic Origin of the Four Gospels* (New York: Ktav, 1979), by F. Zimmermann, in *SR* 10: 131-32.

1982a *A History of Israel* (Philadelphia: Westminster Press, 3rd edn, 1981), by J. Bright, in *SR* 11: 93-94.

1982b *A Manual of Palestinian Aramaic Texts* (Rome: Biblical Institute Press, 1978), by J.A. Fitzmyer and D.J. Harrington, in *JAOS* 102: 181-83.

1983a *Arad Inscriptions* (Jerusalem: Israel Exploration Society, 1981), by Y. Aharoni, in *JAOS* 103: 470-72.

1983b *The Aramaic Proverbs of Ahiqar* (Baltimore: The Johns Hopkins University Press, 1983), by J.M. Lindenberger, in *SR* 12: 342-43.

1984a *A History of Israel in the Old Testament Period* (Philadelphia: Fortress Press, 1983), by H. Jagersma, in *JAOS* 104: 763-64.

1984b *Royal Administration and National Religion in Ancient Palestine* (Leiden: E.J. Brill, 1982), by G.W. Ahlström, in *JAOS* 104: 763.

1984c *Das Zweite Buch der Könige* (Würzburg: Echter Verlag, 1982), by M. Rehm, in *JBL* 103: 641-43.

1986 *Les Inscriptions de Sfiré dans l'Assyrie de Shamshi-ilu* (Geneva: Droz, 1984), by A. Lemaire and J.-M. Durand, in *JBL* 105: 510-12.

1987 *In the Shelter of Elyon: Essays on Ancient Palestinian Life and Literature in Honor of G.W. Ahlström* (ed. W.B. Barrick and J.R. Spencer; Sheffield: Sheffield Academic Press, 1984), in *JAOS* 107: 132-33.

1988a *Ancient Damascus* (Winona Lake, IN: Eisenbrauns, 1987), by W.T. Pitard, in *BASOR* 270: 97-100.

1988b *Critique textuelle de l'Ancien Testament* (Fribourg: Editions Universitaire), by D. Barthélemy, in *JBL* 107: 737-39.

1988c *The Samaritans* (Leiden: E.J. Brill, 1987), by R. Pummer, in *SR* 17: 388.

1989a *Catalogue des sceaux ouest-sémitiques inscrits* (Paris: Bibliothèque Nationale, 1986), by P. Bordreuil, in *BASOR* 275: 74-77.

1989b *A History of Ancient Israel and Judah* (Philadelphia: Westminster, 1986), by J.M. Miller and J.H. Hayes, in *BA* 52: 47-48.

1991 *Les Prophètes* (Ottawa: Novalis, 1990), by W. Vogels, in *Toronto Journal of Theology* 7.2: 268-69.

1993 *Die Beziehungen Altisraels zu den aramäischen Staaten in der israelitisch-jüdäischen Königszeit* (Frankfurt: Peter Lang, 1989), by G.G.G. Reinhold, in *BiOr* 50: 217-19.

1994a *Critique textuelle de l'Ancien Testament* (Fribourg: Editions Universitaire, 1992), by D. Barthélemy, in *JBL* 113: 113-14.

1994b *A History of Ancient Palestine* (Minneapolis: Fortress Press, 1993), by G.W. Ahlström, in *Consensus* 20: 155-56.

1994c *Personal Names in the Nabatean Realm* (Jerusalem: Israel Exploration Society, 1991), by A. Negev, in *BiOr* 51: 155-57.

1994d *Les relations entre les cités de la côte phénicienne et les royaumes d'Israël et de Juda* (Leuven: Peeters, 1992), by F. Briquel Chatonnet, in *BASOR* 293: 92-94.

1995 *Converting the Past: Studies in Ancient Israelite and Moabite Historiography* (OTS, 28; Leiden: E.J. Brill, 1992), by K.A.D. Smelik, in *JAOS* 115: 121-22.

1997a *La Bible en exil* (Neuchâtel: Recherches et Publications, 1995), by C. Jullien and F. Jullien, in *JAOS* 117: 219.

1997b *Deuteronomium 28 und die adê zur Thronfolgeregelung Asarhaddons* (OBO, 145; Fribourg: Universitätsverlag, 1995), by H.U. Steymans, in *Bib* 78: 271-75.

1997c *The Elephantine Papyri in English* (Leiden: E.J. Brill, 1996), by B. Porten *et al.*, in *BASOR* 308: 104-106.

1999 *Deuteronomy and the Hermeneutics of Legal Innovation* (Oxford: Oxford University Press, 1997) by B. Levinson, in *Bib* 80: 116-19.

2000 *Aramaic Documents from Ancient Egypt* 4 (Jerusalem: The Hebrew University, 1999) by B. Porten and A. Yardeni, in *BASOR* 318: 77-79.

# INDEX OF MODERN AUTHORS

# INDEX OF SUBJECTS

INDEX OF PERSONAL AND TRIBAL NAMES

INDEX OF GEOGRAPHICAL NAMES